STUDIES IN THE ANTHROPOLOGY OF NORTH AMERICAN INDIANS

EDITORS

RAYMOND J. DEMALLIE
DOUGLAS R. PARKS

TRADITIONAL NARRATIVES
OF THE
ARIKARA INDIANS

Stories of Alfred Morsette:
English Translations

VOLUME 3

DOUGLAS R. PARKS

Published by the University of Nebraska Press,
Lincoln and London

In cooperation with the American Indian
Studies Research Institute,
Indiana University

Copyright © 1991 by the
University of Nebraska Press
All rights reserved
Manufactured in the
United States of America
The paper in this book meets the
minimum requirements of American
National Standard for Information
Sciences—Permanence of Paper
for Printed Library Materials,
ANSI z39.48–1984.

Library of Congress Cataloging-in-Publication Data
(Revised for volumes 3 and 4)
Traditional narratives of the Arikara Indians.
    (Studies in the anthropology of North American Indians)
    Includes bibliographical references.
    Contents: v. 1. Stories of Alfred Morsette, interlinear linguistic texts—[etc.]
—v. 3. Stories of Alfred Morsette, English translations—v. 4. Stories of other
narrators, English translations.
    1. Arikara Indians—Legends. 2. Tales—Great Plains. I. Parks, Douglas R.
II. Morsette, Alfred. Selections. English. 1991. III. Indiana University.
American Indian Studies Research Institute. IV. Series.
E99.A8T73   1991   398.2'089975   90-12889
ISBN 0-8032-3698-0 (set)
ISBN 0-8032-3691-3 (cl. : v. 1 : alk.)
ISBN 0-8032-3692-1 (v. 2)
ISBN 0-8032-3694-8 (v. 3)
ISBN 0-8032-3695-6 (v. 4)

TiweNAsaakaríčI nikuwetiresWAtwaáhAt:
AniinuuNUxtaahiwaáRA.

Today we remember them,
the ways of the old ones who were:
The good ways that were ours.

FROM THE SONG
MEMORIAL TO THE OLD SCOUTS

Contents

TALES

VOLUME FOUR

Part Two. The Stories of Lillian Brave

NARRATIVES OF THE PAST

TALES

Part Three. The Stories of Ella P. Waters

NARRATIVES OF THE PAST

Part Four. The Stories of Dan Howling Wolf

NARRATIVES OF THE PAST

TALES

Part Five. The Stories of Dan Hopkins

NARRATIVES OF THE PAST

TALES

Part Six. The Stories of Matthew White Bear

NARRATIVES OF THE PAST

TALES

Part Seven. The Stories of Mary Gillette

NARRATIVES OF THE PAST

OF RITUALISM

Part Eight. The Stories of William Deane, Jr.

NARRATIVES OF THE PAST

TALES

Part Nine. The Stories of Eleanor Chase

NARRATIVES OF THE PAST

TALES

Part Ten. The Stories of Esther Perkins

NARRATIVES OF THE PAST

Part Eleven. The Story of Joe Fox

Maps and Plates

Maps

Plates

Preface

Traditional Narratives of the Arikara Indians is a four-volume set comprising 156 oral narratives that represent the only comprehensive collection recorded in the native language of the major genres in the historical and literary tradition of the Arikaras, an historically important northern Plains people who for centuries have lived along the middle course of the Missouri River and today still live by its waters in west central North Dakota, where Garrison Dam forms Lake Sakakawea, the reservoir that divides the Fort Berthold Reservation. Through the contributions of numerous tribal elders, the narratives range in content from mythology and other folkloristic genres to historical accounts and cultural descriptions, embodying a rich selection of what has survived into the late twentieth century of the fundamental attributes as well as the topical diversity and range of stylistic variation of traditional Arikara oral literature.

Volumes 1 and 2 present linguistic transcriptions of the original Arikara oral recordings of these narratives accompanied by literal word-by-word English translations. Each volume also contains one morphologically analyzed text illustrating word composition in the language. The narratives of a single individual, Alfred Morsette, constitute volume 1, while the narratives of ten other contributors comprise volume 2. The preface in volume 1 discusses the tape recordings of the narratives and the conventions relating to the presentation of them as linguistic texts.

Volumes 3 and 4 present free English translations of the stories in which their arrangement parallels that in the first two volumes. An extended introduction in volume 3, moreover, serves the entire collection, covering a variety of topics designed to aid the reader to understand the narratives as fully as possible and to appreciate them as historical and literary documents. To contextualize the collection, the introduction begins with sections that provide a

cultural and historical overview of the Arikara people, the history
of past documentation of Arikara oral traditions, including an
account of this project, and short biographies of the narrators who
contributed stories to the present collection. Against this background there follows a discussion of the structure of the narratives
and their English presentation. Here the topics include a characterization of the nature of this collection, the principles guiding the
translations and redactive form of the narratives, the salient
features comprising the Arikara oral literary style, the structure
and content of the narratives, and a depiction of the performance
situations in which these oral traditions are told.

Because the style and structure of Arikara oral narratives
differ so dramatically from those to which English readers are
accustomed, and because the social and cultural world depicted in
the traditions differs even more dramatically from that of modern
America, these narratives require careful study. Comprehension and
appreciation of the subtleties that characterize the Arikara oral
literary style may be difficult for readers accustomed to the usual
collections of American Indian tales rewritten to conform to Western
literary conventions. Nevertheless, Arikara oral literature must
be approached in its own terms; and for English readers this
effort means understanding the uniqueness of Arikara culture—
particularly, to the extent possible, its worldview and concerns—and
accepting unfamiliar linguistic expression and literary form.

The reward for the effort to understand the narratives as fully
as possible will be at once enlightening and satisfying, since the
accounts recorded here enable the reader, not possible in any other
way, to enter into another cultural world and obtain a glimpse
of a lifeway now lost to contemporary society. Arikara life of the
nineteenth century, like that of American Indian peoples generally,
has transformed dramatically. Many cultural institutions have
persisted, but the concerns of everyday life, together with Arikara
cultural consciousness and its traditional expressions, have been
adapted to the modern world we all now share. The only published
record of the Arikara past from Arikara perspectives is the one
recorded here in the words of the last generation of speakers of
the Arikara language, who have repeated in traditional form the
stories—religious, legendary, historical, anecdotal, and humorous—

which they remembered, stories that formed an intimate, fundamental part of the expression of Arikara culture as it was formerly lived.

To preserve that literary and cultural heritage, the narratives are presented here in the native language with both literal and free translations. This format, established in the late nineteenth century for the publication of such texts, has become the standard in American Indian language study, which for over a century has sought to document as fully as possible the languages and literatures of native America. This format maximizes the accessibility of the collection to the broadest possible audience, one that includes the Arikara people themselves, scholars, and general readers. The presentation of the original linguistic texts in volumes separate from their free English translations enables readers concerned with the texts as linguistic or literary documents to study them separately from, or in combination with, the free English translations, while those readers interested in the narratives as historical or literary texts in translation can read them separately from the native language versions. Volumes 3 and 4 can thus be read either independently or in conjunction with volumes 1 and 2, depending upon the reader's interests.

Acknowledgments

Many Arikara people have contributed to this collection of texts. Foremost among them are the eleven narrators who shared their stories: Alfred Morsette, Lillian Brave, Ella P. Waters, Dan Howling Wolf, Dan Hopkins, Matthew White Bear, Mary Gillette, William Deane, Sr., Eleanor Chase, Esther Perkins, and Joe Fox. Especially impressive are Mr. Morsette's contributions, which constitute more than half of the collection. He was a true raconteur who faithfully remembered the stories told him by older generations, and he was committed to the task of preserving this record of Arikara history. Mrs. Brave and Mrs. Waters, both exceptionally knowledgeable about Arikara traditions, also recorded numerous stories that they remembered in order to make the collection as representative and complete as possible. For them, as for all those individuals whose stories are a part of this collection, these traditional narratives represented a precious, intimate, and fundamental embodiment of their identity as Arikaras, and the decision to share their stories was not lightly undertaken. Theirs was a desire to record and preserve this oral heritage as a gift to future generations, that others, particularly their descendants, might gain some understanding of an Arikara world that is now a part of the past. It is a gift that is sincerely appreciated, especially since of all these narrators only Mrs. Brave and Miss Perkins have lived to see the project to completion; and the passing of these traditional storytellers signals a major transition in the cultural life of the Arikara community.

Fundamentally important, too, were the efforts of various translators—Ella P. Waters, Lillian Brave, Angela Plante, Fannie Whiteman, Nellie Yellow Bird, John Fox, and Melfine Everett—who conscientiously assisted in the demanding process of transcription and translation of the stories. To Mrs. Waters, in particular, I am grateful for an unfailing devotion to this project, which spanned more than a decade of work, lasting until shortly before she passed away in 1983. Without her collaboration, and later that of Mrs. Brave and her daughter Angela, who have worked with me subsequently, this collection of narratives would never have achieved its present state.

Over the years many other individuals in the Arikara community have provided hospitality and assistance, as well as extending many other courtesies to me, all of which have made my work there both pleasant and gratifying. It would be impossible to list everyone, but foremost among them are three individuals now deceased—Mabel Howling Wolf, Wilena Little Soldier, and Alice White Bear—all of whom were warm, generous people and fluent speakers of their language. Other people who have been equally generous with time and friendship include Ramona Flute, David Ripley, Marie Wells, Tom Wells, Florence White, Fannie Whiteman, and Delilah Yellow Bird. To all of them I wish to extend my sincere thanks and express the hope that these volumes do not disappoint their expectations.

Appreciated also is the official support and encouragement of several Fort Berthold tribal organizations. In 1977 the Fort Berthold Tribal Council gave an endorsement by resolution of my linguistic project, and in 1980 tribal chairman Austin Gillette kindly wrote a strong letter of support for the expansion of the linguistic work to document Arikara culture as well, and especially the oral narratives presented here. The White Shield school board and district superintendent, both representing the Arikara community on the Fort Berthold Reservation, have given equally strong support on numerous occasions over the past fifteen years. Among the many school board members who have been particularly helpful are Robert Fox (deceased), Donald Malnourie, Gerald White, Edmund White Bear, and Delores Wilkinson.

It is also a pleasure to acknowledge the critical comments of many colleagues. Wallace Chafe and Ives Goddard offered suggestions on an earlier version of the manuscript that have improved the presentation, while over the past decade my work with the texts has benefited from discussions with Raymond J. DeMallie, A. Wesley Jones, David S. Rood, and Allan R. Taylor. The introduction and translations in volumes 3 and 4 have, in particular, been improved by the careful readings and thoughtful comments of Raymond DeMallie. Helpful suggestions for refining the introduction to volume 3 have also been offered by Loretta Fowler, Lee Irwin, and David Shaul. Lee Irwin, moreover, kindly assisted with the abstracts of each story at the end of volume 4.

Several people have contributed at various stages to the preparation of the texts for publication. Jackie Burke and Holly Ryckman (Mary College) typed initial copies of most of the texts, while Wallace Hooper, Jeffrey Whitmer, and Rita Crouch (American Indian Studies Research Institute, Indiana University) later keyboarded the entire collection and prepared the final copy. To all of them I also extend my sincere appreciation for their efforts in what was a painstaking and at times seemingly endless task.

It is also a pleasure to express my appreciation to each of the individuals and organizations providing the maps and illustrations enhancing the presentation. The maps in the introduction, which illustrate important landmarks in Arikara history, were drawn by Rachael Freyman (Indiana University). Historical photographs were provided by the North Dakota State Historical Society and the Custer Battlefield Historical and Museum Association. Contemporary photographs of North Dakota landmarks were provided by Raymond T. Haas (Baltimore, Maryland), and photographs of several narrators were provided by Faye Seidler of Faye Portraits, Inc. (Garrison, North Dakota), Louis Garcia (Tokio, North Dakota), and James Vranna (New Town, North Dakota).

Support for my study of the Arikara language and specifically for the collection and preparation of the texts has come from a variety of sources. Initially, funds for beginning the study were provided by Idaho State University (1969-1970). Subsequently, more sustained support came from grants made by the following agencies: National Endowment for the Humanities, divisions of Research and Educational Programs (1972-1978); Department of Education, Title III (1974-1979) and Title VII (1984-1988); Smithsonian Institution, Urgent Anthropology Program (1977-1978); and North Dakota Arts Council (1982-1983). It is a pleasure to acknowledge their generous support, without which these volumes would not have been possible. Three institutions—Mary College (Bismarck, North Dakota), White Shield School (Roseglen, North Dakota), and Indiana University (Bloomington)—have also generously provided essential support and assistance that is gratefully acknowledged.

Sound Key

	Arikara	Approximate Equivalent
Short Vowels:	a	*a*go, f*a*ther
	e	b*e*d
	i	pol*i*ce, p*i*t
	o	wr*o*te
	u	fl*u*te
Long Vowels:	aa	sp*a*
	ee	n*ei*ghbor
	ii	mach*i*ne
	oo	g*o*
	uu	r*u*de
Consonants:	č	whi*ch*
	h	*h*it
	n	*n*o
	s	*s*it
	š	*sh*ip
	w	*w*ill
	k	s*k*ill
	p	s*p*ill
	t	s*t*ill
	r	Spanish pe*r*o
	x	German i*ch*, a*ch*t
	'	oh-oh
Others:	i	(Not pronounced)
	u	(Not pronounced)
	æ	b*a*t
	ą	French *an*s
	ų	French *un*
	´	(Primary stress)
	Capital letters	(Whispered sounds)

Introduction to Arikara Oral Traditions

"The desire to preserve to future ages the memory of past achievements is a universal human instinct," wrote James Mooney (1898:141) in the opening line of his *Calendar History of the Kiowa Indians*, the first comprehensive attempt to construct an American Indian tribal history by using native as well as Euro-American written sources. For the Kiowa these native sources were what Mooney called "calendar histories," pictographs drawn on hides or paper that recorded a significant event for a given period—a month, a season, or a year. Like the winter counts of the Sioux and many other tribes, these calendars were mnemonic records of past events that were exhibited at frequent intervals during winter evenings when older men and warriors would recite the traditions represented by the pictographs.

Not all Plains tribes, unfortunately, kept such tangible records formulating tribal history and aiding in its perpetuation, but they all had what the Kiowa pictographs brought to mind: mythic and historic oral traditions that were the substance of the tribe's historiography. Thus Mooney, in his description of the Kiowa calendars, was presenting in essence a collection of oral traditions, albeit ones that because of their chronological sequencing were more systematically organized from the perspective of Western scholarship than most American Indian traditions.[1]

Traditional Narratives of the Arikara Indians presents another Plains historiographic tradition, that of the Arikaras, frequently

---

1. Other tribes also used mnemonic devices to aid in the retention and recitation of ritual knowledge. The Arikara sacred bundle of the Eastern (*huukaawirát*) band, for example, contained a sheaf of thirty-four small sticks that were laid out whenever the bundle was opened and its ritual recited. Each stick symbolized a portion of the bundle's set of religious teachings as well as stages in the development of the world (Gilmore 1929).

called Rees, a group of people who have lived in what is now the
Dakotas for well over two centuries and who are closely related
linguistically to the Pawnees of Nebraska and more distantly to the
Wichitas and Caddos of the southern Plains.[2] All these peoples—
Arikaras, Pawnees, Wichitas, Caddos, as well as the extinct Kitsai—
composed the Caddoan language family and, until the late eighteenth century, formed a nearly unbroken population continuum
extending over the tall grass prairies of the eastern Plains from the
Dakotas to Texas (Lesser and Weltfish 1932). That continuum was
the historical result of a gradual northward movement from the
southeastern Plains of the Caddoan peoples who were the ancestors
of the Arikaras and Pawnees. For the Arikaras, who were in the
vanguard of that movement, the gradual northwestward course
along the Missouri River was divinely sanctioned and became a
religious symbol around which they organized their historical
traditions.

A Cultural Overview

Arikara culture developed over many centuries during which
their ancestors cultivated the soil of the Missouri River bottoms in
what is now South Dakota, where the women planted gardens of
corn, squash, and beans. The crops they raised allowed these people
a more sedentary and secure lifestyle than that of their nomadic
neighbors, who subsisted almost exclusively on the wandering herds
of buffalo. There, generally on bluffs overlooking the west bank of
the river, Arikaras built their permanent villages of earth lodges.
These large, dome-shaped dwellings stood some fifteen feet in
height and thirty feet in diameter, supported by four central posts
and a circle of smaller posts at the periphery, and were covered
with rafters, over which were layers of sticks, grass, and finally

2. In the eighteenth and nineteenth centuries the Arikaras were also
frequently referred to as Arikarees, a name that had many variant spellings
(see Hodge 1907–11, 1:86). The name Rees, a shortened form of Arikarees,
is said to have been the form used by early French Canadian traders
(Lewis and Clark in Moulton 1987, 3:400) and is commonly used on the Fort
Berthold Reservation today by both Arikaras themselves as well as Mandans and Hidatsas.

prairie sod. In the early eighteenth century a typical village was a hamlet of perhaps thirty-five such earth lodges arranged randomly. Somewhere near the center there generally was a ceremonial structure, today called the Medicine Lodge, identical in shape to the residential lodges but much larger in size, having a diameter of up to sixty feet and a capacity to accomodate as many as six hundred people. Later in the eighteenth century, when more easterly tribes like the Sioux pushed westward onto the Plains, intertribal warfare intensified. The Arikaras then concentrated in larger communities, each fortified by a surrounding ditch and palisade to afford protection against enemies, particularly against those tribes from the east who had already obtained European firearms.

Throughout the early eighteenth century the Arikaras had a population of at least 10,000 people living at any one time in twenty to perhaps as many as forty villages extending along the Missouri from the White River north to just above the Grand River. This population was not only much larger but also more diverse than it was a century later. It was not a single, unified tribe but rather comprised aggregates of villages organized into seven or perhaps a dozen bands, some of which—but certainly not all—may have been allied (Parks 1979a). The names of ten of these social units have survived into the twentieth century:

awaáhu (no translation) [3]
tUhkaatákUx 'Village Against A Hill'
NAhuukaátA 'By The Water'
čiNIhnaahtákUx 'Ash Tree On A Hill'
tUhkAsthaánu' 'Buffalo Sod Village'
naakarĭkA 'Tree Branch Sticking Out'
huukaawirát 'Eastern'
warihká' (no translation)
šitʰniišáplt 'They Broke The Arrow'
wiita'uúxU 'Long Haired Man'

---

3. The usual translation for this name is 'Left Behind,' based on an association with the stem *huuriwaa* 'to leave behind, abandon.' It is not certain, however, that the name in fact derives from that stem.

Two other names have been recorded but not corroborated by more than one source: *nakaanústš* 'Little Chokecherry' and Scirihául, a name of uncertain derivation but said to mean 'Coyote Fat'[4] (Gilmore 1927:345).

The population was dialectally diverse as well. Precisely how diverse is unknown today, but based on statements from fur traders and words recorded early in the nineteenth century it is clear that there were at least two major dialect groups, one whose speech was more closely related to that of the Pawnee groups to the south and another whose speech diverged more sharply from Pawnee and more closely resembled that of contemporary Arikaras (Parks 1979b). Less striking dialectal distinctions must have existed within those larger speech groups as well, for in 1804 the fur trader Pierre-Antoine Tabeau, who lived with the Arikaras for two years, wrote:

> The Loups [Skiri Pawnees] and all the different Panis [Pawnees] now on the river Platte, made, undoubtedly, with the Ricaras but one nation which time and circumstances have, without doubt, insensibly divided. The language was originally the same; but, like that of all nations, it has undergone such great changes that it has left many different dialects. Each of the tribes has its own particular one so that no one can say that he knows the Ricara language; for it would be necessary that he should understand in ten different ways the greater number of the words, in which the common etymology is scarely to be recognized. The pronunciation especially differs markedly. [Abel 1939:125–26]

Several fundamental features distinguished eighteenth-century Arikaras from neighboring tribes. The most prominent distinctive cultural traits were corn cultivation—clearly an ancient feature of Arikara life that was deeply embedded in the people's ceremonial life—and patterns of ceremonial and political organization.

Although Arikaras planted other crops as well—squash, beans, and sunflowers—in tribal religious life none of them assumed the fundamental importance of corn. The plant was personified and

---

4. The first element of this form is *sčirir*, the stem for 'wolf, coyote,' and the second part appears to be related to the descriptive stem *ahiht* 'to be fat.' Perhaps Gilmore was attempting to write *sčiri'ahIt*, a word not recognized by modern speakers.

deified as Mother Corn, a bestower of culture and a protector of the people. Mother Corn was intrinsic to religious rites, most of which corresponded to the cycle of corn growth, the teachings of Mother Corn, and the invocation of her assistance. The pervasive role of corn in Arikara life was, moreover, manifested in economy and life-style. Buffalo hunting, while certainly important for subsistence, was not the protracted activity that it was among the Pawnees and other horticulturalists to the south. Corn afforded an economic surplus that attracted nomadic tribes from the high plains to the Arikara villages on the Missouri to barter. In the late eighteenth century those tribes included the Kiowas, Comanches, Plains Apaches, Arapahos, Cheyennes, and others whose names are no longer identifiable today, all friends of the Arikaras, as well as various Sioux bands, sometimes friendly but more often hostile. The nomadic hunters brought to the Arikaras their products of the chase—dried meat, hides, furs, and buckskin clothing decorated with quill work—as well as horses from the southwest, in exchange for which the Arikaras bartered their garden produce and the native tobacco they also grew. So intrinsic, in fact, was corn to the life of Arikaras that it was for them a metaphor for life itself, one that was recognized by other Plains peoples as well and was mani-fested in the Plains sign language designation of Arikaras as 'corn shellers.'

Another striking feature of Arikara culture was a divinely sanc-tioned religious and political organization. Early in human history, when the ancestors of the Arikara people lived underground, the Chief Above (neešaanu' tˀnačitákUx) sent to them Mother Corn, who with the assistance of various animals led them out into the world and along a path beset with many obstacles to reach the land where they lived in the eighteenth century. Finally she gave these ancestors of the Arikaras their religious teachings and ceremonies as well as corn and other plants to cultivate. Through her, too, the Chief Above ordained the office of chief (neešaánu'), the man who would be the people's protector and leader. To him and his lineal descendants was entrusted the sacred bundle, representing the power of the Chief Above and the teachings of Mother Corn; it was to serve as a palladium that drew the people of the village together, binding them as a social unit and giving focus to their religious life

(G.A. Dorsey 1904a:12–32).

Village chieftaincy, a hereditary position, was a status passed down through the male line and was apparently symbolized by family ownership of the village sacred bundle.[5] Through achievements in war other men could become chiefs, who were then leaders in political and social affairs, but their positions could not be inherited; only village chieftaincy was hereditary (Holder 1970:41–45).

Although the chief was the lineal descendant of the original owner of the village sacred bundle, he did not necessarily know its rituals. That knowledge belonged to a leading priest *(kunahUx-čitawi'u')*, whose position also tended to be hereditary in the male line and who actually conducted the ceremonies of the bundle. His duties, like those of the chief, were prescribed at the time of Creation: he was a mediator between the deities and the people. The rituals that he and his assistants conducted in the Medicine Lodge were solemn, measured liturgies composed of offerings and sacrifices interspersed with long cycles of songs recounting events in mythological times, when the world was forming, as well as recitations of the moral teachings given the people by Mother Corn. The purpose of such ceremonies was to gain the attention of the deities—of the Chief Above, Mother Corn, and a host of spiritual beings—and by supplication, sacrifice, and acknowledgment of their deeds to gain the deities' favor, resulting in good fortune and assistance in the people's food quest and in their social needs. Early each spring the ritual calendar began with a renewal of objects in the bundle, proceeded to a series of spring and summer ceremonies marking stages in the planting and cultivation of crops (especially corn), and then continued on to activities associated with the summer hunt. In early fall the ceremonial season concluded with a thanksgiving ritual for bountiful crops, after which life in the winter villages in the Missouri bottom lands was ritually dormant, punctuated by short buffalo hunts on the plains.

Contrasting with Arikara religious life, represented in each village by a sacred bundle and its priest, was the institution of

5. For Arikaras, there is insufficient ethnographic data to confirm that bundles were the property of the chiefs' families, but for Pawnees the association of bundle with village chief is amply documented (Dorsey and Murie 1940; Holder 1970:41–45).

healing, represented by medicines and doctors. Both institutions, the religious and the medical, although conceptually separate, were nevertheless symbolically united in the Medicine Lodge, where the rituals of both were always conducted. The Medicine Lodge was, consequently, the paramount symbol of Arikara social and cultural solidarity.

In Arikara society, doctors *(kunaá'u')* were men not necessarily born to that status but who generally obtained their powers to cure and perform mystical feats from other doctors or from membership in a doctor's society, whose powers ultimately derived from animals. Doctors whose powers came from the same source formed associations. Some doctors, such as those having horse or snake medicine, for example, were loose associations that in the late nineteenth century were of relatively recent origin. Other doctors, however, belonged to older, established societies that had assigned seating positions in the Medicine Lodge for those ritual occasions when its members met there. In the late nineteenth century eight societies comprised the Medicine Lodge—Ghost, Blacktail Deer, Shedding Buffalo, Cormorant, Duck, Owl, Din Of Birds, and Bear—in addition to a group of leading doctors who sat at the altar. Every year during late summer these societies met in the Medicine Lodge, and for a period of a month the doctors lived there, where they performed dances, rituals, and legerdemain daily. Unlike religious rituals, which were solemn, repetitive acts, the doctors' performances emphasized drama. To the accompaniment of song and dance, body parts would appear to be severed, then miraculously reattached; a person would be shot and apparently killed, then be brought back to life; a plant would appear to grow before the eyes of spectators. Those and many other remarkable feats gained Arikara doctors not only the respect and awe of their own people but of others as well, both neighboring Indians and, later, European visitors (Maximilian 1843, 2:394; Curtis 1907–30, 5:70; W. Hoffman 1884; Will 1934:39-48).

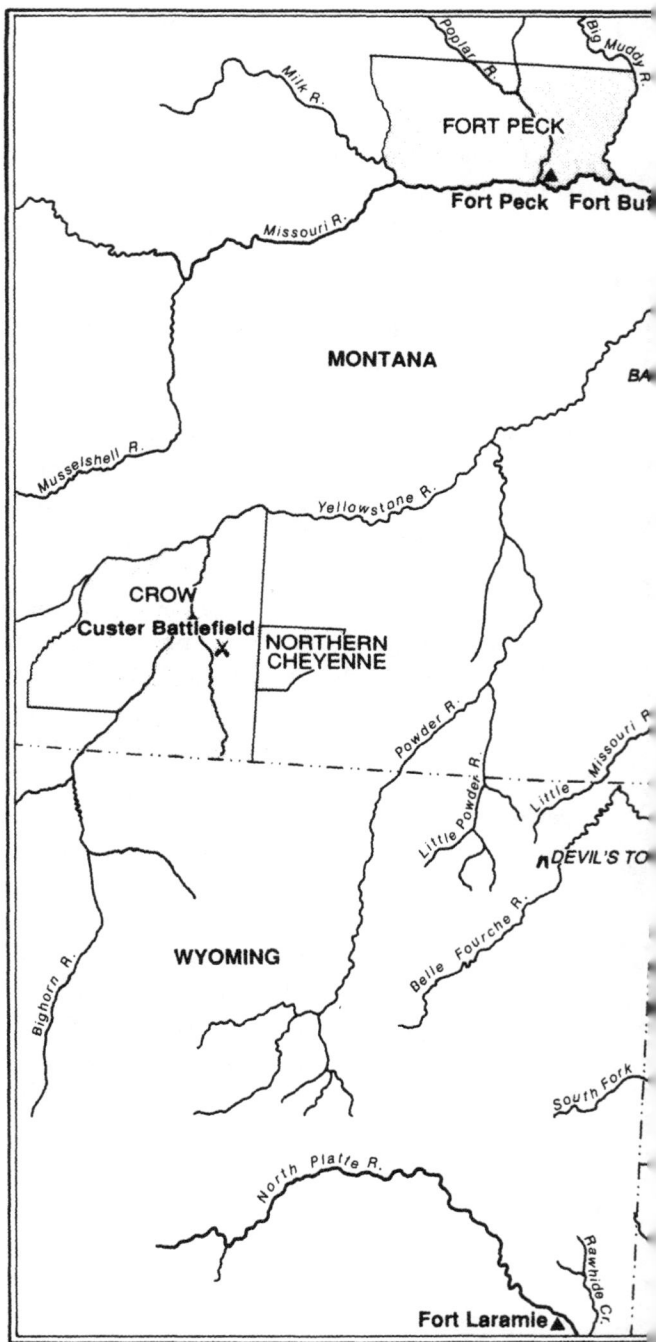

Map 1. The Northern Plains in the Late Nineteenth Century. Shown are the 1897 reservation boundaries.

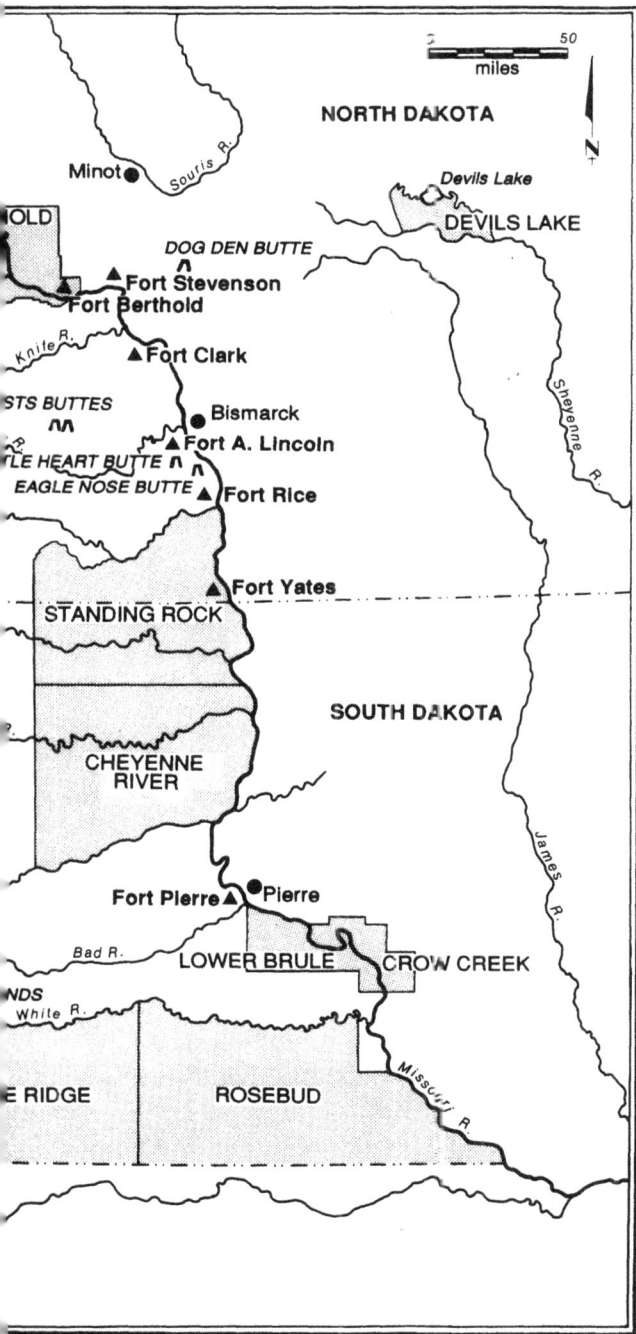

NORTH DAKOTA

Minot

Souris R.

Devils Lake

DEVILS LAKE

OLD

DOG DEN BUTTE

Fort Stevenson

Fort Berthold

Knife R.

Fort Clark

STS BUTTES

R.

Bismarck

LE HEART BUTTE

Fort A. Lincoln

EAGLE NOSE BUTTE

Fort Rice

Sheyenne R.

Fort Yates

STANDING ROCK

SOUTH DAKOTA

CHEYENNE
RIVER

James R.

Fort Pierre

Pierre

Bad R.

LOWER BRULE

CROW CREEK

NDS
White R.

E RIDGE

ROSEBUD

Missouri R.

50
miles

N

A Historical Overview

In the late eighteenth century the Arikara experienced the first of a series of major upheavals that over the next century ultimately shattered their way of life. In 1780-1781 a smallpox epidemic swept over the Plains, inflicting untold casualties among sedentary tribes like the Arikaras. There may have been even earlier, equally deadly epidemics, for the fur trader Jean Baptiste Truteau, who lived among the Arikaras from 1794 to 1796, stated that they had suffered three epidemics before his residency there. Truteau claimed that before those smallpox outbreaks the Arikaras counted 4,000 warriors and lived in thirty-two large villages, but when he was with them, most of the survivors were living in two villages at the mouth of the Cheyenne River, while two additional small groups had gone off, one to reside with the Mandans in the north and the other to visit the Skiri Pawnees to the south; he estimated their population at that time to be 500 warriors, or about 2,500 people in all. The Arikaras, however, anticipating a major onslaught by the Sioux, abandoned the two Cheyenne River villages in 1796, abruptly ending Truteau's stay. Some went north to the Mandans and others went west to the Cheyennes.

In 1804, when Tabeau established residency among the tribe—the same year Lewis and Clark visited them—the Arikaras were again living on the Missouri, now in three villages just above the Grand River, one on modern Ashley Island above the mouth of Rampart Creek and the other two villages four miles north on the west bank of the river. They were still residing there in the two upper villages on the west bank when Henry Brackenridge and John Bradbury traveled up the Missouri in 1811, but the island village had been abandoned some time earlier. During the following decade the Arikaras continued to live in those villages above the Grand River, but in 1823 their life there was disrupted when hostilities broke out with William Ashley's party of fur traders ascending the Missouri. The encounter resulted in the deaths of some fifteen members of Ashley's expedition and immediately prompted a U.S. military expedition to retaliate against the Arikaras. Commanded by Colonel Henry Leavenworth, the American force of 275 men was joined by 750 Sioux. After sustaining Sioux attacks and several days of shelling by the troops, the Arikaras abandoned their palisaded villages under the cover of night, shortly after peace negotiations collapsed, and fled north to the Mandan and Hidatsa villages (Morgan 1964).

George Catlin found the Arikaras living again in the Grand River villages in 1832, but when Prince Maximilian ascended the Missouri in 1833 he recorded that they had moved from the area the preceding year. Driven away by fear of the more powerful Sioux, crop failure, scarcity of buffalo, and potential harassment from American troops in the aftermath of the Leavenworth campaign, most of the Arikaras had gone south to live near the Skiris on the Loup River in Nebraska. In 1835, however, after friction broke out between them and the Skiris, the Arikaras moved into western Nebraska and eastern South Dakota, where they lived for two years as nomadic hunters.

In 1837 small Arikara groups began moving back to the Missouri, continuing their gradual northwestward movement up the river, to settle as a tribe at Fort Clark, the American Fur Company post near the mouth of the Knife River, where the Mandans lived. Immediately upon settling there that year, however, smallpox broke out, brought upstream by a fur company steamboat. The resulting epidemic took a heavy toll on the horticultural tribes of the middle Missouri. The Arikaras lost one half of their population; only some 1,500 survived. Mandan mortalities, however, were even grimmer: some 90 percent of their people perished, reportedly leaving fewer than 150 survivors (Hodge 1907–10, 1:798). Demoralized, the remaining Mandans abandoned their village at Fort Clark and many moved north to join the Hidatsas; later, after a fire destroyed the old Mandan lodges, the Arikaras established their village at Fort Clark, where they remained for over two decades.

Three persistent pressures continued to afflict Arikara life at Fort Clark and took even greater tolls on their already diminished population: crop failures; epidemic diseases that included measles, cholera, and smallpox; and constant Sioux raiding. Finally in 1861, after Fort Clark was abandoned by the fur traders and burned by the Sioux, the Arikaras moved upriver once again, this time to build two villages on the bank opposite Like-A-Fishhook Village, in which both the Mandans and Hidatsas were living. A year later, after more Sioux threats, the Arikaras crossed the Missouri to join them,

Plate 1. Views of Like-A-Fishhook Village in 1872. *Left*, Arikara section, showing palisade in foreground, log cabins and earth lodges in background. *Right*, Arikara section, showing drying scaffolds in foreground and log cabins in background. Photographs by Stanley J. Morrow, courtesy State Historical Society of North Dakota.

Plate 2. Views of Like-A-Fishhook Village in 1872. *Left,* Arikara Medicine Lodge with sacred cedar tree and rock in front of entryway. *Right,* Hidatsa section, showing drying scaffolds in foreground and earth lodges and log cabins in background. Photographs by Stanley J. Morrow, courtesy State Historical Society of North Dakota.

creating in Like-A-Fishhook a combined village in which each of the three tribes maintained its own section. There the Arikaras constructed a Medicine Lodge and tried to recreate their old way of life. At first they were plagued by continuing attacks from the Sioux, but during the following decades their lifestyle was more drastically altered by Euro-Americans. Most previous contact with Americans had been with but one group, the fur traders, who had no intention of radically altering the native lifestyle; now, on a reservation guaranteed them in 1870 by a treaty with the U.S. government, contact occurred with diverse elements of an expanding American society—Indian agents, the military, missionaries, teachers, and settlers—all exerting strong pressures to modify native cultural patterns.

Changes came rapidly for what were now called the Three Tribes[6] on the new Fort Berthold Reservation, the boundaries of which were legally established in 1870.[7] Intertribal warfare, long a bane to the horticulturalists, effectively came to an end after the 1876 military campaign against the off-reservation Sioux and the Battle of the Little Big Horn, in which Arikara scouts served the U.S. government. Once peace was achieved, erstwhile enemies became friendly visitors, and groups of Sioux and Assiniboines, in addition to other previously friendly peoples, came to Fort Berthold to socialize—to visit, dance, and tell stories—while Fort Berthold peoples reciprocated with visits of friendship to neighboring reservation communities in the Dakotas and eastern Montana. The most fundamental changes, however, were ones affecting native culture. Of them, perhaps the most profound was land allotment, the plan of the U.S. government to move Indian families out of tribal settlements and onto individually owned plots of land that they were to farm. The first group of villagers to leave Like-A-Fishhook were Arikara families who took up farmsteads in 1884; by 1886 the entire

6. Later they were officially designated the Three Affiliated Tribes.

7. The first recognition of the territorial claims of the Three Tribes was in the 1851 Fort Laramie Treaty. The boundaries it defined, and the revised ones of 1870, created a reservation that extended on its eastern border from the Missouri River south to the Heart and Little Powder rivers, and on its western border north along the Powder and Yellowstone rivers to the Missouri. The boundaries of this reservation were modified on three subsequent occasions—in 1880, 1891, and finally 1910—in each instance reducing its size. (See map 2.)

Arikara section of the village had been abandoned, thereby ending the community mode of living that the tribe had always known. Equally profound, but not nearly so abrupt, was the elimination, at least overtly, of Arikara religious and curing practices symbolized by the Medicine Lodge. Its public ceremonies were finally suppressed by the Indian agent in 1885, at the same time that families were taking up their allotments.

Shortly after the settlement of families onto individual farmsteads, day schools were established that gave a new focus to community life on the reservation at the end of the nineteenth century, a focus that has continued to the present.[8] The first school was opened in 1895 in the Arikara settlement near the site of old Fort Berthold. Both the school and the settlement there were named Armstrong. Shortly afterward schools were built at Independence, a Mandan and Hidatsa settlement west of the Missouri; at Elbowoods, which was established in 1892 as the site of the new Fort Berthold agency and which became a Hidatsa settlement; and at Shell Creek, another Hidatsa settlement, where most of the members of Crow Flies High's dissident band located after they returned to the reservation in 1894. In addition to the communities that developed around these schools and that later became seats of reservation districts, several other district communities took form: Beaver Creek, an Arikara community; and Red Butte (now Twin Buttes), Little Missouri (or Short River), and Santee (later Lucky Mound), all primarily Hidatsa and Mandan settlements. In addition to the schools in four of them, the initial core of each community was a dance hall and generally a trading post or store. Later, churches were built in some of the communities like Armstrong (later named Nishu), Red Butte, Independence, and Little Missouri (later called Charging Eagle); and a post office, in addition to the one in Elbowoods, was opened in Armstrong. By 1937 each of the

---

8. Earlier schools on the reservation were a day school at the agency, first opened in 1870 but operating only sporadically; one established at the Congregational mission in 1876; and another constructed at the Catholic mission in 1889. When the army closed Fort Stevenson on the eastern border of the reservation, the agency opened a boarding school in the old buildings in 1883 and operated it until 1893, when the main part of the plant burned down.

Territory established by Treaty of 1851

Reservation Boundaries 1870

Reservation Boundaries 1880

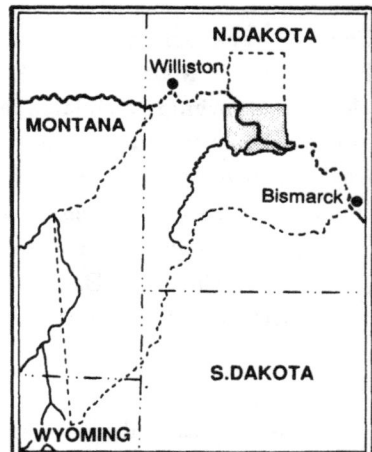

Reservation Boundaries 1891

Map 2. Changing Fort Berthold Reservation Boundaries, 1851–1891.

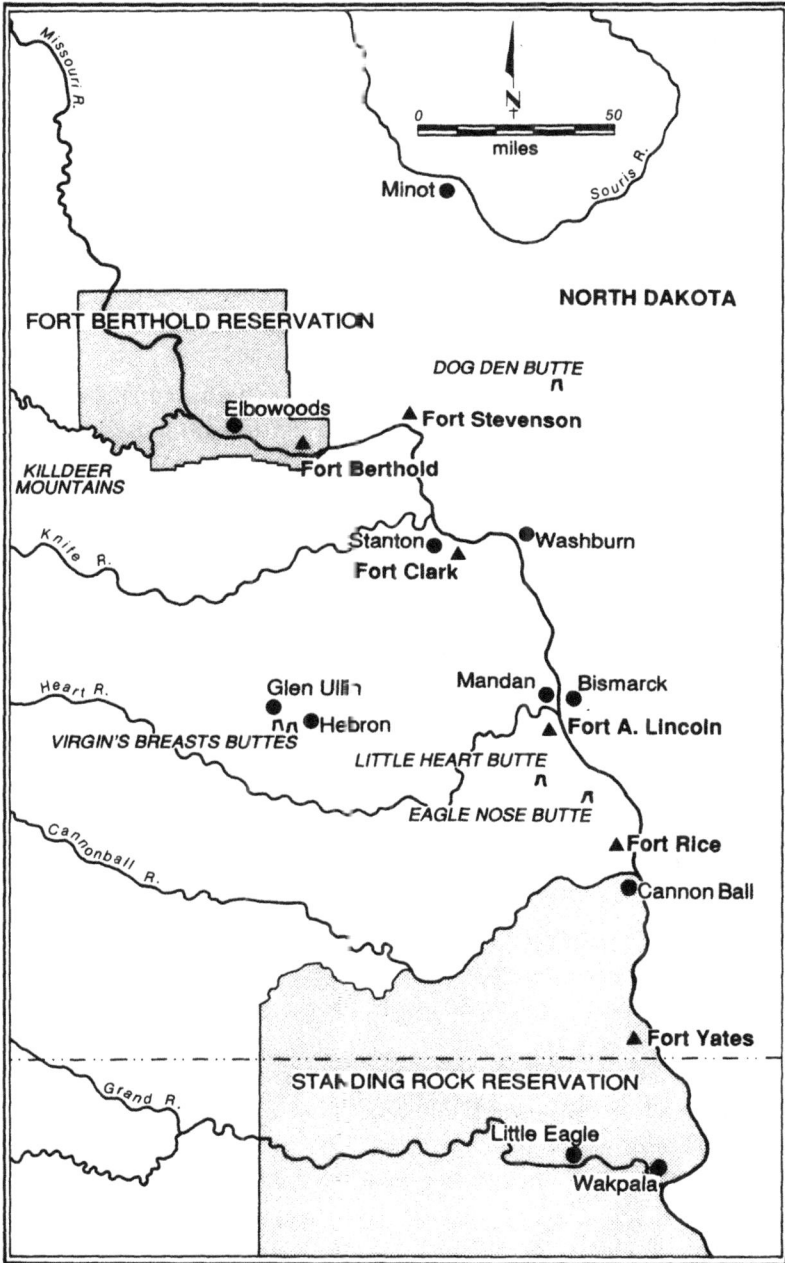

Map 3. Fort Berthold Reservation and Vicinity in the Early Twentieth Century.

eight communities had a day school.

During the first half of the twentieth century, Arikara life on the Fort Berthold Reservation was dominated by efforts to implement government Indian policy charted at the end of the previous century: to educate Indians, primarily by teaching them manual trade skills, and to train them to become successful, independent farmers or livestock ranchers—goals that sought to merge Indian people ultimately into rural American society. Agency and government programs met with general success, although fundamental aspects of traditional Indian culture continued to survive, often in spite of vigorous agency efforts to suppress them. So vigorous, in fact, were those attempts that in 1902 they prompted the anthropologist George A. Dorsey to remark in a letter to Commissioner of Indian Affairs William A. Jones:

> To me, one of the most pitiable things which I have ever seen in all my dealings with the Indians is that of a tribe like the Arikara, for instance, who have been hounded by the missionaries and by their agents for a period of thirty or forty years, and who have been made to think that they had absolutely no right on this earth to think about their own gods, who have literally been compelled to hide away all their religious paraphernalia; and whatever of their rites or ceremonies they have held they have held with fear and trembling—and yet, the Arikara are truly Indians in that feeling and belief as are any Indians of this Continent. [G.A. Dorsey 1902]

Despite the agency and missionary efforts to eradicate Arikara religious traditions, however, at the turn of the century there were attempts in the Beaver Creek district to revive them. Two prominent ritual leaders, Crow Ghost and Red Star, for example, had dreams in which they were given dance songs (story 32); Crow Ghost tried to revive older ceremonies; and a young woman named Winnie Enemy Heart had a vision in which she was told that Arikaras should return to their former ways. Moreover, in 1910 the Arikara Medicine Lodge was revived for Edward Curtis so that he could photograph and describe its rituals for the Arikara section of his multivolume set *The North American Indian* (Curtis 1907–30, 5:59–100). It was a revival that continued sporadically until the early 1930s.

The Arikara population, which had reached an all-time low of

Plate 3. Partial view of Elbowoods, Fort Berthold Reservation, North Dakota. Photograph ca. 1911, by Fred Olsen, courtesy State Historical Society of North Dakota.

379 in 1905, began a slow, steady rise, but simultaneously, Arikara intermarriage with Hidatsas and Mandans increased, blurring many of the distinctive cultural differences among the three tribes, even though each continued to maintain its own communities.

In 1953 still another major upheaval—the last of many—affected life for the Arikaras and their Fort Berthold neighbors when the U.S. Army Corps of Engineers constructed Garrison Dam on the Missouri just below the southeastern boundary of the reservation. Built for flood control and for water diversion to central North Dakota farming areas, the dam created Garrison Reservoir, now called Lake Sakakawea, which flooded all the Missouri bottom lands on the reservation. For the Three Affiliated Tribes, all of whose communities were located in those bottom lands, the flooding necessitated a massive relocation to the upland prairies surrounding the new reservoir. It also meant that the reservation was divided into discontinuous segments even more remote from each other, separated by a lake too wide to span feasibly with bridges. The result of the relocation was only an approximate replication on the prairies of the old communites in the river bottoms. Elbowoods and the agency, as well as the Shell Creek community, were reestablished in New Town in the Northern Segment of the reservation, which continued to be primarily Hidatsa in population. Nishu (formerly Armstrong), the primary Arikara community, moved to the Eastern Segment and became White Shield, named after the prominent nineteenth-century Arikara chief. The old communities of Beaver Creek, Red Butte, and Little Missouri in the Southern Segment joined to form the new community of Twin Buttes; the Hidatsa community of Independence was reformed as Mandaree in the Western Segment; and Lucky Mound was moved to the new Northeastern Segment. As before, the core of each new community was its school, together with housing for teachers and tribal members, and a community hall in which dances, funerals, community meetings, and other social events were held.

Thus by the mid twentieth century the Arikaras had relocated as a group for perhaps the final time in their gradual movement north. It was a journey that had commenced untold centuries in the past, before their modern identification as Arikaras had taken form, when they and their close relatives the Pawnees lived somewhere

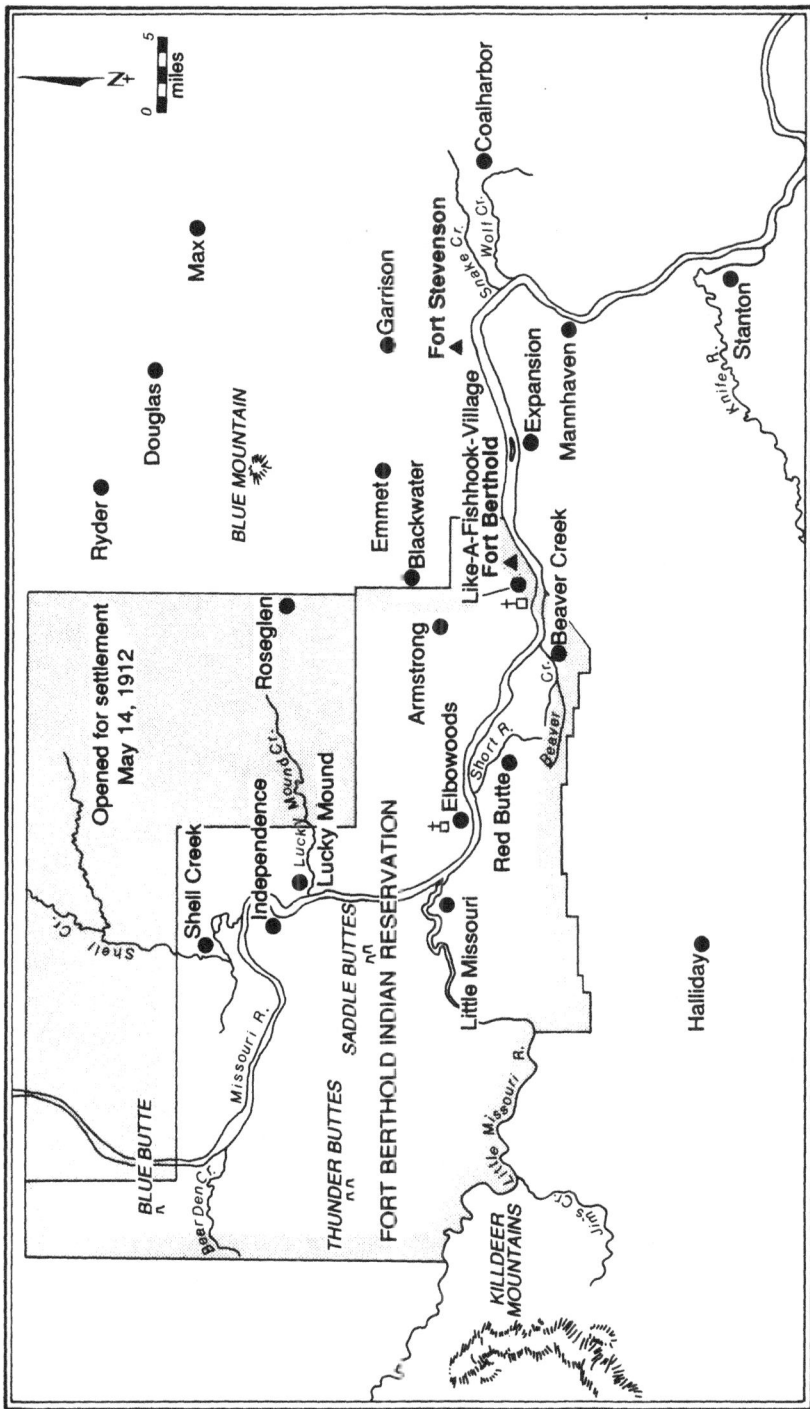

Map 4. Fort Berthold Reservation in the Early Twentieth Century.

farther southeastward in what must have been the homeland of all
the Caddoan peoples. The original group or groups who ultimately
became the Arikaras were the vanguard of those Caddoans who
migrated north to Nebraska and beyond and who were settled along
the Missouri River in South Dakota in the eighteenth century when
Europeans first encountered them. From the late eighteenth to the
late nineteenth century, a combination of disease and warfare dec-
imated their population so that what had formerly been dialectally,
and perhaps culturally, diverse people became an amalgam that
would henceforth be considered a single tribal entity. However, no
matter the specific stimuli—disease, enemies, famine—their history
throughout this period continued to be the story of a northwestward
migration along the Holy Water, the Missouri River, in a general
movement enshrined in myth and ordained in religious belief that
has culminated in their present location in west central North
Dakota.

Recording Arikara Oral Traditions

For a tribe that has received so little attention from anthropologists and other cultural recorders, the body of documented Arikara
oral traditions is both surprisingly extensive and yet frustratingly
meager—extensive in a comparative Plains context because there
is at least one large collection that was recorded at the turn of the
century, and yet meager because even at this relatively early date
the stories were collected at the end of a living tradition, not one
that was still viable.

Jean Baptiste Truteau, during his late-eighteenth-century visit,
was the first outsider to record an Arikara myth. In a discussion of
Arikara religious beliefs in his "Description of the Upper Missouri"
(Parks 1991b), he presented as an illustration of Arikara religious
traditions an abbreviated account of the origins of horticulture and
of human subsistence on game animals followed by divine instruc-
tions for ritual worship of the Great Holy. In their journals nearly
a decade later, Lewis and Clark also mentioned an Arikara tradition, a story about a young couple who turned to stone, which was
related to them during their brief visit with the tribe on their way
up the Missouri (Moulton 1987, 3:169).

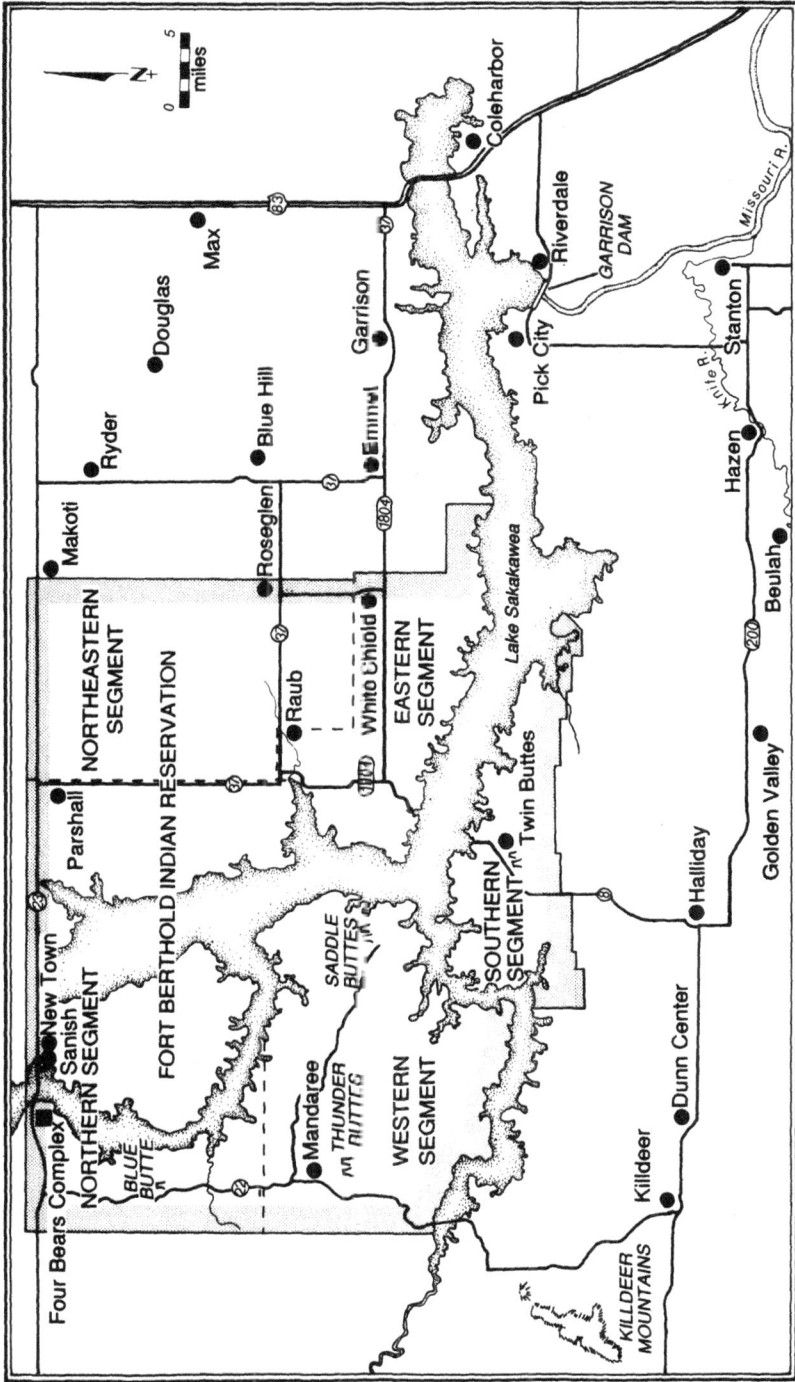

Map 5. Fort Berthold Reservation in the Late Twentieth Century.

Other Arikara stories published in the nineteenth century include the myth of Long Teeth, recorded by the physician Walter Hoffman in 1892, as well as a small number of other stories that appeared sporadically during the last two decades of the nineteenth century in the *Word Carrier*, a newspaper serving the Dakota Mission of the Congregational and Presbyterian churches and printed at Santee, Nebraska. These stories, which include the genesis tradition as well as several myths and fables, were recorded by the Congregational missionary Charles L. Hall and his wife, who first went to the Fort Berthold Reservation in 1876. Hall was not one of those exceptional missionaries who truly appreciated Indian culture and attempted to preserve a record of the vanishing lifeway of the people he served. For him there was no compromise in his missionary calling: the new must replace the old; cultural surrender must be unconditional. And yet, despite his inflexible stance, there was a curious ambivalence toward Indian culture that, for example, inspired him and his wife to record and preserve by publication some of the religious beliefs of the Arikaras.

In 1903 James R. Murie, a mixed-blood Skiri Pawnee educated at Hampton Institute in Virginia and at that time assistant to the anthropologist George A. Dorsey of the Field Columbian Museum in Chicago, visited the Fort Berthold Reservation to make a record of Arikara folklore and ceremonialism as well as to purchase material culture specimens for the museum. The material he recorded, which marked the first modern anthropological study of the Arikara, was to contribute to Dorsey's broad descriptive and comparative study of the mythology and ritualism of the Caddoan tribes. Murie had begun collecting Pawnee oral traditions three years earlier—an effort that over a five-year period resulted in two published volumes of Pawnee traditions[9]—and in the course of a three-month visit to Fort Berthold he recorded eighty-two stories, which were published by Dorsey in 1904 under the title *Traditions of the Arikara*.

Here was a large, representative collection of the repertoire of traditional Arikara folklore at the turn of the century, at a time when the last Arikara Medicine Lodge was a disappearing ruin and

---

9. *Traditions of the Skidi Pawnee* (G.A. Dorsey 1904b) and *The Pawnee: Mythology (Part 1)* (G.A. Dorsey 1906a).

a log church had already been built to serve the tribe. Murie's narrators were prominent tribal members, who included Bear's Head, Four Horns (Four Rings), White Owl, Many Foxes, Yellow Bull, Yellow Bear, Strikes Enemy, White Bear, Snowbird (Nice Voiced Elk), Enemy Heart, Sam Newman (Two Hawks), Joe Reed (Red Hail), and Andrew Little Crow. Some of them as young men had been on war parties, and many were traditional ritual leaders and doctors. Four Rings, for example, was the keeper and priest of the Eastern bundle. Some were educated and were fully bilingual in Arikara and English; but most spoke little or no English, so that Murie, who according to Dorsey had overcome the differences between Arikara and Pawnee speech, took the stories down in an English translation that apparently closely followed the narrated Arikara.

After Murie, no one made further efforts to record substantial amounts of Arikara oral traditions. Edward Curtis, who collected material in 1907 for the Arikara section of *The North American Indian*, did record three long stories, including a version of the genesis tradition, which he published in 1909. And in 1910, when the anthropologist Robert Lowie spent several days interviewing Bear's Teeth, an elderly Arikara man, on the topic of tribal societies, he obtained several stories that he subsequently published (Lowie 1915).

Although not yet oral traditions, the reminiscences in *The Arikara Narrative* are an important part of Arikara oral history. They record Arikara participation in Lieutenant Colonel George Armstrong Custer's 1874 and 1876 campaigns and represent the final major effort during the early twentieth century to preserve tribal history. Finding that Arikara service in those campaigns and their perspective on them had been overlooked by historians, in 1912 O.G. Libby, then director of the North Dakota State Historical Society, gathered together in the house of Bear's Belly the surviving scouts who had served under Custer at Fort Abraham Lincoln. Libby recorded their reminiscences and published them as a volume in 1920.

During the 1920s the ethnobotanist Melvin R. Gilmore frequently visited the Arikaras at Fort Berthold to record material on a variety of topics, including religion, botany, and social organization.

Although he, too, recorded a small number of oral traditions incidental to other projects, one, the genesis myth associated with the Eastern bundle, was published as a separate article (Gilmore 1929). In it Gilmore presented the myth and described the ritual transfer of a sheaf of thirty-four willow sticks from the bundle's priest, Four Rings, to himself. The set of sticks were what the priest would lay out during the bundle-opening ritual to represent stages in the narrative of the beginning and development of all things in the world. Presented here in English translation is a recitation of this cosmogonic component, which was integral to Arikara religious ceremonialism.

More recently, in 1938 the anthropologist Preston Holder spent six months at Fort Berthold studying Arikara culture, and during the course of that work he wrote down in English a small miscellaneous collection of stories that remain unpublished.

Finally, two short selections of Arikara interlinear linguistic texts were recently published as part of a representative collection of Caddoan texts (Parks 1977). One set consists of three narratives collected by Allan R. Taylor in 1960, and the second comprises seven texts, all of which are earlier versions of narratives in the present collection.

Recording the Collection

Despite more than a century and a half of unrelenting assaults on Arikara society by human foes and disease, and despite their cooperativeness with the U.S. government and their more positive attitude toward acculturation than most other Plains tribes adopted in the late nineteenth century, many Arikaras clung tenaciously to their language and distinctive cultural traditions. As a consequence, when I first went to North Dakota in 1970 to begin a study of the Arikara language, there were some two hundred speakers, twenty to thirty of whom still used an old form of the language and remembered many traditional stories.

Over the ensuing two decades I have been engaged in an effort to help preserve as much of this linguistic and historiographic heritage as possible. At the outset my goals were purely academic— to document oral traditions in the language as one means of preserving a linguistic record of Arikara speech. But it soon became apparent that many people in the White Shield community, still maintaining its distinct Arikara identity, were keenly interested in having both their language and their cultural traditions not only preserved but also taught in the tribal school, so that their children would be able to learn there what elders at home were no longer able to teach: their tribal linguistic and historical heritage. Hence my effort developed into a more broadly based one involving many Arikara elders and other individuals in the community.

History of the Project

The history of this project began in Pawnee, Oklahoma, on a hot August evening in 1969, when I went to the home of Dolly Moore, with whom I had regularly worked on the Pawnee language, to bid her farewell before my return to California. Visiting her from North Dakota was a gregarious Arikara friend, Fanny Whiteman, who took a lively interest in our linguistic project and suggested before I left that if I should ever come to North Dakota to study Arikara she would introduce me to her mother, Clara Perkins, an elderly and fluent speaker of the language. Anxious to undertake comparative work with this language, which grammatically is almost identical to Pawnee but is not mutually intelligible with it because of various sound shifts and changes in the meanings of words, I traveled to North Dakota the following summer to spend two weeks there recording Arikara vocabulary from Fanny and her mother. During my visit, Dan Howling Wolf, a blind man then in his sixties, came to Fanny's when she told him I wanted to record Indian stories and songs. Over two evenings we tape-recorded fourteen stories, most of them about Coyote and Scalped Man but including others, as well as forty-six personal songs of military servicemen—the modern equivalent of old warrior songs.

My first visit to North Dakota established warm friendships which developed into obvious mutual enthusiasm for continuing the study of Arikara, but I was not able to return there for a year and a half. Meanwhile, in the fall of the following year, Fanny's mother passed away before we had the opportunity to continue our work.

Nevertheless, in January 1972, during the winter academic break, I flew to Minot, North Dakota, and then took a bus to

Parshall, where I stayed two weeks with Fanny and her father. During that visit Dan and Mabel Howling Wolf and another elder couple, Matthew and Alice White Bear, came to stay for several days. During the daytime we recorded vocabulary, and in the evenings we recorded more stories. Dan told nine, which together with the ones he had told previously, form the inventory of his narratives in this collection. Matthew told eight, four of which are presented here. Subsequently, Fanny and Alice worked with me for several days at transcribing and translating several of them before I had to return to my teaching duties at Idaho State University.

In early June I came back to Parshall and remained in North Dakota throughout the summer. During the first part I continued to work with Fanny and Alice, taking up the linguistic work where we had left off in the winter. Then in early August I visited Mary Gillette, daughter of Little Sioux, an Arikara scout and prominent doctor, and herself a conservative elder member of the community who always participated in traditional affairs. I wanted to record songs and suggested offhandedly that she might, for example, know a lullaby. She mistook my request, however, thinking that I had come to ask her to sing a medicine song for newborn infants that she knew, and set a later date for me to return. When I arrived at her home, accompanied at her request by Fanny, who would be a witness to what she did, she performed a ceremony preparatory to the recording and then sang for me her medicine song preceded by a prayer (narrative 146). Afterward she recorded two stories and a love song with an accompanying explanation in Arikara, all of which are included here.

During that August Fanny took me to White Shield to introduce me to her aunt, Ella Waters, an octogenarian who was noted as a medicine woman and tribal ceremonial leader. We stayed two days at Mrs. Waters's home, working all day and into the night. The experience was exhilarating for me because in Mrs. Waters I had found a person who not only spoke Arikara without peer but who also, because she had previously worked with anthropologists, was sensitive to what I wanted to know and seemed genuinely to enjoy the linguistic endeavor. We arranged to continue working together for the duration of my stay that summer.

I returned to North Dakota the following June (1973) and took up residence in Garrison, a small town twenty-two miles east of White Shield. From there I drove daily to White Shield, a regular commute made whenever I worked in the community over the ensuing eleven years. For a short time while we worked together, Mrs. Waters lived in a house in White Shield, while her own house on a farm four miles west of the community was being renovated. Once the renovations were completed, she moved back to the farm, where we continued our collaboration in a peaceful setting with rare interruptions. There, interspersed with other linguistic endeavors over the course of the summer, I recorded eleven stories. Sometimes her grandson's wife, a young Sioux woman from Manitoba, together with her son, would be present, but frequently I would be the sole member of the audience—an audience which in either case did not understand the narration—told in her living room with its windows open to let the warm summer winds provide a refreshing air flow. After recording the stories, I transcribed and translated them with Mrs. Waters's collaboration.

During the spring of 1974 I accepted a position at Mary College (present University of Mary), a small, private school in Bismarck, North Dakota, to direct an Indian language program established by Elaine A. Jahner (now of Dartmouth College). The goal of the program was to develop college-level pedagogical materials for the languages native to North Dakota so that courses in those languages could be offered as part of the college's developing Indian Studies program, initiated at a time when there was an awakening interest in tribal heritage among Indian students in the state. During the first year of this program, my work, together with that of Janet Beltran, a curriculum designer and writer, was to concentrate on Arikara, but a year later, in 1976, two additional linguists, Robert Hollow and A. Wesley Jones, were added to the staff to prepare reference and teaching materials for the two other Fort Berthold languages, Mandan and Hidatsa. The initial goal of the program was subsequently widened to include the preparation of elementary language lessons that could be used in reservation school classrooms in White Shield, Twin Buttes, and Mandaree. To achieve these goals, two complementary efforts were required: working with older speakers to record various linguistic data—vocabulary for dictionaries; phrases, sentences, and verb paradigms for grammars; and traditional narratives for historical and literary preservation—and developing language lessons derived from the linguistic data and other material collected specifically for that purpose. Thus, over the next few years the agenda was established.

Relocating to Bismarck prevented me from working at Fort Berthold during the summer of 1974, but the new position in North Dakota was to afford me the opportunity to work on the reservation throughout the year rather than solely during the summers and to become acquainted with a wider range of people there—tribal officials, school personnel, and members of the Arikara community. As a result interest in the linguistic project increased, developing it into a more community-based endeavor rather than solely an academic one.

In June 1975 I began again to live in Garrison for a three-month period, during which I recorded another story from Mary Gillette, a number of stories from Mrs. Waters, and three stories from William Deane, Jr., an elderly man with whom I had become acquainted.

The following year, 1976, marked another significant milestone in the project. One day, when casually chatting with John Fox, a prominent member of the White Shield community, he suggested one of his brothers, Alfred Morsette, as a potential source of traditional stories. Although I had never heard of his brother before, I followed the lead. In August I visited him at his home in a remote area west of Twin Buttes in the Southern Segment of the reservation and explained to him the linguistic work I was doing and my desire to record traditional Arikara stories. His response was heartening: he said he knew many old stories about the Arikara past, ones told to him by his grandparents who had reared him and by many other men now deceased, and he would be glad to record them so that there would be a history of the tribe. He insisted, however, on one modification in my plan: I had only asked him to record stories in Arikara, but he wanted to record them in English as well so that anyone who did not understand Arikara—and from his perspective that was nearly everyone in the world—could listen to them. That day we recorded three narratives, all historical in a Western sense, describing the Arikara separation from the Pawnees, the Fort Laramie Treaty of 1851, and the two Custer campaigns culminating in the Battle of the Little Big Horn. Each one was told first in Arikara and immediately afterward in English, a routine subsequently followed every time we recorded stories.

Over the next four years Alfred and I met many times, but always during the winter, which was loosely defined as any time between October and March, since he wished to follow the old custom of telling stories only during that season. At first I traveled to his home, where during each visit we would generally record from two to five narratives, depending on their length. Later, as we became better acquainted, Alfred came periodically to Bismarck—initially, to stay with his son and, later, after he had taken me as a son, to stay with me at my home. On such occasions we would chat and review Arikara vocabulary during the day, and after supper in the evening we would record stories. I would turn on the tape recorder when he was ready, and then he would proceed to narrate, frequently closing his eyes and folding his arms as he recited from memory the details of the story, told, as he would say, exactly as he had heard it. Some stories he had been told only once or twice while a child or youth; others were accounts he had heard later in his life. He had repeated many of the stories to his own children when they were growing up, but many had not been related to anyone since he had heard them originally, so the latter required thoughtful preparation before recording. Then, about ten thirty at night, after recording for several hours, Alfred liked to have "a little lunch" and coffee and then chat until bedtime. In the morning he would always rise early and sit in the dining room singing Arikara songs until breakfast.

Between 1976 and 1979 Alfred recorded a total of sixty-one stories in Arikara, all of which appear in this collection. Then and later he also recorded a number of others that were told only in English and are not included here. The number of stories in his repertoire is impressive, especially given their nature and detail. Certainly no other contemporary Arikara, even those older than he, matched Alfred in the number and variety of stories remembered, all told in a fine narrative style characteristic of an older, all-but-forgotten oral tradition. For him, knowing them was a source of great pride. So, too, was his phenomenal memory for songs. A singer most of his life, he was noted not only for his fine voice but also for his vast repertoire of songs. After he heard a song, he once told me pridefully, he "soaked it up like a sponge" and retained it in his memory. And indeed he demonstrated this capacity one week in spring 1978 when he came to Bismarck to record old songs, most of them no longer remembered by his contemporaries. One set consisted of twenty Pawnee grass dance songs introduced to the Arikaras before the turn of the century; two other groups were also grass dance songs—one set those of Crow Ghost and the other those of Red Star—which were dreamed at the turn of the century (narrative 32). Most of them had not been sung in years. During that week Alfred recorded the old grass dance songs as well as many others representing other genres, for a total of over two hundred songs, and afterward told in English the story behind each one.

In 1977 I also recorded a sample of stories from several other individuals in order to insure that the text collection would be representative of the contemporary Arikara community and illustrate individual variation in both narrative type and style. In September I arranged to meet with John Fox and Dan Hopkins at Fox's house in White Shield. There, in his living room, we recorded all afternoon, the two men alternating stories. They each told four; of these, Hopkins's are printed in this collection. One evening later that month I visited Joe Fox, a grandson of Lowie's informant, Bear's Teeth, at his home in Drags Wolf Village west of New Town. On that visit he recorded two stories, one of which is included in this collection. Again one evening in the fall Mrs. Waters and I went to Drags Wolf Village to visit Eleanor Chase, another fine Arikara speaker who had a strong interest in her heritage. Although, she told us, she wished we had given her advance notice so she could have thought about stories, she recorded three of them, which are included here. Finally that year Mrs. Waters and I visited her niece, Esther Perkins, who then lived across the street from Mrs. Waters's new apartment in a housing development two miles southeast of White Shield. Esther had been crippled all her life and had never attended school. Consequently she grew up speaking only Arikara, learning English later in life. On this visit she took us to her bedroom, where we would be away from the young children playing, and there recorded two stories, both of which are reproduced here.

Through winter 1978 Mrs Waters stayed in Bismarck, where she could work regularly with the language program, aiding in the development of an introductory Arikara language textbook, tape recording lessons, and co-teaching with me an Arikara language course for Mary College students and interested adults. During this period she and I also worked daily at transcribing and translating Alfred Morsette's stories as well as ones that I had recorded earlier from Dan Howling Wolf and others. Mrs. Waters, in fact, assisted me in the transcription and translation process with nearly all of the stories in this collection, with the exception of Lillian Brave's, which are described below. The following year Mrs. Waters returned again to Bismarck for various periods of time to continue the work we had begun the previous fall. At the culmination of this work in spring 1979, at the annual Mary College Indian Student Powwow, she adopted me as a member of the tribe and gave me the Arikara name White Crow *(kaakaataxká)*.

The final chapter in the history of this collection began in 1983, when I came to Indiana University and at the same time began working part-time with a newly funded bilingual education program in the White Shield Elementary School. My goals with the program were to provide further language teaching materials—among them illustrated elementary readers and a bilingual dictionary—and to complete the preparation of this collection of texts. Shortly after the project began, Fanny Whiteman began working with the program and spoke to her aunt, Lillian Brave, then in her mid eighties, about recording some of her stories to be included in the collection. And there began a significant new dimension to the project, since Mrs. Brave was an exceptionally fine speaker of the language—Ella Waters had mentioned to me years earlier that Lillian "spoke the old language"—and knew many old stories. Like Alfred Morsette, she would tell stories only in the winter.

Over a period of several days in January 1984 I recorded nine narratives from Mrs. Brave in the kitchen of her daughter Angela Plante. On each occasion there were at least three of us present— Angela, Fanny, and myself—as well as occasional grandchildren and other relatives, creating an appreciative audience for Mrs. Brave. Afterward I transcribed and translated the stories with the assistance of both Lilly and Angela. In February, after I had returned to

Indiana, Angela recorded another seven stories from her mother and mailed the tape to me. In February 1987 I returned to Parshall, where we recorded six more narratives, all of which, together with the ones previously mailed to me, were then transcribed and translated as before. At the same time Angela shared with me a cassette tape on which in 1975 she had recorded a particularly meaningful story (69) from her mother, and together the three of us transcribed and translated it.

The Narrators

Alfred Morsette, Sr. (Not Afraid Of The Enemy), whose band affiliation was Awahu, was born September 26, 1911, north of Elbowoods in McLean County on the Fort Berthold Reservation. His father was Fred Fox (Holy Owl), the son of John Morsette (Chippewa Child), a Métis from the north, and Squash Blossom, an Arikara woman. His mother was Blanche Meyer, whose father was white and whose mother was Skunk Woman. Alfred lived with his grandparents—Squash Blossom and her second husband, Short Bear, both of whom spoke no English—until he went to Pierre Indian School in South Dakota. There he remained for eight years. When he returned home to the reservation, he lived with an uncle and learned to ride and break horses and then worked locally as a hired hand. At the same time he also took up boxing, but later quit it after losing one eye in an accident. In 1934 he built a house in the old Beaver Creek district from logs that he himself cut and lived there for four years as a bachelor; then in 1938 he married Lena Hunts Along, a Hidatsa who was the daughter of John Hunts Along and the granddaughter of Buffalo Paunch. In that same year Alfred was laid off from his job as a night watchman in Elbowoods and subsequently planted his own gardens, raised horses and cattle, and worked at various odd jobs.

After Garrison Dam was built, Alfred moved to the Southern Segment of the reservation, in a remote area east of Twin Buttes where many other families from Beaver Creek relocated. When I first visited him in 1976, Alfred's son Roy and his family were also living in his home. His wife, Lena, had passed away many years earlier. After several years he moved into an apartment for senior citizens in the Twin Buttes community, where he remained until his

death on December 15, 1989, at the age of seventy-eight. He and his
wife had seven children, two sons and five daughters.

An abiding interest in his Arikara heritage distinguished Mr.
Morsette's life, an interest that was cultivated from the outset by
his grandparents, who were conservative members of the Arikara
community and provided an environment for him early in life that
was rich in traditional culture. Not only did his grandparents and
the relatives and friends who visited them serve as sources for traditional narratives, but when he was a child his grandmother also
encouraged him to go to older relatives to learn songs and stories.
By the time he was fourteen he was singing at the drum, an activity
he continued throughout his life. One of his favorite pastimes, he
used to reminisce, was getting together with friends on winter
evenings—with such men as Wallace Hand, Billy Lockwood, Vincent
Malnourie—who used to come across the river to gather around the
drum and sing for pleasure. When he was younger, Alfred was
recognized as one of the very best singers on the reservation, and
throughout most of his life, whenever he attended a dance or celebration, he always went to the drum. Because of his good voice and
his ability to remember songs, the older officiants at traditional
religious rituals would also ask him to sing. Moreover, he used to
assist his uncle Snowbird, an Arikara ceremonial leader in the
Beaver Creek district, in the performance of such rituals as the
death feast, which was prepared for a deceased person immediately
after burial (see narrative 107); from Snowbird he also acquired the
right to the song that accompanies the smudging of a drum, a ritual
that must be performed preceding a dance after the death of a tribal
member.

The stories told by Mr. Morsette and presented in this collection
represent the full range of Arikara oral traditions. Many of them,
particularly the myths, were no longer known or remembered by
any of his contemporaries. These are stories that he learned from
his grandparents, his father, his uncle Snowbird, Many Foxes,
Running Wolf, Jackrabbit, and other prominent members of previous generations. No doubt in large part because Arikara was
Alfred's first language and the one in which he was most com-
fortable speaking, but also because his narratives were memorized
texts, the vocabulary and grammatical constructions in the narra-

tives are rich in older forms, many of which are no longer used by contemporary speakers; and the narrative style is similarly diverse and eloquent, reflecting an ease of expression in Arikara not found among most speakers of his generation.

What also distinguished Alfred from most Arikara speakers of his generation, in addition to his fluency in the language and his prodigious knowledge of stories and songs, was his attitude toward proper cultural behavior, an attitude that certainly affected this project. He insisted that the stories he recorded must provide a true representation of Arikara history from an Arikara perspective— something he felt had never been recorded—and to that end he contributed a broad range of narratives always told in what he characterized as the proper manner: told a few at a time in the winter and recited in culturally correct form, just as they had been told to him. Many Arikaras, some older than he, had a more relaxed attitude toward Arikara traditions—not just story telling, but behavior as well—and when they neglected or fell short of traditional expectations, Alfred was always critical of them, sometimes outspokenly.

Ella P. Waters (Yellow Bird Woman), who passed away at age ninety-five in 1984, was born on the Fort Berthold Reservation in 1889. Her father was Paul Yellow Bear (*kuuNUxtAhkáta* Yellow Bear), a noted Arikara doctor and later in his life a lay reader in the Episcopal church on the reservation. Her mother was Buffalo Sod Village Woman, a name designating the band to which she and Ella also belonged, since band membership descended in the female line. After attending the Congregational mission school at Fort Berthold, Ella was a student at Wahpeton Indian School in South Dakota. Not long after returning home, her parents arranged her marriage in the traditional manner to Albert Simpson, an older Arikara man trained as a blacksmith and who owned a store in Beaver Creek. For several years he also served as the McLean County assessor.

Both Ella and her husband took a keen interest in traditional Arikara life, especially in its religion, doctoring, and social activities. As a young man in the decade before 1920 and later, Mr. Simpson had been an interpreter for the ethnobotanist Melvin

Gilmore on his frequent visits to the reservation, and at times Simpson himself had served as consultant for Gilmore. With Ella assisting him, Simpson learned what he could from the older men who were traditional doctors, in particular Bear's Belly and Yellow Bear, and kept several of them, including George Howard, Sr., and Crow Ghost, in his home when they were elderly; later, after these men died, Simpson carried out many of the rituals they had conducted and healed people with the medicines he had obtained from them. Ella, for her part, used to take food to the doctors in the revived Medicine Lodge, manifesting what she characterized as "having holy feelings." In the preface to one narrative (108), in fact, she tells that beginning at the age of eighteen she regularly went to the Medicine Lodge to fast, make sacrifices of food and goods, and ask the doctors' societies for blessings. Later she, too, became a doctor; and then just before the death of her aunt, Julia White Bear, the sole female member of the Ghost Society, Mrs. White Bear gave her position in this doctor's society to Ella.[10]

Throughout her life Ella Waters was prominent in the Arikara community. From the 1930s to 1953, when Garrison Dam was constructed, she and three other women (Hanna Fox, Daisy Ross, and Mary Lockwood) formed the female chorus *(swakaatakúxu')* for the Dead Grass Society, a men's dance organization that was also influential in community affairs. Like her father, she was active in the Episcopal church throughout her life. During World War II she was president of the Nishu chapter of the War Mothers.

When I first met Mrs. Waters in 1970, she had recently lost her third husband, Levi Waters. For the next decade she continued to live on their farm four miles west of White Shield; then in 1980 she and her daughter Grace moved into an apartment for senior citizens in White Shield. Throughout the fifteen years of our friendship, Mrs. Waters was a ceremonial leader for the Arikara community, maintaining such traditions as the death feast and the public bestowal of Arikara names on individuals—rituals formerly performed by men but which by then only she knew and had the right to conduct.

Because of her intense, lifelong desire to learn and maintain

10. Most of the medicine societies had one female member.

Arikara traditions, Ella Waters was unsurpassed over the last two decades of her life as a source of information on the Arikara language, and particularly on older usages. A proud, confident woman, she always responded unhesitatingly and authoritatively to language questions, and she translated the stories of other narrators, no matter how challenging to understand, with ease and a strong sense of what was correct Arikara speech. After I began to work with her, she became completely dedicated to the project of preserving the Arikara language through whatever media were available—written stories, a dictionary, classroom materials, tape recordings, personal instruction—and with a clear, unflagging sense of mission she always gave highest priority to this endeavor, most of the products of which, unfortunately, she did not live to see completed.

Lillian Brave (One Kernel Of Corn Woman), whose band affiliation is *čiNIhnaahtákUx*, is in 1991 the oldest living Arikara speaker. She was born July 20, 1899 in her parents' home in Elbowoods. Her father was Sam Newman (Two Hawks), an educated Arikara man who frequently interpreted for government officials and also served as Hidatsa interpreter for anthropologist Alfred Bowers in his studies of that tribe during the 1930s. Lilly's mother was Jenny Strikes Enemy (Squash Blossom), whose father was Black Trail, a leading Arikara doctor and nineteenth-century political leader who was one of the signatories to the Fort Laramie Treaty. While Lilly was growing up, several prominent Arikara ritualists stayed at her parents' home, among whom were Weasel Heart, Little Crow, and Crow Ghost. Crow Ghost, a cultural revivalist, taught the men in the family the ritual for opening a sacred bundle, how to sing Sage (purificatory) and other ceremonial songs, and recounted numerous traditions. It was in this environment—a home in which some of the most prominent, conservative Arikaras lived, men who were determined to maintain their traditions despite the radical social changes engulfing their lives— that Lilly lived during her early years, save for the periods when she attended boarding school, first at Wahpeton and then later at Bismarck Indian School. And it was this environment that enabled her to become familiar with many facets of traditional Arikara life unknown to most of her contemporaries and that instilled in her a strong, lifelong Arikara identity. It was this environment, too, that nurtured her conservative Arikara speech, which has many old features not found in the speech of her contemporaries.

Mrs. Brave lived most of her life in the Elbowoods community, but after construction of the dam she moved to Parshall, where she continues to live. Although she began work with me relatively late in the course of this project, Lilly, like Ella Waters, has demonstrated a deep, serious commitment to it, a commitment that is a measure of the importance she attaches to her language and culture. She nevertheless loves to clown and joke, often bawdily, and is deftly able to enliven any social situation, no matter how serious, without trivializing it. The latter trait, combined with her solemn, earnest attitude toward her language and culture, have made Lilly an extraordinarily pleasurable person to work with.

Lilly was formerly married to the late John Bad Brave, a noted Hidatsa traditionalist, and has two daughters, one of whom (Angela Plante) speaks Arikara fluently.

Mary Gillette (Red Eagle Woman) was a cousin of Lilly Brave and a classmate as well when they both attended Wahpeton Indian School. She was born in Beaver Creek district on April 4, 1899. Her mother was Sioux Woman, a first cousin of Jenny Newman. Like Mrs. Newman, her band affiliation was *čiNIhnaahtákUx*. Mary's father was Little Sioux, an Arikara who was part Sioux Indian. He served as an Indian scout in the 1876 campaign against the Sioux and was a traditional doctor who owned both horse and snake medicine.[11] Mary was married first to Walter Plenty Chief and later to Albert Gillette. She lived in Nishu until the dam flooded the river basin in 1953, when she moved into Parshall, the first Indian to live in this small town that has only recently been recognized to be within the borders of the Northeastern Segment of the reservation. Parshall was her home from that time until her death on

11. Various individuals owned these medicines, and those who possessed one of them (e.g., snake medicine) formed a loose-knit society. They were not, however, members of the older, established doctors' societies that had positions in the Medicine Lodge. A short biography of Little Sioux, which he apparently dictated, appears in Libby (1920:191–193).

July 26, 1976, at the age of seventy-seven.

A close friend of both Ella Waters and Lilly Brave, Mary Gillette shared with them a deep sense of pride in her Arikara heritage. When I first visited Fort Berthold, she was recognized as one of the most knowledgeable members of the community and an excellent speaker of the language—one who, as I learned, spoke slowly and precisely, always with exceptional clarity. She was also a gregarious individual, generous to friend and stranger alike, who was noted for usually having a pot of food simmering on the stove and for inviting friends who passed by her house to come in to eat. Whenever I visited at her home, she was unfailingly cordial and warm, an outgoing person whose conversations in a heavily accented English were always spiced with humor, and who was happy to contribute her knowledge to this project.

William Deane, Jr. (Lone Chief) was a proud, serious man, then in his late seventies, when I knew him. He was born July 11, 1897 at Armstrong. His parents were William Deane, Sr. (He Is Yellow), an Arikara subchief, and Grace Parker. After attending day school at Armstrong, Bill Deane, too, went to Wahpeton Indian School to complete his education. From 1917 to 1918 he served in the U.S. Army, and upon discharge he returned to Fort Berthold, where in 1920 he married Leona Yellow Bird.

Throughout most of his life, Bill ranched. He started the first Hereford ranch on the Fort Berthold Reservation and operated it until his retirement in 1960. In his youth he was noted as an outstanding saddle bronc rider and, like many young men on the reservation, competed in rodeos in North Dakota and surrounding states. Later he became involved in tribal government and served on the tribal council, holding the position of treasurer. He also held positions with the Bureau of Indian Affairs as relocation officer and credit officer. An active member of the local chapter of the American Legion, he served as its commander several times and helped to reorganize the post at White Shield. He also served as precinct committeeman for the Republican Party from 1942 until his death.

Bill Deane was a member of the Prairie Sod Village band. The last tribal subchief, he possessed the personality traits traditionally associated with that status: generosity, thoughtfulness, and security born of confidence. Although he devoted most of his life to ranching and tribal government, he was an active participant in Arikara tribal functions. He spoke fluent Arikara and Hidatsa, as well as English, and when I came into the community he was recognized as a linguistic and cultural authority.

Dan Howling Wolf (Standing Wolf), born on April 11, 1906, in the Nishu community, was the son of Lawrence Howling Wolf (Bear Crosses The Water), a minister of the Nishu Congregational Church, which was a branch of the reservation mission at Elbowoods. His mother was Stella Rogers (Curlew Woman). In 1927 Dan married Mabel Bear, daughter of Floyd Bear, who in turn was the son of Sitting Bear, the leading Arikara chief at the end of the nineteenth century and the son of Son Of Star. For most of their lives, Dan and Mabel lived in the country near Nishu, where Dan ranched, working cattle and horses, and did a little farming. From 1931 until 1953 he was a member of the Nishu singers, a group of younger men who succeeded the older Grass Dance society singers in the community and included Vincent Malnourie, Harvey Hopkins, Dan Hopkins, Davis Painte, and Marvin Painte. After the Nishu community relocated to the present White Shield area, Dan continued singing with those men, who then came to be known as the White Shield singers. Most of his sons also took up singing, and today several of them are active members of the White Shield singers.

When I first met Dan, he was living in the country several miles west of White Shield. Now blind, he was still an active singer and was a fluent speaker of Arikara who loved to tell stories, be they traditional Arikara or contemporary ones. He was, like Alfred Morsette, a generation younger than the more elderly speakers like Ella Waters, Lilly Brave, and Mary Gillette. Yet he and Mabel spoke Arikara in the home, one of the few families to maintain active use of the language. As a consequence, their older children speak Arikara, and the younger ones understand it. Dan was an amiable, generous person, always helpful to anyone who approached him. He passed away on July 5, 1974, at the age of sixty-eight.

Dan Hopkins (Rabbit Goes In The Middle), a World War I veter-

an, was born on August 26, 1900, in Nishu. He was the son of Ernest
Hopkins (Snowbird) and Ida Sherwood (Chippewa Woman), and was
an Awahu band member. In 1930, after two previous marriages, he
married Ruth Eagle. Except for the period of his military service, he
was a lifelong resident of the Fort Berthold Reservation, where he
ranched and farmed. When I became acquainted with him, Dan was
living alone in the country, several miles west of the homes of Mrs.
Waters and the Howling Wolfs. A contemporary of Dan Howling
Wolf, he, too, was a singer most of his life. Before Mrs. Waters
passed away, he learned from her the ritual for the death feast and
conducted it occasionally during the several years before his death.
He passed away on November 26, 1982, at the age of eighty-two.

Matthew White Bear (Together With The Bear), born May 31,
1900, in Elbowoods, was the son of Paul White Bear (*kuuNUxtaáka*
White Bear) and Annie Sitting Bear (Yellow Calf Woman), and was
a member of the *čiNIhnaahtákUx* band. He was a nephew of Sitting
Bear and a descendant of White Shield and Son Of Star, all prominent nineteenth-century Arikara chiefs. In 1924 he married Alice
Eagle, and together they lived on a farm near Nishu, not far from
the site of old Like-A-Fishhook Village, where Matthew raised crops
and ranched and was active in the Catholic church.

When I met the couple in 1970, they were living on their farm
southeast of White Shield. Both were noted for their knowledge of
Arikara culture. They spoke their language fluently, and Matthew
had in his keeping a tribal pipe and a sacred bundle. He was a
quiet, reflective man who spoke softly, sometimes almost in a
whisper. Alice was an active, prominent member of the White
Shield community; and Matthew, by virtue of his father's social
position, was himself a leader in the Arikara community throughout
his life. On January 21, 1975, he passed away at the age of seventy-
four.

Eleanor Chase (White Bear Woman), born April 12, 1906, was the
daughter of Red Bear and Julia Bull Neck.[12] Her parents, too, were

---

12. A short biography of Red Bear, apparently one he himself dictated,
appears in Libby (1920:200–202).

prominent members of the Arikara community at Fort Berthold. Her father served as a scout under Lieutenant Colonel George A. Custer on his 1876 expedition to the Little Big Horn and was appointed tribal judge in 1915. Julia Red Bear, her mother, worked with Melvin Gilmore and later Preston Holder when those two anthropologists visited the reservation.

After attending Flandreau Indian School, Eleanor worked as a cook and matron at Pierre Indian School in South Dakota. Later she returned home to Nishu, where she worked as a cook at the day school. In 1929 she married Joseph White Bear, Sr., who farmed near Nishu, but he passed away four years later. In 1940 she married Frank Chase, a Mandan from the Twin Buttes community. After their marriage the couple lived near Nishu, where they farmed. Throughout her life Eleanor maintained a strong interest in Arikara ways, an interest that after her marriage to Frank Chase was expressed in part by her beadwork and by her participation in Indian dances. After dam construction the couple moved to Bear Den, and, later, after the death of her husband, Eleanor moved to Drags Wolf Village, where I visited her in 1977. She was a large, outgoing, confident woman who spoke clear, crisp Arikara at a rapid tempo, certainly faster than any other speaker I ever heard. She passed away on December 31, 1980.

Esther Perkins (Young Elk Woman) was born in her parents' home in the country near Armstrong on March 15, 1916. Her father was Henry Perkins (Afraid Of The Soldier), an older brother of Ella Waters; and her mother was Elizabeth Price. Because Esther was born with a congenital ailment that prevented her from walking, she did not attend school. During her early childhood she lived with her grandfather Yellow Bear and his wife, who spoke no English, and consequently she grew up speaking Arikara as her first language. Later, when living with her parents, who spoke English as well as Arikara in the home, she learned English by listening to them.

Esther lived with her parents until they died, and since then has lived with a sister and her family. Despite her handicap, she is always cheerful and jocular. She, like most in her family, is active in the Episcopal church in White Shield.

Joseph Fox (Little Elk) was born January 8, 1904, in Nishu, where he was reared. His father was Isaac Fox (Red Fox); his mother, Julia (Last Child). After attending Bismarck Indian School, he returned to the Fort Berthold Reservation and in 1920 married Susan Many Bears. They farmed in the Nishu area until 1943 and then moved to Minot, where Joe worked in construction. In 1963 he moved back to the reservation and lived first in White Shield and later in Drags Wolf Village.

Throughout his life Joe was noted as a good dancer. He was, in fact, the last surviving member of the Grass Dance society. I knew him from only one visit to his home in 1977, when he recorded two stories and a song. Those recordings proved him to be fine speaker of Arikara, whose diction was unsurpassed for clarity and smoothness of delivery. He passed away on September 21, 1978.

Nature of the Collection

A Typology of Arikara Oral Traditions

In 1976, when I first approached Alfred Morsette with my request to record traditional Arikara stories, his response revealed a fundamentally different perception of what I wanted. He translated the Western category of "traditional story" into something meaningful from an Arikara perspective, and replied that he would be happy to tell stories of the Arikara past—those he had learned from his grandparents and other individuals of preceding generations—so that there would be a written history of the tribe. For him the stories that he would tell were *history*, not myths, tales, or other folkloric categories. Similarly, Lillian Brave made the same identification of oral traditions with history, although she revealed her understanding of Arikara historiography through an example. Before commencing our first recording session, she asked what precisely I wanted her to tell. I asked her to relate something about Arikara history, about some incident that had actually occurred in the tribal past. For several minutes she sat silently and then began to recount a story (70) about a brother and sister mesmerized by an elk spirit and subsequently given power by that animal. From a Euro-American perspective this narrative is a myth, but for Mrs.

Brave, as for any older Arikara, this is an account of a historical event, an important incident that happened in the past—in a time very different from today—when an elk bestowed supernatural power on the brother and sister, who in turn conveyed certain traditions to the Arikara people. For Arikaras this story, together with the total aggregate of those known to their people, preserved over countless generations through oral transmission, constitute their history.

All the narrators in this collection classified oral traditions into two fundamental categories: true stories; and tales or, as Arikaras call them in English today, fairy tales. In Arikara the latter are termed *naa'iikáWIš*. True stories have no special denotation. If one must specify a story as true, he simply says, *tiraanaáNIš* 'It is true.' Thus, true stories are, to use a linguistic expression, an unmarked category, whereas tales are marked by a denotative term, so that unless an Arikara story is characterized as or known to be a tale, it is assumed to be true.

True Stories. True stories cover a wide range of themes but are not subcategorized into named types. There is, however, again a native distinction between two general types: the sacred story that tells about "holy" or mysterious events in the past, and the non-sacred story that is not as remote in time and lacks the overriding supernatural element of sacred traditions—generally what from a Western perspective would be called historical narratives. Although most stories fall clearly into one of these two general categories, and although finer subgroupings within each type can be distinguished, Arikaras have no more than a general sense of such a classification, which is based primarily on named protagonists or on functions such as explanations of the origin of particular institutions. The boundaries between types are not hard and fast, but rather blend into one another; so that in actual fact sacred and secular stories and their subtypes form a continuum along which stories cluster, a continuum which, in the last analysis, is for Arikaras a single category: the true story or history.

The most specialized type of sacred story is the genesis tradition, or the traditions associated with the tribal sacred bundles. Formerly, when Arikaras lived in autonomous or semi-independent villages, each village had its own sacred bundle that symbolized the history of the group and its covenant with the deities. The origin of each village traced back to a supernatural experience or encounter, during which the deity instructed the dreamer to make a bundle of objects, some to recall what happened in the dream and some to be used in subsequent rituals. As a result of the decimation of the Arikara people in the late eighteenth and nineteenth centuries, by the early twentieth century all these village origin stories, except for that of the Awahu, were apparently lost. What did survive, however, was a genesis story that accounts for the origins and migration of all the Arikara people, a story that may have formerly belonged to one band. This tradition was recorded from many individuals in the late nineteenth and early twentieth centuries (Hall 1891:32; Grinnell 1893:122-128; G.A. Dorsey 1904a:12-35).

Another type of sacred story comprises what are generally termed myths—traditions of incidents that occurred during a period before the earth had fully taken its present form, before or at a time when human institutions were developing. Arikaras refer to this as the holy period, the time when mysterious events occurred. Stories set in this era are said to be holy (*tiraa'iitUxwaáRUxti'* 'it is a holy story'). It was a time when animals were the actors in dramas and deities came down to earth from the heavens above, when animals killed humans and buffalo ate people rather than the reverse—a period when a dangerous natural world was evolving into the present one in which man hunts animals and rides horses and lives much as he did previous to the arrival of Euro-Americans.

A third type of sacred story is the legendary event. Here there are several discreet types to be distinguished. One of the most common is the etiological narrative that accounts for the origin of a particular rite or tradition. This is a dream or vision story that relates a supernatural encounter between a human and some animal spirit or other agency who teaches an Arikara a ritual for the benefit of the tribe. Related to this type is the dream story, in which a poor boy or some hapless young man stumbles upon an animal or other supernaturally endowed agent whom he is able to help or please and who subsequently pities him—or "blesses" him, as Arikaras say in English today—by endowing him with supernatural powers for hunting, warfare, or healing and becomes his spiritual helper. Still a third type of legendary narrative is one that recounts some supernatural occurrence, as when, for example, a priest pouts and turns into stone or a girl is shamed and turns into stone.

In contrast to these sacred stories are the nonsacred ones, which in general describe events that are more recent in time and, more importantly, do not have a predominant supernatural component—although nearly every story has some supernatural reference. War stories, which relate incidents that occurred during the period of intertribal warfare, form a prominent group. So also do narratives describing recent historical events such as the Arikara tribal migration to Pawnee country immediately after the Atkinson campaign, the Fort Laramie Treaty, or the Custer campaign. Still another group of nonsacred stories are personal anecdotes, generally telling of a supernatural encounter but lacking the bestowal of power—what might be characterized as testimonials to the existence of supernatural beings or events, to phenomena that ostensibly are humanly inexplicable—the sort of attestation that assures people that the world about them is still imbued with mysterious power and that skepticism is foolish.

Tales. As with true stories, there are different sorts of tales, but most common are those that have the trickster Coyote or some other animal as protagonist. Unlike many other tribes, the Arikaras do not put Coyote into the role of a divine being. He is endowed with mysterious power *(waaRUxtiťu')*, but he is always portrayed as a tricky, deceitful character who tries to outwit others but invariably bungles and generally dies through his own folly. Only secondarily is he a transformer. Frequently these tales are etiological ones that end with an explanation of some feature of the natural world, but on the whole Arikaras attach little significance to Coyote stories since they are primarily told to evoke laughter or to entertain children. Alfred Morsette, in fact, told me that it would be a waste of time to record them, even though he always relished a good Coyote story.

Other stories, like that of Bounding Head, are more like European Mother Goose stories and, like Coyote tales, were told on winter nights for diversion, frequently to lull children to sleep.

Unlike Coyote and other animal tales, however, they are not humorous but have a more serious, often frightening, tone and a primarily human cast of characters. The characters in these tales are often the same ones that appear in myths, and so these stories sometimes seem to be categorically transitional between myth and tale. In one version of the Bounding Head story (6), in fact, the narrator states in his introduction that "I certainly never saw him [the one-eyed Bounding Head], but I have heard of him through the stories they used to tell about him." Because of this and a similar ambivalence expressed by some narrators toward the historical validity of many stories that otherwise would unequivocally be considered to be tales, these stories have been arranged with the myths in this collection with the caveat that the line between myth and tale is fine indeed. What are true myths for some Arikaras today are tales for others. For many stories, in fact, it is doubtful that consensus in regard to their historical validity could be achieved now—or even, perhaps, could ever have been achieved in the past—since in no culture does everyone hold identical beliefs.

The oral traditions in this collection are grouped by narrator and then arranged to reflect the basic Arikara distinction between true stories and fictional tales. These two divisions are designated here as Narratives of the Past and Tales, respectively. Within the category of true stories are four types, which again reflect the genres discussed above: Of Ancient Times (myths); Of Power Bestowed (legends); Of Historical Events (historical narratives); and Of Mysterious Events (anecdotes of supernatural occurrences). A fifth type, designated Of Ritualism, also fits into the category of true stories. These narratives include descriptive accounts of ritual procedures like personal name bestowal (107, 108), prayers (110, 144), song texts (146, 147), and an account of the origin of the death feast (107). In contrast to true stories, tales, the second major division of narratives, are grouped by protagonist: Coyote, Stuwi, and others, the latter of whom may be other animals or human characters. Table 1 summarizes the classification of Arikara oral traditions in this collection and the content of each category.

Table 1. Typology of Arikara Oral Traditions

Arikara Classification	Table of Contents Designation	Narrative Type
TRUE STORIES	NARRATIVES OF THE PAST	
Sacred	Of Ancient Times	World origins, mythic dramas
	Of Power Bestowed	Visionary encounters, legends
Nonsacred	Of Historical Events	Historical narratives
	Of Mysterious Incidents	Supernatural occurrences
TALES (naa'iikáWIš)	TALES	
	Of Coyote	Trickster tales
	Of Stuwi	Trickster tales
	Of Others	Animal tales; adventure stories

Characters

Although many of the same characters reappear in the myths and tales of all Plains tribes, albeit with different names, each tribe has its own set of favorite characters that recur in many stories and thereby become distinctive in the traditions of that people. The Mandans, for example, have Corn Silk Woman, a beautiful young woman transformed from corn, about whom there are many accounts (Beckwith 1937; Bowers 1950; Lévi-Strauss 1968:314–323). Other tribes tell of this same woman—Corn Woman among the Arikaras and the Omahas, Reed Woman among the Sioux, for example—in the widely diffused story of the corn wife and buffalo wife—but she appears in only this one story and no others. The Sioux, for another example, have the mythical Double Face, who appears sometimes as a man and sometimes as a woman in numerous stories and is peculiarly Sioux even though, like the Mandan Corn Silk Woman, Double Face parallels characters in the traditions of other tribes (Deloria 1932).

In Arikara stories, too, there are familiar characters, ones who return again and again in different narratives; some are named and some are nameless. The named characters appear primarily in two groups of stories, myths and tales, although some of them occasionally occur in legendary stories as well. Nameless persons are most frequently the protagonists of myths and legendary stories and are often a favorite personality type representing an actor in an old story whose name has been forgotten or perhaps may never have existed, or for an actor in a story borrowed from another tribe whose name would lack significance in its new social context.

Named characters. Among the most common of the named characters is Lucky Man *(wiitakaWAhaánu'),* whose name, according to Mrs. Waters, signifies a person who is a successful hunter and is able to provide for his family. He is a good man, whom Mrs. Brave characterized as "sort of a chief," indicating that he is wealthy and never in want, and is always willing to share what he has with other people and help those in need. His roles vary from being the father of a protagonist (e.g., 4, 64, 65) to being a protagonist himself (e.g., 69).

Stays In The Lodge Dressed In Finery *(tshaahkaákUx)* is another stock character who is a frequent protagonist. Said by some Arikara narrators to be a Hidatsa character incorporated into Arikara stories, he is portrayed as a young dandy who stays at home, spending his days on the earth lodge roof and never venturing from the village with war parties or hunters. Although he represents the antithesis of what a young Arikara male should be, Stays In The Lodge always vindicates his aberrant social role, which is invariably a mask for a person who possesses mysterious power.

Bloody Hands *(štaanápaa'At),* the Burnt Belly of Skiri folklore and Wets The Bed of Wichita stories, is a favorite personage, an archetype of the widespread Plains poor boy. Known also as Hands *(štaánu'),* a shortened form of his name, he is a small, poor boy who lives with his grandmother in a tipi among the dung heaps on the outskirts of the village. Although in some stories (4, 5) his physical appearance is not mentioned, he is usually said to be short, ugly, and swaybacked and to have a scarred potbelly and deformed feet. His grandmother, too, is short and heavyset, with a large stomach. Despite his ugliness and poverty, Bloody Hands has mysterious powers that always enable him and his grandmother to triumph in situations where other, socially more fortunate individuals fail.

Old Woman Spider *(suxtiikIsĭš)*, a spider who appears in the form of an old woman, is in some stories a neutral, background character who helps people to accomplish an otherwise insurmountable task (e.g., 85, 89), while in others she is an evil personage who, like the spider, ensnares adversaries in her web (e.g., 62, 65).

A ubiquitous character, uniquely Arikara and Pawnee, is Scalped Man *(tshunúxu'* 'scalped one'), who appears in a variety of roles.[13] "Scalped one" is the term for a person who was scalped in warfare but who, though mistaken for dead, somehow survived, generally, it was believed, through the act of some supernatural agency like Night. Of such a maimed person it was said, *ti' ičiwiniítu'* 'He is transformed; he is different,' signifying the belief that he was no longer human but had become a spirit forever doomed to live a solitary existence outside the pale of human society, shunning human contact. Arikara and Pawnee traditions about Scalped Man abound. In some anecdotes and stories he is a historical character, sometimes simply a misfortunate person who survived scalping and is later accidentally encountered by someone, while at other times he is a malevolent spirit who steals human possessions as well as women and children. In the latter role he is a bogeyman, an object of fear whom parents frequently used to threaten misbehaving children. In still other stories Scalped Man is a legendary figure who is the benefactor or bestower of supernatural power on some man, generally a solitary hunter, who discovers him and receives war or healing powers in return for keeping his existence secret. Occasionally, too, Scalped Man appears in myths (e.g., 1) and tales (e.g., 81), in which he may be either a serious or comic character, becoming in the latter role a trickster much like Coyote, who bears little or no resemblance to the historical personage.

Occurring in several myths are two men who are said to be

13. A fuller discussion of the scalped man appears below and in Parks (1982).

stars in the heavens associated with the buffalo on earth and who
come down to earth, where they appear in human form. They are
holy men who have supernatural powers, particularly the ability to
summon buffalo herds, powers which they use to save people from
starvation. Consequently they are portrayed as benefactors. In none
of the stories in which they occur (15, 16, 85), however, are they
named; in the Arikara versions they are referred to simply as "two
men" or as "fathers" of the protagonist, while in English Mr.
Morsette speaks of them as the "two holy men" and "star fathers."
They appear in Mandan and Hidatsa myths, too, in which they are
named Two Men (Beckwith 1937:43–52, 257–58; Bowers 1965).

Coyote *(sčirihtš)* is the Arikara trickster who, like the animal
after which he is named, is noted primarily for his cunning and
deceit, particularly in his quest for food and sex, and his wild
conceits. He is known by two other names that are also used in
these narratives, Mischievous Coyote *(sčiRIhtšutaRAháxu')* and
Coyote Chief *(sčiRIhtšuneešaánu')*, the latter a name frequently
used when referring to him in English. Mrs. Brave characterized
Coyote by a single term, *aawaaniix* 'foxy, tricky,' while Eleanor
Chase said of him, "Coyote is the one we have who always does
wrong things . . . who has no sense and who does mischievous
things." In the conclusion to one Coyote story (60), Alfred Morsette
gives a similar portrayal: "That is the way Coyote was, always
telling lies when he was looking for food for himself." Despite his
trickiness and virtual indestructibility, Coyote is always overcome,
either by his own ineptitude or by an adversary; and although
he generally dies at the end of a story, he is never ultimately
vanquished.[14]

For one narrator, Mrs. Brave, a character epitomizing the traits
of Coyote is Wolf *(sčiRIhkaapinát)*, whom she portrays as "the main
Coyote, who is the *really* tricky one." At the outset of several of her
stories (75–78) she interchanges Wolf and Coyote as protagonist but
eventually settles on Coyote as the name she uses throughout the
remainder of the tales. Although no other narrator represented in

14. A classic description of the Winnebago trickster, who is not unlike the
Arikaras' Coyote, appears in Paul Radin (1956). For a more recent
comparative study of Coyote in American Indian folklore see "The Natural
History of Old Man Coyote" by William Bright (1987:339–87).

this collection employs Wolf as the trickster, her usage and insistence that Wolf is the real trickster are significant in light of a
parallel role Wolf was formerly said to play in Pawnee tales:

> There is reason to believe that, while the Pawnee were in Nebras-
> ka, the Coyote was rarely or possibly never used in connection
> with these [trickster] tales, and that they were called instead Wolf
> tales, the Wolf being the mean trickster and not the Coyote. These
> Coyote or Wolf tales, in general, suggest to the Pawnee the mis-
> chievous performances of the Wolf sent by the Wolf-star, who, in
> attempting to steal people from Lightning, introduces mortality on
> earth, and through Lightning's failure to sacrifice Wolf the earth
> becomes subject to warfare and death. Thus the original wolf is a
> transformer of far-reaching consequences and at the same time a
> veritable trickster. [G.A. Dorsey 1906a:10–11]

Another character who appears only in Mrs. Brave's stories is
Kit Fox (*pAhkáts̆*), whom the narrator describes as "the littlest fox"
and red in color. He is a comic character and Coyote's nemesis,
always mocking Coyote and giving him away by announcing pub-
licly his foibles. Although no other contemporary Arikara narrator
tells stories in which Kit Fox appears, the character is undoubtedly
an old one. His name appears in Maximilian's Arikara vocabulary
recorded in 1833, where it is translated as 'god.'[15] Even earlier, in
1796, Truteau mentioned what must be the same character in his
description of doctors' performances in the Medicine Lodge, when he
wrote that "two young men, the most sprightly, to whom they give
the name of 'little foxes,' imitate and mimic the gestures and contor-
tions of the others [doctors] almost as clowns among our comedians
mimic the actors" (Parks 1991b).

A female character who appears in tales is Stuwi (*stuúWI*),
whose name has no translation.[16] She is a sexually loose, meddle-
some woman who is something of a clown. Mrs. Brave characterizes

15. Maximilian (1843, 3:211) recorded the name as "pachkátsch," with the
note that *ach* was pronounced as the German guttural. In the orthography
used here the word would be *pÁxkáts̆*, differing slightly from the form used
by Mrs. Brave.

16. The Pawnee equivalent of Stuwi is *Ctú'u'* (Witch Woman), who has
the same attributes of the Arikara character. For a description of her, see
George A. Dorsey (1904a:334).

her as a 1920s flapper who tempts men and fools people, while Mr.
Morsette similarly likened her to a modern go-go dancer or stripper.
Like Coyote, Stuwi is said to be tricky *(aawaanúx)*. Because of her
overtly sexual nature and the reticence of most narrators to tell
such stories, there are only two about her in this collection. In one
(81) the Stuwis of the world are portrayed as responsible for creek
water, which they cause to flow by urinating, while in the other
(80), a fine example of ribald humor, Stuwi is a sexually insatiable
woman.

In addition to the foregoing personae, every story has its distinctive character who generally does not appear in other narratives.
Among the best known of the mythical ones who are named are
Bounding Head *(pAxukúku')*, Shwahit *(šwaáhii'It*, no translation),
Old Woman's Grandson *(súxtIt iNAhniítš)*, and Long Teeth *(aáhčes)*
and his brother, Drinks Brain Soup *(pAxčiRAhčiika')*, each of whom
has a consistent portrayal in all the versions of the story in which
he or she occurs.

Unnamed characters. In Arikara mythical and legendary traditions unnamed protagonists are far more common than named
ones. Among the stories recorded by Alfred Morsette, for example,
primary characters are named in three myths and are unnamed in
nine, and similarly they are named in ten legends but are unnamed
in twenty-six. Such unnamed characters are referred to simply as
a boy, a young man, or a man, or, if female, as a girl, a young
woman, or a woman; and frequently the designations boy and young
man, or young man and man, are used interchangeably in the same
story for the same individual, as are also the parallel female sets,
girl and young woman, or young woman and woman. In some
stories (e.g., 23, 46, 90) the name of the protagonist or another
character is not given until the very end of the narrative, where its
specification typically serves as part of the conclusion.

Secondary characters in such stories are almost always unnamed, too, depicted only as, for example, a young man, boy, or
woman, depending upon the person's sex and age, and perhaps
referred to as 'the one who was his companion' or some similar
descriptive designation. Frequently, however, secondary characters
are relatives of a major character, and then kinship terms are used

when referring to them.

Character types. Arikara traditions, like oral traditions throughout the world, usually lack character development. In most Arikara stories, in fact, characterization of the personality of the protagonist or members of the supporting cast generally consists of a simple summary statement. The named characters discussed above, like Bloody Hands, Coyote, and Stays Inside The Lodge, are culturally renowned personae representing types with which all Arikaras are familiar, so that it is unnecessary to describe them. Most stories, however, have a protagonist who appears in only that narrative. Since that narrative generally depicts only the protagonist's actions, the listener must construct a visualization of the character on this basis alone and never becomes intimately acquainted with the individual or directly learns his motivations. There is, nevertheless, among the many characters in the "true" stories of this collection, a small number of recurrent personality types that typify Arikara oral tradition and, significantly, contrast with the personality norm in Arikara society.

A favorite Arikara literary figure is the poor boy, represented archetypically by the mythical Bloody Hands, who, despite an outward appearance of ugliness and poverty, is in reality a handsome young man endowed with mysterious powers that enable him to accomplish feats beyond the capabilities of men who are socially prominent. The poor boy character is represented equally well in the tale of Eats Ashes (14≤), who also lives in poverty with his grandmother. After befriending a wealthy boy who has everything, Eats Ashes determines to go on a war party with his companion to accomplish something noteworthy. Although his grandmother futilely tries to dissuade him from going, she finally gives him a burnt marrowbone to take on the expedition. Its ashes are to be his food, but in fact the bone is the source of his power, enabling him to kill many of the enemy and return to the village as a person of renown who is given a seat among the chiefs. The protagonists of many other stories are similarly poor but achieve fame after some supernatural power pities them.

Many stories recount the exploits of young men who are socially deviant: those who are lazy, reclusive, backward, or even retarded.

Eats Ashes, the triumphant poor boy, for example, is also characterized as backward. The story of Young Hawk (28) tells of a lazy
young man who is mysteriously endowed with hawk power that
enables him to achieve success in war, while in the account of the
origin of the Hidatsa Crazy Dog Society (30) the young man who is
chosen to forewarn his people of an impending attack on the village
is a disinterested fop. Representing the dandy who never ventures
from the village is Stays Inside The Lodge Dressed In Finery.
Others like him are the boy with the feathered staff (23) and the
boy who had coyote or wolf power (156). All are reclusive young men
who, though seemingly unmanly in their behavior, have power that
ultimately allows them to achieve success in war and vindicate their
socially abnormal manner. At the extreme of this type is the simple-
minded, or actually retarded, young man (96) who once ate snake
flesh and subsequently became a snake himself. After he was put
into the Missouri River, he was thereafter commemorated by
warriors who made offerings to him whenever they wished to cross
the river safely.

The reckless young man, sometimes arrogant but always a foolish daredevil, is another typical protagonist spanning the temporal
range of Arikara traditions. Mythically, he is represented by the
wild Long Teeth, who brashly leads his brother, Drinks Brain Soup,
into one dangerous adventure after another. In legend the same
character type appears frequently. The story of the two Foolish
Ones who killed the beloved snake child (14, 88) provides an example in which such behavior was institutionalized in a men's
organization and, in this story at least, brought grief to the Arikara
people; while the story of Red Dog and the Four Stars (18) illustrates this personality in a man who also had the power to call the
buffalo, a power which he used successfully to save his people from
starvation. In another example, the story of a wild buffalo (134), the
protagonist is a poor daredevil who teases the fearsome animal
despite the warnings of his companions. Although the buffalo chases
him for countless miles and kills his horse, it ultimately pities the
young man and enables him to achieve success in war.

The foolish daredevil personality is depicted in war stories, too,
in which the deeds of reckless young men figure prominently. Exemplifying this personality is the account of a Sioux attack on Like-A-

Fishhook Village (47) in which the enemies lay in ambush on the
bank of the Missouri opposite the village and used decoys to lure
impetuous young Arikaras into their trap. Despite the warnings of
older, experienced warriors, according to Mr. Morsette's account,
"there always are some who won't heed what they are told," and
they rashly gave chase to the decoys. Three of those brave but
reckless Arikaras were killed. As a matter of interest, the same
scenario in which Sioux attackers lured reckless young Arikaras
into their traps on the bank opposite the village is a familiar one
that was first described in 1796 by the fur trader Truteau (Parks
1991b) and was reiterated throughout the nineteenth century in the
accounts of white observers on the Upper Missouri.

A related character type common in Arikara literature is the
skeptic who scoffs at conventional wisdom—the individual who does
not believe in spirits and in the mysterious power resident in holy
objects. Such a skeptic is the leader of a war party in an Arikara
version of the story of the gigantic snapping turtle (25), a widespread legend on the Plains. When the party encounters a large,
strange object—the something-out-of-the-ordinary sort that typically
marks it as holy—the leader, characterized as a nonbeliever, cannot
resist the temptation to climb up onto it despite the admonitions of
one member of the group who has appropriate respect for the holy.
The leader's skepticism, of course, proves to be fateful for both
himself and the companions who follow his lead. A similar, common
type of tradition is exemplified in the account of a young man who
does not believe in ghosts until he encounters one (56). That encounter proves to be fateful, too, until the young man acknowledges
the ghost's existence and pays it proper respect, after which the
man enjoys success in hunting and as a result becomes a believer.

Another character recurring in Arikara traditions is the man
who, after being pitied by some animal or other supernatural being,
abuses the powers conferred on him until he becomes thoroughly
evil. Such individuals appear frequently in myths as the antagonist.
The story of the man with the sharpened leg (8) is a short but typical example. In it a young man courts a beautiful young woman,
and after he marries her the father-in-law pursues him to kill him
with his leg, just as he has done before to many other young men.
This young man, however, is saved by the tree that had previously

given the father-in-law his power, since the tree is finally outraged
by the older man's repeated evil deeds. Many legends also tell about
a pitiful young man who is given power and for some time afterward performs good deeds with it, but finally begins to abuse it.
Sometimes, as in one version of the young man pitied by a wild
buffalo (134), his behavior simply becomes reprehensible; but at
other times, as in the story of Mice Mouth (20, 89, 112), his actions
become so intolerable that he must be killed.

Although most of the prominent character types in Arikara oral
traditions are male, there are at least two recurrent female roles.
The more stereotyped one is the outcast grandmother who lives in
poverty with her grandson, either Bloody Hands or another poor-boy
character like Eats Ashes. In most of the stories in which she
figures, the grandmother usually serves as a counterforce to her
grandson's ambitions, always trying to dissuade him from attempting to achieve his aspirations. So, for example, in Lillian Brave's
stories of Bloody Hands (64–68) and Mary Gillette's story of Eats
Ashes (144), the grandmother initially scoffs at her grandson's
presumption to want to go on the warpath like young men of higher
social station do; in one story (68), in fact, she steadfastly forbids it,
ultimately to her everlasting regret. Also characteristic of her in
this role is her pride in—or perhaps resigned determination to
uphold—her impoverished lifestyle; so that, even when her grandson does achieve social prominence (e.g., 64, 66), she refuses to leave
her humble lodge among the dung heaps to live in a better one
among the wealthy families. Despite her destitute state, however,
in some stories the grandmother, like her grandson, possesses
mysterious power that she finally demonstrates. Before Eats Ashes
goes on the warpath, for example, his grandmother gives him a
marrowbone that miraculously enables him to kill many enemies
and become a great warrior.

The chief's—or alternatively a wealthy man's—daughter is another common female character whose customary role complements
that of the protagonist. This young woman, often a background
character with little or no involvement in the action of a story, is
always beautiful and unmarried; her ultimate fate is to be the
wife of the protagonist, often the lowly poor boy, who wins her in
marriage through his exploits.

Translation and Presentation

All the narratives in this collection were recorded in Arikara, the first language of each narrator and the language in which each one learned the stories. Most of Alfred Morsette's and one of William Deane's stories were afterward retold and taped in English as well, providing parallel versions of a substantial portion of the collection, but the Arikara versions, which are to a large extent memorized texts, are the primary documents that preserve the stories in the original language without the interpretive reworking that characterizes versions either translated into or told in English. The English versions are thus primarily of comparative interest and illustrative of the differences between accounts told in the original and in a second language.

The narratives are presented in two forms. One is an interlinear format that consists of a systematic phonetic transcription of the naturally told Arikara together with an accompanying word-by-word literal English translation conveying the grammatical and semantic content of each word. This paired-line format, standard for the publication of linguistic texts, provides both an accurate written version of the oral documents and an English translation that allows for their future linguistic and literary study and interpretation. The interlinear presentation of the collection appears in volumes 1 and 2 of this work.

The second mode of presentation is a set of free English translations that presents the texts as literary forms. Until recently, when translating American Indian traditions, linguists and other recorders have generally recast them into free English translations that conform to our own standards of good English written style but generally ignore literary devices and stylistic features integral to the native rendition. The results all too frequently have been vapid translations that are neither good stories in English nor faithful representations of the native originals. Over the past few decades, however, a number of literary scholars have become interested in American Indian oral traditions as oral literature, and they have raised the translation process to a new level of concern and sensitivity, insisting on fresh standards that give primacy to native literary features and structure (summarized in Hymes 1981 and Tedlock 1983). The goal of this recent work is, at least ideally, a translated text that is as close to the original as can be achieved in a rendition in another language. It is this goal that has guided the free translations of the Arikara stories presented here.

Where the translations in this collection depart from certain contemporary trends in textual presentation, however, is in redactive form. One recent convention is to replicate the oral performance in written form: pauses, voice modulation, and other performative features are indicated typographically in the translations so that the reader can "participate" in the original performance, reading back from the printed page to the vocal presentation, even though the language of the printing and the auditory medium are removed, and different, from it (Tedlock 1983). The other major approach, in which performative features play no role, is to portray underlying linguistic patterns, marked by morphological and syntactic features such as verbal inflection or sentence initial particles, by numerical repetitions, and a structuring of the narrative into a hierarchy of divisions that includes lines, verses, acts, and scenes, all of which give the text a construction much like a drama (Hymes 1981). Although these two models of redaction differ in the attention they give to performance and linguistic patterns, both share an assumption that native American texts are literary documents that are fundamentally poetic in structure and should be presented in verse, rather than prose, format.

Both of these models have developed out of individual efforts to deal with texts in specific languages.[17] One has evolved out of recordings of narratives performed before audiences, where the performance itself became as important as the words, while the other has developed out of a study of philological texts and oral recordings in which the performative context was minimized. Neither approach seems entirely appropriate to the presentation of this collection of Arikara texts. Although during many of the recordings narrators accompanied their tellings with gestures and dramatic vocal modulation, the recitations were generally subdued, not staged performances, since there was either no audience present (other than the recorder) or it was at most a small, intimate one.

17. Mattina (1987:129–48) and Krupat (1987:113–28) provide recent discussions of alternatives and problems in textual redaction.

Narrators' attention, instead, centered on narrative detail—on remembering all the pieces of the story and rendering as full a version as possible. Similarly nothing in delivery style or morphological and syntactic arrangements of narrative material suggests a line-verse structure that would more accurately portray an underlying Arikara narrative form than what is achieved in prose.

The presentational format employed here, which evolved out of the translation process itself, recognizes three basic units: sentences, paragraphs, and sections.

Sentence boundaries have been established on the basis of a combination of criteria: pause and intonational contours, occurrence of particle introducers, and grammatical composition. Minimally, a sentence consists of one independent verbal form (i.e., a verb inflected for one of the independent modes) in addition to any number of optional subordinate verbal forms (i.e., verbs in one of the dependent modes). Elliptical sentences, in which the verb form has been omitted, are the exception to the rule. Sometimes they occur in narratives, particularly in statements introducing dialogue, where the speaker's identity is given but the specification of his action—for example, "he said"—is understood and therefore omitted. Although Arikara sentences often contain only a single verb, they frequently have, in addition to an independent one, a long string of satellite subordinate forms, some of which translate best into English as independent sentences. Similarly, a sentence may be a concatenation of two or more independent verbs, sometimes, but not always, connected by the conjunctions *na* or *a* 'and.'

Paragraph boundaries are defined by several criteria, the most prominent of which are a variety of transitions. Topical changes, actor and dialogue switches, topical changes within a long dialogue, and temporal and scene changes mark paragraph breaks. Thus paragraphs are generally short, topically self-contained units.

Interacting with these transitions are two forms of discourse bracketing (see Style, below) that frequently introduce and/or conclude a paragraph, thereby helping to define the paragraph as a discourse unit. One form sets off quoted speech: the introductory form is, for example, *uitiwaáko'* 'He said,' or *taanikuwitiwaáko'* 'This is what he said,' and the concluding statement is *taanikuwitiwaáko'* 'This is what he said.' An action or series of concatenated actions is similarly bounded by statements like *taanikuwituúta* 'This is what he did.'

In addition to the transitions marked by paragraph breaks there are greater temporal and topical discontinuities—what in drama are changes of scenes or acts. Frequently introduced by a temporal distancing clause like "It was some time later" or "It was a long time later," these shifts from one part of a story to another are indicated here by additional space (i.e., a blank line) between paragraphs. Most stories also begin with an introductory paragraph or section, which backgrounds the narrative and precedes its onset, and ends with a concluding paragraph or section following the end of the story. These introductions and conclusions are also set off by additional space. If that blank line occurs at the top or bottom of a page, where it might not be obvious, a pair of facing guillemets (« ») marks the transition.

In several stories, moreover, there are major transitions between separate episodes that are nearly equivalent to independent stories (see pp. 86-87). These transitions are marked by three pairs of facing guillemets (« « «   » » ») wherever they occur.

One overriding criterion has guided the translation process: to reflect faithfully the original Arikara text. In making the translations, careful effort has been exercised to reproduce the Arikara narrative, with all its complexities and subtleties, as closely as possible in idiomatic English and to maintain the stylistic devices of the original language, even though adherence to those principles has often resulted in a mode of expression that sounds somewhat stilted in English.

The translations, moreover, have been given in formal English since the Arikara speech style is itself formal. In dialogue, however, English contractions are used so that the speech there approximates English spoken style more realistically than uncontracted forms.

Although translations conform closely to the original Arikara, there are a variety of situations in which explanatory information has been inserted so that the English text reads unambiguously. One instance is the specification of a name or noun for an actor who is unspecified in Arikara. Frequently, in Arikara as in other American Indian oral traditions, in describing situations in which individuals are interacting with one another, the names or other nouns denoting the actors are omitted, although sometimes a narrator will use gestures to differentiate among actors;[18] literal translations, therefore, result in an ambiguous interplay of two or more third person singular pronominal subjects (e.g., multiple *he*s and *she*s). For clarity, appropriate designations specifying these actors have been introduced in the translation when confusion would otherwise result.

Similarly, occasional details that are not overtly stated in the Arikara version—details that are generally understood by an Arikara audience and consequently not mentioned, or details that have accidently been omitted in the particular telling but are essential to the story—have been silently provided in the English translation.

An example of an implicit, culturally understood omission occurs in story 140, where the text translates literally as 'thunderbirds were shooting it [a water monster]'; the free translation reads "thunderbirds were shooting it with lightning bolts." Since an Arikara listener understands that a thunderbird shoots lightning bolts, the narrator does not state it explicitly. Likewise, in the opening paragraph of story 142 there is the literal statement, "Then they said, 'Let's go gather ground beans.'" Since no subject other than "they" has been introduced up to this point to identify who the subjects are, the phrase "a group of young women" was added to the free translation since it is culturally understood that women (who happen to be young in this story), and not men or children, would be going to gather the beans. Still another randomly selected example comes from the same story (142) when the protagonist and his three companions discover an apparently unoccupied lodge in their travels. In dialogue the protagonist assigns two of his companions to beds, and then the text reads, "That was the way it was"; to this literal statement the translation adds the explanation, "each had a bed to sleep on," since that is what the Arikara expression implies.

An example of a simple explanatory detail that is not explicitly stated in the Arikara but has been supplied in the free translation

18. A common gestural means of differentiating two actors is to use a hand, index finger extended upward, to represent each person and then to move forward the hand that represents the actor who is being referred to or quoted.

occurs in story 4 when Long Teeth, one of two protagonists, becomes angry and states, "I have power just like you do." Because it is not immediately apparent who "you" is in this context, a clarifying "he said to the tree" has been added in the translation. Another illustration of a silently added detail appears in story 5 when the protagonist, a star boy who is disguised as a poor, ugly human boy, tries to maintain his disguise by riding a decrepit horse and shooting arrows here and there. After the story had been recorded the narrator explained that the boy had been shooting at prairie chickens, so the translation was expanded to "he . . . began to shoot here and there at prairie chickens."

There is, finally, one additional type of editorial insertion in the free translations that occurs only in the stories told by Alfred Morsette. Occasionally, narrative sequences that range from a sentence to a paragraph or more were accidently omitted in the telling of the Arikara version but were included in the English rendition. When such omissions were deemed important to the story, either as helpful explanations or as integral details, they have been inserted in the free translations and are identified by angled brackets.

In the presentation of the traditions in English translation, each narrative is preceded by an introduction that provides background information intended to facilitate the reader's understanding and appreciation of the story. To this end the introductions vary in content: they may contain comparative observations, clarify obscure references or passages, elucidate relationships among narrative elements, or highlight the significance of the story or an episode in it. Whenever a narrator provided relevant explanatory information outside the recording session, that material is also included.

Style

Perhaps the characteristic that most distinguishes individual American Indian literary traditions is the oral style in which their stories are told. General stylistic features such as narrative perspective, the use of quoted material, narrative sequencing, abbreviatory devices, and numerical patterning, as well as specific morphological and syntactic traits serve to shape what is typically an Arikara story and differentiate its delivery style from that of a narrative in English or other American Indian literary traditions. Since the stylistic features of Arikara have been assiduously preserved in the translations of the narratives in this collection, it is important to recognize and understand them so that for the English reader they are an enhancement rather than an impediment to the appreciation of this literary tradition.

Narrative Perspective

In Arikara a narrative about some past personage or event is usually told in such a way that the teller is distanced from the story line. Generally the teller is repeating what he or she has heard or has been told and relates the activities of the character or cast of the story from a *third person perspective*, in which those actors, even though named, are referred to by the pronouns 'he,' 'she,' 'it,' and 'they.' In Arikara, like many American Indian languages, the narrative is further characterized by what are generally termed evidentials, formal linguistic elements that in different languages may be prefixes, suffixes, or even independent words that usually occur with verbs, tagging their actions as something that the teller has not witnessed or cannot verify from his own experience.

There are two evidentials in Arikara, both verbal prefixes, which occur most extensively in narratives and serve to define a story as a tradition. One is *wi-*, the quotative, which occurs with verbs in the indicative mode and indicates that the speaker is repeating what he heard, not what he observed. The quotative is rarely translated into English by Arikaras. When pressed to explain its use on a verb, they merely attribute it to the story, remarking that it indicates something that is told. It is the equivalent of what in other American Indian languages is frequently translated as 'it is said.' The other evidential, *an-* 'evidential proper,' which usually appears in the form *Ah-*, is prefixed to verbs in modes other than the indicative and signifies that what the verb denotes was not seen by the speaker—that something "apparently" was the case. It, too, is generally not translated; Arikara speakers simply consider it an attribute of the way words appear in a story. Since Arikara speakers do not consider these evidentials as features to be translated into English, both are omitted in the free translations presented in this collection.

Contrasting with this more common narrative perspective in Arikara, however, is an alternative one that is extensively used in historical accounts of war and other incidents that occurred during the nineteenth century. It is a *first person perspective* in which the narrator, rather than distancing himself from the narrative activity, relates it from the perspective of a participant, nearly always a major participant. Here the first person pronoun 'I' predominates, and the third person pronouns are used for other characters in the story. In a narrative told from this perspective, the narrator actually repeats the words of the original actor or participant, telling the story as if the narrator himself had been that person and is now relating what he did and saw. When a narrator recounts a story told in this style, he generally begins with an introductory statement that he is repeating the words of another person, the one who related it to him. So, for example, in story 45, Alfred Morsette begins an Assiniboine war story with the declaration that "Now I am going to repeat the words of my uncle Snowbird," who, as he later explains, had been told the story of a war party that came to Like-A-Fishhook Village sometime during the nineteenth century by the Assiniboine who had led it.

In relating a story from this first person perspective, the narrator does not use the evidential prefixes since he is giving the account from a participatory perspective and thus as something he actually witnessed. Since the narrator is repeating the words of the original participant, in fact, the entire account is one long sequence of quoted speech. Consequently, in translation the entirety of narratives told in this style are set off by double quotation marks, and the speech of other actors in the story is in turn enclosed by single quotation marks. (And if one of those actors repeats someone else's speech, that dialogue is then in turn enclosed by double quotation marks within the single ones.)

Rarely, however, is a narrator entirely consistent in maintaining this first person perspective throughout a long story, since the style apparently requires considerable concentration and effort to execute. Six stories in the collection of sixty-one told by Alfred Morsette illustrate use of this perspective style, and of those six narratives, only two (45, 55) are told entirely within the first person frame. A mixture of perspectives occurs in the other four stories: in one (49) the first person perspective predominates, while in the other three narratives (46, 47, 58) it occurs only sporadically. The same combination of perspectives predominates in Pawnee historical stories as well.

Since the mixture of perspectives in some narratives creates potential confusion for English readers, the first person perspective is set off typographically in these volumes (**using this boldface sans serif type**) to distinguish it from the usual third person perspective. This typographic change occurs in narratives 45-47, 49, 55, 58, and 108-9. In the latter two texts the change represents the actual words recited during the public bestowal of a personal name and contrasts with the narrative description of the ritual procedure in them.

General Features

Direct discourse. One of the most pervasive characteristics of Arikara oral narrative style is its heavy emphasis on quoted speech. So extensive, in fact, is the amount of dialogue in some stories that those narratives take on the appearance of scripts for dramas in which the interplay of dialogue is bound together by a thin narrative thread. Much of the time dialogue is introduced by a statement like "then he said," often preceded by a name or noun designating the actor who is speaking, but almost as frequently there is no introduction. The words of an actor simply appear. Similarly, the dialogue of one character often follows that of another in back-and-forth exchanges throughout which it can become difficult to keep the speakers correctly identified, particularly when the printed rendition lacks the gestures and intonational changes that generally characterize narrative delivery.

This emphasis on dialogue and the attention paid to verbal interaction among characters in narratives correlates with the general tendency in Arikara stories to neglect descriptive detail, a trait once commented on by Mrs. Brave's daughter after we had transcribed a long story. She remarked that "Indian" (here Arikara) stories gloss over many details and that narrators, when pressed, never seem able to provide them. She particularly remembered that as a child when she asked her grandmother about details she had not mentioned in her stories, the grandmother could not provide them, stating that she was just telling the story as she had heard it.

Contributing to the extensive occurrence of dialogue, too, is the lack of any indirect discourse in Arikara. The Arikara equivalent of an indirect statement in English is a direct statement or quotation. The English sentence "He said that he would go there," for example, would translate literally into Arikara as "He said, 'I will go there.'" As another example, the Arikara statement "You'll tell the men, 'This is the kind you should make,'" would translate into idiomatic English as "You'll tell the men that they should make this kind."

The Arikara insistence on direct discourse requires, of course, that quoted material be embedded in dialogue, as the preceding examples show. Such quotations within quotations are common in the language, and freely combine with dialogue interplay, as illustrated in a woman's account of how she had been mesmerized and abducted by a bear:

> Then the woman told what happened. "This is what happened. Here it must have been a bear—a bear—that I had been seeing. Then it was a man who was going into the woods. And it got the best of me. 'I think I'll go there. I wonder who you are, you who are coming out of the woods and then going back into them.'
> "This is what I did: I went and walked into the woods. He passed in front of me. And there it was a bear! This is what it said: 'Now you must have come.'
> " 'I did come.'
> " 'Now let's go over there to my dwelling!'"
> "And this is what I did: it took me to its den where you found me. It took me inside where you found me. Now this is what the bear did." [story 119]

Moreover, three levels of embedding are not uncommon, as the following paragraph illustrates. In it a young man is instructing his sister to quiz another sister who had become a bear:

> [He said,] "You should go find out things from your bear sister. You must say to her, 'You and I are living here alone. It might happen that the enemy will find us. You say, "They cannot kill me. No one can kill me." However, what will happen if they do kill you? Where can you be wounded?'" [10]

Thoughts, too, are presented as dialogue in Arikara, so that what an actor thinks, wants, or wishes appears in the translations within quotation marks. For example, a young man sees a buffalo in the distance:

> Then he thought, "How can I sneak up on you?" [11]

Another example illustrates the common sequence of a stated action followed by the thought motivating it:

> The next morning the girl went out. "I think I'll go off for a while! I think I'll look around!" She went up into the hills wandering around, and then went to where her brothers were. [10]

A similar example:

> When a party was out going around on the warpath . . . they just did not find anything. Then they started back home. "Let's go home! We haven't found anything." [25]

Because dialogue is such an integral feature of the Arikara oral style, the translations in this collection retain all the direct discourse that appears in the original Arikara, no matter the amount of embedding.

Sequencing. The sequencing of actions and description illustrates yet another fundamental difference between Arikara and Western narrative style. A frequently used technique in Arikara is to state a result *first* and then relate the events or actions that led up to that result, the reverse of normal English style. In Lillian Brave's version of Bounding Head, for example, the listener is first told that Old Woman Spider came and caught in her web the people who were trying to smash Bounding Head, her brother. Then in the next paragraph the narrator goes back in time to relate how the people were trying to smash Bounding Head and nearly did so:

> But finally Spider was the one who had caught them. Then they were defeated by him. They were defeated by Bounding Head [i.e., Spider, Bounding Head's partisan]. [62]

The English reader at this point is left wondering, "But I thought that Spider had *already* caught them in her web; is this a second incident?" The answer, of course, is no; the latter sequence actually explains the result that was previously stated.

Another example of stating a result before mentioning the action that led to it occurs when children were misbehaving in the lodge of Fire Maker:

> And finally they [the children] were jumping over the fire. Then they were doing it: now they were jumping over the fire.
> Then after a while he [Fire Maker] said, "Now, see, you have spoiled it!
> When one of them jumped over it, he farted—a big fart. Then he farted on the fire. [84]

Such narrative sequencing frequently presents the English reader with a story that seems full of contradictions, but which, in fact, are not contradictions at all. Understanding the story requires an appreciation of this sequencing device.

Related to this type of sequencing is another common one in which the actions of an unspecified actor are stated first and only afterward is the actor identified, as in this example:

> A man touched him. "Now I've come to tell you. I know what you are seeking. You're seeking your wife. Your wife is not lost. This is what he's been doing. Why, now he's overstepped his limits. A black bear is the one. [22]

Similarly, finer specification or description often follows a more general statement. For example:

> Then he went into water. There he crossed to the other side. It was a lake. [20]

Discourse bracketing. A prominent feature of Arikara oral style is to preface an action or sequence of actions with an introductory statement "This is what he did" and frequently to conclude the description with a repetition of the same statement. Alternatively, this formulaic statement may appear only once, either before or after the description of the action. For example:

> Now then that is what they did: when spring came, when the
> green grass came up, he said, "Plant what I gave you!" And then
> that is what they did. [11]

> And as was his custom, he just wouldn't do anything. Whenever
> the party stopped, he would eat. He would sit there way off
> somewhere on the prairie. He would walk around on the prairie at
> a distance, looking all around. That is what he would do. [28]

The same kind of discourse framing occurs with spoken or
thought dialogue as well. A quotation is generally preceded by
either "Then he said" or "This is what he said," and frequently it is
concluded with a repetition of the same remark. In the following
example left and right (i.e., opening and closing) framing co-occur:

> Then the man said, "Hidden Man, I called you purposely since we
> who live here are always hungry. On this earth you are out-
> standing in the ways of hunting. And I am hungry as I sit here
> wanting something to eat. You never think, 'My uncle lives over
> there,' and you never come." That is what this man was saying.
> [15]

The following paragraphs illustrate right framing:

> Coyote awoke. He did not have the hoop around his neck. Now he
> darted around anxiously as he looked for it. "Oh, where could I
> have dropped it? Oh, I certainly had it around my neck when I lay
> down." That is what he thought. [12]

> "Oh, why don't you come in? You're causing dirt to drop down on
> us. I have some meat boiling." That is what she was saying over
> and over. [12]

Repetition. As a stylistic device repetition of a statement, either
in whole or in part, is commonly used for emphasis, often dramatic
in tone, when effected with appropriate voice modulation, as can be
seen in the following examples:

> While he was searching around, there lay something on the

ground! It was the remains of an elk that had apparently been
there a long time. Its bones were there. Its bones were there. The
skull was there with the horns still on it. [22]

Then one of them said, "Hidden Man, we have come purposefully." Then they gave him two arrows. They gave him two. [15]

Now this is the reason we ride horses: to chase the buffalo as
they roam. That is what the plan of the horse was. That was what
he planned for himself. [3]

Repetition for dramatic effect and emphasis also occurs in
slightly modified restatements, in which a word is either replaced
by a synonym or the word order in the restatement is changed, as
in the following examples:

Then all the water disappeared. There was no more water.
Wherever the creek and river valleys were, the water disappeared
entirely. And the boy would go to different places looking for water
while he just wandered all around. When he came to a bank there
would be only mud there. [2]

There he sat on a hill, on a high hill. It was a high hill where he
was sitting on top. [53]

When the name of a person is first introduced in a narrative, the
statement is commonly repeated with the order of noun and verb
reversed:

Now there once was a man who was chief of them. He was named
White Horse. White Horse is what he was named. [40]

Verbal repetition is also commonly used to indicate spatial
extension—a long, long ways—as shown here:

Then Coyote ran off as fast as he could, coming, coming, coming.
Now, after four days his strength left him. [1]

He followed and followed the couple, shooting at the elk until he
used up all his arrows. [21]

It also denotes temporal extension, as in the following:

Then the young man cried and cried while he was at the edge of
the water. Oh, then it became dark. Just before morning the young
woman came to the surface. [21]

Indeterminacy. An emphasis on specificity characterizes Arikara
narrative style. Verbal accounts must precisely stipulate such
details as quantity, location, identification, occurrence, and action.
If, for example, a group of men leaves on a war party, an account
of it must specify the number of men in the party. If they reach a
certain location, it must be named. If certain actors are mentioned,
they must be named; and if a certain activity is alluded to, it must
also be described. Frequently, however, a narrator cannot supply
such details, either because he cannot remember them or perhaps
because he was not told them when he learned the story. In such
instances, he is constrained to note the indeterminacy of detail by
a special verbal construction in which the verb stem is preceded by
niikohna-, a sequence consisting of the general deictic prefix *nii-*
followed by the dubitative *kah-* and the absolute modal prefix *na-*.

Such formations translate into English in one of two ways. One,
which occurs more frequently in these translations, signifies 'whichever,' 'whoever,' 'however many,' or 'whatever,' followed by the
English meaning of the Arikara verb, as in the following examples:

After he lay down and fell asleep, some birds came flying up to
Coyote, whatever kind they were. Whatever kind of bird it was, it
picked Sun's child up and turned back with him. [1]

And then they followed behind the group as it went off after
the weather was cold in late fall. After leaving the village, they
traveled for however many days it was. [15]

Once when he was traveling around, when he was going around
hunting, well, wherever he was going, he crossed the water,
wherever it was, to the other side when the ice was floating on the
river. [15]

Then the young man gave it the stick, whatever kind it was. [17]

Then the other one said, "Now be strong for a while! Our village
is close by. You must come there! We're living there with the man

who is now my father-in-law"—whatever his name was. [15]

Depending on context, this indeterminate construction sometimes translates into English better as either 'I don't know what/who/which' or 'it isn't known what/who/which' followed by the English meaning of the Arikara verb. The following passages exemplify this translation:

> It occurred long, long ago, somewhere along the way when the Arikaras—the ones I am telling about—were migrating this way upriver. . . . It is not known whether this incident occurred near where we are living today [or whether it happened when we were farther downriver]. [13]

> Then he went to look for a hoop since his son wanted to have one. It was the kind of hoop used in the hoop and pole game. I don't know whether it was a large or small one. [12]

Arikara stories abound with these constructions, which are one of the most distinctive features of their narrative style.

Abbreviatory devices. Arikara narrators employ several conventionalized expressions either for abbreviating narrative repetition or for skipping over stretches of time.

The abbreviation of repetition generally occurs after an actor has undergone some experience, an episode described in the story, and finally returns home, where he relates what has happened to him. Here the actor says, "This is what happened," a conventionalized expression symbolizing the sequence of events he is recounting. The expression commonly occurs at the end of stories, as several examples illustrate. One is the conclusion to a story in which a young man has vanquished his evil father-in-law, then returns to his village with his wife and mother-in-law:

> Then they did it: they arrived at the village. Then they told about it: "This is what happened. So this is what the man who used to come here has been doing." [8]

In another story a boy returns home after a series of adventures in pursuit of his hoop:

Then he said, "Father, mother, I was looking for my brother, the poor thing, after my hoop disappeared. And I've found him. This is what happened." [12]

Another type of abbreviatory device occurs when the narrator wishes to move from one time period to another. In a story about a woman who was abducted by a bear (142), for example, the narrator, Matthew White Bear, describes how the bear has the woman in its den, and then the narrator wishes to jump ahead to the period after the woman has had a child by it. To do so, he says, "Meanwhile this tale goes fast," and then takes up the narrative from that point. After another episode, the narrator again uses the same device to move the story forward. A similar technique occurs in a true story (148) told by William Deane. There he, too, wishes to take the narrative from the time when a child is small to when he has become older; he states, "As the story goes, it suddenly happened that the child had grown up. Then he became a boy."

Numerical patterning. Two numerals, four and seven, give structure to Arikara traditions. Of the two numbers, four is used far more extensively and figures in most narratives. In the myth of the race between the horse and the buffalo (3), for example, both the animals that race are said to be four winters old, and at the conclusion of the story four horses are said to have their stations in the heavens among the celestial powers, where each is one of the four sacred colors and represents one of the four directions. In the story of Red Dog and the four stars (18), as another example, the numerical pattern of four occurs repeatedly: there are four men, later stars; the wife of one of the stars lays the pipe down in front of the men four times; and Red Dog sends scouts out to look for buffalo four days after he performs a ritual. Likewise, whenever there is a sequence of tests or hurdles in a story, they occur in a set of four, although occasionally in a performance a narrator will inadvertently omit one. So, for example, when the four young women are fleeing from Bounding Head in Mr. Morsette's version (6), they take turns throwing four objects (an awl, comb, knife, and mirror) that create obstacles for him; but in Esther Perkins's version (154), only three young women throw objects (a comb, awl, and a looking glass). Likewise, in Miss Perkins's version of the Long

Teeth story (155), the two brothers subdue only two holy beings, whereas in most versions of this story the number of encounters is four (or more).

The number seven also occurs in stories but not with the same frequency. In the story of the young man who is pitied by spotted buffalos (17), for example, there are seven animals; and in the narrative of Carries The Antelope (19), the protagonist is confronted with seven paddle-shaped coup sticks, of which he is to choose one.

Morphological and Syntactic Traits

A wide variety of morphological and syntactic features characterize Arikara oral style, giving stories their distinctive texture.

Sentence introducers and connectors. Two interjections, *nawáh* and its shortened form *wah*, are the particles most commonly used to introduce a sentence. They both translate best as 'now' but also convey the meaning 'well,' and are frequently used to open a conversation or greet a person as well as to conclude a conversation or bid farewell. Narrators vary in how frequently they use these particles; some use them very often, others sparingly.

Verbs generally take one of two proclitics that serve to situate a statement in time or to connect it to other statements. One of these is *we-* 'now, at this time,' which has only a vague temporal signification. In addition to 'now,' it also translates into English as the present and past perfect forms of verbs. Arikara speakers occasionally translate it into English as 'now,' but more frequently do not give it any discreet meaning. The other proclitic, *noo-* 'then, and then, so' is a connector that has a fainter semantic force than its English equivalents and that may or may not be preceded by the conjunctions *na* and *a* 'and.' It occurs commonly; in fact, it appears on verb after verb in stories, so that in translation it impresses an English reader as a monotonously redundant feature. Generally it is translated here as 'then' and 'so,' but in many instances it is not translated at all.

Existential constructions. Two existential constructions, each having a distinctive connotation, are prevalent in Arikara narratives. One is the indicative existential, *inoowitii-*. It is composed of the quotative prefix *wi-* and the third person indicative modal prefix *ti-* followed by the sequential *i-;* those elements are preceded by a compounded form of the distal deictic *i-* 'there' and *noo-* 'there.' The construction translates as 'there there [verb]' or 'there he [verb],' and serves to point out emphatically the existence or occurrence of someone or something. Examples of its use are:

> When he went inside where she lived, a heart was hanging there with blood dripping from it. [7]

> Then they were very anxious, so they got up. Then each woman went to her cache pit, and there there were plenty of different kinds of corn, just as the crier had said. [11]

The other construction is the contingent existential, so called because it consists of the independent particle *či* 'here' followed by the contingent modal *i-* and second person subject pronominal prefix *š-* and the evidential proper prefix *an-*. It is translated as 'here it [verb]' and connotes a sense of surprise or of the unexpected, as in the following examples:

> And the children moved toward the woods where the plum bushes were. Then the young girl charged out of the brush, and here she was [now] a bear! [10]

> Then they killed the snake. And here it was the favored child of the snakes, the one that they killed! [14]

The particle *či* 'here' occurs with the absolutive mode *(na-)* as well, and in such combinations the English translations are similar to those of the contingent existential; for example:

> Then her husband said, "And here this is what you are doing when you come here! I'm going to punish that one." [13]

Demonstratives. Demonstrative pronouns are used extensively in Arikara, not only where they are normally used in English but also very often where either the English definite article is used or where in English neither a demonstrative pronoun nor a definite article normally occurs. Proper names and nominal subjects are usually preceded by a demonstrative pronoun, usually 'this one.' In story 1, for example, in most occurrences of the characters' names— Raven, Scalped Man, Coyote, and Sun—there is a demonstrative preceding it that translates literally as 'this Raven,' 'this Scalped Man,' etc. Similarly, in story 2 there are two primary actors, a boy and a spring peeper, and generally when the nouns designating them appear in the narrative, they are preceded by the demonstrative. In these and other instances where a demonstrative is not used in idiomatic English, it is either not translated or is translated as the definite article, whichever is more appropriate.

Exclamatives. Another characteristic feature of Arikara oral style is the prevalent use of four exclamatives, each of which adds a certain emotive tone to statements and which, because they are used far more extensively than similar elements in English, give Arikara narratives a distinctive flavor.

The most common of these interjections are *uu* and *aa*, the equivalents of English 'oh' and 'ah' respectively, which add an element of surprise, intensity, or emphasis to a statement. Exemplifying the use of *uu* is a passage in which Long Teeth suspiciously enters the lodge where Drinks Brains is:

> Oh, the other boy [Long Teeth] looked all around inside the interior of the lodge, at the four main posts; oh, he looked all around. Then he came inside. [4]

In another example from the same story:

> There in the distance was a village. Oh, it was a big village! And then that is where he went. [4]

Examples of *aa* occur in the following, in which Raven instructs Scalped Man to take the hoop:

> And you, Scalped Man, will take the hoop. And after you get out, they're going to chase you. Ah, they're watching. They're watching over him. You'll go in, and as soon as you come out, I'll be right there. You'll put the hoop around my neck and I'll come flying north, ah, for as long as my strength lasts. [1]

A similar interjection is *čiríkU* 'oh, my; why!' It, too, adds an element of surprise, as illustrated here:

> And so the spring peeper went to a mud flat where the ground was damp. The spring peeper put its two forelegs into the mud and then backed off. Oh my, then water emerged! And as the water came out, it grew in volume. Why, now this boy began to drink his fill! [2]

Different from these is another exclamative, *wačéh* 'poor thing,' which appears in apposition to an animate noun and is also extensively used. It expresses the narrator's sympathy for a person who, in the Arikara mind, is in a pitiful condition. Sometimes the significance of its use is apparent to an English reader, but at other times it is somewhat elusive as the following passages illustrate.

> Now the spring peeper, poor thing, became very frightened since the boy was kicking it around, molesting it. [2]

> She caused the village to turn up when the fire swept through it, there where that village was. And it burned everything in it, including the men and women, the poor things, who burned up. Then everything was lost, except for the people, the poor things, who fled in different directions—the ones who ran up the hill or who ran into the water. [4]

> Now I am going to relate a story that my grandmother used to tell. Maybe she is listening now, the poor thing, to what she used to tell when she and I were living alone when my grandfather had gone somewhere. . . . [26]

Decedents. When speaking of someone who is deceased, an Arikara usually qualifies the reference with a past tense participial form, which sometimes is *nuúxU* 'the one who was' and other times is *nuuxAxaáNU* 'the one who was named.' In the introduction to story 24, for example, Alfred Morsette states, "I heard the story from the one who was *[nuúxU]* Bear Goes Out; he was named *[kuwituuxAxaá'A]* Bear Goes Out." Another set of examples occurs in story 104, in which Ella Waters tells about a trip her parents made to the Standing Rock Reservation sometime near the turn of the century. In it she refers to her parents as 'my mother who was' and 'my father who was,' since both were deceased when she

recorded the narrative. In the historical narrative about the Fort
Laramie Treaty (41) the qualifier 'the one who was named' precedes
the first mention of numerous individuals, and at the conclusion of
story 53 the narrator states, "This is what I used to hear from the
man [who was] named Enemy Heart."

Still another usage for introducing a deceased person's name is
what translates as 'they used to call him,' or its subordinate form
'the one they used to call.' These forms also appear in narrative 41;
for example, "Then the chiefs summoned another man. They used
to call him Stone."

Similar qualifiers that occur in the narratives include 'my father
who was living,' (104) and 'when I was the old man's son-in-law'
(i.e., 'when my father-in-law was living') (30).

Intensification. In Arikara there are three common ways of
intensifying a statement. The one that occurs most frequently is use
of the particle *Axtóh.* This particle is, in fact, so extensively used
that it, too, gives a characteristic flavor to Arikara narrative style.
Most of the time it translates as 'surely, truly, certainly,' as, for
example:

"It sure would be nice if it were warm. . . ." [1]

"Say, there surely is a being living who controls things where it is
summer." [1]

Then Coyote said, "Truly no one ever overtakes me. . . ." [1]

Occasionally, however, it translates best as 'why, . . !":

Then this Drinks Brains said, "Why, he said, 'Don't go there!' He
doesn't want us to do that." [4]

Another method of expressing intensification is with a negative
verb form. A verb inflected for the negative has a double meaning:
usually it indicates the negative, but it also sometimes serves to
intensify a statement. In the latter instance, the negative form
translates into English as a positive statement together with 'really,
very, so' or sometimes 'indeed.' Although this archaic usage is no
longer understood by most Arikara speakers, it occurs frequently in

the narratives of Alfred Morsette and others. Examples are:

Then these horses, the poor things, became fearful. The buffalo was *so* strong. [3]

Surely that man who's coming has gone too far. . . . We blessed him previously, but now he's gone beyond the limit with these things that he's been doing. [8]

Now he threw an awl. And when he threw it where they had just come from, there was a thicket of thorn apple bushes. Oh, there was indeed a multitude of them! [10]

It was certainly [lit. not] true that this horse was swift when it ran. [50]

Still another way of intensifying an utterance is to lengthen a vowel in a word. So, for example, the adverbial expression *nuu naapakúhtu'* 'long, long ago' can be exaggerated by lengthening *nuu* 'then' to *nuuuu*, the equivalent of lengthening English 'long' to 'loooong.' The same effect can also be achieved by lengthening the vowel of the first syllable in *naapakúhtu'*, especially when *nuu* does not precede it; thus, *naaaaapakúhtu'* 'loooong ago.'

Sentence types. Word order in Arikara, as in many polysynthetic languages, is quite free. When a sentence has an independent nominal subject and object, for example, the only requirement is that the subject precede the object, but otherwise nearly every permutation of the two nouns and verb is possible. Speakers concur that no one order is preferable to the others, although each person tends to use certain ones; and speakers do not correlate any of the permutations with specific word orderings in English. Consequently, the English translations here often do not reflect Arikara word order, particularly when an Arikara sentence is long and complex.

The sentences in the translations do, however, reflect the structural complexity or simplicity of the Arikara, and therein lies a basic stylistic contrast in the language. Arikara narrators alternate between sentences that, from an English perspective, are long and unusually complex and ones that are short and simple.

Long, complex sentences occur most commonly in description,

where they illustrate a propensity in Arikara to form sentences by stringing many subordinate clauses to a single independent one. The following two paragraphs vividly illustrate this structural preference:

> The young man also had a friend. But his friend was active, going all around, going around hunting and going off on war parties. But this other one was just passive, as they used to say, never going on a war party and never looking for things for his mother and father—just walking around in the village where people made fun of him. [23]

> And when it was morning the man who had had the crippled legs walked around inside. Then he was tremendously thankful, being thankful that he was able to walk all around again after they had made him well—after they had taken away his crippledness. [15]

In stark contrast to complex sentences like the preceding are short, direct ones, which are usually employed in recounting sequences of action. Here, too, the integrity of their simplicity is preserved in the translations, even though the style is not valued in English. The following examples illustrate the concatenation of simple sentences:

> Then the boy went on. Then he went home. Then he went inside. Then he said, "Mother, make a fire! I've returned."
> Then she said, "Oh, why, they're making fun of me!" [12]

> Then this young man started out. Then he went back to his lodge. Then he untied the dogs. He packed some moccasins. Then he came on. Then he arrived at the village after dark. [22]

More common, however, is a balance between the simple and the complex:

> Then he prepared a sweat lodge. He took the boy inside. He made him vomit everything—the things that he used to eat when he lived in the water of that lake. After he had vomited everything—the worms, frogs, and whatever other things, everything that he ate—then the man gave him different medicines to drink. [4]

Narrative Structure

Beginnings

Narrators vary in the manner in which they begin their stories. Some open them with a formulaic statement, while others offer an introduction containing background information that situates and authenticates the version of the narrative being told. Still others begin directly with the story.

Unless she is telling historical narratives of recent origin, Lilly Brave illustrates the first-named pattern and nearly always opens her stories, whether true ones or tales, with the formula *kuwitee-tuunú'a'* 'the village was coming in a long procession,' an allusion to a village on the march. It has no known historical reference, although it probably refers to the Arikara migration upriver. It is now a formal opening to a story, equivalent to the English 'once upon a time.'

Most narrators, however, generally precede their stories with an introduction. Alfred Morsette prefaces almost every narrative he recorded in this collection with the most elaborately stylized introductions. The prefatory statements of other narrators, although containing some of the same information, never have the detail of his. He generally opens with the statement that he will now tell an old story, which he often characterizes either as holy or one that actually happened, frequently qualifying his statement with an avowal that he did not witness it himself. For myths there may also be a statement that the story occurred during the holy period and involved star beings from the celestial world above. Myths and legends, however, are nearly always said to have occurred "long, long ago when our people were coming this way," the reference being to past centuries when the Arikaras were gradually moving upriver in the northwesterly direction of the Missouri River; this general frame is followed by a more precise locational reference, when it is known. Then Mr. Morsette, like many narrators, generally names the person who told him the story and sometimes tells how he came to hear it. Since the sources of his stories are always people of social rank, who are today, as they were previously, accorded respect, the mention of their names serves to authenticate his stories as well as simply to supply background information.

(Sometimes, however, he does not name his source until the conclusion of the narrative.)

Eleanor Chase also begins both the one myth and one tale she recorded with the now formulaic introductory statement that the story occurred sometime "when our villages extended along the Missouri River," an anachronistic localizing term not unlike Alfred Morsette's that refers to a former period when small Arikara villages were strung along the banks of the Missouri.

Other narrators, especially Ella Waters and Matthew White Bear, frequently open a story with one of several closely related verbal forms that translate as 'there was a village.' This statement is often modified by a tribal name or a geographical characterization. Such an introductory line serves to situate the story in an indefinite, or at most a loosely defined, temporal and spatial setting that is usually either unknown or of no concern to the narrator, much like the opening line in English stories, "Once upon a time there was a . . ."

Another term used to situate historical stories is *nuuneesawatuúNU* 'there over the hill,' which Arikaras have used during this century to refer to the location of former Arikara villages at Fort Clark and sites farther south. For Mr. Morsette this term designates the Fort Clark village specifically, but for Mrs. Waters it has a more general reference, denoting village sites along the Missouri below Fort Clark.

Although many tales commence with a short introduction that often includes one of the opening statements characteristic of myths or other narrative types, they generally move directly into the story. In Coyote stories, which comprise the majority of these narratives and are the most stylized of all, the opening line is typically one in which Coyote is said to be wandering around or trotting along, often followed by a picaresque reference to his being hungry as usual—introductory assertions that invariably evoke immediate smiles or laughter from Arikara listeners.

Episodic Structure

Long stories are composite texts of episodes set between an introduction and a conclusion. Even though details may differ, the overall structure of different versions of most stories, particularly

myths and tales, whether told by the same or a different narrator,
is generally very similar or identical. People learn stories in different forms, of course. Sometimes one person's version is longer than
another's and contains embellishments or particulars that do not
occur in the other's; or certain details may vary, reflecting the
different forms in which myths are told and transmitted. These
differences also derive in part from the specific situations in which
narratives are told. Depending on such variables as a narrator's
mood, memory, or other personal factors as well as the narrative
situation itself, the teller may lengthen a story by adding episodes,
elaborating on details within an episode, or both, as well as by
creating new episodes and details or by utilizing existing ones.
Similarly, given the same variables, the narrator may abridge a
version to its primary components, omitting one or more episodes as
well as neglecting or excluding embellishments and other details
considered superfluous to the outline of the story. Rarely, then, are
two recitations of the same story by the same narrator identical in
all particulars.

Examples of versions of stories that differ in their episodic
structure abound in this collection. The story of the girl who became
a bear offers a simple illustration of how details within an episode
differ. Three of the four versions of this story (10, 86, 141) are
identical in structure except for the one episode in which the bear
sister's siblings flee from her. (The fourth version, 151, is radically
different.) Two versions (10, 36) have the same sequence of four
hurdles that the siblings create for their pursuer before they finally
escape by climbing onto a rock that rises into the sky, but the third
version (141) omits the obstacles altogether.

Although some stories have a set number of episodes, others
have a seemingly indefinite number and thereby allow for greater
variability in structure. Two examples are the stories of Long Teeth
and Drinks Brain Soup (4, 63, 155) and The Star Husband and Old
Woman's Grandson (85, 111), in both of which the young protagonists—two brothers in the former, one boy in the latter—embark
on a series of adventures. In one of the versions of the Long Teeth
myth (4) four adventures are described, whereas in another version
(155) there are only two; moreover, between the two sets there is
only one common exploit. A similar contrast occurs in the two

versions of Old Woman's Grandson. In one version (85) there are
eight episodic adventures, but in the other one (111) there are only
four, all of which occur in the longer version. In stark contrast to
the versions of these two stories is one telling of the Long Teeth
myth (63) that is actually a composite of that myth and the story of
The Star Husband and Old Woman's Grandson. In this narrative
the two brothers undergo a series of three exploits, of which only
one matches any of those in the other versions (4, 155).

The myth of The Star Husband and Old Woman's Grandson
illustrates another feature of narrative composition: the creation of
a story by combining two different narratives into a single, longer
one. This Arikara story, similar to many versions found throughout
the Plains (see Lowie 1942; Thompson 1953:93–163), is a composite
text of two common myths—one the widespread story of a woman
who marries a star and the other, its sequel, a hero tale about the
exploits of Star Boy—that are tied together by the survival of the
star wife's child when he and his mother drop to earth.[19] Another
example of this method of creating one longer story by linking two
separate ones is the story of The Young Man Who Became a Snake
and Carries The Antelope. Both versions of it presented here—one
by Alfred Morsette (19) and the other by Dan Hopkins (133), which
are nearly identical—consist of two subparts that for other Arikara
narrators are separate stories: one about a young man who eats
snake flesh and subsequently becomes a snake himself and takes up
his abode in the Missouri River; and the other about a young man
who is taken up into a thunderbirds' nest, where he kills a water
monster eating the thunderbirds' children. For Mrs. Waters (90, 96)
and Matthew White Bear (140), as well as for other Plains tribes
(e.g., Pawnee in G.A. Dorsey 1904b:167–68, Grinnell 1893b:171;
Cheyenne in Grinnell 1926:154–57), these are separate stories, but
for Mr. Morsette and Mr. Hopkins they have become combined into
a single narrative.[20]

Similar in construction is William Deane's version of The Man
Married to Buffalo Woman (148), which is a simple juxtaposition of

---

19. The combination of these two stories into a single myth occurs among
many Plains tribes, and was not developed by the Arikara alone.

20. They are interrelated in Hidatsa myth, too (Bowers 1965:360–62).

two stories, one an account of a clinging old woman who attaches herself to a young man,[21] and the following one the story of the man who married a buffalo woman; in this telling the two parts are not explicitly related to each other.[22] Another version of the second part of Mr. Deane's story is told as a separate myth by Lilly Brave (69), as in fact it is in many versions among neighboring tribes (e.g., the Omaha in J.O. Dorsey 1890:147–62).

The creation of longer narratives is illustrated here by yet another technique: the combination of different accounts of an event into one story. In his narrative of a nineteenth-century attack on Like-A-Fishhook Village (47), for example, Alfred Morsette gives a loosely integrated account of the attack and its aftermath composed of separate versions that he heard from three older men, each one providing a different perspective on the action. Similar in construction is Mr. Morsette's narrative of Custer's expedition against the Sioux in 1876, culminating in the Battle of the Little Big Horn. This version is actually a conflation of accounts of two separate expeditions in which Arikara scouts served under Lt. Col. Custer's command—the 1874 exploring expedition to the Black Hills and the military campaign against the Sioux two years later—that portrays the two maneuvers as a single one. Two other narratives told by Mr. Morsette, one about Arikara-Hidatsa relations (39) and the other about the Fort Laramie Treaty of 1851 (41), are compositions similarly built up from accounts of many separate events.

Explanations

Many stories end with a moral or an explanation of why some facet of the world is the way it is today. Myths, which frequently are accounts of the origin of some feature in the world, are etiological. The story of "How Summer Came to the North Country" (1), for example, tells how summer was first brought to the northern latitude where the Arikaras were living and why summer and

21. Lévi-Strauss (1968:54–85) analyzes and traces the distribution of this myth throughout North and South America.
22. A version of this story recorded by Edward Curtis in 1907 also is composed of these two parts, but in it the relationship between the clinging old woman and the buffalo wife is made explicit.

winter have alternated annually ever since. Similarly, the story of
the girl who became a bear (10, 86, 141, 151) explains the origin of
Devils Tower, a natural landmark in northeastern Wyoming, as well
as of the Pleiades. In both stories, these explanations are given at
the end. The mythical and legendary stories of the poor boy—Bloody
Hands, Eats Ashes, and others—typically, but not always, end with
a moral, which is usually that the poor person who is humble
ultimately triumphs, as Mrs. Brave eloquently states:

> And now today that is the reason that the person who is poor is
> the one who becomes a chief. And the one who is a chief is the one
> who will come last. The poor person is the one who will arrive in
> the lead. This is the reason that when one of us is poor, that
> person comes in the lead. For this is what [Bloody] Hands did. [66]

Many legendary stories are also explanatory, particularly those
that account for the origin of a rite, a society, or a man's name, or
which relate an incident that is reputed to have resulted in a
natural feature or landmark. The story of the origin of the Hidatsa
Crazy Dog society, for example, ends with the declaration that the
incident related in it explains why Doorway songs are sung at night
among the Hidatsas. The war story (46) of an Assiniboine of the
Watopa band who led a raiding party to Like-A-Fishhook Village
and stole two kettles of food from an Arikara lodge illustrates how
a man acquired the name Two Kettles, and how the Arikaras gave
his people the designation Two Kettles' Village. As still another
example, the story of the priest who pouted and turned to stone (53)
is typical of several in this collection that account for landmarks.

Tales, like myths, frequently end with an explanation, but in
tales this formulaic element tends to be more facile than serious,
usually accounting for a mundane phenomenon, and often seems to
be tacked on to the story to give it significance more to children
than to adults. In Alfred Morsette's version of "Coyote and Beaver"
(61), for example, Coyote is ultimately frightened by Beaver's power,
and so the narrator ends the tale with the statement "this [incident]
is the reason a coyote is afraid; when it sees someone, it runs off."
Two other narrators, William Deane and Eleanor Chase, utilize the
same formulaic explanation as an ending for two entirely different
Coyote stories. Both tales end with Coyote's demise beside a rock,

so the incident is cited to explain why people today often find bones lying near rocks. Not unlike these explanations is the one given at the end of the tale of "Fire Maker and Why Children Misbehave" (84), a story of how children once ruined a fire in the fireplace in the lodge of the man who controls fire. Their misbehavior is said to account for why children misbehave today.

Endings

Sometimes narrators end a story with no concluding statement. The story of the man with the sharpened leg (8), for example, simply ends when the protagonist returns triumphantly to his village with his wife and mother-in-law and tells people what happened to him. Sometimes, too, the explanatory statement serves as the finale. Most narratives, however, end with a formal statement like "This is how the story goes," "This is the extent of the story," and "This is what happened," or "This is what I used to hear." Alfred Morsette, for example, nearly always uses one or a combination of these forms for a conclusion, any two of which are rarely identical. Other narrators like Mrs. Gillette end their stories with the simple statement *nɔwáh* 'Now' to indicate the conclusion (e.g., 144–46).

For true stories, in contrast to tales, narrators often qualify the concluding statement by designating the person who told them the story, particularly when that information has not been given in the introduction. Mr. Morsette, for example, concludes one narrative (15) with the statement, "Now this is what I used to hear when my grandmother told the story." He ends another narrative (53) by saying, "This is what I used to hear from the man named Enemy Heart," who was a prominent Arikara doctor and warrior. By specifying the source of the story in such a manner, as noted above, the narrator validates his version, and he may even mention that the person who was its source gave the narrator the right to tell it. Mary Gillette makes this point at the conclusion of her story about Has The Horn and the Sioux raiders (145), when she says, "This is the way Has The Horn used to tell it. She gave me the story."

Still another conclusion to a story is one of the two formulaic statements that signal not only the end of a story but also the end of a narrator's story telling (see pp. 117-118).

Narrative Content

Recognition of both the predominant themes that constitute Arikara traditions and the major cultural symbols that pervade them are equally essential to an understanding and appreciation of the Arikara literary tradition. Themes, or topics, are cultural perceptions of natural phenomena and human events, real or imagined, which Arikaras have deemed to be sufficiently significant to remember in tradition and which constitute their notion of history. The cultural symbols imbuing them, in contrast, help to flesh out the themes with distinctively Arikara elements; they are the cultural analogues of stylistic features at the linguistic level. Together, those compositional elements, combined with character types and linguistic features of style, create and define the essence of Arikara oral literature. For Arikaras, that literature fulfills the role of history, and the historicity of stories—evaluated by criteria fundamentally different from Western notions of historiography—is an important measure of their validity. At the same time, Arikara oral tradition does not neglect humor; some stories are told solely for amusement, and humorous episodes are introduced into historical narratives for comic relief.

Cultural Symbols

Holiness. Fundamental to these traditions—indeed, permeating almost all of them—is the Arikara concept *waaRUxtii'u'* 'mysterious power, holiness, sacredness.' It signifies an awe-inspiring, inexplicable power or quality resident in the forces of the universe *(awaaháxu')*.[23] Those forces or beings, perceived to be animate spirits whom people generally refer to and address by kinship terms, include not only celestial phenomena—stars, Sun, Moon, Rain, Thunder, Night—but such natural features of the earth as rocks, rivers, and trees, as well as animals and birds. They are, in fact, anything in the world that is remarkable or unusual. Each

---

23. Mrs. Waters and Mrs. Gillette translated *awaaháxu'* and its semantically related form *t'naawaáhAt* as 'the elements,' referring to the elements of the universe that have power. Mrs. Brave's translation, 'the Universe; the amorphous, expansive power above,' is similar.

possesses a mysterious power enabling it to effect the extraordinary, to achieve spectacular actions or feats beyond the capabilities or comprehension of human beings. That power may be manifested in what is observable, like the flash of lightning, the ferocity of a grizzly bear, the cure of an herb, or a feat of magic; or it may be exhibited in what is only indirectly apparent but for an Arikara is just as real, like the rain that falls after a ritual has been performed, the death that occurs after a sacrilege has been committed, or the accident that befalls someone after another person who is reputed to possess "medicine" has done something out of the ordinary that appears to be an act of witchcraft.

Arikaras conceive of a supreme power, which is denoted by several terms. During this century the most common designation for him is the Chief Above (*neesaánu' tⁱnačitákUx*, literally 'this chief who sits above'), but he is also known as Our Father Above (*atí'Ax tⁱNAxčitákUx*, literally 'your father who sits above), and in one story in this collection (11) he is also referred to as the Great Holy One (*šeeniiwaaRUxtiNIhuuíNU*). Among elderly Arikaras he is characterized as an amorphous power who is overhead in the heavens and is the ultimate source of the world and everything in it. In story 11, for example, Mother Corn tells the people that he is seen in the sky, that he is the one who put everything in the world, and that he is to be called Father by people here on earth. After recording this story, Alfred Morsette explained that the Great Holy One *is* the Heavens, who looks down on Mother Earth and people here but who does not help people by doing good things for them. Primarily a neutral force, he does not intervene directly in human affairs.

Mother Corn, in contrast, is his intermediary on earth. She is the one who came down to earth from the heavens and is the Mother of people; she is the deity who has helped the Arikara people in the past and continues to help them in times of need. At the beginning of human history she led the Arikaras' ancestors out of the underground world and into the one here on earth; she led them on a journey beset with obstacles to their historic location in the Missouri River valley; she gave them their cultural institutions and moral teachings, and provided them with horticulture, including corn itself. It has been primarily Mother Corn to whom Arikaras have turned for help during the past.

Below the Chief Above and Mother Corn is a host of powers, all of which are subsumed under a general term that occurs in several alternate forms based on the stem -awaahak 'to be an expanse.' The most common of those forms are awaaháxu' and tⁱnaawaáhAt, both of which are translated in various ways by elderly Arikaras, but in essence refer to the totality of powers in the universe.[24] Although today many speakers associate the terms with the Christian God-head, others recognize the difference between an older Arikara concept of multitudinous powers and the more recent association with a single Christian God. Ella Waters and Mary Gillette, for example, preferred to translate both awaaháxu' and tⁱnaawaáhAt as 'the Elements,' an English term that they felt encompassed both animate and inanimate powers. And so in one story (99) told by Mrs. Waters, the Elements include the wind, stones, sticks, and straw that blow up into the air and make war whoops when saving the helpless inhabitants of an Arikara village being attacked by a Sioux war party. In the narrative describing her naming ritual (108), moreover, Mrs. Waters distinguishes between two types of Elements, or powers: heavenly and earthly.[25] The former includes celestial beings, such as Sun, Moon, and the various stars, while the latter includes features of the landscape, here enumerated as the Grandfather stones on hillsides and Mother River and those things that are on her banks. Lillian Brave, in contrast, translates both awaaháxu' and tⁱnaawaáhAt as 'the Universe; the amorphous, expansive power above,' an English rendering that emphasizes the heavenly powers, although it does not exclude the earthly ones. In volumes 1 and 2 of this collection of narratives, 'elements' has generally been given as the translation for these concepts, following the preference of Mrs. Waters; but in the free translations in volumes 3 and 4, 'powers' is the English term used throughout since it is less ambiguous for most readers. Sometimes the distinction between heavenly and earthly Powers is made, and occasionally a

24. The terms are cognate with Pawnee tiraawaahat and awaahaksu', which are usually translated as 'the Heavens' or 'the Expanse Of The Heavens.' As with Arikaras, many contemporary Pawnees associate Tirawahat with God.

25. Pawnees make the same fundamental distinction between heavenly and earthly powers.

modifier like 'holy' is used.

The mysterious powers of the universe are ambivalent—they can be either malevolent or benevolent—and are frequently unpredictable. As malevolent, what is *waaruxti'* is dangerous and to be shunned, unless, of course, a person knows how to handle it properly, as through ritual. To avoid its malevolent effects, a human must treat a force imbued with holiness with respect and maintain a proper distance from it. But mysterious power may also be beneficent, and a person may receive some of this power from the being possessing it. An individual may get it as a token of appreciation after performing some service for the being, as when the poor boy retrieved the children of the distraught mouse couple and for this act was blessed with their power (20); or, more commonly, he may acquire it after making himself pitiable so that the force gives him power out of sympathy for his plight. Fasting on a hill, in a cemetery, or in some other appropriate spot, where the lone supplicant neither eats nor drinks and cries for days and nights, is the institutionalized manner of obtaining a spiritual benefactor and some of its power. The nature of that power varies, naturally, depending on the capabilities of the being who bestows it. At the outset of one story (17), each of four animals endows a young man with its characteristic power. The mountain lion's power is the gift of bravery over the enemy; the eagle's is the ability to hunt proficiently; the rabbit's is fleetness and the ability to overtake someone when running after him; and the ant's is the power to find hidden objects.

Arikara doctors possess more powers than any other members of their society; among them they have all three of the types of power that supernatural beings confer on people. One, already mentioned and undoubtedly the most important, is the power to cure, the methods of which vary from herbal treatment to ritual acts (e.g., story 73). Another is the ability to perform feats of magic, illustrated by the doctors' spectacular public demonstrations in the Medicine Lodge that were staged to convince people of their powers and to inspire awe (e.g., stories 55, 102). Finally, there is the power to 'shoot the spirit' *(assawanik)* of another person, producing a trance state that enables a doctor to render that person passive or helpless and thereby to control his or her behavior. The exercise of this power, translated here as 'to mesmerize,' is exemplified in these narratives only by animals, who generally transform themselves into human beings to mesmerize women and then abduct them (e.g., 21, 26, 70, etc.). In one story (70), however, a brother and sister are mesmerized by an elk spirit so that powers can be conveyed to them—powers that they were to take back to the Arikara people.

Frequently when a person is blessed with power, that power is embodied in a little animal spirit said to reside in the individual's chest, the locus of the human spirit and of emotions. When the little spirit manifests itself, the individual becomes suffused with its power and actually manifests the animal's behavior.[26] Such a transformation is illustrated in the story of an Assiniboine raid (45), when the warriors are "performing the things they say to become holy," thereby taking on the behavior of the animal power each possesses. In this instance the men conjure up the animal spirits within themselves.[27]

Sometimes, however, the spirit overtakes an individual without any conscious effort, exemplified in two anecdotes told by Ella Waters. One incident occurred when an Arikara doctor named Bear's Belly and his wife were visiting her parents and the couple stayed overnight. Mrs. Waters's father, Yellow Bear, and Bear's Belly, who had bear power, slept beside each other on pallets on the floor. During the night, according to her father, Bear's Belly suddenly began to growl and then act like a bear and several times started to bite at Yellow Bear's neck. The next day Yellow Bear recounted the frightening behavior of Bear's Belly when the bear spirit "came on him" during the night.

The other incident related by Mrs. Waters occurred just before the death of Strikes Two *(titaraawičé)*, a doctor who had jackrabbit power. Just before his death while this man lay ill in bed, too weak to move, he asked to be taken outside. Once there, he seemed to regain his strength when, uncontrollably, he proceeded to sit on his

26. The belief in little animal spirits residing in the chest is common among neighboring tribes on the northern Plains (see, e.g., Cooper 1957:283–85, 332 for Atsinas; DeMallie 1984:239 for the Teton Sioux). The Pawnees apparently do not share this belief.

27. Maximilian (1843, 2:343) discusses the same belief in animals in the body among the Mandans and Hidatsas.

haunches and jerk his head while making the cries of a jackrabbit. Then, after the spirit in him "calmed down," he lay down weak again, and no sooner had he been taken back into the house than he died.

Respect. Intertwined in part with the concept of holiness are symbols of respect, which are the same symbols used to honor a person, such as a distinguished visitor. Within the lodge, the west end opposite the entry is the area of honor *(huNAhtAhtiš)*. In the Medicine Lodge the altar is located there and is the place where the leading priests sit during rituals. In the lodge of a keeper it is also the area where the sacred bundle hangs from a rafter, and in other lodges it is the location of a family's private altar or shrine. Visitors are seated at the west end of the lodge when one wishes to show them respect.

Further signs of respect are offerings of food and tobacco. Hence, in all Arikara ceremonies, religious and curing, the three standard offerings made to the deities and spirits of the deceased are the smoke offering of tobacco and the two food offerings of corn and meat. Similarly, when an honored guest arrives at a home, the host shows his respect by seating the visitor in the west and giving him tobacco to smoke and having food served to him.

There is, in addition to these standard forms of extending honor, another overt set of symbols denoted by the term 'to clothe someone' that Arikaras extend to the living as well as to spirits. This custom is illustrated in several narratives here. In one (24), a family wishes to honor a she-bear who visits their lodge, and besides seating her at the west end and giving her food, the family paints her face and put a feather on her head. In another story (54), in which a bear and a buffalo bull fight and kill one another, a party of Arikaras who witness the battle wish to pay honor to the animals' spirits. As in the previous story, they paint the faces of the dead animals and put feathers on them, and because they are males, they offer them smoke.

The same symbols are employed to honor a human and are frequently combined with a magnificent set of clothing that is put on the person. Vividly illustrating this form of honoring someone is a historical account of how its symbolism was employed to end a battle in 1862 between two camps, one of Arikaras and the other of Hunkpapa Sioux, who had been trading with each other until a fight broke out over a horse race. During a lull in the fighting the Arikara chief went forward and called for Sitting Bull, the Sioux leader, who came and was led to the Arikara's tipi:

> Inside the tipi, the Ree chief helped Sitting Bull undress. Then he brought out several bags of fine clothing. . . . He honored Sitting Bull by dressing him in these fine clothes with his own hands. He put on him two fine scarlet trailing breech-cloths, a foot wide, reaching from his belt to the ground, before and behind. He helped him into a pair of handsome leggings of soft, pliant buckskin, decorated with a broad bead stripe down the leg, and having heavy twisted fringes from the hip to ankle. On his feet he placed moccasins with stiff rawhide soles and flexible elkskin uppers covered with designs in dyed porcupine quills. Over Sitting Bull's head the Ree chief slipped a shirt of mountain-sheep's skin, with trailing fringes, decorations of quillwork across the shoulders and chest, and tassels of hair in rows on either side. This shirt he laced up the side, and tied the sleeves to fit. . . . Having painted Sitting Bull's face, he then took from a painted cylindrical rawhide case a swagger war-bonnet and put it on his head—a splendid headgear, with an upright crown of glistening plumes from the golden eagle, a beaded brow-band, and a long tail of feathers cascading down the back to his heels. The Ree tied the chin-straps under Sitting Bull's chin, and belted the tail of the bonnet around his waist.
>
> Leading him outside the tent, the Ree made him mount a fine black horse with a bald face. A war-bonnet was tied to the mane of this horse and another tied to the tail, and its back was thick with blankets. When the horse moved, the tails of the war-bonnets dragged the ground. The Ree chief led this horse to the open space between the lines of hostile warriors. [Vestal 1934:22–23].

This symbolic gesture ended the hostilities.

Yet another way of conferring honor on someone in Arikara society is through sponsorship of the *piireškáni'*, or child-naming, ceremony. The Arikara name means literally 'many-handed child' and is cognate with the obsolete Pawnee name for the ceremony, *kskári'* 'many hands.' This early twentieth-century ritual appears to have been a development from one or both of two separate ceremonies of the late eighteenth and early nineteenth centuries, one for piercing children's ears and the other for adopting children

(Parks 1991b; Abel 1939:214–16; Will 1934:33–39), the latter a form of the widespread Calumet Ceremony.[28] The *piireškáni'*, at least in its twentieth-century form, is sponsored by parents who wish to honor a child by having him or her named at a public celebration before the entire tribe. In the ceremony the child not only receives a new name but is also painted and reclothed, all honorific symbols representing the new period of life that a candidate is entering—a period marked by new religious and social responsibilities. A child so honored is known thereafter as a beloved, or favored, child (*piiraasštawí'u'*).

Pitifulness. Another pervasive Arikara cultural symbol occurring in narratives is that of pitifulness (*kaapaačišu'*), denoted by the two synonymous descriptive verbal stems *kaapaačiš* and *takaahuun* 'to be pitiful, poor.' This state is to some extent relative, as illustrated by the Pawnee use of the term 'poor ones' to designate Indians in general, in apparent contrast to white people, who are so richly endowed by their 'power' (*waaRUxtii'u'*), manifested by their technology. In Arikara society, however, the poor person is one who has no relatives, the orphan or the widowed who have no kin to help them in the accumulation and social distribution of such valuable commodities as food, hides, and horses. Not able to provide adequately for themselves or to participate in the interchange of goods, they have no social status and are objects of pity. In Arikara lore Bloody Hands and his grandmother embody these traits: they live in a tipi rather than an earth lodge, located by the dung heaps on the outskirts of the village, where they eat the scraps thrown away by more affluent families, and they have only a swaybacked nag for a horse.

The notion of pitifulness, though, is extended to circumstances other than social status. The invalid, the sickly, and the simple-minded as well as the old person who is no longer able to lead an active life or who is beset by the infirmities or feebleness of advanced age are all said to be pitiful, too. In contemporary life as well as in traditions, elderly Arikaras, in fact, regularly intersperse

28. The Pawnee Calumet Ceremony is best known as the Hako, a term Alice Fletcher gave to it in her classic study (Fletcher 1904).

their conversations with an appositional *wačéh* 'poor thing; poor me' in reference to their own condition, just as narrators frequently do in stories when describing a person portrayed as pitiful.

Sensibleness. There is, finally, another cultural concept that occurs repeatedly in Arikara stories as well as in ordinary conversation. It is the notion denoted by the verb *asškaxa* 'to have sense, to be sensible.' The term is used most frequently to describe a child who has matured to the stage where he is consciously aware of his surroundings and is able to reflect on them. When he has reached that level of maturity, usually about age six or seven, he is said to be sensible or have sense. The term, however, is also used in its negative form to describe an adult who engages in antisocial behavior—who lies, steals, kills, or violates social custom. People say that such a person "has no sense."[29] He is an object of pity or scorn; they accord him no respect and do not listen to him.

Related to this characterization is another one, 'to be no good,' which is commonly used in Arikara and contrasts with English usage. In English there are many forms of varying negative intensity and social opprobrium to describe a person who transgresses social mores: whose behavior is, for example, insensitive, cruel, terrible, evil, insidious, horrible, or outrageous. In Arikara, in contrast, only the one expression "He is not good" is used to cover this semantic field. No matter how mildly or intensely bad a person's action or behavior is, an Arikara always describes it with this single term, which to an English speaker generally seems a flat understatement.

Kinship. Integral to the Arikaras' world view is their conception of kinship relationships, which are extended not only to a broader group of people than Euro-Americans generally recognize but also to various nonhuman beings with whom the latter recognize no affinity at all. Among Arikaras, as among most Plains Indian peoples, the orientation of individuals to the people in their world

---

29. Truteau noted this Arikara expression and its Sioux equivalent 'to have a bad heart' as early as 1796 and described the significance of the characterization (Parks 1991b).

is ordered through kin ties, real and fictive. Their social relations are regulated by the behavior prescribed by those ties, and their verbal interactions are marked by terms of address and reference symbolizing them.

In addition to a wide net of consanguineal and affinal kin relationships with the people in their own village and extending to individuals in other Arikara villages, and even among other tribes when such relationships are created through marriage, Arikaras commonly forge kinship ties with nonrelated individuals through ritual adoption. It is not uncommon for a couple who either has no children or who lose their sons in war to adopt a child in another family or perhaps even in another village. That child will not necessarily move into the adoptive couple's lodge, but the parent-child relationship will be established and will henceforth govern interaction between the families of the couple and the child.

During intertribal visits Arikaras frequently establish kin ties that symbolize friendships formed with individuals in the other social group, and those relationships thereafter govern interaction between the two who adopt one another as well as between their families. Similarly, when an outsider enters an Arikara community to live and interact with its members, it is common for an Arikara who is particularly close to that individual to adopt the person and incorporate him into the kinship network. Historically, this adoption was frequently extended to traders and other whites who worked with Arikaras, and today it is still informally practiced. When I began working in the Arikara community, for example, several of the female narrators in this collection took me for a grandson, two of them even giving me an Arikara name, while Mr. Morsette took me for a son. In all cases, appropriate kinship terms have been used and the expected behavior associated with these fictive ties has prevailed.

For Arikaras, however, as for most American Indian peoples, kinship ties extend beyond human society to include animals, trees, and other forces of the universe that have mysterious power, and these ties regulate the manner in which an individual symbolically interacts with the beings in activities like rituals, prayers, and dreams. These relationships are commonly illustrated in Arikara oral traditions, in which, for example, Moon, Corn (as personified by

Mother Corn), and sacred bundles are mothers. The cedar tree, in contrast, is grandmother. And so when an Arikara addresses one of these powers in prayer and refers to one in conversation or narrative, the person will use the appropriate kinship term, mother or grandmother, for the culturally understood relationship (e.g., see 11, 108, 109, 146), just as a human relative would be addressed and talked about. Similarly, Sun and the Chief Above are fathers, while the male spirit in a buffalo skull and the spirits in rocks are grandfathers (see 59, 109). In the story of Hidden Man (15), the two holy men who are Hidden Man's benefactors are his fathers, as are benefactors in many spiritual encounters, and Hidden Man's wife is, by extension, the daughter-in-law of these men.

Directions. Illustrating the numerical patterning of four in Arikara culture is directional representation, another set of symbols permeating Arikara religious life that is occasionally reflected in this collection of oral traditions.

Directional symbolism, which divides both heavenly and earthly space into two primary axes, north-south and east-west, is fundamental to the religious thought of Arikaras as well as most other Plains tribes. The four quarters of the world recognized by Arikaras today are the cardinal directions—north, south, east, and west— but based on a combination of ethnographic data and narratives collected earlier in the century, the testimony of several older people today, as well as historical Pawnee usage, it is clear that formerly the four primary directions were the semicardinal points of the compass (i.e., northeast, southeast southwest, and northwest, which correspond to east, south, west, and north respectively).[30]

Particular deities are associated with each of these semicardinal world quarters, to whom prayers and offerings of smoke and food are made in all Arikara rituals (G.A. Dorsey 1904a:20, passim). In the earth lodge there are four pillar posts that represent the world quarters, and in ritual gatherings the members of bands seat themselves in the quarter of the directional post in the lodge with

---

30. The semicardinal points are, for example, the symbolic directions in narratives Murie recorded at the turn of the century (G.A. Dorsey 1904a:20, 40, 54, 105; Gilmore 1927:336). For Pawnee usage, see Murie (1981:109–10).

which their band is affiliated (Gilmore 1927:344–45). The west side of the lodge *(huNAhtAhtis̆)*, which is opposite the entryway in the east, is, moreover, the area of the altar in the Medicine Lodge where the leading priests or doctors always sit when conducting ceremonies; and it is the area in the lodges of individuals where a sacred bundle or other holy objects hang and where honored guests are seated.

Colors. In Arikara culture four symbolic colors are distinctive: black, yellow, red, and white. The same set of colors occurs in the religious symbolism of the Pawnee and Siouan tribes, among whom each color is associated with one of the four directions in rituals. In the literature on the Arikaras there is not sufficient information to determine whether there was ever the same ritual association of colors and directions, but there is a suggestion of it in one narrative in this collection. At the end of Alfred Morsette's story of "The Race between the Horse and the Buffalo" (3), he refers to four colored horses in the heavens, each one having its station among the powers at one of the points of the compass. Here a black horse is in the east, a palomino (yellow) in the south, a sorrel (red) in the west, and a white horse in the north. (Historically these colors were associated with the semicardinal directions as follows: black and northeast; yellow and southeast; red and southwest; white and northwest.) Whether the symbolism in this story reflects an earlier Arikara usage or borrowing from another tribe is not clear.

Nevertheless, the four symbolic colors pervade various aspects of Arikara culture. In oral traditions holy objects, powers, and characters often occur in sets of four, and they are inevitably associated with the same four colors. In the story of Bounding Head (6, 154), for example, there are four spinsters, each of whom grows a certain color of corn—red, black, white, and yellow—after which she is named (thus Red Corn Woman, White Corn Woman, etc.). Similarly, in the legend of the young man who carries a feathered staff (23), the protagonist jumps into a body of water where he encounters four bears, each one of which is one of the four symbolic colors.

In Arikara personal names, which often derive from individual religious experiences, only the four symbolic colors occur as nominal

modifiers, so that when a person is named after an animal or other
spirit being, the latter will be red, black, white, or yellow if a color
is specified. Moreover, some of these colors have symbolic associations. White, for example, when modifying an animal name refers
to the favored child of that species.

Blessing. Rubbing or stroking an object or the body of another
individual, a symbolic form of blessing, is a gesture that occurs
extensively throughout the oral traditions of the Arikaras and their
kindred Pawnees, reflecting its prevalence as a cultural symbol
among these people. The act is denoted by one of two closely related
verb stems *(in...ut...ištawi'a* or *ut...ištawi'at),* both literally meaning
'to stroke, pass the hands down over in a brushing movement,' and
generally is translated in these narratives as 'to stroke in blessing;
to stroke in appreciation.'

Arikaras nearly always translate these two verbs into English
as 'to bless,' but for them the gesture has a somewhat wider range
of meaning. It is a frequent act in rituals, illustrated, for example,
during a smoke offering. After being given the pipe, an individual
draws in smoke while simultaneously stroking the pipe toward
himself; and then as he exhales he first rubs his hands in the
smoke and then rubs them over his head, drawing the power of the
pipe to himself. Generally, too, the man who leads the smoke offering will conclude the ritual with a "blessing" of the pipe after he has
emptied the burned ashes from the bowl, just before returning it to
the altar. Here the act is a symbolic form of reverence or thanks
that closely approximates the Western religious notion of blessing.

It also symbolizes appreciation, as when, for example, one
person grants something to another and the recipient then strokes
that person's head and arms in thanksgiving.

Supplication. The custom called "carrying the pipe" to someone
is illustrated in several narratives in this collection. This is a formal
symbolic gesture to which a person may resort when one individual
becomes estranged from another person or from a group and then
is reluctant to comply with a request or fulfill some duty. In such
a situation an individual who wishes to persuade the estranged
person to reconcile himself to the other party and become con-

sentient will take a pipe filled with tobacco, lay it on the ground in front of him in the prescribed manner, and beseech him to reconsider the situation. Although such a formal supplication generally changes the heart of the disaffected person in real life, in the stories in this collection it does not always accomplish its aim.

An instance of carrying the pipe occurs in the story of Red Dog and the four star men (18), in which a young woman marries the leader of four star men who come to the Arikara village. Later she is unfaithful to her star husband. When he discovers that she has been seduced by Red Dog, he forsakes her, and together with his companions he leaves the Arikara village. As the four men travel off the young woman follows them and entreats her husband to return with her by taking a pipe to him and laying it down in front of him four times. He refuses to accept it, but since a person never steps over a pipe, he steps around it, alternately from each side, creating a winding path that is replicated in the heavens when the stars return there. Other examples of this custom occur in stories 65 and 67. The act of laying the pipe before someone is also illustrated in the Bloody Hands stories (65–67).

Cultural Themes

Most Arikara traditions center on the theme of power acquisition: how a person gains and uses supernatural power. Those experiences, frequently called visions in the written literature, are said by Arikaras to occur during dreams, typically when a person, generally a young man, fasts and puts himself in a pitiable state. Then some animal or other being comes to him and out of compassion confers on him certain power together with a symbol or symbols representing it. This power may be for achieving success in hunting, war, or doctoring, and sometimes for all three of those endeavors, which are the routes open to a man who would achieve prosperity and prominence in Arikara society. War stories that relate an individual's exploits are generally accounts of how that person's power enabled him to achieve his feats, and in a like manner the narratives of doctors who perform miraculously are descriptive attestations of their power.

So dominant is the theme of power acquisition, in fact, that in addition to its being the primary topic of all the legendary and some of the historical stories in this collection, it has been integrated into many of the myths as well. Such a widespread myth as "The Race between the Buffalo and Horse" (3), for example, is not only an explanatory narrative of how humans came to ride horses and hunt buffalo, but in this Arikara version it is set within the context of a dream in which two star beings appear to a young man and tell him what to do to help transform the primordial condition in which buffalos killed and ate human beings. Likewise, in the story of a boy and the hoop and pole game (12), several mythological themes are combined with the familiar one of power bestowal to create a larger drama.

Within the more general context of power acquisition, there are many other contingent or subsidiary themes occurring in legendary narratives that give to each a distinctive significance. A popular theme is the abuse and subsequent loss of power, a theme that occurs in two plot types. One is exemplified in the story of the man with a sharpened leg (8), in which a person who has been given power uses it to kill so many young men of his own tribe that he finally oversteps the bounds of tolerability and causes his supernatural benefactor to kill him. Illustrating the other plot type is the story of Mice Mouth (20, 89, 112), who at first uses his power in the performance of good deeds but then begins to abuse it until he, too, goes beyond the limits of social tolerance.

Another popular subsidiary theme, described above, is that of the poor boy who raises his social status and achieves prominence either through power that he or his grandmother already has or through the acquisition of it by evoking compassion in a supernatural being. Related to this type is yet another theme, also previously described, the vindication of abnormality, in which a reclusive boy who is thought to be unmanly actually possesses power that his passive behavior masks, and, finally, after deciding to demonstrate his abilities, achieves social prominence.

There are other equally common themes intertwined with that of power acquisition, two of which account for power used for social rather than more strictly personal ends. Stories that recount the origin of a cultural tradition, especially dances and rites, exemplify one of the themes. In such narratives an animal or group of animals wishes to convey a tradition to the Arikara people and uses a young

man or young woman as the intermediary who brings the dance or
rite to the people and who instructs them in it (e.g., 29–32, 70–72).
The other theme is relief from starvation, in stories about which a
young man acquires the power to summon buffalo herds toward the
village so that the animals can be killed to provide the hungry
village with meat (e.g., 15, 16, 18). A variant of the latter is the
story of how on several occasions Mother Corn and Buffalo Woman
saved the Arikara people from starvation (11).

Another related popular theme is the abduction of a human
being by an animal. Sometimes the victim is a man, but more often
it is a woman. When it is a female, the animal usually turns itself
into a human and mesmerizes the victim before taking her. In one
scenario of this type the animal is hunted down and killed, where-
upon the human captive is released (e.g., 22, 119), while in another
common version the animal takes the person to its home or into
another world, generally underwater, where he or she is forever
destined to what is said to be a difficult life but where the person
also becomes an intermediary between the animal captor and
human beings, conveying to the latter power or good fortune from
the animal (e.g., 21, 23, 25). Another variant of this theme is the
marriage of an animal to a human. In one example (24), a man has
sexual relations with a she-bear that result in a human child, and
later, when the father is rearing his son, the bear mother confers
power on both father and child. More commonly, though, the human
partner is a woman, and again the union results in power bestowal,
for example, on the woman's husband (26) or on her brother (29).

Many other narrative themes do not result in power bestowal.
One of these types is animal aggression toward human beings, the
topic of several myths (e.g. 2, 3). Related to it is aggression resulting from a disrespect for the holy, as when, for example, a
husband tries to kill a bear that is having sexual relations with his
wife but is actually conferring power on the husband *through* his
wife (13, 87); or the story of the two Foolish Ones who kill the
beloved snake child (14, 88). Lack of respect for the holy crosscuts
other thematic types, too, as when, for instance, the simpleminded
boy imprudently eats snake flesh (96), or when the leader of a war
party recklessly climbs onto the back of a giant turtle despite a
companion's warning (25).

Historicity

Vividly illustrating a difference between Arikara and Western notions of historicity is the type of story that Arikaras consider true and historical: myths and legends, as discussed previously, were as historically real for them as they were unreal for the Euro-Americans who first encountered the Arikaras in the eighteenth century.[31] Also within the Arikara rubric of history, however, are traditions that do correspond closely to what Euro-Americans consider to be true, albeit perhaps skewed, accounts of the past. The narratives of tribal separations (37, 38), for example, and of the Fort Laramie Treaty of 1851 (41) and the Custer campaigns (42), as well as war stories, (e.g., 43–51) correspond closely to the Western notion of history.

There are, nevertheless, differences between what Arikaras and their Euro-American counterparts consider to be the substance of history, and so to appreciate the Arikara perspective it is necessary to recognize the features that are inherent to it.

Timelessness. One fundamental contrast is an Arikara indifference to chronology. Dates and historical periods do not occur in Arikara accounts or in their conception of the past. Instead, events take place simply in the past. Myths and legends generally begin with the formulaic time frame marker "long, long ago when our people were moving upriver" or a similar expression that places them in a remote past. Recent historical accounts similarly fix the temporal setting with a general statement like "when our villages were below Fort Clark," although incidents that occurred more recently, when the Arikaras were living in Like-A-Fishhook Village, are said to have occurred, for example, "when our people were living in the old village."

Nondevelopmental. Early Arikara history—the holy period described in myth and legend—is not, moreover, developmental or even sequential. There is no chronological ordering, for example, to

31. In his Description of the Missouri River, Truteau discusses at some length the traditions and beliefs of the Arikaras, to which he gives no historical validity (Parks 1991b).

the events recounted in myths. Narrators, at least today, tell mythic and legendary traditions in random order and do not perceive them to belong to a recognized historical sequence. Once, for example, in a discussion with Alfred Morsette about the order in which to present his myths and legends, he stated that the best grouping would be according to the type of animal that figures most prominently in each story (so that all stories of bears, for example, would appear together). He also gave a general sequence for narratives, placing what are here grouped as myths in an earlier period and what are legends in a later time frame, but he could not provide a finer succession and did not perceive one event or story to build on another in either mythic or legendary times.

Interpersonal topical focus. Another feature distinguishing Arikara historical narratives from those of Euro-Americans is their subject content. In contrast with the Euro-American tradition, in which there is a focus on events and their outcomes, in the Arikara tradition there is an emphasis on interpersonal relations, often reduced to either a single putative incident or to a sequence of incidents, which is associated with the outcome of an event even though it may only be incidental to it. In the two narratives of tribal fission (Crow-Hidatsa and Arikara-Pawnee), as illustrations, the splits between groups are attributed to social discord—to a dispute over the division of the parts of a butchered buffalo in the Crow-Hidatsa story (37) and to recurrent social hostilities in the Arikara-Pawnee account (33)—and not to any other motives or causes, as though there were no wider historical context to the event beyond the discord described. In the narrative of the Fort Laramie Treaty (41), as another example, the treaty council on Horse Creek and the trips to and from there serve to establish a general narrative framework, but the topics that fill in this outline are again predominantly interpersonal matters: how the Hidatsa chief Four Bears does not want to go to the treaty council and is said to be a coward when the delegation of Arikaras, Mandans, and Hidatsas enter enemy territory; how one member of the Arikara party, Young Fox, becomes ill and has to return home; how the American soldiers feed the Arikaras splendidly; how during treaty negotiations the Arikaras, led by Son Of Star, establish the precedent that is subsequently followed by all the other tribes in attendance; and how Son Of Star slights Carries Moccasins at a celebration after the treaty has been concluded. Although the general stipulations of the treaty and its social aftermath are mentioned, they are not considered to be any more important to the narrative than are the outstanding social topics of the trip.

Oral repetition. Still another characteristic of the Arikara historical tradition that contrasts with the Euro-American is the manner in which it is transmitted and by extension how its authenticity is established. Unlike the written history of Euro-Americans, the Arikara tradition is oral, and narrative authenticity is based on the presumption of faithful repetition, beginning with what an eyewitness or participant told and continuing with the words of his story as repeated by individuals since then. Consequently, these orally transmitted narratives contrast with Euro-American written ones in that the former may be by their nature more subject to individual reworking, whether purposeful or accidental, whether through misunderstanding or memory lapse, during the transmission process, even though the Arikara tradition insists on exact repetition (see Performance Evaluation, below). The oral tradition must, of course, rely on an absolutely faithful repetition from one telling to the next over time, a process which is obviated by a written tradition in which words, once committed to paper, achieve a permanence that is altered only by rewriting or by destruction.

Temporal displacement. Another marked contrast between Arikara and Western notions of historicity, at least from the Euro-American perspective, is the displacement back in time, and so the displacement in narrative type, of a character or story—a displacement that apparently results in part from generations of telling. Stories of Scalped Man in Arikara and Pawnee traditions offer an instructive example of how a character diffuses through time and role type (Parks 1982). Scalped men were, of course, historical personages: ones who survived scalping during warfare but who, according to Arikara custom, were not able return to their village or reenter human society because, after scalping or even maiming, they were thought to exist in a transformed state as spirits who were no longer human. Because they were forced to shun human contact but yet necessarily lived on the outskirts of areas populated by Arikaras, where they occasionally came in contact with people, diverse traditions developed about these scalped men. Some are accounts of encounters with them (e.g., 98, 122, 123, 124) and are what from a Euro-American perspective are historical anecdotes; but other traditions go beyond the simple encounter and move toward an association of the scalped man with a spiritual benefactor. Thus, in some transitional stories the scalped man becomes a provider for a lone hunter or some other person whom he meets (G.A. Dorsey 1904a:149–51, Gilmore 1933:39–43), giving him horses, meat, and eagle feathers, for example (e.g., 94–95, 113); but in other narratives the scalped man takes on the attributes of a truly legendary figure, becoming a spiritual being who bestows hunting and curing powers on individuals, just as celestial and animal beings do (e.g., 34, 35, 36). Moreover, Scalped Man also appears as a figure in myths (e.g., 1) and even tales (e.g., 81), illustrating his transformation into a mythologized or trickster character.

A similar kind of development is probably exemplified in many stories that appear to have originally been dream, or vision, stories accounting for some individual's power but that through time have become more public and ultimately more mythological. The story of Hidden Man and the two holy men (14) illustrates this apparent development. It is, first of all, an account of a man who is pitied and given the power to bring the buffalo herds toward the Arikara village during times of starvation. Such a story would originally have been the personal account and property of a man who had had the vision in which he was given this power. But over time, as the story was retold by him and perhaps later his children, it would become widely known and retold in turn by many other individuals so that its original significance was finally lost. And so after the episodes of buffalo calling in the Hidden Man story, there is the addition of a long episode embodying the common mythological theme of the triumph over abuse of supernatural power, in which Hidden Man is led by a buffalo bull to an evil man who enslaves him and then subjects him to a series of tests. The latter subplot, certainly not a part of the original story, was combined with it subsequently.

The narrative of Red Dog and the four stars (18) is a similar example in that it, too, is a combination of what were formerly apparently two separate stories. Red Dog also has the power to call the buffalo, a feat he accomplishes during a period of starvation, suggesting again an original vision story; but the beginning of this narrative has another plot—the marriage of a woman to one of four star beings who come to earth—that was apparently added to the story of Red Dog. The two parts of the narrative are connected when Red Dog seduces the young woman after she has married one of the star beings, with the result that, despite her entreaties, her star husband and his three companions return to the sky, where they form a constellation.

That the significance of traditions changes over time through public dissemination and frequent retelling was also noted among the Pawnees by George A. Dorsey (1904b:xxii). After pointing out that each bundle ceremony and each dance had its origin tale that was the personal property of the keeper or owner of the bundle or dance, he states:

> Naturally, these myths of the origins of bundles and dances do not always remain the exclusive property of the priesthood; they find their way among the ordinary people, where, when told, they lose much of their original meaning. Thus, by a gradual process of deterioration, they come to be regarded as of no especial religious significance, and are told as tales are told.

Although among the Arikaras origin stories for bundles and dances are no longer owned by individuals or societies, they clearly were formerly, just as vision stories were individually owned. Hence the evolution of religious stories from the secret, individual sphere to the public domain described for the Pawnees undoubtedly occurred among the Arikaras as well and evolved, moreover, with episodic embellishments of the sort illustrated above.

Humor

The stories in this collection that are intended to provoke laughter are tales. In fact, every one of the tales with animal characters is humorous. Some, like the ones about Lumpy Toad (82,

83) and about the war party of insects (132, 150), are told for the amusement of children but still are considered to be cute by adult audiences. Stories of Stuwi, in contrast, are sexual in content and appeal primarily to adult audiences, who generally find them uproariously funny. Among Arikaras, however, it is Coyote tales that epitomize humor. The trickster Coyote is always a comic character, never a serious one, whose name, whenever it is mentioned, invariably brings smiles to the faces of listeners and whose antics always evoke laughter, no matter the age of the audience.

Ordinarily the content of true stories, which tell about the holy and other historical events, is serious and not given to humor. There are, however, occasions when even acts of desecration can be funny—when, it would seem, a satirical episode allows the tensions inherent in ritual seriousness to be released socially as humor. One illustration of such satirization appears in the story of a scalped man and an eagle trapping party (59). When the party of men set up a hunting lodge in which to eat and sleep, their leader makes an altar composed of a buffalo skull and an ear of corn representing Mother Corn. During the day while the men are in their individual traps, a scalped man steals into the empty hunting lodge and paints a face on the Mother Corn and rubs soot over the buffalo skull. After he repeats this desecration for several days in a row, the members of the party determine to catch the culprit; and when they finally surprise him in the act, they cause the scalped man to die of fright. To the narrator, Alfred Morsette, this story—both the scalped man's antics with the sacred objects and the narrative climax—was hilarious.

A different example appears in a narrative of two undisciplined young men who are urged to go on a vision quest when an older man thinks that a religious experience would help them mature and become men (125). They fail in their attempt, however—first by breaking the rule of fasting and finally by running home when they hear strange, frightening sounds near the spot where they are fasting. Their experience, a story of irreverence and cowardice, is also a source of humor.[32]

32. In a collection of Pawnee narratives, Weltfish (1937:vii) notes two examples of the vision told in humorous parody.

In contrast to the satirical themes that turn on religious observations, another form of humor frequently occurs in true stories:
comic relief. That technique is illustrated repeatedly in the stories
of this collection, always by the introduction of Coyote, the supreme
comic. In one example, the story of a star boy who comes down to
earth to live with human beings and experience their wars (5), the
protagonist comes to a village where he encounters Bloody Hands
and his grandmother and decides to live with them. After moving
into their lodge, the star boy doctors Bloody Hands to cure him of
bedwetting. Just as he finishes this serious endeavor, Coyote comes
onto the roof of their lodge and urinates on the fire, putting it out
as he always does, and so the star boy nocks an arrow and shoots
Coyote in the testicles, causing him to run off yelping. This type of
brief comical interlude also occurs earlier in the same story in an
episode when the village chief seeks to learn the identity of a
mysterious young man, in reality the star boy, who is killing the
invincible enemies of the village. To determine who the young man
is, the chief shoots a marked arrowhead into his leg and then has
his crier announce through the village that not only can he, the
chief, extract it but he will also give his daughter in marriage to the
stranger if the latter makes himself known. At that point, Coyote
comes onto the scene, dragging one foot as he enters the chief's
lodge, and pretends to be the young man. The chief, however, is not
fooled by Coyote's deceit, and throws him out. Similar intrusions of
Coyote into otherwise serious narratives form a common literary
technique of comic relief.

Performance

When the recording of this collection of narratives began in
1970, the Arikara oral tradition as an ongoing feature of tribal life
had vanished long ago. Older people no longer told stories among
themselves, and they no longer told them to younger people. As Ella
Waters commented in describing her naming ritual, "We had sacred
ways—all the rituals that the Arikara tribe used to perform. No one
knows those ways now. Dust has covered all the old traditions. But
now only a little is known" [109]. What remained were memories
from a bygone era—the stories that many elders remembered

hearing when they were younger, either from parents or grand-parents, or perhaps from some other relative or elderly person—while the last generation of participants in that tradition still lived. During the course of my work some older people, particularly Alfred Morsette and Lillian Brave, remembered numerous stories, often in full detail, and had in fact told many of them to their own children, while other narrators remembered fewer and frequently had for-gotten many of the details of most of the ones they knew or, as some lamented, they confused parts of one story with those of another.

In this situation, then, it was no longer possible to observe a living tradition. It was necessary to question people about it and to ask them to tell the stories they remembered.

Performance Settings

Formerly, nearly every social occasion offered a context for telling stories. Whenever people got together and chatted or when-ever old men or women visited one another, they generally told stories. When an older couple would visit another family, whether friends or relatives, the older ones would tell stories. Settings were also diverse: in a living room, around the kitchen table, on the front porch or seated on a bench by the house, in a wagon or car, in camp or in a park.[33] Wherever it might be, story telling was an integral part of social interaction among adults and particularly older people, who were purveyors of knowledge and instructors of the young.

Intertribal visits were, and still are today, another popular context for story telling. During the period of intertribal warfare that preceded the 1880s, not only tribes friendly with each other but even enemy villages would sometimes camp together, if only for a short time, to trade and visit. Based on interviews with the Minneconjou Sioux chief White Bull in the 1930s, Stanley Vestal (1934:18–19) describes such occasions when Sioux and Arikaras

---

33. G. A. Dorsey (1904b:xxii) says that Pawnee men told Coyote tales whenever they assembled during the winter months—at home, on the hunt, and on the warpath. This characterization clearly held for Arikaras, too.

would declare a truce that permitted economic and social interchange:

> Such a truce was always interesting. In those small nations, every
> prominent man was well known to his enemies by name and
> record, and, when there was a truce, the warriors would get
> together and discuss last season's battles, checking up on any of
> their own side whose claims to *coups* might require verification,
> and giving evidence, when asked, as to the deeds of their enemies.
> Thus, if a Hunkpapa had claimed to have wounded a certain Ree,
> the Hunkpapa might ask the Ree to show his scar, and thus make
> sure of it. In this way, warriors and chiefs became well acquainted
> between fights, just as rival football teams might become ac-
> quainted and talk over old games.

Immediately after intertribal warfare ended on the northern
Plains in the late nineteenth century, groups of people from tribes
that had formerly been at war began visiting each other, intensifying an older tradition of camping, visiting, and dancing for a
period of several days, just as groups from friendly—and frequently
unfriendly—tribes had done previously (see stories 45–47). In the
1880s, for example, groups of Sioux from reservations like Standing
Rock, Cheyenne River, and even Pine Ridge visited Fort Berthold,
where men who had been at war with each other only a few years
earlier now exchanged stories as an integral part of social interaction, frequently reliving old battles and comparing accounts as
they had always done. Arikaras reciprocated with visits to those
communities, where the process of narrative interchange continued
(see, for example, story 47).

Although story telling was not restricted to any time of the day,
the evening was particularly congenial, especially after a meal when
people were sitting around in their homes or in camp and could
continue into the early hours of morning if so inclined. Evening, too,
was a favorite time to tell myths and tales to children, and today
many people remember their grandmothers telling them stories at
bedtime when they were youngsters. Nevertheless, a younger person
might be told stories by an older person in the household at any
time when the opportunity arose, and men certainly would tell
stories whenever they were together.

Another setting in which stories were frequently told was when a boy or youth was urged by his mother or grandmother to take some meat or tobacco to a certain old man, frequently an uncle, and ask the older person to tell him stories and sing songs that he might learn. Alfred Morsette s grandmother used to do this when he was young. She would give him food to take to old men like Snowbird to learn songs and hear stories. Often, too, a young boy might be the companion of an older male relative, when each had the responsibility of looking after the other. An Arikara man who passed away recently knew many old songs he had learned in this way as a youth when he used to stay with his uncle, Albert Simpson, for whom he was a companion.

Whenever one approached a person to ask him to tell a story, it was customary to give that person a small gift, generally food, as a form of payment. The present might be a cornball or a small amount of dried meat, or it might be tobacco, but there must be some tangible offering, which then obligated the recipient to tell a story. If a token sacrifice was not made, people used to say that the story was not valued and so there was no reason to tell it since the hearer was not really interested in it and would not remember it. One elderly lady today relates a humorous anecdote that vividly illustrates the seriousness placed on payment for a story. When her grandparents came to visit on one occasion, she and her siblings—all young children—asked the grandparents to tell them stories. For each one they told over the course of the evening, the grandchildren gave the old couple one of the farm animals that their parents owned. The grandparents went home that night but returned the next day, pretending to claim the animals and thereby leave the family without any for food and work. Ostensibly surprised, the parents scolded the children to impress on them the gravity of this custom.

Another custom associated with the oral tradition was a restriction on the season when certain stories could be told. The Arikara narrators represented in this collection of narratives agreed that in former times myths and tales were to be told only during the winter months. Some affirmed that if a person told a story during the summer, when snakes were not hibernating, he or she would be bitten by one. Two individuals, Alfred Morsette and Lillian Brave, insisted on observing the custom and generalized it to include a prohibition on all storytelling during the nonwinter months. For Mr. Morsette the story-telling period was approximately bounded by the first snow in the fall and the breakup of the ice on the Missouri River in early spring. For Mrs. Brave the timing was similar, but she insisted that the end of the winter period was actually marked in the February sky by the appearance of a constellation whose Arikara name is *NAsaahaanu' šiniinaáhNA* 'invalid being carried.' No one can identify it any longer.[34]

Mr. Morsette adhered to yet another custom: once he told a story he would not retell it during the same season. His reticence to repeat a story arose several times during the course of our work together when, after telling a story, we discovered that the tape recorder had malfunctioned. In every instance he insisted that we wait until the next winter to record it again.

Performance Interaction

Public performance of oral tradition was predominately a male activity, in part because men had the leading roles in ritual and social contexts. During social gatherings, as Ella Waters once remarked, women were usually engaged in cooking or other domestic duties that minimized their opportunities to listen when men were exchanging stories. Nevertheless women did learn and tell traditional narratives. They heard them in the home from family and visitors, in rituals when spectators were allowed, and in formal

---

34. This constellation is perhaps the same as the one known to the Skiri Pawnees as *raaruka'iitu'* 'Stretcher,' also referred to as *raarukitkucu'* 'Big Stretcher' to distinguish it from a smaller constellation named *raarukitkiripahki* 'Little Stretcher.' The former has been identified as Ursa Major, the latter as Ursa Minor (Murie 1981:41; Parks 1991a).

The Skiri had a similar restriction on telling tales in the summer and associated it with the appearance of a star. According to George A. Dorsey (1904b:xxii–xxiii):

Such tales are not told during the summer months, or rather during those months when the snakes are visible; for it is supposed that the tutelary god or star of the snakes is in direct communication with the star of Coyote, for during these months the Coyote-Star is early visible in the eastern horizon, and, not liking to be talked about, directs the Snake-Star to tell the snakes of those who talk about him that they may bite him.

situations when, for example, a doctor imparted his knowledge to a man whose wife assisted him in learning the secrets. Women also exchanged stories among themselves and told them to children, frequently at bedtime.

The story-telling situation, no matter its setting, was a performance in which there apparently was fairly constant interaction between narrator and audience. When a man began a story, he frequently would name his source for it and listeners would voice a grunting sound to indicate their acknowledgement or agreement, and then throughout the narration listeners would periodically utter *híni'*, which has no exact translation but is the equivalent of 'Go on!' serving as a signal to the narrator that his audience is listening attentively and wants him to continue with the story.

When men were gathered telling stories, there was also an ongoing interaction among them as narrators in which, for example, after one man told a story another might tell a different version of it. Or the interaction might reflect the interrelatedness of many stories and their episodic structure. In reminiscences today, elderly men have commented how in the past one man would begin a story and tell so many episodes—perhaps all he knew—and then another person would take up the narrative with other episodes and still another man might continue with it, leading the narrative thread into another story. Sometimes an incident mentioned but not described in one story might serve as an opening point for another man who knew that story. In William Deane's version of the buffalo wife (148), for example, the buffalo woman's husband and his son escape from the buffalo by climbing onto a rock that rises upward, taking the two of them out of the reach of the buffalo. At that point Mr. Deane says, "There is a story about when they sat there on the rock," and then continues with a subsequent episode. Formerly, another man knowing that story would have taken the cue to tell it after Mr. Deane had finished.[35]

Older people today still remember several formulaic statements that were used when tales were told. If the narrator wished to

---

35. For discussions of the interrelatedness of narratives among other tribes, see Wissler and Duvall (1908:5) for the Blackfeet, and Beckwith (1937:268) and Bowers (1965:290–304) for the Mandans and Hidatsas.

conclude his story telling, he would say *wetAhneesi'it* 'Now I am
letting go of the gut' at the end of his last story, thereby signaling
that he was finished and that it was now another's turn.[36] At the
end of the last story of the evening, the one telling stories would say
wetireskaá'At 'Now the gut has gone in.' If a listener wanted the
teller to continue with another story, however, he would say *we-*
tatuhneesáhUt 'I am holding onto the gut' before the narrator said
wetAhneesi'it or *wetireskaá'At*, thereby forcing him to tell another
story. A similar expression was *wetatuhneesuunîkUt* 'I have caught
the gut,' which a listener could also say at the end of a story if he
wanted the narrator to tell another. The original significance of
these expressions is no longer known.

   Although there rarely was an audience during the recording of
most of the stories in this collection, there were small ones on the
first two occasions when I began recording stories in 1970. That
winter in particular the situation was a relaxed, intimate one, in
which Mr. and Mrs. Howling Wolf, Mr. and Mrs. White Bear, and
I were staying at the home of Mrs. Fanny Whiteman. Over a period
of several days the two men told stories, first one man relating one
or two stories, then the other man picking up with a story that he
remembered, while the women were either sitting close by listening
or were engaged in sewing or cooking and partially listening. In this
situation while each man recited a story, the other one or one of the
women would occasionally say *híni'* to encourage the teller to
continue. Similarly, the women would respond to actions in the
story, laughing when a line was funny or gasping when it was
frightful. Beyond that, Fanny would often tell one of the two men
to say *wetireskaá'At* at the end of a story as a conclusion to it, even
though the expression was more correctly reserved for the last story
of the evening.

   During the recitation of stories, narrators varied in the amount
of dramatic voice modulation and gesture they employed. Men
consistently gesticulated more dramatically to act out certain

---

36. Dorsey (1904a:xxii) notes a similar term used by the Pawnees and
explains its origin: "As the tale is finished it is the custom for the teller to
say, '*We na netsu ut*' (Now the gut passes), referring to the custom of an
individual passing his dried fat buffalo entrail to the one next to him after
he has satiated his hunger by chewing upon it, when upon the march."

aspects of a story, but they did not accompany the oral narrative with a running version in signs. Although women used their hands to gesture, too, they employed them less for dramatic effect and more for explanation. Men would, for example, use their fingers to indicate the number of times something happened, perhaps pointing one finger forward at the first occurrence of a sequence, then two fingers at the second occurrence, and so on. At dramatic moments they would typically punctuate a statement with a clap of the hands. When size was being specified, however, all of the narrators usually indicated it with the hand brought to the appropriate height above either the floor or a table, which served as a base line, or with one hand opposed to the other. Direction was indicated gesturally in a similar manner, particularly when two contrasting reference points were being described.

Performance Evaluation

It is not possible to specify precisely all the criteria an Arikara employs for evaluating a narrative performance. Throughout the period during which these stories were recorded and translated, I posed the question many times to elderly speakers of the language, but it was never satisfactorily answered, in part because they were loathe to evaluate critically the aesthetics of another person's performance. But today at least, when so few individuals know traditional stories, what seems to concern Arikaras most, older and younger alike, is a familiarity with narrative details, while stylistic elegance is clearly of secondary importance.

A comment frequently made by any older person listening to a story told by someone else, particularly a younger person, is that some of the details are not exactly as he or she heard them—sometimes simply noting that this version differs somewhat from the one he or she knows, but more often suggesting that the teller has not recounted the story correctly. Although such an evaluative statement serves to reinforce the authority of elders, the perspective also reflects a fundamental Arikara concern for reproducing a tradition in exactly the form in which it was learned. When Mrs. Waters talked about ritual performances, for example, she never neglected to state emphatically that the old people had always admonished her to do *exactly* as one was taught and neither add to nor neglect any part of it. Hers was a cultural concern for exact reproduction, reiterated by other contemporary Arikara elders as well, which applied to myths, songs, and chant recitations as well as to other ritual acts. For that reason she refused to record stories that she could only remember in part or that she felt she had confused with other stories.[37] Alfred Morsette reiterated the same concern when he used to assert that he had recounted a certain story precisely as he had heard it—that he had not elaborated on it or added to any of its details. Thus it can be said that one primary criterion for evaluating a good Arikara narrator is the ability to reproduce a traditional account precisely as it was heard.

In many cultures, and perhaps nowhere more so than on the Plains, a raconteur's creativity—his or her ability to utilize culturally patterned techniques of expression in novel and aesthetically pleasing ways—is highly valued.[38] Among Arikaras it is not clear exactly what role the creative aspect of performance played in story telling since the tradition is no longer a living one and the language is no longer actively used. Myths, legends, and other true stories were at least in principle patently more subject to the criterion of exactness in verbal performance, while Coyote stories and other tales, which were told for pleasure and laughter, were undoubtedly less stringently held to it. But whatever the story type, linguistic creativity apparently did play an important role in defining an outstanding raconteur; on numerous occasions one elderly man stressed that the sign of a proficient Arikara speaker is the ability to create and use new, compositionally complex words. Earlier in the century Gene Weltfish (1937:vi) noted a similar value placed on word creation among older Pawnees:

> The dominant tendency of classic Pawnee to compound and integrate ideas into one complex is also falling into disuse.

37. Radin (1915:35–36), for example, notes this same concern among the Winnebagos: "The Indian has a firm belief in the existence of a 'correct' version for each myth, which seems to evidence itself in his refusal to tell a myth unless he knows it perfectly."

38. During the early part of this century Robert Lowie studied Crow culture when its oral tradition was vibrantly alive and later wrote about the value of linguistic creativity in it as well as what distinguished a good raconteur (Lowie 1935:104–13).

Conversations with older people indicate that this type of integration has a very real aesthetic value for speakers of the older language. On a number of occasions verbal complexes which were compounded of many involved ideas were enjoyed by informants as "beautiful words."

Thus it seems reasonable to conclude that linguistic creativity was another significant criterion for distinguishing a good narrator.

Beyond those two criteria, however, only social status has been observed to influence the evaluation of verbal performance. Elderly people, particularly those descended from prominent families—ones in which members were chiefs, priests, doctors, warriors or others with valued social roles in the nineteenth century—who themselves have carried on Arikara traditions and who have led exemplary lives are today recognized as important repositories of the tribal past and are highly valued in this role.

Conclusion

Although a people's oral traditions have various functions, fulfilling artistic as well as recreational needs, their fundamental purpose is to answer the human quest for knowledge about the world in which people live: how one's physical environment took its present shape, how one's cultural world came to have its present form, where one's social group came from, and what and who were eventful in its past. For a preliterate society, oral traditions contextualize the individual's existence in this world, giving it meaning and temporal as well as spatial orientation.

The oral traditions presented here are representative of the Arikaras' literary heritage. The narratives span its full range, from sacred traditions of a mythical past, through legendary stories of prominent figures and their deeds, to relatively recent historical accounts set in the late nineteenth century. They include ritual descriptions as well as short anecdotes telling about mysterious occurrences, both of which, like the historical traditions, are intended to be instructive. And they include tales illustrating the stories Arikaras told to make one another laugh and the stories parents and grandparents told to entertain their children.

The Arikara historical tradition, composed of its sacred myths and legends as well as other more recent narrative accounts, is not finely sequenced, with each story having its acknowledged position in a temporal order, nor is it developmental, except in the loosest sense. The myths of the earliest period in human history tell about a primordial world in which humans were helpless and had no control over the elements in their environment—when animals hunted and killed people, in a time before humans had learned horticulture. With the intervention of star beings, however, this order was changed so that man became the hunter rather than the prey, and later humans received corn as well as mysterious powers for curing and summoning the buffalo—events that created the order found in eighteenth- and nineteenth-century Arikara life. But beyond those two important developments, Arikara history is primarily an aggregate of timeless narratives, set in a period "when our people were moving upriver," which describe the accretion of rituals and social customs as well as recount the exploits of heroes and malefactors.

A relatively small number of themes predominate throughout Arikara historical traditions. The fundamental one is the belief in a mysterious power *(waaRUxtii'u')* that pervades the universe and is capable of doing both good and harm. This power, which resides in a host of celestial and earthly beings, must be respected and propitiated. One must not be skeptical of it or tamper with the beings—the animals, natural objects, or celestial beings—possessing it since they can do people irreparable harm. These beings can, however, bestow some of their power on humans and thereby give them good fortune: the ability to cure and to achieve success in hunting and war as well as to control such natural phenomena as rainfall. If a person wishes to prosper and succeed in life, he or she must seek a "blessing" from a spirit being, which imparts some of its powers on the individual and remains his or her spiritual guardian throughout life. Thus the central theme of the Arikara historical tradition, extending through the centuries when they were gradually moving northwestward up the Missouri River, is human interaction with spirit beings and the resultant power bestowal. Most of the traditions, then, are either accounts of men and women who were blessed with certain powers because they were pitiful or in some other way were deemed worthy, or are

accounts of those who refused to accord respect to the holy and
suffered the consequences.

That pervasive theme is, of course, also characteristic of the oral
traditions of other Plains tribes. In fact, Arikara traditions, like
those of other tribes in the region, include stories that have passed
back and forth between tribes during the friendship visits and
trading fairs that have been a part of their lives for centuries past
and that have continued up to the present. For the Arikaras, stories
represented here have come from the Pawnees, Sioux, Hidatsas,
Mandans, Cheyennes, Crows Assiniboines—indeed, from all the
surrounding peoples with whom they have had contact over the past
two hundred years or longer, maintaining a pattern of story exchange that over millennia diffused myths throughout both North
and South America.

What distinguishes Arikara traditions is not so much their basic
themes but rather the particular cultural symbols that permeate
the expression of those themes in combination with the person-
alities—the individual characters—appearing in them and the
linguistic features of style that create an Arikara narrative form.
The latter compositional elements, built into more widespread
themes that have been adapted to specific cultural context, to a
large extent give Arikara stories their distinctive texture and
identity.

This collection of narratives represents the Arikara oral tradition at its end. The individuals who contributed the stories here
belong to the last generation who grew up speaking Arikara as
their first language and were privileged to hear tribal traditions
recounted as they always had been. During their lifetimes they have
seen the use of their language overwhelmed by an ever-growing use
of English and simultaneously have witnessed interest in Arikara
traditions dissipate as the acculturative processes begun over a
century ago have continued unabated. In this changing world,
where Arikara culture has been almost completely replaced by that
of a dominant Euro-American society, they have retained only in
their memories what survives of Arikara oral traditions, since the
generations below them neither speak the language nor maintain
a distinctively Arikara lifestyle. Consequently, when this collection
was recorded, some narrators remembered a larger number of

stories than others, and some recalled structural details in them more closely than others.

Yet despite its adverse context, this collection clearly represents the content and quality of Arikara oral traditions as they existed throughout this century. The earliest, and only other, comparable collection is the one compiled by James R. Murie and published by George A. Dorsey (1904a) at the beginning of the twentieth century, nearly eighty years preceding the recording of this one. The range of story types and narrative diversity in the two collections are quite similar. In fact, twenty-four of the stories in Dorsey's monograph appear here as well, many of them told today by the sons and daughters of the men who recorded them for Murie in 1903. The quality of the narratives in the two collections likewise does not seem to vary significantly. Many here are recounted in almost identical form to what Murie recorded. Alfred Morsette's version of the young woman who married an elk (21) is, in fact, richer in detail than Standing Bull's narrative (G.A. Dorsey 1904a: 127–29). Similarly, Ella Waters's version of the star husband myth (85) and Lilly Brave's rendition of one Bloody Hands story (66) are virtually identical to their fathers' versions (G.A. Dorsey 1904a: 45–55, 69–70). In contrast, however, are a few others here that are abridgements of what were formerly much longer stories (compare, for example, story 93 with G.A. Dorsey 1904a:109–14).

Most importantly, though, the renditions here are the first to be recorded in Arikara as well as, rather than solely in, English and to be presented in a translated form that carefully attempts to preserve the literary devices of the original language. Although the oral traditions of the Arikara are no longer passed down in the native language, this collection, which has been preserved through the efforts of the most knowledgeable elders of the last generation of Arikara language speakers, preserves for the future an authentic record of the tribal legacy that enables Arikara people to reenter the world of their forebears and allows other people to share in it. For Arikaras, then, it serves as a primary link with their people's past, and through written form many of these traditions may take on new life as they are retold in English and passed on to future generations.

PART ONE

THE STORIES OF

ALFRED MORSETTE

(Paatúh Kananuuninó Not Afraid Of The Enemy)

Plate 4. Alfred Morsette, Sr. (*Paatúh Kananuuninó*, Not Afraid Of The Enemy). Photograph by Douglas R. Parks, 1980.

Narratives of the Past

Of Ancient Times

1

How Summer Came to the North Country

This story is an Arikara version of the widespread Promethean myth, which, in variant forms throughout North America, accounts for the origin of daylight or fire on earth. Here it accounts for the origin of summer on the northern Plains. Distinctive of this version is the incorporation of Scalped Man, usually a legendary or historical character in Arikara stories but who here joins the ordinary cast of animals in stealing the Sun's son. The narrator heard this story twice, once from his grandfather Short Bear and once from Harry Gillette (White Shield).

Long, long ago when we people were not yet living on this earth, when the ways on this earth were holy, there was no summer here in this country. It was always cold then, always winter. Oh, it is not known how long the time was when it never got warm, when it was always very wintry.

Well, now Raven came along, wherever he came from. It is not known where Raven came from. And Coyote, wherever he came from. Coyote. And this Scalped Man I talk about. Now Scalped Man was one. Now there were three of them.

Then one of them said, "Say, everything sure is difficult for us when it is winter like this all the time, never getting warm, just winter, winter." It is not known how long it had been that way. "It sure would be nice if it were warm and green grass were to come up for these buffalo and the other creatures roaming around here to eat, instead of its just being winter. It makes things difficult." That is what these three were talking about.

Then this Raven said, "Say, there surely is a being living who

129

controls things where it is summer. [It is Sun.] If we were to steal Sun's child and bring him here, Sun will come looking for his child. He'll come pursuing us."

Then one of the others asked, "Well, now how will we do that?"

Then Raven said, "Now, we'll go south to where he lives. Truly I know where he lives—where Sun's lodge is. I know."

Well, then they went. Then they went as a war party. They went after summer so that it would be warm some of the time here where we live. Then Raven took them to the place, wherever it was.

"This lodge here is the one. This is Sun's lodge, and here is where his child lives. Now this one—this Scalped Man is the one who is going to go inside. Then he'll bring the child while his father is sleeping. The child is a hoop that is hanging there.

Sometimes the hoop is round there where Sun hangs. Then we say it's wintry when Sun is making summer.

"And you, Scalped Man, will take the hoop. And after you get out, they're going to chase you. Ah, they're watching. They're watching over him. You'll go in, and as soon as you come out, I'll be right there. You'll put the hoop around my neck and I'll come flying north, ah, for as long as my strength lasts.

"Now this one here, Coyote—when I arrive where it's winter, then Coyote will be the one to take the hoop. Then Coyote will be the one to take it. Now he'll carry it for as long as his strength lasts, and then Scalped Man will be the one to take it. Now meanwhile the heat is going to follow us, so that summer will come while they are chasing us."

And so that is what they did. Then Scalped Man entered the lodge. Since he could see well at night, he looked all around. He found the hoop. He took it. He took it around the inside of the lodge and went out. Now he gave it to Raven; he put it around his neck.

Then Raven flew up into the air. Now he fled with the boy as the tribe of beings—whoever they were I surely do not know—were yelling back there. This is what they used to say.

They began chasing after Raven, and meanwhile this Scalped Man was the one holding the pursuers back. He was the one holding them back so that they would not shoot Raven. He was holding them back while Raven came north.

Finally Raven said, "Well, my strength is gone now," and, oh, then he arrived where Coyote sat. Then the ring was put around the head of Coyote.

Then Coyote said, "Truly no one ever overtakes me," saying this over and over. Then Coyote ran off as fast as he could, coming, coming, coming.

Now, after four days his strength left him. Four. Then Coyote tired. Then he sat down. "I'll sleep for just a little while and then I'll regain my strength."

After he lay down and fell asleep, some birds came flying up to Coyote, whatever kind they were. Whatever kind of bird it was, it picked Sun's child up and turned back with him.

Now, there, that is where the boundary of winter is, here where we are living today. It isn't known how things would be if Coyote had kept his strength up. But he tired and lay down to sleep a little while. "I think I'll just sleep a little while!" Had he gone still farther north, it isn't known what things would be like.

Now this is what happened when summer first arrived here. It became winter again, and then it became summer. Now this is the reason things came to be as they are now.

That is what I myself heard. The old-timers who used to tell stories, the ones who were storytellers, have all died.

This is the reason things came to be as they are now. This is what happened.

2

The Holy Boy Who Stopped Animals from Killing Humans

The setting for this myth is the earth at a time when large animals and birds were the aggressors and human beings were the victims. To change this primordial relation-

ship, a holy boy, actually a star, comes down to earth to
punish the animals and birds. After subduing them and
insuring that they will no longer molest humans, he returns
to the heavens, where he is one of the stars visible even to
this day in the night sky. The narrator heard this story from
his grandmother Squash Blossom.

Now I am going to tell a story. It isn't a long story.

Long, long ago when mysterious things occurred during the holy
period, the different kinds of animals that roam around today used
to hate us human beings. When they would see a human, the stags,
buffalo, or whatever they were, would burn him. And these birds
that fly around—geese and cranes—would fly in a circle over a
human whenever they saw him. Then while he was looking for food
for himself, the poor thing—whether a man or a youth—he would
become dizzy as he watched them and be knocked to the ground, as
he went about wherever he was going, seeking to find food for
himself. Things were not good for human beings during the holy
period. I don't know when that time was.

Well, then a boy came down from up there in the sky. Before he
came down here, he said, "I don't like what these animals are doing
down there, molesting human beings, the poor things. Now I am
coming. I'm going to hurt them." Well, then he came down to earth.

Then as he traveled around, he would nock an arrow in his bow
and shoot it into the brush. In this way he felled stags, elks, bears,
and other ferocious animals when he shot at them. He would also
fell a buffalo whenever he released an arrow and let it fly somewhere. Likewise, whenever he shot an arrow up into the air, it
would land and then there would be a flock of dead geese or cranes
lying there.

Then the living powers became angry. "Eh, he has killed a
multitude of us, this holy boy who goes around shooting us. Now let
him die of thirst!"

Then all the water disappeared. There was no more water.
Wherever the creek and river valleys were, the water disappeared
entirely. And the boy would go to different places looking for water

while he just wandered all around. When he came to a bank there would be only mud there.

One day while he was looking at things along a dry bank, he saw what is called a spring peeper, the one that makes sounds in the evening at the edge of a creek or spring.

Then this boy sang:

> Tell me where the water is, and I shan't jab you.
> Tell me where the water is, and I shan't jab you.
> Tell me where the water is!
> Tell me where the water is, and I shan't jab you.
> Tell me where the water is!

Now the spring peeper, poor thing, became very frightened since the boy was kicking it around, molesting it. Then it stood up and thought, "I might save myself."

And so the spring peeper went to a mud flat where the ground was damp. The spring peeper put its two forelegs into the mud and then backed off. Oh my, then water emerged. And as the water came out, it grew in volume. Why, now this boy began to drink his fill!

Then the boy said, "Now, you creatures who did this to me, my vengeance will fall upon you."

And after he nocked an arrow, he felled an elk or whatever kind of animal it might be, as he was killing different ones. "Now do not do it again!" he warned. "If I return, the consequences will be even worse." When he shot an arrow into the air, he brought down geese and cranes, killing them, too. "Let that also be all of your killing of these human beings of mine, the poor things! If I must come again, it will be even worse."

Then the boy returned to the sky.

Now that is why animals no longer molest us poor human beings like they used to do long, long ago. When the different kinds of wild animals used to oppose us in those times, they must have been ferocious. When the stags bellowed, they burned a person up. The stags and elk and other such animals were fierce and attacked human beings. [Then this boy came and] here they were the ones that became frightened! The boy said, "It's no longer the way it used to be. It's not going to be that way again."

And then this boy went back up into the sky to wherever he had come from.

3

The Race between the Horse and the Buffalo

This story, like the preceding one, is set in the period when animals preyed on human beings. Here the primary aggressors are buffalo. In a dream two star beings appear in human form to a young man. They instruct him to teach his people to make bows and arrows and then arrange for a meeting among all animal kind to determine whether animals will continue to kill humans or humans will hunt animals. In a race between a horse (representing this breed as well as wolves, coyotes, bears and eagles) and a buffalo (representing his species as well as various types of wild cats), the horse wins, establishing a new order in which humans hunt buffalo and ride and care for horses.

Unlike versions of the mythic animal race found among surrounding tribes, this Arikara narrative has the typical form of a vision story and concludes with an explanation for the origin of horse medicine, a doctoring power that many individuals among Plains tribes possessed to cure horses of maladies. The ending is significant, moreover, because it integrates four horses, each of them one of the four sacred directional colors—red, black, white, and yellow—into Arikara religious symbolism, where the horses assume their stations in the Heavens together with the powers of the four directions.

Our people used to tell about how things were when we were

moving upriver. Long, long ago things were not good. The buffalo used to come to a village whenever they smelled humans. That is what they used to say. Then the buffalo attacked the people. They did away with us, killing many people when they attacked, and tore the village down where it stood. The buffalo killed lots of people and ate the bodies they obtained, eating the dead human beings. That is how the buffalo were. They used to do that.

[After they had attacked a village,] they moved off. And after they had departed those people who had survived came back to the village and then put the remains of the dead, the poor things, on scaffolds after the buffalo had torn up the bodies and eaten them.

Now there once was a boy going around who was sixteen winters old. He was pitiful after his father and mother had been killed. The boy would go to the scaffold on which one of his parents lay and would cry. Then one time he lay down after he had been crying and became tired. Then he dreamed of two men.

One of the men said, "Now you are strong as you go around crying, here where you have been crying. Now we have come here to do something for you because of what the buffalo are doing, because of their eating you people. Now you people are going to be saved. Those who have been killed will become alive again. You'll see your father again, and you'll see your mother again.

"Now in the morning you are to go to your village there in the woods, and you'll tell the men and young men." Then these two men instructed him: "This is what bows are like. This is how you'll make a bow. And you'll make arrowheads and arrows. You'll tell the men, 'This is the kind you should make.'

"Now you'll go to the different bodies lying on scaffolds there. <The flesh has not spoiled yet. It is still good.> Then you'll touch the body and say, 'Wake up quickly! Fix yourself up!' Then they will get up and come back to the village. 'Now all of you must get yourselves ready!'

"After you people have finished making the bows and arrows, after you have finished doing it <we are going to a different world>. The different kinds of animals, the different kinds of us creatures, are all going to gather together. They're going to talk about different things. Now this is what will be the main topic: what is going to happen—whether or not the buffalo will continue to eat you humans. Now that is what they're going to discuss. And we'll tell you what is decided, what is going to happen."

Then this boy went off.

Now when the different animals—the buffalo, elks, coyotes, bears, the different ones—gathered together to plan how things on this earth would be, the horse said, "Now I'll be the one who is first to say something."

Then this horse said, "I don't like what this buffalo is doing. After you abuse some pitiful human being, a weak human being, you kill him. Then you eat him. But here is grass, the thing which was intended for you to eat as you roam around. The human being is helpless now that you have cut his life short."

Then the buffalo said, "No one is telling me what to do as I roam around. Now we'll race. If you beat me, you'll win. But if I beat you, it will be the way it is now. Things will remain the way they are now. I'll eat human beings. I like eating human flesh." That is what he said. "I'll have my way, as I think it should be."

Then the horse said, "Now I'm in agreement. Let's race!"

There was one buffalo standing out in front. He said to the other buffalos, "Now who is going to be the one to run?"

Then one put his forepaw out. He was the one, a bull, a young one who was four winters old. "Now I'll be the one. I'm the fastest. No one can equal me."

Then everyone became fearful.

Now a horse, a palomino, one four winters old, said, "Now I'll be the one to race him. I'm fast. I can run four days straight. That is the strength I have to run. Now I'll be the one. We'll race. On the land passing by here, on this bare land, is where we are going to race. Oh, the goal will be the edge of the water—the edge of the water. Now if you beat me, you'll win. But if I reach the edge of the water first, I'll beat you."

Now the two of them planned it. Then these horses, the poor things, became fearful. The buffalo was *so* strong.

Then the two raced. When they went, this horse was *really* fast when he ran on the course they took. And then this horse got in the lead. Then he got in the lead. The buffalo fell behind and then swerved to one side.

Now when the buffalo did that, the humans yelled out. Then they mounted the horses and chased the buffalo, shooting them, too.

Now the horse who was racing went on. Then he arrived at the goal. But this buffalo ran off, running away after he was beaten—after he had been saying, "No one can outdo me."

Now this is the reason we ride horses: to chase the buffalo as they roam. That is what the plan of the horse was. That was what he planned for himself.

Well, then the horse said, "I have saved you. And now I want you to keep me, poor me, and I'm going to take care of you, seeking out things for you. Wherever you want to go, I'll take you there. Meanwhile you are going to keep medicine for me here, too."

This was the horse's plan. That must be the reason we rode horses when our people traveled around long ago. We are still doing it, riding horses.

The horse said, "Now I am standing here. I'm the black horse." In the east here on this earth is where he stands. A palomino stands over there in the south; a sorrel horse, in the west; a white horse, on the bare land in the north. Now there is where they have their stations among the powers in the sky when we pray for things to the Chief Above, the one who looks after us who are living here on this earth.

Now this is how the story goes. This is what I used to hear from my grandmother when she told it. And my father used to tell the story, too.

4

Long Teeth and Drinks Brain Soup

This story, widespread throughout the Plains and one of the most popular Arikara myths, tells of the adventures of

*two brothers who are taken from their mother's womb after
she is killed. One of them, Drinks Brain Soup (a name frequently shortened to Drinks Brains), is so named because his
father nurses him on deer brain soup; the other, named Long
Teeth, develops from his brother's discarded afterbirth and
grows up wild. After a sequence of episodes leading to the
capture and taming of Long Teeth, the two brothers enter on
a series of adventures in which they overcome powerful,
destructive beings on earth, thereby making the world safe
for humans.*

This story that I am going to relate is one that they always talk
about. It is about two boys when they were growing up. One was
named Drinks Brain Soup; he was raised by his father, who took
care of him. And the other one, named Long Teeth, grew out of his
afterbirth. This is what I used to hear.

There once was a village, wherever it was, and a prairie fire
came up. Then a woman came, whoever she was. She was an old
woman who set the fire. She caused the village to burn up when the
prairie fire swept through it, there where that village was. And it
burned everything in it, including the men and women, the poor
things, who burned up. Then everything was lost, except for the
people, the poor things, who fled in different directions—the ones
who ran up the hill or who ran into the water.

Meanwhile this one man had gone hunting. He had gone off
hunting, traveling around hunting. Then he came back. He returned
to where the village had been. Everything there had burned, including the people, the poor things, who had burned up after the fire
broke out in the village.

Then the man began looking for his wife. She was pregnant. As
he was going along, there she lay partly in the water. She must
have run to the water for safety. After he found her, the poor thing,
he cried.

Then he touched her on the abdomen. There inside, in her
stomach, there was movement. "But you who lie here are dead."

Then he cut her stomach open and took the baby out. And then
he removed the afterbirth. Then he wrapped it up and threw the

afterbirth into the water. And then he washed the baby all over.

Then he fixed up a lodge. It was an earth lodge.

While he was taking care of the little boy, his son, he would kill deer, and the soup made from their brains and milk is what the baby drank. And so he reared him.

And then he reared the boy until he was a certain age. They used to say he was perhaps five winters old, when he was at an age to understand things.

Then one time the boy saw another one. The other one began peeking into the lodge through the smokehole.

"Drinks Brains, where did your father go?"

Then he said, "Why, he went hunting."

Oh, the other boy looked all around inside the interior of the lodge, at the four main posts; oh, he looked all around. Then he came inside.

The boy was the same age as Drinks Brains was.

There was food lying around for Drinks Brains to eat, meat and ribs that his father had put by the fire.

Then this boy ate everything up.

Now, after they had played for a while, the boy said, "Now your father is coming." Then he ran off. Then he ran into the water.

Then the father arrived. His boy had apparently eaten up everything.

"You must have eaten well. You must have eaten it all."

"Yes, that's what I always do."

Now what this boy who came out of the water did occurred many times.

Oh, he had two long teeth—two of his teeth were long.

Then this man, Lucky Man, said, "Eh, boy, now you are older. Tell me why it is that when I leave food for you, you seem to eat up everything?"

Then the boy said, "Yes, I'll tell you. A boy always comes inside. He always comes out of the water over there. Then he comes here. When he comes inside he looks all around where these lodge posts are here inside where we live. Then he sits down. 'Let me have something to eat now!' When he eats, he consumes everything.

"After we play, he says, 'Now your father is coming.' Then he goes off. He jumps into the lake."

Then the man realized who he was. Then he said, "He is your brother. This one who keeps coming inside here is your brother. Now I'll catch him."

Now this man was himself holy. Then he changed himself into a fire poker. They call it a poker, to stoke the fire and rake the embers together.

After he had changed himself into it and lay there by the fire, the boy came running. He came inside.

"You here, Drinks Brains, where has your father gone?"

"Eh, why, he went hunting."

After he looked all around he said, "You're lying. There he is." Then he found him.

The boy turned back around. Then he went into the water.

And now while they were doing this—while the man was spying to catch him—he was seen by the boy no matter what he changed himself into.

Now one day this man said, "I'll catch him. You'll play with him and then you'll grab him quickly. You'll call me and then I'll take hold of him."

Then this man changed himself into a blade of grass. He was under one of the upright lodge posts while he watched for him.

There was the sound of someone coming. Then he came inside.

"Ah, Drinks Brains, where did your father go?"

"Why, he's gone hunting. He's going around hunting. He's never at home."

Then the boy eyed everything carefully as he looked all around. Then he said, "Now let me eat at last!"

He ate, and after sitting there doing it, he finally finished.

Now while they were playing, while he and Drinks Brains were wrestling with each other, Drinks Brains clutched him around the waist.

Then he said, "Father, I'm holding him!"

His father appeared in sight. Then the two of them took hold of

Long Teeth. The man tied his hands while he struggled with him.

Then the man filed his teeth with a stone. Oh, he ground the teeth down.

Then he prepared a sweat lodge. He took the boy inside. He made him vomit everything—the things that he used to eat when he lived in the water of that lake. After he had vomited every-thing—the worms, frogs, and whatever other things, everything that he ate—then the man gave him different medicines to drink.

And he had a deer bladder which was inflated with air. Then he tied it to Long Teeth's head. He tightened it.

Now he released the boy.

Then the father said, "Follow Long Teeth there! Go on! Follow him there!"

Then this boy Drinks Brains followed him after he ran off.

Now Long Teeth jumped into the middle of the water there. But the inflated bladder brought him up to the surface of the water. Again he dove down in the water, trying to submerge. But then Long Teeth tired.

"Now let's go! Surely you're tired now. This is our home here."

So then the two boys began going around playing together.

Then this Lucky Man said, "Don't go over there! A woman lives there. She grabs people when they go around there. She snatches up whomever she wants. Then she turns him into a sack. Don't go there."

And after the man went off somewhere, this Long Teeth said, "Let's go where your father said, 'Don't go there.'"

Then this Drinks Brains said, "Why, he said, 'Don't go there.' He doesn't want us to do that."

"If you don't want to, I'll bite you!"

Now he was afraid of Long Teeth.

"I'm your brother who had the long teeth!"

And so they went off. Then they went into the woods that their father had warned them about.

Then Long Teeth said, "Let's see where her lodge is."

After they had gone into the woods there was a trail there. Then two girls were coming through the woods following it, as the two of them were coming along. Now they stopped.

Then he said, "Where did you two come from?"

Then one of these girls said, "We're living with our grandmother over there. Our house is there in the thick woods. That's where we came from. We're gathering wood. That's what we came after. We came after wood. We're going to sing bundle-opening songs tonight.[1] Our grandmother is going to sing bundle-opening songs. That one, the younger one, knows the songs really well." This one, the older girl, said, "I haven't been able to learn them."

Then Long Teeth said, "Why, sing a song!" Then he and his brother went up to them. Now they all stood there.

Then he said, "Why, sing a song! Let us hear you. What does she usually do?"

She said, "When my grandmother performs, she blows into someone's mouth. Then he becomes a sack. That is what my grandmother does."

"Ah. Now sing a song!"

And then she said, "This girl, the younger child, knows how to sing. I don't know how."

"Let us hear this girl. Do it!"

Then this girl began to sing.

Then Long Teeth said, "Hey, I can't learn the song." This Long Teeth said, "Now it would surely be better if we kiss, and then perhaps we could learn them."

Now this young woman, the older one, was willing. Well, then these two boys kissed them. While they were kissing them Long Teeth blew into her mouth. Then he turned to Drinks Brains: "You do the same!"

Then the girls rolled over, skinless.

Then right there where they had stood Long Teeth and Drinks Brains changed themselves into the girls. After they had killed both girls they put on the skins that the girls had worn.

Then they brought the wood to the lodge. The old woman was inside. She was cooking meat.

"Heh, put the wood down! Now at least try to learn the song that we are going to sing."

Oh, now this time the girls were certainly different.

---

1. The ritual songs priests sing when a village sacred bundle is opened.

They all sat down as this woman was telling them things while she was catching birds in a basket as they flew around. Then she put them on the fire to cook so that they could eat them, whatever kind of birds they were. That is what this woman, the old woman, was doing.

And then she caused a prairie fire when she put a pair of moccasins on. They were rabbit skin moccasins. After she put them on sparks shot out from under them. That is what she used to do, what they were watching her do now.

And it got dark. Then they began singing bundle-opening songs while they sat there. But Long Teeth could not learn them.

"Hey, you don't seem to be able to learn them."

Then he said, "Grandma, perhaps if we were to kiss I'd be able to learn them."

Then this old woman did that. "Alright." Then Long Teeth and the old woman kissed each other. When he and the old woman kissed each other, he blew into her mouth. Then he killed the old woman.

"Now let's put her on the fire!"

Then they put her on the fire. They burned her. Then they picked up the skins that she wore. They put everything on the fire.

A heart was hanging there. Then he took the heart down. Then he threw it onto the fire there. They burned everything.

[Then Long Teeth took the rabbit skin moccasins and put one on his foot.] Then when he stamped his foot the sparks came flying out.

"Hey, my gosh, look! Put a moccasin on yourself!"

The other one, Drinks Brains, put one on his foot. When he stamped his foot down, sparks came flying out.

"Hey, they'll be good for my father."

Then they departed for home. Then they took the rabbit skin moccasins.

"Why, father, we've brought these moccasins for you. You'll wear them on your feet. <And we have this basket.>"

Now he looked at them. "Now surely they're nice for me to have."

Then later he burned them. He disposed of the things that were holy.

Then their father said, "Don't go over there. There's a buffalo in the woods. Oh, it's no good, and it might kill you."

And after their father went off somewhere Long Teeth said, "Let's go to where your father said, 'Go there.'"

And then Drinks Brains said, "Why, he said, 'Don't go there.'"

"Well, if you don't go I'll bite you."

Then they went. They went there into the woods. And there in the woods was the buffalo. Oh, it was no good!

But now with the power that they had Long Teeth said, "Let's shoot it!"

Then Drinks Brains proceeded to do it. Then the buffalo charged him. Then it was butting him and knocked him unconscious.

Then Long Teeth charged. He grabbed the buffalo's horns and dragged it around. Then he broke its neck. Then he skinned it.

Then he went over to his brother. Then he kicked his feet and said, "Get up! Don't sleep. We're traveling around."

Then Drinks Brains got up. Ah, he was rubbing his eyes. "Hey, I must have slept."

"Don't be falling asleep. We're traveling around."

And there lay the buffalo that had run into him.

Then the two went off. They made some ropes. Then after returning Long Teeth roped the buffalo.

"Let's go back to where our father lives. We'll pretend the buffalo is charging us."

There in the distance was the lodge where they lived. There was their father going about over there, whatever it was that he was doing. That is where they went.

"Hey, father, the buffalo you talked about is chasing us!"

Oh, the buffalo was right there behind the younger boy. But it was already dead. But they were pretending it was alive.

Well, then the man picked up his bow and arrows. Then he said, "If my boy Drinks Brains is killed, I'll kill you, too."

Long Teeth's feelings were hurt. He was not able to stop as he cried and cried.

"Father, what you said to me was not nice. You said, 'I will kill you.'"

"No! I meant the buffalo bull: 'If you run into him, I'll kill you.' That is what I was saying."

Then Long Teeth felt better again.

"Ha, it's only a buffalo hide. We'll use it for our bedding. We'll use it for bedding."

But this Lucky Man knew that this buffalo was not good. He threw it away over there.

These two boys had many such adventures. One time they went off. There was a tree. It was a tall tree. On top of it was a nest.

Then Long Teeth said, "Climb it! Drop the baby bird down!"

Then Drinks Brains climbed up. After he had climbed so far, it became difficult for him. The tree began swaying back and forth. While it was doing that, Drinks Brains, the poor thing, fell down. He was killed. Now he lay there dead after he was killed.

Then this Long Teeth got angry. "I have power just like you do," [he said to the tree].

He climbed up the tree angrily. Now he did what Drinks Brains had done. The tree was twisting itself as it had done previously.

Then he went on to the top. He reached the top where the nest was. He took the baby birds. He killed them. He also killed the mother. Also the father. They were large red birds, whatever kind they were.

Then he brought them down. He went to the spot where his brother lay; and then he said, "Hey, Drinks Brains, you who have been sleeping, you have been lying there sleeping long enough! Get up!"

Then he got up, and there stood Long Teeth with the birds that had been in the nest.

Then the two of them went off. Then they arrived at their home.

Then Long Teeth said, "Hey, we have brought these birds for you! They're pretty. They're red."

"Why, I'll lay them here. How good these are for me!"

But after the boys went off somewhere else, their father burned the birds. Then he threw them away. Now it was not good that they should be killing the various holy beings.

《   》

Then the two boys went off. They both carried arrows when they went. When they lay down to sleep, they placed the arrows upright in the ground beside themselves. Whenever a snake came along, whatever kind it might be, an arrow would fall and hit the boy in the face. The same happened to the other boy. They would jump up.

Now the powers of the universe were spying on the boys in order to kill them, because the boys had spoiled things many times by doing away with various holy beings.

Now one time they were lying asleep on top of a hill. And then an arm suspended in the air came down. Then Long Teeth was the one it picked up first. Then it took him up there into the sky, into this sky.

Then this Drinks Brains awoke, and his brother was no longer lying there. Then he began to look for him. He searched everywhere.

Now he lay there looking around at the sky up above. He was looking, and there in the sky was a hole.

Then Drinks Brains changed himself into an arrow. Then he flew up. He disappeared as he went up into the sky. He was holy.

Then he got there, and as he was traveling around he saw that it was a different world where he was looking for his brother.

There in the distance was a village. Oh, it was a big village! And then that is where he went.

As he looked on, there in the center of the village they were dancing a victory dance. And there was his brother Long Teeth. There he was, stretched out on a scaffold, as he watched him—as they watched him.

Then Long Teeth knew his brother was there. He had great power!

Then he said, "Now hurry, brother, I'm burning! These people living here have done their worst."

Then this boy Drinks Brains went off. At the far end of the village was a lodge. An old woman lived there.

Then he changed himself into a little boy.

"Hey, grandma, I have come. I'm hungry."

"Yes. You must sit down. You'll eat." Now this old woman was cooking.

Then he said, "Grandma, what's this commotion all about?"

And then the old woman answered, "Why, they brought a boy here, one of those from the world below. These two boys destroyed all the holy beings that were down there below. They destroyed them. Now that's why one of them was brought here first. And one remains. After they kill the one who's stretched out here, they'll go after the remaining one."

And here he was the one, this one who sat there listening!

"Now, grandma, let's go see them dance the victory dance over there."

Then the two of them went. She packed him on her back. Then she got close to the crowd.

Then the old woman was dancing around among the dancers.

Then the little boy said, "Now, grandma, let's go! I'm sleepy."

Meanwhile he had told his brother, "I'm going to come. I'm going to take you down."

Now he and this old woman arrived back at her lodge.

Meanwhile, the noise of the people singing and dancing died down. Then this little boy got up, and then he took a knife of hers. Then he ran to where his brother was stretched out.

Now the flames had died down where the fire was. Then he cut the rope.

Now his brother was weak from hunger. Oh, he laid him over his shoulder. Then he ran off with him. Meanwhile he kept the knife.

The two reached the hole in the sky. They came flying down to earth. The long arm with the hand was coming after them. And when the hand reached close to them, Drinks Brains cut it. He cut the hand off. Now that is the reason there is an image of a hand outlined by stars in the sky.

And then the two boys dropped down. They returned to earth here. Oh, they went back home.

Then their father said, "Ah, where have you two been?"

One said, "We've gone all around this world. We traveled all around. Then we came home."

Now this is the end of the story I heard about Long Teeth. This is where the story ends.

5

Bloody Hands and the Star Boy

This is the story of a star boy, the son of Morning Star,
who lives in a celestial world. During the mythological
period he comes down to earth to live among humans and
participate in their wars. His visit is filled with a series of
adventures. First he encounters an evil man who can trans-
form himself into a whirlwind. Later he goes to live in a
village of people, and there one by one he overcomes the four
enemies who are harassing the village. Incorporated into the
story is the popular mythological character Bloody Hands,
a poor boy who lives with his grandmother on the outskirts
of the village. Here, however, Bloody Hands lacks the mys-
terious power that he possesses in most Arikara and Pawnee
stories. Nevertheless Bloody Hands triumphs when the star
boy raises him and his grandmother from their poverty,
enabling them to live with the chief's family. The story also
explains the origin of the contemporary woman's name Sage
Woman.

Now I am going to tell another story that my relatives—my grandmother and my aunt—used to tell me. My mother died when I was a baby, but I used to listen when they told stories, when my grandmother would tell one.

Now, there are beings who live in a world up in the heavens beyond the sky. I surely don't know about it, but this is the story as it was told.

A boy there said, "Father, I like it. I want to be among the people living in the world down below. I like their wars. I want to be among them and do what they do in that other land."

And then his father said, "You're a man now. It will be as you wish. You can go. And after you are satisfied, you can come back here again. You'll come back after you're satisfied with what you're going to do in that place there where you're going to live."

«   »

And so this boy descended. I don't know what he did or what happened when he dropped down, but he reached here where we were living on this earth.

Now after this boy had come here from above, he was going along, just wandering all around looking all over the land. As he was going, he noticed smoke coming up in the direction he was headed. There was smoke there. Then that is where he went.

This boy came to it. There were earth lodges there. They were well built. The lodges were sturdy.

Then he went up to them. As he approached a man just came out of one.

Then the man asked, "Where did you come from?"

"Myself, I'm just wandering around. I'm looking for some place to live for a while."

And then this man—he was a heavyset man—said, "Say, it's sure good that you came here. I'd like you to stay here awhile to do some work for me, to do some things for me that I need to have done."

And then he said, "Alright, I'll certainly do that. I'll watch over things for you." Now this boy was going to work for this man.

Well, then morning came and the man said, "Now you're going to gather up things for me. But that lodge close by, where the door is facing us—don't go there. Don't ever open the door!

(Now right here I wanted to find out from my grandmother when she was still living—I asked, "Why did he give him keys? Surely there weren't any keys around at that time.")[1]

"Don't open that door! But you can look around the other lodges. And you can enter those where I have my things. But I don't want you to lay a hand on that lodge."

And then that morning the man was just not around. He must

---

1. This parenthetical remark was intended to follow a statement—which the narrator neglected to make in this rendition—that the man had a set of keys to open the earth lodge doors.

have gone somewhere.

The man had a horse, a white horse. Oh, it was nice looking! It had a chunk of meat. That is what the horse was eating. When the boy came up to it, it stopped.

And the man had a bear that was tied up. Oh, a big black bear! It was large. It had hay. It was tied up, too. The bear was eating the hay, and the horse was eating that meat. That is what this man was doing with the two animals he had, forcing them to eat what he gave them.

And then this man went off somewhere while the boy was working for him, while he went all around working for him, getting meat for the horse and cutting hay for the bear.

After the boy had been up on a hill, he came down. The lodge must have been at the base of the hill where he had been going around.

Then the boy thought, "I wonder why he doesn't want me to look in that lodge. I wonder what's inside it."

Then this boy went there and tried out the keys. Now he must have gone to the place where the keys were kept. Then he opened the door and when he peeked inside he saw them. Oh, dead people! There were many dead human bodies piled up inside, human beings whom the man had apparently killed. But the boy certainly did not know what tribes the different kinds of humans were.

<"Oh, so that's where he gets the meat that he gives to the horse! The horse is eating human flesh.">

Now when he wanted to lock the door, it would not lock easily. Oh, it was with great difficulty that he locked it. Then the key got bloody as blood dripped down all over the door.

Then the boy went over to the man's lodge. As soon as he entered it, the horse over there said, "Now hurry! You've made a mistake. Now quickly!" And it said, "Give me that hay over there! And you can give this piece of meat to that one over there."

And so that is what the boy did. He picked up the meat. Then he gave it to the bear. And then he gave the hay to the horse.

Then the horse began eating the hay. It said, "Let me fill myself up! We're going to go far, far off."

Then the horse said, "But first go into that pond!"

Then the boy went into it [to wash off the smell of dead human flesh]. Oh, he had nice looking hair on his head! His hair was golden.

Then the horse said, "Put those things hanging up over there on yourself!"

Oh, they were nice clothes [armor], and a wooden sword. Then the boy got himself ready.

And then the horse said, "Put one of those saddles on my back! Now you're going to ride me. You and I are going to run away. He'll do something evil when he comes back. The three of us here will be dead if we stay. [The man is a whirlwind.] Now let's go quickly!"

Meanwhile the bear had already run off.

Then this boy mounted the white horse. Then the two of them went off.

Then the horse said, "Now we'll head south there [where he can't go]. Now whip me! Our flight is going to be very difficult! He'll be fast when he comes after us."

Then he mounted it. Then he made the horse run fast. It ran exceedingly fast as it went.

"Now keep looking back! He must be coming."

He looked back. Oh, black clouds were rolling toward them as a big storm came, coming, as hail beat down and the whirlwind came forcefully. Meanwhile this young man whipped the horse.

It said, "He's coming exceedingly fast, but you and I will leave him behind."

They went on, went on, until, oh, it was morning. Then this horse said, "My speed is slackening. Now bark like a coyote does when it yelps!"

Then that is what the boy did, yelping the way a coyote does, the way a big white wolf does. And then this horse regained its strength.[2]

Then it said, "Now he's going to turn back."

Then, after they went on, the sky cleared up. "Now we've beat him. He's turned back. He's gone back there."

So they went on, with the boy riding the horse.

---

2. The motif of a man barking like a coyote or wolf to reinvigorate the horse on which he escapes is a recurrent one (cf. story 91).

«   »

Now at last the horse said, "Now, my brother, there's a village over there, one like you want for the life you wish to lead and the things you want to do. It's a village of human beings. Oh, it's a big village!

"Now this is where I'll stay. This is where I'll roam. Now then, when you get down, you'll take off the things you are wearing. You'll tie them onto the saddle I have on myself. And then you'll kill me. You'll strike me on the head with the wooden sword you have. Then I'll be dead.

"But when the enemy comes to attack, you'll come here. This is what you'll say: 'Black horse of mine, come! Now we've found each other.' Or 'Yellow horse of mine' or 'Sorrel horse of mine' or 'Now white horse of mine'—however many times it may be that the enemy comes, and whatever your strength may be. Now this is what I have planned for you: you are going to go around on the warpath and I'm going to watch over you while you accomplish different things for yourself."

It said, "Now disguise yourself [since you are from a different world]! I know where you came from."

Then that is what this boy did. He took off the armor that he was wearing. He tied it to the saddle. He struck the horse on the head. It fell over. It disappeared.

Then the boy went on. As he was coming along he climbed up a hill. As he looked all around, he saw a line of smoke over yonder. Then that is where he headed as he went on. Then he went to the edge of the village. There at the end of the village, oh, there at the end of the village, was where the smoke was coming out. Then he went on.

There was a boy there playing around. The little boy was not very old. He had an old buckskin horse picketed there. Oh, he and his grandmother had a lodge there.

This boy got there. "Hey, I have come!"

Then the little boy said, "Where did you come from?"

Then he answered, "Myself, I'm just wandering around." He had his head covered with a honeycomb tripe. It made his head appear as if it had sores when someone looked at him. Then he said, "I want to play with you—for us to be companions."

"Let me tell my grandmother first!"

Then he ran off.

"Grandma, a boy has come here, and he says, 'I want to play with you.'"

"Oh, they always do that. They always beat you up. Don't do it. Don't pay any attention to him."

He ran off. Then this Bloody Hands said, "Uh, my grandma said, 'They always beat you up. Don't pay any attention to him.'"

This one said, "I certainly wouldn't do that. I'm poor like you are. I wander around because I don't have any relatives."

Then this Bloody Hands swung back around. He said, "Grandma, he says, 'I don't have any relatives. Poor me, I just wander around. I'm poor like you are. And I want us to be companions, and I want to live with you, where you and your grandmother live.'"

"Alright, let him come in!"

Then he said, "My grandma said, 'You can come in.'"

Then the two of them went inside. When this old woman saw him, she thought, "He's different. He isn't a human like we are who live here."

"Now sit down, sonny, you who are just wandering around!"

Then she fed them and they ate. Meanwhile the boy told Bloody Hands's grandmother various stories while she scrutinized him, thinking, "Here you are different! And here you've come from far, far off!"

She said to Bloody Hands, "When you two are sleeping together, don't pee on him. You're a bed wetter."

The boy said, "Oh, there's nothing to that. There's nothing to it." Then he doctored Bloody Hands for what she had said he did by rubbing ashes over his crotch.

Now as he always had been doing, Coyote came onto the top of the lodge to urinate, to urinate on their fire from the top of the lodge and put the fire out.

This time this boy Sore Head nocked an arrow in his bow. Then he shot him. He shot him in the testicles, and Coyote went running off into the distance yelping.

A long time passed now, and when each morning came, Bloody Hands had not wet the bed.

While they were telling stories, Bloody Hands said, "In the evening I always go swimming. Our chief has four daughters. Oh, they're fond of me when we play, and they push me under the water when we're swimming. You'll see them."

Then the two of them went off. He took Sore Head around.

In the evening Bloody Hands said, "Now the girls have gone there."

Then these two went there. Then Sore Head sat down on a bluff, but Bloody Hands went down to the stream. These four young women—the maidens—were happy to see him and began to play with him.

"And over there Sore Head is sitting."

And then they said, "Oh, his head must smell bad." They began calling him names, but the youngest one began to take a liking to this Sore Head. She liked him. She looked at him, unable to take her mind off him. He was really quiet while the other young women called him names.

Then the young women went home.

Then Bloody Hands asked, "Did you see them?"

Sore Head said, "Yes."

"Don't pay attention to what they say when they are looking for something to say!"

"I know what they were saying."

Once when they were going back to the river bank, however many times they went there, the crier announced, "The enemy is coming to attack! Hey, we are going to have a battle! And this is what our chief has said: 'Iron Shirt is among the enemy. Whoever kills him will be the one to marry my daughters.'" This is what the crier was announcing as the men went off to fight. I don't know how many times he did this.

And then this Sore Head said, "Ah, my friend, let me mount the old buckskin gelding! I'll go there. I want to see the action—to see what happens where the fighting is."

Then Bloody Hands said, "Grandma, he says he wants to go to where the fighting is."

"Ah, grandson, don't go close to it! They might wound you. Oh, it's not good! They aren't careful where they shoot."

"Oh, I'll go anyway. I just want to watch them. I'll peep over the hills here and there."

The boy mounted the old buckskin horse and rode on while men passed by him, going to fight in the battle. Everyone passed ahead of him.

<"Where are you going?" they asked. "You should go home. You might get killed.">

Then he got off the old buckskin and left it. Then he quickly climbed the hill where his horse had been. Then he said, "I have come. I want to ride a black horse."

Then there was a loud rumble and a cloud of dust. There stood a black horse. Oh, it shone!

Then he put the armor on himself. Then he charged up the hill, too.

Then, in the fighting between the enemy and the villagers, he killed the warrior who wore the metal shirt. He scalped him. He ran off with the scalp. Then he hid.

Then he made the black horse disappear as he had done previously. After he made the horse he had disappear, he took the scalp. Then he mounted the old buckskin gelding and began to shoot here and there <at prairie chickens> as he came along slowly.

Men were passing him by while the battle raged. "Hey, this one isn't going to be the one who killed Iron Shirt." That is what they were saying [ridiculing him because he was going so slowly on the old horse].

Later this boy Bloody Hands arrived at the creek where the maidens were.

"Hey, Bloody Hands, did you see it?"

"Eh, I saw the battle."

"Did they kill him?"

"Say, I don't know. I don't know what happened. I don't know if they killed him."

He did not reveal it when one of them pried to see if he had been the one who killed Iron Shirt. That is what the maidens were asking him over and over.

Finally the youngest one lost her patience. She couldn't take her mind off this boy [Sore Head] she liked. Finally she began to come to the lodge of Bloody Hands and his grandmother.

Then the young woman came. "I just brought moccasins for the boys, your grandsons, who live here with you."

"Oh, these boys will be *so* thankful!"

This boy Sore Head was the real reason the young woman came to play with them.

Finally the boy began to sleep with her. Meanwhile she persisted in coming and bringing things.

But her sisters did not approve of what she did. "Whatever does she want to do with someone who has a sore head—whose head smells rotten!"

But this young woman did not care when they said those things. She could not take her mind off him.

Now there were other battles. Then Sore Head killed Iron Ear. And Iron Hand. And Iron Hair. There he killed the fourth one. That was the number of those who were the major enemies of this village. These were the bravest warriors who came to fight the people in this village.

When the village crier announced, "The enemy is coming! There is going to be a battle!" this Sore Head mounted up. "I think I'll go watch!" Then he mounted the old buckskin gelding. The men, when they were passing by him on their faster horses, said, "Why, this one won't be the one to kill Iron Hand!" And all of them went up the hill to the battle.

And then the boy ran to the spot. Then he said, "Yellow horse of mine, come!"

Oh, then there was a buckskin horse, a fine-looking horse!

Then he put on himself the things that were hanging from the horse. He hurried to join the fighters where the battle was. Then he killed Iron Hand. Then the Sioux ran away.[3]

Then this young man slipped off unnoticed after he killed Iron Hand. He made the buckskin horse stand there and tied onto it the things he wore. Then the buckskin disappeared.

Then he mounted the clubfooted old buckskin. While he was coming through the valley shooting arrows here and there, men said, "Why, you going through the valley here, you aren't going to be the one to do it. You should be like the one who killed Iron Hand!" They said things like that. Everyone went on.

Then Sore Head returned home. Then he said, "Grandmother, here are some prairie chickens."

She plucked them.

Then Last Child,[4] that young woman he was sleeping with, arrived. After they all went to bed and he lay with her, she forgot the holy things she had said.[5]

Now when Iron Ear was the one who led the enemy when they came to fight, the young man rode a white steed.

"Whoever kills Iron Ear will be the one to marry this daughter! Whoever he is who has been killing these enemies—the one who is the brave warrior—we don't know him."

And so the chief, the father of these young women, made an arrowhead and an arrow. He made a groove around the end of the arrow, where the arrowhead is. Then he joined the fighters to spy on the unknown warrior.

Then the white horse the young man was riding suddenly appeared as he got to the front line. The young man charged this Iron Ear. He yanked him off his horse. He scalped him. Then he swung around and rode along at the edge of the fighting.

Meanwhile the chief shot the arrow somewhere into one of his legs, whichever leg it was. I don't know.

This young man continued on, though. Then he quickly rode down the hillside. He hid from them. He put his things on the white

3. In Arikara oral traditions the term Sioux frequently has, as here, the more generalized meaning of enemy.

4. A name for the youngest child in a family. Here it refers to the chief's youngest daughter.

5. An obscure reference.

horse.

His leg was aching where he had been struck. So he broke off the arrow shaft, realizing that someone would recognize him as the one killing the enemy warriors.

Then he returned to where he was living. After they had boiled some meat and, oh, as they were eating, the young woman Last Child walked around inside the lodge. His grandmother watched the young woman.

Then this Sore Head said, "Hey, my wife, my leg hurts me terrifically. Your father is the cause of it. He shot me in the leg with an arrow, and the arrowhead is in it and now my leg is swollen. It's really paining me."

Meanwhile, there in the main part of the village, the crier was calling out, "The chief says, 'I grooved my own arrowhead. I want the man to come. I'll doctor him. I'll take it out. And he'll be the one to be my son-in-law.'"

Now Coyote came into the chief's lodge, wanting to be the one to marry these young women. Coyote dragged his leg inside.

This chief: "Hey, he's different. Take him outside!"

They threw him out, Coyote, Mischievous Coyote, as he underhandedly tried to marry these young women.

And then this young woman ran up to her father's lodge. She said, "Father, I have come. My husband wants you to doctor him. You shot an arrowhead into his leg. Now his leg is paining him. His leg has swollen up."

"Eh, what are you doing? Bring him over here!"

Then they took this young man up there. They laid him down. Then this man the chief extracted the arrowhead with a stick. He pulled his arms. Then the wound healed.

"And here he's the one who killed all of them—who counted coups on the ones molesting us! Now he is my son-in-law. Now he's my son-in-law. Now, you people of this village, this son-in-law of mine owns the village."[6]

6. The expression 'to own the village' is a metaphor designating the position of village chief.

Then this Sore Head said to the daughter, "Let things be as they were. You and I are together. That's good enough. Nothing else matters. Your father has the village. Meanwhile we are now all together. And it wouldn't be good if I moved my grandmother's things away. Nothing else matters, just that we're together."

Then she told her father what he said. "This is what he says."

"Well, it doesn't make any difference. You two are together."

Now the other sisters of this Last Child, when they brought moccasins and war shirts to him, they would be told, "Ah, he doesn't need it. He has one of those. You were always calling him names."

When she said that, the three maidens left. They said, "Ah, we made a mistake when we did that, calling him names."

And here he must have been a handsome young man all along! For then he did it: he took the covering off from his head. Here he was a handsome man!

Well, then he married this young woman. Well, then she had a baby for him. It was a girl that they had.

Then he said, "Now, my wife, now my spirit wants to go home. My father is calling me. I'm not one of you people living here on earth. There in the sky is where I came from, where my father is, where you see the star that comes up just before daybreak. The big star [Morning Star]—that one is my father. Now he's calling me. He wants to see this child of mine."

Well, then the young woman cried as she mourned, not wanting him to do it.

He said, "It doesn't matter. You don't need to feel bad. My father and I will watch over you. But I must take this girl. But you will have another one. She'll look like this one. Now I want you, Last Child, and her to be together. And I want her to look like me."

Now they made a sweat lodge. They went inside. They went inside the sweat lodge.

When this young man called out in prayer—after he and his father had spoken—then he said, "Now, grandmother, I want you to say how old you would like to be so that you can be young again."

Then his grandmother said, "Now, my grandson, you have taken care of me. You have taken care of us and what we have been doing.

Now we feel bad that you are going to leave us.

"Well, I want to be as old as a young woman who has had four children, one who is thirty winters old. I'll be that age."

"Now, my brother, how old do you want to be?"

Then the boy said, "I want to be as old as you—a man like you are."

"Well, that's good. It's going to be that way."

Then he began to splash water on the hot rocks.

"Now, Last Child, open the door!"

Then she opened the door. There she sat: there sat his grandmother. She was a young girl. And the other one, his brother Bloody Hands, sat there. The two of them [Bloody Hands and Star Boy] looked like twins.

Then they all went out.

Then they ate after Last Child cooked a meal. Oh, they ate!

Then this young man said, "Now the night has passed. Let's go up on the hill! Let's go up!"

Then he and his wife took the baby girl. They were dipping water while they talked. "This is how you people here are going to fare. You are going to be thus" [foretelling their future].

"Now, bring me a bunch of sage! White sage!"

Then she brought it. She wrapped the sage up into a bundle. It looked like a baby.

"Now, this bundle will be like this girl. Now I'm going to go. My father is calling me—my father, the one there looking down on you. My father sees you.

"Now turn that way to face the west!"

Then the young woman stood up there. Then he put the bundle of sage on her back. He put a robe over her shoulders, so that the sage was wrapped like a baby.

Then he said, "Now you're going to go back."

He turned her around.

"You're going to go back to where you live. Now this baby will begin to cry; when she gets lonesome, she'll cry. Don't pay any attention to her, but watch over her.

"As soon as she begins to hang down, hanging down over your shoulder, take her in your arms. You'll nurse her. The white sage is going to be like mine. Put her on your back. Nurse her. Now this one will be just like the child we have.

"You'll know that my grandmother is waiting for you where she lives, and my brother Bloody Hands. You three will be together. And if my brother wants to be chief of the village, that is how it will be."

And it happened that way for this young woman, just as he said it would. When morning came and the baby cried, the young woman thought, "Now it's time, just as he said."

She took the bundle. "Why, here this sage is mine!" Then she took it. Then she nursed it.

Then she and the baby went on. They arrived where she, the old woman, and Bloody Hands lived, and they all mourned there.

Then she told them, "Now we're all going to move to my father's lodge."

Then they gathered their possessions and went up to the lodge in which the young woman's father lived.

"Now my husband has left. Here this boy had come from a great distance away, from another world! The star that comes up in the morning, the bright one, the big bright one—that one is his father."

Now, this young man Bloody Hands became a great warrior. Bloody Hands became chief of the village. And this young woman raised that girl, Sage Woman.

Now this is what happened. These young women and older women who today are named after the sage, who are named Sage Woman, get the name from this incident. But there is no man among us who is named Sage.

6

Bounding Head and the
Four Young Women

*The myth of Bounding Head—or Rolling Skull, as the
name has been more frequently translated—is found in
many versions throughout the Plains. Among most tribes the
character has an ambiguous form: he or she is a head or
skull who can travel with extraordinary speed by rolling, yet
who behaves in most respects as a fully formed human. In
this Arikara version the character is a one-eyed man who
travels by bounding through the air. As a persona in
Arikara myths, Bounding Head is noted for his attraction to
women and his devious ways of seducing them. The version
related here was told to the narrator by his grandmother
Squash Blossom.*

Now I am going to tell about Bounding Head. I certainly never
saw him, but I have heard of him through the stories that they used
to tell about him.

Once there lived some young women. There were four of them.
One was named White Corn; and one, Yellow Corn; and Red Corn;
and one, Black Corn. Now there were these four. White Corn was
the oldest one. Yellow Corn was the second oldest; and the other
one, Red Corn, was in the middle. Black Corn was the youngest
child.

Now they lived there, planting their corn. Now one planted red
corn; and one, yellow corn; and one, white corn; and the other, black
corn.

Now while they were hoeing their garden, this man Bounding
Head was lurking around there. He had one eye in his forehead.
After he would bound into the air, he would land somewhere off in
the distance. He also knew how to hunt.

Well, then he desired to marry one of these young women, the spinsters[1] who lived there. And so he killed a deer. Then he took it. He laid it at the entry to their lodge.

Then the oldest one went outside. "Oh my, you sisters inside, there's a deer lying here! It must have suffocated."

Then she took the carcass inside and butchered it. Then there was plenty of meat.

Meanwhile Bounding Head was peeking around to see if they had picked up the carcass. "Now it's not lying there. They must have taken it inside. They must have butchered it." That is what he was thinking.

Again early the next morning he did the same thing. He laid an antelope at the entry.

The middle sister, Yellow Corn, said, "Ee! Get up! There's an antelope lying here at the entry. It must have smothered. Here it lies. What are you doing? Let's butcher it, too!"

Then there was plenty of meat.

That is what Bounding Head did repeatedly, however many times he did it.

Now the youngest one, Black Corn, thought, "I wonder what's happening—that the carcasses of these deer—the whitetail deer—and antelope are lying at the entry? I wonder what the cause is? I'll find out."

Oh, then really early in the morning she arose to peek out. Then a man appeared. He was carrying the carcass of a buck elk. Then he laid it in front of the spinsters' doorway. Then he bounded up and flew quickly out of sight in the distance.

Then Black Corn touched her sister White Corn. "Get up! Peek out! The one who has been bringing these different things that we have eaten—here he isn't human! Here Bounding Head is the one bringing these different kinds of animals. Get up! Put on different clothes! Put on another dress! Put your moccasins on!"

Then she told Yellow Corn the same thing, and then she told Red Corn the same thing, too.

Then they ran around and around inside their earth lodge,

---

1. The Arikara term used here refers to women, young or old, who choose not to marry—generally women who do not like men.

running around inside the room. Then they went outside, and also ran on top of the roof of the lodge. "Well, now we'll get ahead of Bounding Head's power. We have power, too."

Then they ran off. Oh, I don't know how far they had gone. "Keep looking!" [Black Corn warned them].

Meanwhile that Bounding Head was peeping over the hills. What he now brought and left at the doorway remained there. No one took the carcass inside. "Ah, I wonder what the matter is? I think I'll go over there and find out."

Then he went. He entered the lodge. They were each still lying there on their beds.

Then he went to where White Corn lay. He said, "Move over! I have come."

Then the spirit of that young woman said, "Oh, go farther on to where she lies! Lie down with her over there!"

Then he went farther on to where Yellow Corn lay. "Hey, move over a little farther! I have come."

"Ah, go farther on, to that one over there!"

Then he went on farther to where Red Corn lay. "You who are going all around, lie with the one farther on!"

Then he went to where Black Corn lay. Then he checked: no one was lying there. Hey, he became furious! There were only wads of hair there.

And then he himself ran around inside the lodge just as the spinsters had done. He flew outside and onto the roof. Ah, there their tracks were!

Then he did it: he chased them. "You aren't going to go anywhere! Why, you're my wives now."

When he bounded into the air, he went an enormous distance.

Meanwhile the young women kept looking back. "Oh, now he's coming! He's coming. Run faster!"

Now he was gaining on them.

Then the oldest one threw an awl. Oh, here there was a thicket over there, a thicket of sharp thorn apple bushes![2] Oh, then Bound-

---

2. A local name for red haw (*Crataegus* sp.). Its thorns were used as awls.

ing Head came along the edge of them as he was quickly passing through them. Then he bounded up and, oh, he dropped right into the middle of the thicket! Now the thorns were pricking him. Oh, he barely got across!

Then he did it: he bounded into the air. He gained on them.

"Now he's coming on!"

Well, then this Yellow Corn threw a comb. Oh, now there was a huge, thick patch of cactus—sharp cactus—spread out there. He bounded up and then landed in the middle of it. Oh, then the needles lacerated him all over!

And he passed through it. "You're mine." Then he began to bound along as he went on.

Now it was Red Corn's turn. Then she threw a knife. It landed over there in the distance. Then there were cracks in the ground. There was now a deep, bluish valley there.

Bounding Head came flying to the bank of it and he went along the bank. Then he jumped. Oh, he almost reached the other side, when he rolled and, oh, he fell down the cliff over there. Then he began to go around at the base. He barely got up the precipice.

Meanwhile the spinsters had covered an enormous amount of ground as they went on. Then he chased after them again. Then he caught up with them.

"Now, Last Child, it's your turn!"

Then she threw a mirror, whatever kind of mirror it was. Oh my, there was a valley there filled with water!

Now he came to its bank. "Hey, I'll overtake you nevertheless. That was your last shot!" Then he bounded up. Oh my, he landed in the water! Then the water began to take him in its current, and he barely got across it.

Oh, then he bounded into the air. Then he gained on them as he was bounding along. He caught up with them.

Now these young women became frightened. Now they said, "Our grandmother lives here. Perhaps she might help us in some way."

Then she opened the door for them.

"Now we have come! The one coming has been chasing us."

"Now quickly!"

They ran inside. They fell down. Foam was frothing from their mouths. The door closed.

Then Bounding Head began to go around the lodge. "Oh, let them out! Let them come out! I tired them out for myself. These young women inside are my wives."

Old Woman Spider said, "You must move on since you're frightening my grandchildren. Go on!"

"Now let them come back out! I've tired them out for myself. They're my wives." That is what he was saying.

Then Old Woman Spider said, "You who are scaring my grandchildren, now it's my own turn to strike back."

Then it became wintry.

"You who were yelling, now come inside!"

The sound died out. And here he froze! Oh, there was deep snow there. Now, he froze. "We've frozen him."

In the morning the heat came inside the lodge from the sunlight. And out there lay Bounding Head frozen in the snow.

Now at this point I don't know whether they went back to their lodge or whether they went to a different place. What I have told here is the story that I know.

7

The Young Woman Who Swallowed a Stone

Representing another popular Plains mythic theme are stories of Stone Boy, who was born after his mother swallowed a stone. The story presented here is one of two such myths known to the narrator. (The other one was not recorded because of its sexual content.) In this one the young woman's brothers are killed by an old woman whose breath reduces men to empty skin bags. Stone Boy, who has mys-

terious powers because of the holiness of his stone parentage,
vanquishes the old woman and restores life to the young
men, who together with their sister ascend into the sky to
become stars and there enjoy eternal life.

Now I will tell a story that occurred when they lived long ago,
when the Arikaras were coming this way upriver. I surely don't
know that it happened, but my grandmother, the poor thing, used
to tell me stories when she reared me, telling me different stories,
telling me tales. I surely don't know that what I am going to tell
actually occurred, but it is what they used to tell.

There were four young men living together. They had one sister
who cooked for them when they went around hunting and brought
back deer meat. She made dried meat and made moccasins for her
brothers.

One evening the young woman went after water. It isn't known
how old she was. She felt downhearted and, the poor thing, she
cried and cried as she went along. She was mourning for her father
and mother, who were no longer alive. Her brothers were the only
ones she had; there were no other living relatives. People lived far
apart then and they did not see each other regularly.

Now after this young woman had gone, after she had gone down
to the creek, there was a stone there. It was transparent. Then she
picked it up. Then she looked it all over and put it in her mouth. "I
think I'll keep it in my mouth!"

For some reason it slid down her throat after she put it in
her mouth. She swallowed it. Now she just stood there. She had
swallowed the stone. Then she went on, dipped water, and brought
the water back. Then she began to boil meat. Her brothers returned.

Now some time later this young woman became pregnant.
Her brothers then asked, "Ah, what has happened? Our sister is
pregnant." They were looking for the reason.

Some time later the moment arrived and this young woman
bore a child. It was a boy. This boy, the child, was light complex-
ioned. His uncles were happy to see him. They cuddled him. Oh,

they loved their nephew, whom they brought various things, like deer brains and milk. Then this boy grew up. Oh, the boy was very stout as he grew up and went all around!

Then the young woman's brothers began to disappear. And here it was she, Shwahit,[1] who was making bags of them. For some reason, when her breath struck a man's mouth, it caused the man's flesh to peel and fall off, leaving him skinned. And then he became a bag.

That is what Shwahit was doing: she went around doing away with people. When they wandered around, she would find out where they were staying and would then go there. Then that is what she would do: she would kill them, killing various ones.

Then this boy asked, "Mother, why is it that we live here alone? Wherever I go, I don't see anyone."

Then the young woman said, "Now that's how it is. You're right. Your uncles were living here. While you were growing up as a child, they loved you. Then they disappeared! I don't know what happened. One went off and never returned. Another went and then he didn't return. All of them disappeared for some reason! I don't know what happened."

This boy was very holy since he was a stone. As he wandered around, looking everywhere and watching over things where he and his mother lived, he saw that woman Shwahit. Oh, she was fast when she ran! Then he began to spy on her, and then she and the boy encountered each other.

Then she said, "Ah, grandson, you who are wandering from afar, now come!"

When the boy looked at her, he said, "I surely am not related to you."

"Now come!"

Then this woman Shwahit began to think of this boy, "I think I'll blow on him!" That is the way she did things: when she would blow into someone's mouth, the poor thing, he would fall over dead

---

1. This name is an anglicization of *šwaahii'It*, the Arikara term for Indian hemp, here used as a personal name.

and turn into a bag after the flesh peeled off. That is what she would do.

But this boy was a stone. The boy was very stout!

When he went inside where she lived, a heart was hanging there with blood dripping from it.

Then he made a fire. He made a fire.

Then he asked, "Why is it that you do these things? I wonder, where did my uncles go? Where did you take them? You must have killed them."

Then the woman came charging at him, wanting to blow into his mouth. But he now had the heart. He hit it. Then this Shwahit was thoroughly disconcerted.[2]

Then he said, "If you tell me where you took my uncles, wherever they are, I won't put you into the fire."

And so she said, "Surely they are there! They are there! Those are your uncles."

There they lay in the back of the room: they were bags. They were all wrinkled up, since they had lain there a long time.

Then he said, "Now I know. Now you'll die, too. And here you're the one who did away with my uncles!"

He threw the heart into the fire. This Shwahit flopped over. She was burned. Then the young man went and picked up his uncles who were bags and talked to them.

Then he arrived back home.

Then he said, "Mother, make a sweat lodge! We'll go into it."

Then she did that, and they went into the sweat lodge.

He spoke. He said, "Mother, my uncles are going to come back. I've found them. While we have been living here pitifully, I found them. Now they're going to come back."

He said, "Now, mother, close the door!"

Then he brought them inside, those uncles, the dried hides. He put them down. He began to pray to the heated stones, the stones that were like himself. He began to splash water on them.

2. The heart is the source of Shwahit's life and power. The hanging heart as portrayed here, representing the power of an evil being, is a recurrent Arikara motif (cf. stories 4 and 15).

Then those bags lying there began to talk: "Eh, I feel good now."
That is what each one of them was saying.

He continued splashing water on the stones. When the water
was gone they were all talking.[3]

Then he said, "Now, mother, open the door!"

When she looked, there sat her brothers!

"Now my uncles have come back. I've brought them back. Now
this is what happened to them after a woman killed them. And I got
rid of the woman so that nothing bad like that will happen again."

Well, the young men arose, and the young woman cooked a meal
for them. Their sister boiled meat for them while they walked
around. Now it isn't known what happened after that.

Then the boy said, "Now, mother, you and I are going to go
inside the sweat lodge. You have reached maturity and now it will
be thus: I'll turn to face the way from which I came, and I'll go back
where I came from, now that we have all been together. But now
you all are going to go on alone for a long life; you will all be headed
for an eternal life. But I'm going to go back to the stones from
where I came."

And so that is what happened: when it dawned they were there.
Meanwhile they had gone up into the sky to become stars. But this
boy went back there where he was a stone. Then he went back
there.

3. The rejuvenative powers of the sweat lodge as well as its power to
restore life are common motifs in Plains traditions, illustrated elsewhere in
this collection (story 72).

8

The Man with the Sharpened Leg

This myth is an Arikara version of the widespread
northern Plains story of the man who sharpened the end of
his leg to use as a weapon to kill people. Among tribes like
the Arapahos, Assiniboines, and Crows, it is a young man
who sharpens his leg and then kills his companion and
frequently other people as well, whereas in this Arikara
account the antagonist is a man with a beautiful daughter
whom he uses to lure young men to his winter camp and
there kill them. This narrative also exemplifies a common
Arikara mythic theme: an evil old man, generally a father-
in-law, who abuses power that he has been given and so is
in turn killed, usually by or with the assistance of his
benefactor, after he oversteps the bounds of tolerability.

Now I am going to tell the story of a man who used to sharpen
the end of his leg. After he would sharpen his leg, he would call his
son-in-law and tell him, "Now we are going to kick each other." And
that is what he did. Then when it was becoming spring, this man
would come back to the villages of whichever tribe it was, whether
the Arikaras, Hidatsas, or Mandans. This is what they used to tell.

Now there was a village, and when it was becoming spring that
man came there. He had a young daughter. Oh, she was beautiful,
a nice-looking young woman. She would mingle among the people
during the summer, and then when autumn came her father would
say, "Now we are going to go back to where we always stay during
the winter. I hunt there, where there are plenty of antelope, deer,
and buffalo. But, poor us, we're the ones who are full."

Oh, there were young men who liked the daughter of this man,
and every year one of them would follow her when she and her
family left for the winter. There had been many of them who had
done this, following after the young woman.

Well, so one young man went. And then he said, "Hey, surely

there have been many young men whom this young woman has led off. Then when spring comes, the young man does not come back. Then he disappears. I just want to find out about it. I wonder what's happening?"

And so that was what happened when the man went off, leaving with his wife and daughter. "And now we are going where we usually go for the winter." And then this young man followed along with the young woman, going with her family to the badlands.

There was an earth lodge there in which they used to stay. And then the father-in-law said, "Now this other one will be your lodge, son-in-law." There were two earth lodges. "This other one is the one where my daughter always lives. That is her lodge."

The two of them lived there, and this young man would go out hunting and bring back deer, antelope, and buffalo. Whenever an animal was killed, he brought back the meat. Oh, there was plenty of meat. Meanwhile the man stayed around his lodge. Oh, there was plenty of dried meat for them to eat during the winter when it was cold! Oh, they lived in a nice meadow at the base of a hill! Oh, it was nice land!

[After there was a sufficient supply of meat stored to last through the winter,] this man said, "Now, son-in-law, get ready! We are going to kick each other. We'll kick each other. And if you beat me, my daughter is yours. You're going to have the one you are living with."

Then he did that: then there was a pounding sound in the lodge where the man and his wife lived. Then there was a pounding sound.

Then the young man thought, "I wonder what that is?" Then he went to the other lodge where his father-in-law lived. Then he opened the door, and there went the man's wife off into the brush at a distance where her gardens were.

Then he asked, "Are you ready?"

After that sound began inside, the young woman said, "Now he's doing what he always does. This is what my father always does. Oh, there have been many young men he has killed—ones I was going to marry. This is what he does."

After the young man opened the door, he peeked inside and saw his father-in-law sharpening the end of one of his legs. Then the leg came to a point.

"Now I'm ready. I'll charge outside. Now be ready! We'll kick each other."

And then this young man hurried outside.

Then the young woman told him, "You won't be able to kill him even if you shoot him. You aren't going to be able to kill him. Run away! He's really fast."

This young man ran outside with the bow and arrows he had. Then he ran onto a flat.

Then the father-in-law came charging out. When he saw the young man his leg was sharpened. "Hey, where do you think you can go? Now I'll kick you." Then he ran after him. Now the man was extremely swift: he would hook his leg into the ground and then spring forward. Now he was gaining on the young man.

And there there was a tree. Oh, it was a big tree! Then it said to the young man, "Hey, come closer! Surely that man who's coming has gone too far. Come closer!"

The boy quickly came up close to the tree, and then he climbed up it. He got to the top. Then the tree got higher.

Then the man rushed to the base of it. Then he sprang up. He said, "I'll stick you in the ribs and then bring you down." That is what he was saying.

When he sprang up he stuck his leg into the trunk of the tree. The leg stuck straight out. Then he was not able to get down. Now he was hanging there.

And then this tree said to the young man, "Now go on! He can't get down. He'll hang from here. He won't live. We blessed him previously, but now he's gone beyond the limit with these things that he's been doing.

"Now go on home! You'll go back to the lodge and then you'll go home to your village. But meanwhile he'll hang here until he dies."

Then the man said, "Now by all means take me off! You're making a mistake. I surely was just teasing you." That is what he was saying over and over.

But the young man went to his lodge. Then he arrived there. Then he, the young woman his wife, and his mother-in-law got themselves ready.

Then the old woman said, "Yes, he's gone beyond his limit doing the things he's been doing here. But now you have beat him. Now let's flee! Now let's go home quickly!"

Then they did it: they arrived at the village. Then they told about it: "This is what happened. So this is what the man who used to come here has been doing."

9

The Young Woman Who Married the Moon

This is the story of a young woman who, despite the entreaties of her brothers, declines all offers of marriage. Finally, in reproachful anger they ask her if she wants a husband as handsome as the moon. Shamed, she decides to follow their ironic suggestion and marry this heavenly being. The narrative tells of her journey, accompanied by a ball that is her source of power; of the obstacles they overcome; of her marriage to Moon; and of her eventual return, with a child, to her people. The portrayal of Moon here as a man is unusual, since in Arikara religion Moon is a female deity referred to and addressed as Mother.

This story occurred long, long ago when our people were coming this way, when they were moving upriver. It is not known where it happened or how many winters ago it was. I surely don't know, but I do know the story.

There once was a young woman who was an only daughter, and she had four brothers, and a father, a mother, uncles, and all sorts of relatives.

The relatives of various young men came to the family of that young woman to ask for her, that she marry certain ones. She refused. She did not want to marry them. There were many young men she treated that way by declining their requests.

Then her brothers became angry with her. "What you are doing—your rejecting all these suitors—certainly isn't good. What do you want your husband to look like? Do you want to marry the moon? Do you want the man you marry to look like the moon, since you are rejecting these young men—someone to be with and to be a provider?" That is what her brothers and uncles were saying repeatedly as they reproached her.

And this young woman had a ball, whatever kind it was. And here this ball is what blessed her. <It had something inside it, like fur, which was medicine. She had played with it when she was young. She had always taken good care of it. And now whenever she went anywhere, she would always carry it on her back. And when she went to bed she kept it by her for protection. It always told her what was going to happen—when the enemy was coming close, when game was coming close, when something was going to happen.>

Then this young woman said, "Alright. Now I'll go off somewhere. I don't like your reproaching me. I don't want to marry anyone. Now I'll go off somewhere."

Now her brothers and uncles also disapproved of this; they did not want her to go off somewhere.

Now this young woman got ready. Then she carried the ball on her back. She also took moccasins for herself, however many pairs of moccasins she had. Then she went off toward the east.

After she had been going and going in that direction, it became daylight. Now it became dark again. Morning came again and then night.

Then different kinds of holy beings began to block her path. But this ball always warned her. It would say, "Don't do anything! They will deceive you. But we're going where Moon is. That's where we're going. <That's a better place there. Life is forever. One never gets old.>"

<As she went she met a wolf who wanted to marry her, but she just kept going. Other animals—a bear, an elk, a buffalo—met her

and wanted to marry her, but she continued going.>

<Finally this ball said, "You're going to meet Night, the spirit
of Night who controls the night. But he's not comparable to Moon.
This one is going to meet you and make you stay up for four days
and nights. He's going to try to outdo you, and Sun is going to try
to get you, too. Where we're going there is no water and everything
is hot. Sun is trying to get you by drying everything up and tiring
you. But Moon is after you; he's waiting for you. And I'm taking you
there. I'm just like that Moon: I'm round.">

Then as this young woman was going along, Night overtook her.
He overtook her. <He was all dressed up in his war finery. He, too,
wanted to marry her, but the young woman refused.> Then they
each sat down, with Night wanting to put her to sleep so that he
could marry her in her sleep.

Then Night said, "We'll stay awake four nights. If you go to
sleep before the fourth night is over, I'll win. I'll marry you. We'll
get married. But if you outdo me—if you don't fall asleep for four
nights—you'll be saved. You'll go where you want to, wherever you
are going."

Then he and this young woman made a fire. Night sat on one
side. He faced the other way, toward the west, while this young
woman faced east, as they told stories while they stayed awake.

Now three days passed and three nights. Then after the fourth
day, when it was becoming the fourth night, the young woman
tired. Then she started to go to sleep. She began feeling sleepy.

Then this ball that was her companion said, "Now go to sleep!
I'll stay awake. He and I will be the ones to compete."

Now this ball <which turned itself into human form> replaced
the young woman; and he and Night told stories while they stayed
awake. Then it got to be evening. At midnight Night began to
slacken. Then he, too, began to fall asleep. He was tired. He was
barely talking now. But this ball was awake. He was strong. <But
Night would doze off, and the ball would wake him.>

Now when it was nearly morning this Night said, "Alright. You
have beat me. Now you're going to go where you want. Why, you are
strong! Why, you are certain to go where you want to!"

Now he left her.

Then it became daylight and the ball woke the young woman. "Now we've beaten him. Now hurry! Let's go quickly!

"There remains one more obstacle. Night was the last one [to attempt to prevent you from reaching the one you want]. Now we're going to see the main one, the one you want."

And then that is what they did, as they went on, wherever it was.

Then the ball said, "Now you're going to see a young man. He's the one who'll be your companion. He's waiting for you. There's no obstacle now. Don't be afraid! He's the one you are seeking, just as you want it to be.

"But I'm watching for the time when we'll go. It'll be dark then. Moon is going to rise. When he appears in the sky, a young man will come. He's the one."

And then that is what happened.

"Now I've come here, just as you wanted. And I'm the one. I'm waiting for you. I'm the one who caused you to come here. And I'm thankful that you didn't succumb to their deceptions while you were coming—that you were not deceived. Your coming the right way is how I wanted it to be.

"Now I was blocking the attempts of Sun. I was blocking the attempts of Sun, who was throwing rays of heat down. He wants to tire you and make you thirsty for water by drying up all the streams and lakes. But I'm the one who's responsible for bringing you two here, you two who have come."

Meanwhile he was watching her closely.

"Now we're going to go where I live. My grandmother and grandfather are waiting for you."

Then he led her off. Then they went up into the sky and into the clouds. He lifted her up quickly.

Then there was a country that spread out before her. It was a different land. There was a tipi there.

"Now this is the place."

Now while the young woman was living with this young man, different ones were bringing <deer> meat to her for them to eat. Now they were stars, the ones who were bringing the meat for her.

Now this young woman said, "I'm downhearted now. I just feel that I should go back home to my village."

And after awhile this young woman had given birth to a baby. She had a baby, a little boy <who was now four winters old>.

Then her husband said, "Now I'll take you two back. There's no obstacle to your returning. But I'm going to remain here. For so many nights and so many days I'm going to come along. I'll be coming, and I'll watch over you. I'll come to where you two live.

"But I'm not going to die. No matter how far off the time may be, when you die you're going to come here where I live, here where I go around. And you and this little boy are going to have everything.

"Now I'll take you two. I'll keep a watch over both you and Sun. Now we're going to go. It's going to rain, but he's going to be looking for you nevertheless. You and the boy are going to ride on that cloud. Now that is how you're going to go. The cloud will make Sun forget."

Then they came. But now Sun spied on her in order to get rid of her. What he wanted was for this young woman to die. But Moon was hiding her and brought her back to the village, wherever it was.

Then the young woman and her son arrived there. People had forgotten her. Then that young woman just appeared when she arrived back. Then her family was glad to see her. And there she led a little boy!

Then she said, "Now you were exaggerating my thoughts when you said that I wanted to marry the moon. But that's what happened. Now that's where I went. I traveled to where Moon lives. Now this boy is his son.

"Now I don't know how long this boy and I will be together, but it isn't going to be difficult for him to find things. Things aren't going to be difficult for him. Now you can't make up a story about me again. That's all."

Now this is the end of the story. I do not know how long she lived, and then she died. It is the same with the boy: I did not hear whether he married, and I do not know how long he lived. This boy died, too.

Now this is the story that I used to hear.

10

The Young Woman Who Became a Bear

One of the most spectacular geographical features on the northern Plains is Devils Tower, a large, solitary butte that rises dramatically 865 feet from its base on the Wyoming plains northwest of the Black Hills. Because of its symmetry, geological uniqueness, and prominence—it can be seen from nearly a hundred miles in some directions—it inspired awe among the many tribes who lived near or visited it. To most northern Plains peoples Devils Tower was a sacred site where men went to fast and pray when seeking power or a supernatural blessing. So deep was the impression created by it that early in this century Kiowas still remembered the landmark in tradition, even though sometime before 1800 the tribe had moved to the southern Plains from their homeland in and west of the Black Hills.

The Arikaras and Kiowas have nearly identical myths about the origin of Devils Tower. Both tribes tell how a girl and her brothers escaped from their sister, who had turned into a bear, by standing on a rock that rose into the sky to become Devils Tower, and how they then became the stars of the Pleiades. Other tribes tell similar variants (but sometimes lack the star transformation ending). The version recounted here, told to the narrator by his grandmother Squash Blossom, is a fine example of what is one of the most widely known stories among contemporary Arikaras. Today there is no Arikara name remembered for Devils Tower, but to Arapahos, Crows, Cheyennes, and Sioux it is known as Bear Lodge. The origin of the English name Devils Tower is uncertain.

Now I will tell an old story. It happened a long time ago, long ago when the people were migrating this way. It is what I used to hear when my grandmother told the story. It is a holy story.

When the people were wandering around as a group long, long ago, traveling somewhere, wherever it was, in the land to the south, it happened while the children were playing, when the chokecherries and plums were coming on but were not yet ripe.

The children were playing. There were many of them playing. Among them was one girl who was a little older than the others; she was fourteen winters old. Then they told her, "Now it's your turn to be a bear." They were imitating a bear as it charges out of the brush, and the children would run away. "A bear is charging!" they would say as they played. And then they told that girl, "Now it's your turn to be a bear."

The young girl, however, did not want to do it. "I don't want to. Let me be! Ask someone else!"

But they continued to ask her.

Finally she gave in and said, "Now it will be that way."

The girl's sister was younger. She was ten winters old. Then the girl told her sister, "Now go on! Hide somewhere in a dog's den, where she has had her puppies. Go in it and hide there! When I arrive, you'll come out. Now what is going to happen is not going to be a good thing."

Then the young girl went into the woods.

She was fourteen winters old when she turned into a bear. And the children moved toward the woods where the plum bushes were. Then the young girl charged out of the brush, and here she was a bear! She chased the children, knocking them down as they yelled, "A bear is charging!" They began shooting at her, but they were not able to do anything to stop her. She killed various ones. Then she even included those who were her relatives. Then she killed her brother. And she did away with her sister, her mother, and her grandmother. Oh, finally she must have satisfied herself, for she came back after everyone else had run away.

The village was now empty except for the bodies of the dead lying all around after she had killed them.

« »

Then she went around and said, "Magpie Woman, wherever you are, I have arrived."

This girl came out of the den there where a dog had had her puppies.

Then the young woman said to her sister, "Now let's go up into the hills somewhere! Let my wounds heal where they shot me and where they cut me! Now I was afraid this would happen. I didn't want to play, but they insisted on it."

When the girl mourned after she saw the dead bodies of her mother and father, her older sister said to her, "Cease your crying! I'll kill you if you continue doing it."

Then the girl followed her sister as they went up a hill, up a high hill.

Then this bear woman began to dig a hole in the woods, wherever it was. Then she said, "Here is where we'll stay."

And when they finished their digging, the two went into the hole.

Then the bear woman told her sister, "Now make a fire! And bring dried meat from our village. There must be dried meat there. Bring some of it!"

Then this girl went back to the village, and then she began picking up the dried meat that people had stored. She brought it back, and then they cooked it.

While they were eating the bear sister said, "When you go outside, you must look all around. Our brothers went on the warpath. When you see them coming back, you must tell me. I'll kill them, too. I don't like what has been done to me, the way I am. I didn't want it."

The girl now went out early the next morning and climbed up where she could look all around while she was digging Indian turnips here and there. This incident must have occurred when summer was beginning, since the turnips were still in the ground for her to dig up to bring back to her bear sister.

Then the girl said, "It's terrible back in our village. Flesh and other things are rotting. It's not good."

Then her bear sister said, "Let it be! Don't go there. Go somewhere else!"

Then the girl said, "There aren't any turnips growing close by. I must go far off."

The bear sister said, "The chokecherries and plums must be ripe now. Those are what we'll eat."

So the girl went out and went up on a high hill where she could look all around and pick chokecherries, Juneberries, and whatever else was growing on the trees.

Then she saw her brothers. There they came. There were four of them. So the girl went. Then she went to meet them.

Then she said, "Something bad has happened. Our sister is a bear now. I'm living with her. She's killed our father, our mother, and our grandmother. She killed them. No one is living there in our village now. They've gone off in different directions. They've apparently taken their possessions secretly. They must have been coming back for the things they left behind."

Then the young men said, "Now we'll stay here awhile."

Then they helped her pick plums.

"You should go find out things from your bear sister. You must say to her, 'We're living here alone. It might happen that the enemy will find us. You say, "They cannot kill me. No one can kill me." However, what will happen if they do kill you? Where can you be wounded?"' The brother continued, "She will tell you. That's what you should say."

Then the girl went back to where she and her sister lived. Then she entered the den. Then the bear sister said, "You have the strong odor of a human. Have our brothers returned? You must tell me. I must kill them."

Then the girl said, "Surely no one is around. I went to where our father and mother lie, because I'm lonesome now that we are living alone."

The bear woman calmed down after having become angry.

The next morning the girl went out. "I think I'll go off for a while! I think I'll look around!" She went up into the hills wandering around, and then went to where her brothers were.

Then they told her, "Now you must eat!" They had killed a deer. Then she finished eating.

After she had eaten, one brother asked, "Now what did she say?"

She said, "I asked her. Now this is what she said: 'They cannot kill me, even if they were to shoot me. But if they wound me here on my little toe, either of my two little toes, that's when I'll die. Then they'll kill me. But if it should happen that any blood spurts out, I'll come back. Then it will not be good if I come back. I'll be different.'" And so this girl related to her brothers what she had been told.

Then one brother said, "We'll make preparations now. You stay here awhile! Wander around here on the sides of the hills close by! There are enemies around and they might see you."

And then these young men went and picked a cactus and the branches of a thorn apple bush. Then they broke the thorns off and brought them to the girl.

One said, "Now lay these around outside the hole in the ground where you two live. The sharpest ones, the cactus thorns, you must lay closest to it. Now, after you have done this, you'll come tell us."

Then that is what the girl did: she laid them around while the bear sister, who was a deep sleeper, slept inside. The girl's hands moved around rapidly as she set the thorns of the thorn apple bush and cactus all around in the ground. She prepared everything in front of the entrance.

Then she came to where her brothers were. Then she said, "I'm finished doing it."

Then one young man said, "Now go there! Rush inside and say, 'The enemy is chasing me!' When you run out, go over there to the left. You must run up the hill. Your sister is going to head straight to the entrance. She's not going to see you. Now we're going to rush her. We'll kill her and then burn her."

And then that is what this girl did: she ran there. Then she ran inside where her sister was. Then she said, "The enemy is coming! They're chasing me!" Then she swung around and ran out.

And now the bear sister manifested her mysterious power as she jumped up angrily and ran outside. She ran on the cactus and apple thorns. Then as she rolled over growling, the young men cut off her toes. Then she lay still after they had killed her.

Then he said, "Quickly!"

Now they gathered wood which they brought. Then they set it on fire. Then they put her on top of the fire. And then they burned all around the spot while her body flopped around. They burned everything.

"Now let's flee! Let's go quickly! She's going to come."

Then they ran off. Then these young men put the girl in the lead. She led as they told her where to go: "You go there!"

Now they must have gone far. It was a long time later.

Then they said, "Now there she comes."

And there she came. Now there was no telling what had happened: some blood must have splashed onto the ground; wherever it was that the blood lay on the ground, it must not have burned. Then she chased them.

The bear woman was fast as she pursued them, especially because she was angry. Now she was gaining on them.

The eldest brother then said, "I'll do something to slow her up. She's catching up with us."

Now he threw an awl. And when he threw it where they had just come from, there was a thicket of thorn apple bushes. Oh, there was indeed a multitude of them! And as the bear woman came up against them, she started to look for a place to go through the thicket. She was barely able to pass through.

Now she came on. "There's no place where you're going to run to. I'm going to kill all of you."

Now the second brother threw a knife. Then it cut the ground open; it made cracks in the ground. And where the ground was cut open, the crack was very wide.

The bear woman nearly reached the top of the precipice. When she was about to climb up over the edge of it, she fell back. She fell to the bottom. She began to jump around.

Then she came up. Again she ran after them.

Why, now another brother threw something: a comb. And there there was a large cactus patch! When the bear woman reached it, she began jumping around as she went into it. She barely crossed it, too, as the thorns pricked her paws. Then she ran after them again.

While they were going, the youngest brother said, "Now we are dead."

Now he took a grooved stone, a black stone, the kind one would have to sharpen knives, and he said to it, "Now, grandfather, do something! Quickly! She's tired now, and I can't do anything with her."

And there there was a stone. It was so big around. Then they all stood on it. Then this stone grew upward. Then it expanded higher and higher.

Now after it was high up the bear arrived. She began jumping up, throwing herself against it so that she might knock it over. At first her claws reached the top of the stone, where they stood on top. But the stone got higher.

Then the stone said, "Don't be afraid. She isn't going to harm you, for the land slopes downward where we are standing. She isn't going to be able to knock it over."

Then the bear woman said, "Now you've outdone me. Now you are safe. Now I shall never see you again. But now I'll go in the other direction. I shall roam around over there, in the land over there in the west. You've outdone me."

Then the stone reached up against the sky there.

Now when people roamed around in that barren country they used to see it over there. The butte was the way it was when the bear woman jumped against it: there were claw marks on it. They used to say that one could not see the top of the butte.

Today, when airplanes fly over and people look down at it, there is something on top. It is white, whatever it is. But these [the girl and her brothers] went up into the sky. They are the five stars that are bunched up.

Now this is what I used to hear when they used to tell the story.

11

Corn Woman and Buffalo Woman

Arikaras believe that corn originated among them and that it subsequently spread to other tribes. Such peoples as the Teton Sioux and Omahas, who tell similar stories of its origin, support this tradition.[1] Indeed, corn was so integral to the life of the Arikaras that in the Plains sign language they were known as corn shellers. Certainly the cultivation of corn thoroughly permeated Arikara life, providing not only a major part of their subsistence but forming the most important symbolic element in their ritual life as well. Among the Arikaras and Pawnees, the veneration of corn culminated in the personification of the plant as Mother Corn, a spiritual manifestation of corn sent to earth as a woman by the Great Holy One, or Chief Above, to give the people food and assistance in times of distress.

There are two major mythic accounts of Mother Corn's role in Arikara history. In one, the origin story, she led the people out of the underworld and along their path of flight, after which she gave them their cultural institutions and moral teachings. In the other, exemplified in the account presented here, she revisited the people at a later time. The present narrative, however, is actually a concatenation of three separate stories: how the corn plant first came to the Arikaras; how Mother Corn, a personification of the plant, came to the tribe to save them during a period of starvation; and how Buffalo Woman, a human manifestation of the buffalo people, came to save the tribe during another period of starvation. The narrative thus presents a neatly balanced description of how in the past representatives of the two primary sources of subsistence—corn and buffalo—have come in human form to the Arikaras in times of need to give them succor.

---

1. An Omaha account recorded at the turn of the century, said to be of Arikara origin, is remarkably close to the first part of Mr. Morsette's version presented here (Fletcher and La Flesche 1911:76–78).

Now I am going to tell a story that I used to hear when they told stories. They are all dead now. I was interested in the old stories that they told—of what had happened when the people came this way from wherever it was that the villages used to be clustered when they were migrating this way upriver. There were many Arikaras then.

Now one time when a young man went hunting, when he was wandering around hunting, why, all at once he saw a buffalo! It stood far off on the prairie, on the level prairie. As he watched it, it stood there facing the east. Then, after searching for a way to get nearer, this boy thought, "Why, there is nowhere to hide so that I can get closer to where you are standing to shoot you!" Oh, then he gave up. Then he returned home. Then he arrived at the village, where the villages were clustered.

When morning came he went out again. Then he arrived where he had seen the buffalo standing. Now it was facing south. Oh, while he sought a way to get closer to where it stood, it was still too difficult for him! When it was sunset he came home.

Now again morning came and he went out. When he saw this buffalo, it was facing the other way: west. Oh, it was big! Then he thought, "How can I sneak up on you?" Then he gave up when it was too difficult for him. Then he came home.

Once again it was morning, and then he went out. He arrived there, and now it stood over there facing north. It seemed to see this young man as he ran furtively about, trying to sneak up on it to shoot it. He gave up. "Why, it's impossible for me." He came home; he arrived where he lived.

Then he thought, "Why don't I go to where I have been seeing the buffalo!"

It was no longer standing there. Then he arrived there. Now he looked all around. There were tracks where it had stood. Something was growing there. There was a clump of stalks growing here, and also over there, and also in the middle. After he looked at them, he came home.

Then he told people, "Something has happened. I tried to sneak around a buffalo that was standing there. Oh, the land was level where it stood. It was impossible for me to get close to where it

stood. Now, look, I just now went there, and a clump of stalks is
growing there, whatever they are. These things that are growing,
whatever they are, are puzzling."

Then he gathered the holy men, the leading priests, the ones
who had the holy ways. Then they went there to look at them. "Say,
they are something. We don't know what these growing things are,
these stalks growing in a clump."

Then they drove sticks into the ground to fence them off so that
the buffalo and antelope roaming around would not eat them. "Let
them grow! Let them grow up so that we can find out what they are
going to be," they said as they watched over them.

Now in midsummer something strange was there: ears of corn
were growing on the stalks standing there. When they looked at
them they did not know what they were. And one man said, "I'll try
it. Let me eat one of them! Let's see what happens to me. I'll cook
it, since it appears that one must cook it."

Then they made a fire. Then this man began to roast it. Here it
was green corn. "Surely it's cooked now." Then he took a bite as he
sat there and ate it. "Why, say, it tastes good!" Then he gave one of
them another ear; then he gave each one of them an ear.

"Why, say, this is something! It's edible. Now let it grow up!"

Then as they watched over it, the corn got fully ripe. I do not
know what happened when they discovered that it was corn, but
then they divided it up among the people. After they shelled it, they
divided it up. "In the spring you shall plant it as it was; you shall
do it thus, the way it was when it was growing. Then put soil over
it."

Now then that is what they did: when spring came, when the
green grass came up, he said, "Plant what I gave you!" And then
that is what they did.

Now it was not a long time before clumps grew here and there,
sprouting as they had seen them do before. Then ears hung from
the stalks.

Now that is where the corn increased. After people gave it to
one another and after they planted it, the corn increased as the
people migrated this way upriver. They had corn. Oh, it tasted good!

≺   »

Now I don't know how they happened to acquire squash and beans, and what are called ground beans.[2] But the ground bean is different. Now what I have told here is the limit of my knowledge.

« « «   » » »

Now, sometime after corn had appeared among us, while this one man, one who was holy, was sitting there examining this ear of corn, he said to his wife, "Say, make a dress, a woman's dress! Then put the dress on this ear of corn! I just have a notion that she is holy. It just appears that I'm seeing a woman."

Then this woman, his wife, made a dress. Then she clothed it. Then she put a shawl on it, and wrapped it around the ear.

Then he took it to the Missouri River and said, "Now I'm going to name you as a relative. Now you are my Mother. Now make haste! Come back quickly!" Then he threw her into the water. She floated downstream.

Now sometime later they saw a woman. They did not know who she was as she went among the people. She just came. They did not know who she was.

Now the priests sought her out. "Call this young woman who is going around so that we can see who she is and where she came from!"

Now they got things ready. Then they called her. The young woman came into the lodge. Then she sat down. They did not recognize her.

Now, wherever the man who had dressed the ear of corn had been, he entered. Why, he said, "Hah, my wife made the dress for this young woman and I put it on her. And I called out to her, 'I want you to be among us so that we may know you. We shall call you Mother from now on, since from my observation you are a

2. Ground beans (*Amphicarpa bracteata*), also called hog peanuts, are both aerial and underground beanlike seeds that were gathered and used as a food item, especially during the winter, by Arikaras and other Plains tribes.

woman.' Now this is the one."

Then this young woman said, "Now you are right. You are the one who sent me floating downstream. What you have said is the way it is—I have come here. Now I have come back so that you may know: now I am the one, your Mother. You have found me. Here on earth different things will appear: the green grass coming up, and the corn when it has been planted. Now I am the one who has come onto this earth. You see the Big Holy One in the sky. He is the one. All these different things are what He put here. This one whom you call your Father is the one: He is your Father. But you are mine. I am the one, your Mother."

Now this is the end of the story of this young woman when she was going among the people.

It was sometime later, a long time later. It was one of those years when there is no rain, when everything is dry, when the grass barely comes up because there is no rain.

Then this young woman said—after she prayed to the powers, she said, "I will do something for you. Before morning comes, when the sun has not yet risen, at dawn, then you will have things ready. Open your cache pits! Clean the ground! Clean the interior of the pits! Now I am going to pass by them. Now you are going to tell me where you store your corn. You must tell me which ones are the kinds of corn you value most among the ones you plant.[3]

"Now this is what I am going to do: I will pass by there. Early in the morning, before the sun has risen, when the crier calls out, when he announces it, you will know that I am going to start out as I said. You women who are heads of households, stand where your cache pits are, telling me where your cellars are. That is why I am going."

Then that is what this young woman did. "Now what do you have in your cache pit here?" she would ask.

"This is where I store my white corn, yellow corn, blue corn, red corn, and squash."

"Now cover it!"

3. Will and Hyde (1917:299–300) give a provisional list of eleven varieties of corn grown by Arikaras.

Then she would cover it over. Then the young woman would pass by.

After the young woman finished, she entered the Medicine Lodge. Then she said to the crier, "Now after four days have passed you can announce, 'Open up your storage pits to see what I have done for you.' Now that is what you will do!"

Well, then this man called out, "You now know that in the morning each of you will go to where you have your storage pit. Open it up! Now this is what is yours."

Then they were very anxious, so they got up. Then each woman went to her cache pit, and there there were plenty of different kinds of corn, just as the crier had said. Oh, they all became lively, and then they planted again. Then they all became lively again when the ears of corn were whole and the corn could be shelled.

Now this is what she said, "I am the corn that you are going to shell. Wherever there is a stalk with an ear of corn on it, I am that corn. Now I am Mother, the one who leads us. That is why I hurried when I returned, just as this man, the one who clothed me, planned for me to do."

« ‹ «   » › »

Now while they were migrating this way, the people began seeing a young woman. They did not know her, either. Now this is what she did: she did not eat meat, or dried meat; but she ate corn, squash, plums, chokecherries, and wild artichokes. She did not eat meat. Now the other one, Corn Woman—Mother Corn—did not eat corn. This was the difference between them.

Now things became difficult when the buffalo did not come near the village, when they did not roam close by—when, alas, a famine occurred.

Then this young woman said, "Now I am the one who came in the herd. I like being among you people, eating this corn, eating this green corn. I prize it. I do know that you are getting short on meat, which you value most. Now I want you to make me four pairs of moccasins so that I may do something for you."

Now a woman who knew how to make moccasins sat down. She finished them. "Now here are the moccasins." Also another pair.

Then they went into the Medicine Lodge. After they had prayed
to the powers and had offered smoke, then she said, "Now I am
going. I am starting out."

There where the four upright lodge posts were, there on the left
on the other side, she started out, going and going. Then she arrived
at the post there, where she took her moccasins off. The ones she
had worn were worn out.

Then she put another pair on her feet. Now again she did the
same thing: she also did it, going to that post there. She got to it
and took her moccasins off. The moccasins were worn out.

Then she put on another pair. Well, then she did it: she got to
the other post and, as she had been doing, she arrived there with
ragged moccasins.

She put a different pair on her feet and then she did it: she
arrived [at the post] where she had started from. She sat down.
They offered smoke.

She said, "Now I have gone all over this world.[4] The buffalo
have gone far, far off in different directions. I have seen my grandfather and grandmother. Now I did beg them, the poor things, to
cause the buffalo to move closer toward here where we are living.
Here where I am going among you people I appreciate being able to
eat fresh corn, corn balls, and squash.

"Now, after four days have passed, pick out four young men,
four who know how to hunt. Before the sun has yet risen, they
should run up that long hill and look all around to see if the buffalo
have come.

"Now listen. Now I am tired. I have been *all* over the land."

Four days passed; then they picked them. "Now, we have faith
in this one. This one is dependable." Also another, and another.
"Now you are going to go up the long hill, this long hill. You can see
whatever is going on in the village."

Well, then they ran up the hill. Oh my, the buffalo had drawn
near! Then they began to call out, shouting, "Now there's a multi-

---

4. Although the spectators see Buffalo Woman walk only from post to
post, her spirit actually travels throughout the world searching for the
buffalo. Her spirit's travels are represented by the four pairs of worn-out
moccasins.

tude of them! There's a large herd of them!"

Then the men mounted, then they rode up the hill, and then they attacked them. They killed the buffalo, and then they ate their fill of the meat.

So this Corn Woman, when she ate, her favorite food was meat, and dried meat—that is what she herself liked. But this other one ate corn and corn balls.

Now this Buffalo Woman said: "I face the west as I travel. That land over there is my favorite." This one used to come from the west. That is where she came from. "I face that way. No matter how long it takes, we will continue to go that way. If you turn me around, if you face me the other way, toward the east, it will not last a long time—the village will not last after I die."[5]

Now, this is the end of what the old timers used to tell. Now what I have told is what I used to hear. There is no one living who knows—who knows the story. I was interested in things, in what I heard when they used to tell stories.

12

The Boy and the Hoop Game
of the Buffalo

In Arikara and Pawnee mythology the hoop and pole game is derived from buffalo. In some stories two young bulls turned into the first set of poles, or javelins, and a buffalo cow turned herself into the first hoop; in others a

---

5. Here Buffalo Woman ordains that the Arikara people, if they are to survive, must always travel in a northwestward direction and that the buffalo skull in the Medicine Lodge must face the west, the direction from which the buffalo come.

*man was directed in a dream to wrap two poles with strips
of tanned buffalo hide and to cover a hoop with a cow's
vulva. The hoop and poles, moreover, are frequently associated with buffalo calling rituals.*

*In this Arikara story there is the same association of the
game with buffalo, but the game is already in existence, and
the symbolism is somewhat different. A chief's son wants a
hoop with which to play the hoop and pole game, and so a
male buffalo—the chief's spiritual benefactor—changes himself into one to become the boy's companion. In the ensuing
drama several widespread mythological themes are combined to develop the plot. One is the motif of the stealing of
light, in which a hoop usually represents the sun (cf. story
1). In this story first Coyote and then mice steal the hoop
and take it to another world below this one. Three animals—
Mole, Shrew, and Badger—enable the chief's son to get to
that underground world by boring a passage through the
earth, a motif found in the Arikara origin story. Once in the
other world, Bloody Hands and his grandmother appear as
characters to aid the chief's son to regain his hoop. In its
conclusion the story becomes one of power bestowal, the
theme of most Arikara stories, in which here the buffalo
resumes his animal form but promises to watch over the boy
and help him achieve whatever he might wish in the future.*

*The narrator learned this story from his father, John
Morsette, who in turn had learned it from Red Corn Woman.
Mr. Morsette noted that he had never witnessed the game,
and from his description of it here it is unclear which of the
two variants that were found among the Arikara—one using
a hoop and poles, another employing a ring and barbed
darts or arrows (Culin 1907:420–41, 461–69)—is referred to
in this story. The narrator calls the projectiles "arrows."*

It was many winters long, long ago when the old man, my
father, told this story to us when he would come to our home to stay
for a few days. He had many stories that he told—ones that he had
heard—including this one that I am going to tell.

«   »

One man had a boy who wanted a hoop—who kept asking him for a hoop. "Father, make a hoop for me! I want to have a hoop."

And so the man went out. Then he went to look for a hoop since his son wanted to have one. It was the kind of hoop used in the hoop and pole game. I don't know whether it was a large or small one.

Now this man had been blessed by a buffalo, one that was four winters old. Now it said to him, "I'll be the one. I'll be friends with your son. We'll play the hoop and pole game. I'm like he is: I like the game very much. That's what I want: that the boy I'm going to be friends with and I win prizes."

Now this buffalo turned itself into a hoop. It was a buffalo, a male buffalo four winters old.

Then the man brought it home. Then he said, "Now, my son, it's good for you to have this hoop. The two of you are to be friends. This hoop is holy. The hoop is holy. When you play hoop and pole and have had enough of the game, bring it home. Then set it down nicely. And don't just throw it around."

And so that is what the boy did, taking good care of the hoop when he played the hoop and pole game. Then he took prizes whenever he played.

Now there were people who were jealous when this boy won prizes. Mischievous Coyote was one. During one game he lay down near the point where the hoop was always thrown and would come to a stop.

After the hoop was thrown, two men, one on each side, would throw an arrow, trying to send it through the hoop. When the hoop stopped, the arrow that lay closest to it was the winner.

But now Coyote Chief, the one who always plays pranks, lay there close by the goal watching the boy win various prizes for himself. Coyote lay there close to the spot where the hoop stopped after it had rolled. Then he put it over his head. Then he ran off with it while the players looked for it. Oh, it had disappeared.

Coyote—Mischievous Coyote—ran off with it. Oh, after he had gone so far, Coyote, being tired, lay down on the side of a hill. He had the hoop around his neck while he slept.

Well, then some mice stole the hoop that Coyote had around his neck. The mice stole the hoop. Then they took it under the ground. There must have been another country down below.

Coyote awoke. He did not have the hoop around his neck. Now he darted around anxiously as he looked for it. "Oh, where could I have dropped it? Oh, I certainly had it around my neck when I lay down." That was what he thought.

Meanwhile the boy began to search for his hoop, standing on different hills crying as he mourned for his lost hoop. Well, then he went up one hill, and, oh, as he cried someone said, "Why don't you come in? Whoever you are, you're causing dirt to drop down all over."

Then the boy went down the hill, and as he was looking all around a door just opened into the ground. There was a lodge there. He entered it. There sat a woman.

"Why, grandson, you who have come from far away, now sit down!" Then she cooked dried meat for him. "Why, my grandson is hungry!"

Then she said, "Ah, grandson, you have come from such a *long* way off! I know the reason. Now, we'll do it for you—we'll give you a blessing. We'll help you achieve what you want. Now, farther on your grandmother has her home. She is going to be eager to help. I'll go right over there."

And then she told the boy, "Now go! If you cry like you were doing, she'll call you."

Then the young man went out. Then he went to a hill over there. Then he went up it and cried like she had said.

"Oh, why don't you come inside? You're causing dirt to drop down on us. I have some meat boiling." That is what she was saying over and over.

Then the boy went down the hill. As he was looking all around for the door, there it was. "Over here!" Then the two women took him inside.

"Hey, grandson, you who have come from far away, now sit down! You must eat."

Then they fed him while they, too, ate.

"Grandson, I know what you're after. Now, your grandmother has a home over there. You go over there to her! Now meanwhile we'll go over there, too." The first grandmother whom the boy had visited previously had already arrived. "She and I will go right over there, too. We'll follow behind you. Over there you'll learn the truth. We're going to reveal what you want to know—where your friend is. He feels the same way you do: he's tired in spirit and he's hungry. We must hurry!"

Well, then he went there. Then he arrived.

Then she said, "Hey, whoever you are who is a visitor, you're causing dirt to drop down all over. Come in quickly!"

Then the door opened. Then she led him inside. Oh, there sat a woman. She said, "Ah, grandson, you have come from such a long way off!"

Meanwhile the two women whom he had previously visited had already arrived. Now there were three of them as well as the boy.

Then this third woman said, "We'll do it right away, here where my home is. We'll start from here. Your friend is near here."

Now there were three of them: Mole, Shrew, and Badger. Now these sitting here were the grandmothers of this boy.

Then Badger said, "Now I'll be the first one." Then she went into the ground, boring a hole and going in and in. The others followed behind her as she tunneled her way.

Then she said, "Now one of *you* go on! You do this, too! Let me rest for a while!"

Then another one, Mole, took her turn.

Oh, and then the other one, Shrew, did the same thing, too, boring through the earth as she went.

And then it was the boy's turn to bore through the earth.

Now each of the four had had a turn. Then one of the grand-mothers said, "Grandson, we have gone through to the village. Now be smart! That one will quickly calm down when he's told what's happening."

When the boy emerged he changed his form. (I have forgotten what he turned into.)

And there they were playing the hoop and pole game. The hoop they were throwing was the one: it was the hoop he was looking for.

When the hoop came to where he was, he said, "My brother, I have come here."

Then that hoop said, "Yes, I know. I know that you have come. Oh, I'm starving to death! I haven't eaten anything yet. When they take me inside, they hang me up. I'm not able to eat anything. I'm hungry. Now hurry!"

Then the game ended. Then they set the hoop down. Now they watched over it.

Meanwhile the boy watched where they took it. Oh, there he stood on a hill with the entire village extending in sight over there. And there at the end of the village smoke was coming out. The smoke was wafting upward.

Then the boy went over there. He went onto a knoll. There was a boy there. He was playing. Then he went to where the boy was, and then he said, "Ah, I've been watching you here."

And then this boy asked, "Who are you?"

The one who had just come there said, "I'm just wandering around. Let's play."

Then this short boy, Bloody Hands, said, "Let me tell my grand-mother first!"

He ran inside. He said, "Grandma, there's a boy wandering around who wants me to play with him."

And then his grandmother said, "Hey, they always fool you. Then they whip you. Then they make you cry. Be careful!"

Then Bloody Hands went back and said, "My grandma said, 'They always whip you after they fool you.'"

The other boy said, "I certainly won't do that. I'm just wandering around. I had no place to go when I came here. We'll be companions. I want us to be brothers."

Then Bloody Hands ran inside. Then he said, "Grandma, he says, 'I don't have any place to go to stay overnight, and I came here. I want us to be brothers—for us to be together with your grandma, for all of us to live together. I'll help you two in various ways.'"

"Well, now that's fine. Bring him inside!"

Then they all lived together.

Now the old woman, whoever she was, was holy.

Then she said, "Hey, you two eat!" Then she set boiled dried sweet corn down for them.

And then they all lay down to sleep.

Then Bloody Hands said, "Grandma, he wants us to sleep together."

"Hey, you are a bed wetter. Don't urinate on him!"

Then he said, "My grandmother says, 'You're a bed wetter. Don't urinate on the brother you have now!'"

Then he said, "That doesn't matter." Why, now this boy was also holy.

After they had told various stories, Bloody Hands said, "I have to urinate."

The boy then said, "Now wait! You'll get cured of this bed wetting."

Then he went and took some ashes. Then he rubbed the ashes on Bloody Hands's abdomen. "Now you'll get over it."

Then he did not wet the bed.

It was morning. "Well, I suppose you wet the bed, Bloody Hands."

"Grandma, this boy doctored me. I didn't wet the bed."

Oh, his grandmother was thankful. "Why, it's certainly a good thing!"

He said, "Nothing must ever happen here where you people live."

Then Bloody Hands replied, "Yes, I'll tell you. Our chief has a young son. He wanted a hoop. And Coyote brought one—one that he stole. He brought it here. Then it was taken from him. He had wanted them to buy it, but they just took it from him. They stole it. Now our chief has it."

They had brought it here for him—the ones who lived above [in the other world] are the ones who had brought that hoop. This boy was the one. He was the one—this one looking for it.

Then he said, "Say, the story you have told is good." He asked, "Where is the lodge where they keep it?"

Then Bloody Hands answered, "There in the middle of the village is where they keep it. It's hanging there where the medicines [i.e., the sacred bundle] hang.[1] Oh, they watch it carefully."

Now the boy decided to tell him. So he said, "That hoop you told about is what I have come for. Now that's what I came for. I'm the owner of the hoop." That is what he told Bloody Hands.

Then he said, "Grandma, this boy has come from where they live at the end of the sky, and he has come for the hoop that they have here. That's the reason he came here. He wants us to get it so that he can take it home."

Now the old woman said, "Hey, grandson, I'll do something for you now myself, since you cured my grandson when you doctored him for his bed wetting. You made him well. Now I'll do something for you in turn. Now I'll take the hoop from them. Now I'll get it."

Then she said, "Now, you two here, be ready! When I bring it back, you two are going to run away with it. If they catch up with us, all of us will die. They'll kill all of us here. Now to the best of my ability I'm going to try to bring it back."

Then she continued, "I'll go there first. I'll observe everything. I'll observe things where they always keep the hoop hanging. And then when I go back there a second time, I'll pick it up. Now you two be ready!"

Then this old woman, their grandmother, went there. She went to visit at the lodge of their chief. Oh, the family was happy to see her, but meanwhile she was observing everything. There the chief had the hoop hanging. She looked all around the area where it hung in order to determine what to do when she returned to get it. She took note of everything. Then she came home.

Bloody Hands said, "Grandma, what did you learn?"

She said, "I'll get it. I now know what to do when I get there where it's hanging. Now, you two be ready! You two will take it from here. You two are going to go where you came from. You'll change yourselves back into little boys." They were both young men now.

Then, after everyone had gone to bed, the old woman went there. While the family had told stories [on her earlier visit], she had observed everything. Now she changed herself into a mouse.

---

1. A reference to the chief's lodge in the center of the village, in which the sacred bundle hung.

Then she ran along the wall to where it hung.

"Now, my grandson came after you."

The old woman ran out with it into the dark. She took it to where her two grandsons were waiting.

Then they took the hoop, and then the old woman went to her lodge.

[At the chief's lodge they discovered what had happened.] "Oh, the hoop has disappeared! It's been stolen!"

Then they set out to search for it in the morning. But Bloody Hands and the boy had already run away with it.

Then Bloody Hands turned back. "Now, my brother, go on! When everything dies down, I'll be a handsome young man like you are."

Now, meanwhile, as the searchers went through the village, they said, "There was a boy living here. Where did he go?"

"Oh, I don't know where he went. He just wanders around."

Then Bloody Hands returned.

"Where did your friend go?"

"Say, I don't know where he went. Why, I'm not friends with anyone. When I'm together with anyone, I always get whipped." Now he was acting pitifully.

They gave up their search.

Now the young man passed beyond the boundary of that country back there [as he brought the hoop back to where his three grandmothers were].

"Now, grandmas, you have pleased me by doing all that you have done for me. Now my brother [the hoop] and I are going back."

Then he came back up to this earth.

"Now, brother, go back to your range!"

He threw the hoop. And then a male buffalo jumped up. It was lean from hunger.

While it began grazing, it said, "Brother, you have saved me. When I get full, I'll go to where my uncles, my father, and my mother roam. But I'll watch over you. Whatever you desire will come to pass."

«   »

Then the boy went on. Then he went home. Then he went inside.

Then he said, "Mother, make a fire! I've returned."

Then she said, "Oh, why, they're making fun of me!"

The father of the boy said, "Ah, you have nothing now, old woman. Get up! Make a fire! Our son died. We had only the one."

Then the woman arose. Then she made a fire, and there sat the young man, her son.

Then he said, "Father, mother, I was looking for my brother, the poor thing, after my hoop disappeared. And I've found him. This is what happened.

"And now he's gone back to his range, where he roams. Now he's gone back. He who was mine must have been starving to death while he was in the form of the hoop. But he told me that he would watch over me wherever I go, and whatever I desire will come to pass."

Now, this is the end of the story.

Narratives of the Past

Of Power Bestowed

13

When the Bears Attacked the Arikaras

Several times early in their history, according to tradition, the Arikara villages were attacked by hordes of a particular animal species—buffalo, bear, and snake—just as at an even earlier period humans were the victims of the animal world at large. In two accounts of such attacks—one by bears and another by snakes—the animals' aggression was precipitated by human passion and a lack of judicious restraint. In the story presented here, a young man discovers that his wife is meeting another young man in her garden and having intercourse with him. When the outraged husband shoots the young man, his wife's paramour turns out to be a bear—in fact, the favored child of the bear people. Although the Arikaras are able to repulse the subsequent attack on their village by a horde of bears seeking revenge, the husband is doomed never to find power or have good fortune in war. For Arikaras the irony of this incident lies in the fact that the bear, by having intercourse with the young man's wife, is thereby giving the husband power; but because he shoots the bear out of jealousy, the man never again is able to obtain it. The story illustrates a general Plains Indian belief in the transmission of power from one man (or animal) to another through sexual intercourse with the recipient's wife.

Now I am going to tell another story. It is not really a long one. It is what I used to hear from my grandmother, who was the one who told us the story.

It occurred long, long ago, somewhere along the way when the Arikaras—the ones I am telling about—were migrating this way upriver.

There was a nice-looking young woman who had a garden in the brush. That is where the women used to have their gardens—in the brush. It is not known whether this incident occurred near where we are living today [or whether it happened when we were farther downriver].

Now this young woman would be in her garden planting corn, squash, and beans. There were no potatoes at that time when they used to hoe their gardens. Her husband would wait for her to return from the garden, and it would be late at night before she at last came back to the lodge.

"Ah, you sure must have a big garden!" The man did not like what the woman was doing. When the women and young women would come up from their gardens in the brush, the sun would already have set when they returned home, but this man's wife would not have started to come back. Oh, it got dark. Then at last she would appear. That is what she was doing all the time.

Meanwhile this young man did not like it. He thought, "I wonder what you're doing."

Then this young woman would get up really early in the morning again. She would go off into the brush to her garden.

And this young man did not like what his wife must be doing. So one day he took his bow and arrows and lay in wait for her.

As soon as the young woman got up, she did as she always did: she got up really early in the morning, and then she went out. She went off. Then her husband jumped up from bed. Then he sneaked after his wife as she went along. Then she went down into the bottomlands, oh, as he secretly followed her and watched her.

Oh, then someone came out of the brush by the garden. There at a distance in the garden sat a young man. Then this young woman went there, and, oh, they embraced each other where this young man sat in the garden. Then the two of them went off. They went into the brush.

Meanwhile the real husband of this young woman followed at a distance when the two went into the brush. Now the young man lay on top of the young woman and was having intercourse with her. And then the husband came out of the brush with his bow and arrows. He shot this bear several times. And here the young man having intercourse with the young woman was a bear when he jumped up screaming!

Then her husband said, "And here this is what you are doing when you come here! I'm going to punish that one." Then he shot the bear repeatedly until the arrows were sticking out of him as he ran in the brush.

And then the young man drove the young woman ahead of him as he was whipping her and whipping her. Then he drove her out of the brush.

Then he said, "You are not going to come back to where I live. You can go wherever you want to go. You have not treated me well after I have been supporting you. And here this is what you have been doing!"

Now when he was shooting it, why, here he discovered it was a bear! It had turned into a white bear—a white bear, a bear that was white all over. He must not have killed it. He must only have wounded it in various spots when he was shooting it with arrows. But now, the bear was holy. Then it just disappeared.

Then sometime later it became foggy. Then this young man, as he was going around, was warned by a bird, whatever kind it was. It said, "They have sent me to tell you what you did when you wounded the bear. He is the beloved child [of the bear people]. Now from all over the entire country the bears are coming here to your village. They're going to kill all of you. But now I have told you. You are numerous! There certainly are many of you people. Get all of yourselves together! Put up a palisade! Put a palisade up around your village! Make it strong! The bears are coming. There's a horde of them. Now get your arrows ready! You're going to battle the bears."

Well, then that is what this young man did. Then he came home. Then he told his father. Then he began to call out from the top of his lodge.

Then the people of this village were willing to do what he said. Then they put up a palisade. It had four rows of posts. Now this village—the entire village—was ready. The young men and the older men made arrows in order to be ready. "Use them freely when the bears come!"

Then it became foggy. There were two days of fogginess. Everyone was uneasy. It was getting dark. And here it was the breathing of the bears when they were coming! Here the bears were the ones causing it to be foggy by their breathing!

Then the people said, "They must have arrived."

Oh, a large horde of bears arrived and came against the palisade while the people in the village were shooting them and, oh, killing the bears. <They kept shooting and shooting; they kept killing them and killing them. And the bears knocked down the outer row of the palisade and then the second one.>

Now only one row of the palisade remained to be knocked down. But there were many bears killed and wounded by the shooting.

Finally one bear said, "There are certainly a lot of us, but we haven't accomplished anything, the way we thought we would! They have beat us. Now, those of us who remain, let's withdraw!"

And then the bears retreated. But now there were carcasses lying all around.

And then this young man said to his father, "Now announce this: they can butcher these bears. They're the ones who took my wife away. They took my woman."

And so that is what he did. "Butcher them! These bears lying here are meat."

Now this is what happened.

Well, then misfortune befell this young man whenever he thought that he would do something. And so he had no success on the warpath. He was not able to find anything for himself. Everything that he attempted was a failure for him as his life progressed. Well, he never was able to get married again, either.

That woman—and, through her, the bear—was the cause when she brought on misfortune for him. The bear took his wife in order to bless him, but this young man did not allow it. He did not like what was being done. Whether he killed the bear, I don't know. And then this woman died from grief. She did not feel right about what had happened to the bear.

◄   ≫

Now this that I have told is the story.

14

The Foolish Ones Who Killed the Beloved Snake Child

Most Plains tribes had a society or group of men who acted by doing the opposite of what they were bidden. This contrary behavior was found, for example, in the Children of the Iruska Society of the Pawnees, the Heyoka of the Sioux, the Fool dancers of the Assiniboines, and the Contrary (or Bowstring) warriors of the Cheyennes. Among the Arikaras these men were known as Foolish Ones (sakhuúnu'), a term that connotes reckless, crazy, or foolish behavior—behavior, that is not socially normal or acceptable. At any one time there were never more than two men who were sakhuúnu'. Besides being fearless, Foolish Ones were reputed to have strong medicine and thus to be good doctors.

This story continues the theme of animal aggression from the preceding narrative. Here its cause is a lack of respect for what is holy. Arikaras feared snakes, believing them to have mysterious power, and consequently avoided them. In this incident, however, a pair of Foolish Ones recklessly kills a small snake that all the other members of a returning hunting party have encountered on the trail and cautiously bypassed. This snake, like the bear in the preceding story, is the favored, or beloved, child of the snake people—a chief's son. As a result of the killing, the Arikara village is attacked by a horde of snakes. Although the two Foolish Ones are able to fight them off, the story illustrates the consequences of antisocial behavior, particularly a disregard for the holy.

This story was told to the narrator by his grandfather Short
Bear. In 1910 Robert Lowie recorded a nearly identical
version from Bear's Teeth.

Now I am going to tell a story that happened long, long ago
when mysterious things used to occur. I surely don't know that it
happened; it is what I used to hear when someone told it. Now my
grandfather [Short Bear]—the one who reared me—was the one I
heard it from when he told this story that I am going to relate.

It happened somewhere long, long ago when our people were
moving up the Missouri River. I do not know the location, but I will
relate the story as I heard it.

Now it happened when all the people were out on a communal
buffalo hunt, wherever it was that they were roving about after the
buffalo had withdrawn from the vicinity of the village. The people
were still doing that long ago, going on communal buffalo hunts.
Now it occurred this way: they had traveled around camping here
and there until they had got enough meat. [Then they said,] "Now
let's go back to our village!" Meanwhile there were people living
alone in the village, ones who had been left behind and remained
living there alone.

Then they returned <toward the middle of summer>. Then they
were coming back as a group. Now they had just about reached the
outskirts of the village, and there lay a snake coiled up in the
middle of the trail, guarding it. That is what I used to hear.

Now we are afraid of snakes. So the party was bypassing it,
going around it so that they would not disturb it where it lay coiled
as they traveled by. They were going into the village there.

Now there were two young men who were what they used to
call Foolish Ones. They did things differently whenever they did
anything. If someone said, "Get angry!" they would not get angry.
But when someone said, "Don't get angry!" then they would get
angry. They would start charging about after turning around to
fight, just as if it were the enemy who used to count coups on us
long ago when there were intertribal battles all over. Both of these
young men were fierce.

When the two of them were coming along, there that snake was, lying coiled on the trail. "I don't see why they're afraid of it. There's nothing to fear." Then they killed the snake. And here it was the favored child of the snakes, the one that they killed!

Then they went on into the village.

Now sometime later when the young men were out watching the horses, there on the surrounding hills everything was shining brightly. When the sun came up the surrounding hills shone.

"Now whatever might it be?"

And then those two Foolish Ones said, "Now, all of you here in the village, hurry! Make a palisade with four rows of poles. Get things prepared really well! What you see there shining on the ground are snakes. I think something mysterious must be happening." These two were the ones who were the cause, but they were not telling about it. "Now those are snakes that are shining on the ground. They're coming to attack."

Ah, then everyone in this village became excited as they went about erecting the palisade and tightening the posts so that no snake might crawl through. Ah, they got things prepared!

"Now get yourselves ready! Have some sticks ready to hit on the head the ones that are going to come through the palisade. The snakes aren't going to be careful."

But these two Foolish Ones themselves were fierce when they began killing the snakes outside the palisade, shooting them with arrows from their bows.

Now over there the same thing was occurring. There were many snakes, a multitude of them. Then they started coming over the palisade where the poles were crossed. Whenever someone was bitten by a snake, he was killed.

And then the snakes started coming into the earth lodges where people were inside, coming through the smokeholes and crawling through any cracks in the walls. Now innumerable people were killed!

Meanwhile these two Foolish Ones were going back and forth doing away with many of the snakes, killing the ones that were biting them, that were biting their legs.

And then the two went. Then they went into the Medicine Lodge, where the sacred objects were inside. Then they restored the flesh to their legs, the way they had been before, and then they went back out and killed a huge number of snakes again. <After they had killed many of them, ones that bit the flesh off their legs, they went back into the Medicine Lodge, where their flesh was again restored. I don't know how many times they did that, whether four times or more.>

Then many people, the poor things, died as each one was crying. Their sounds ceased after they died, when the snakes did away with our people.

Now these two Foolish Ones climbed up onto a drying scaffold. Then they sat down back to back. They faced in opposite directions, each young man hitting a snake on the head as it came up. The snakes dropped down, one after another. Then they killed a multitude of them, killing them and killing them. Then the dead bodies of the snakes were piled up.

Now the snakes became frightened. "Why, we can't do anything to these two boys! They are exceedingly holy! We haven't hurt them at all. Now let's retreat far away from here!"

Now whatever snakes were remaining, they withdrew. They crawled away.

Now these two Foolish Ones went into the Medicine Lodge, where they sang their holy song; and where the flesh on their legs had been bitten off, there their legs were, restored just as they had been before!

Now, the two Foolish Ones came among the bodies of the dead and injured, the pitiful ones who had been bitten by the snakes. "Now get up! They've gone. The snakes have withdrawn."

The dead people got up, for these two boys were holy. The two made the village alive again. Then they also dug holes for burying the dead snakes.

"Now, you people, get yourselves ready! Let's move to a different location!"

And then that is what they did: all the people in the village got themselves ready. Then they moved off as a group. Now they began to head toward the west, here where we now live.

Now this is what I used to hear when I listened to what they told. Now this is what happened.

15

Hidden Man and the Two Holy Men

A poor boy living with his grandmother is the protagonist of this story. Social outcasts, he and his grandmother choose not to accompany the people on their communal winter buffalo hunt but to return instead to remain alone in the permanent earth lodge village. There the boy is pitied by two strange men who name him Hidden Man. These men are in reality stars, but are related to the buffalo on earth. (Hence they eat only horticultural products—corn and squash—but not meat; and they remain out of sight during the buffalo slaughter.) They cure Hidden Man's father-in-law, save the people from starvation, and kill an evil man who has enslaved Hidden Man as well as Big Star, the leader of the buffalo herd that has come to the village. The story thereby combines the themes of curing, buffalo calling, and triumph over abuse of supernatural power to explain the name of a poor boy who acquires celestial benefactors, enabling him to perform good deeds.

This story, like many others told by Arikaras, is nearly identical to one told by Hidatsas. Both groups claim the story as their own. Although they have shared a reservation for more than a century and have increasingly intermarried, Arikaras and Hidatsas have maintained distinct cultures and tribal identities. Yet they have inevitably borrowed much from one another, especially apparent in oral traditions. In a Hidatsa version of this narrative recorded from Bear's Arm in 1929 by Martha Beckwith, Hidden Man has the name Unknown One, while the two star fathers are referred to as Two Men but are identified as Lodge Boy and Spring Boy, the Hidatsa counterparts of the Arikara characters Long Teeth and Drinks Brain Soup (see stories 4, 63, and 155). The exploits of Lodge Boy and Spring Boy, however, are primarily told in other Hidatsa stories, and their association with the two star fathers seems adventitious.

Now I am going to tell a story. It is about a personal name from long, long ago when the people were coming this way. It is what I heard from my grandmother—what she told. Also I heard it from someone else. It was the same story that he told; I think it was Ray Gough. I think it is the same story that my grandmother always used to tell—about when they gave this name Hidden Boy to the boy they found, because the boy and his grandmother were poor. They lived in an earth lodge, living in it by themselves [on the outskirts of the village].

<It was in the fall, when it was getting cold.> Then the chiefs in this village planned it: "Let's go somewhere far off, where the buffalo have gone! The buffalo aren't close by around here now. They must have gone far off. Also the deer are diminishing in number. There aren't any around. They must have gone far off. Now let's all go as a group to a different place! And then we'll come back; we'll return here when spring comes."

And then they got themselves ready. Then they were going to leave the village as a group.

Now this boy and his grandmother, the poor things. . . . <They were getting along. The boy was about fourteen winters old. He would go out to hunt prairie chickens and rabbits, and his grandmother had a supply of corn, squash, beans, and chokecherries. They were getting along.>

Then the hunting trip was organized. There were the marshals, the "forbidders," who enforced the rules. That is what I used to hear. But today they call the ones who watch over things "scouts." Now that was the position for the young men who were fearless, who were brave warriors, when the village traveled.

"Now we are leaving. We are going to go off somewhere. After setting out, if anyone wishes to turn back, these soldiers are the enforcers. They will come and kill your dog, the one you have. Even if you have a bunch, say thirteen, they'll kill all of yours." Now this was the custom.

Then the people left as a group. Meanwhile this old woman—the grandmother—and the boy decided to go. "Well, let's go! There is no choice. We have only our one dog, and they might kill it. A soldier might kill our dog that carries wood for us."

And then they followed behind the group as it went off after the weather was cold in late fall. After leaving the village, they traveled for however many days it was.

Now, but the boy who lived with his grandmother—then he said to her, "Hey, grandma, let's turn back! It's nice where we live in our lodge and I always go around hunting and we eat cottontail rabbits or prairie chickens. But now it's difficult going somewhere far off. I'm just lazy. Now let's go back home!"

Then his grandmother said, "Yes, we should do that. Why, that's just how I feel: I'm just too lazy to go on. Now let's do it! Let's turn back!"

Then the boy said, "Well, I'll go early in the morning, before it's daybreak yet. I'll take this dog of ours. We'll go back there. We'll hide. And when the village starts moving on, I'll come back in the evening. Then we'll go home.

"If the enforcers come, you should say, 'He went after meat. He must have killed a deer. He's the one I'm waiting for. And as soon as he returns, we'll go on. I'm ready now.' And that's what you'll say."

Early in the morning—*really* early in the morning—this boy got up. Then he ran off with the dog that they had. Then, wherever the place was, he stopped with the dog to wait there.

It got to be daybreak. Then the camp crier began calling out, "Now get yourselves ready! Our camp is moving. We are going on until we reach a nice location, where there are woods and where there is plenty of wood and water. Those are the main concerns. That is the purpose of our going. And when the weather begins to get warm again, we will be coming home." That is what was planned.

Then the group began moving on.

Meanwhile, this old woman, the poor thing, took down the brush shelter she and her grandson had. Then she was ready. Then the young men, the enforcers, came. "You aren't ready."

Then she said, "I'm waiting for my grandson. He went after meat. He must have killed a deer. That is what he went after. As soon as he returns, then we'll go on."

Then they went on. The young men, the enforcers who were

hurrying everyone, left her.

In the evening the boy arrived. Then he and his grandmother loaded their gear onto the travois pulled by the dog. Then they went back to their lodge in the village. They arrived there.

"It's good to be back home safely. It's too much trouble making a camp all the time. One no more than puts up a lodge than one takes it down again." That is what he was saying repeatedly.

He went hunting, shooting cottontails and prairie chickens. And that is what he and his grandmother ate.

Early one morning the boy arose and went up onto a hill to look all around. There was smoke coming out of one earth lodge there in the village. Smoke was coming out of it.

Then he came home. Then he said, "Grandma, I stood on top of that hill over there. In the village there's smoke coming out of one lodge. Someone must be living in it. Maybe someone else turned back, too. Perhaps you should find out! Go there!"

Then his grandmother said, "That family never goes anywhere. They're living there. The man's legs are paralyzed. That's the reason they're not with the village on its trip. I'll go. I'll go to see them. I'll go into the village."

After the boy went hunting for prairie chickens, cottontails, jackrabbits—these kinds of things—his grandmother went through the village to where they lived.

Then this family was happy to see her—that man and the woman who was his wife and the young woman who was their daughter. Oh, she was nice looking, this young girl who was about fourteen or fifteen winters old.

Then the grandmother came home in the evening. There sat her grandson inside the lodge.

Then the boy said, "Grandma, I killed a cottontail. I'm boiling it."

Then she said, "I went through the village where you said, and they're living there. Now they've invited us to their lodge to live with them during the winter."

Well, then he said, "Well, it will be that way, but first I think I'll go somewhere to hunt for a while!"

Then his grandmother took her belongings to where the two of them had been invited.

"Well, my grandson and I are going to come here."

Then the man said, "Where did your grandson go?"

"Oh, my grandson went hunting."

Then he said, "Well, I want my daughter to marry your grandson since I'm not able to go around hunting anything. I want this boy to be my son-in-law to help me."

"Now I'll ask him."

Then the boy arrived. They were calling him. Then they told him.

Then the boy said, "Well, it'll be that way. I'll marry this young woman."

Then that is what he did: then they married. Then they lived together for a while, however long it was.

Meanwhile, nothing was difficult for this young man when he went out hunting and killed various things. Even if it was a deer, he killed it. Then he brought the meat back.

"Oh, son-in-law!" Now his father-in-law was thankful. "Ah, that's what I want: to eat well. I'm just not able to go hunting for anything myself. It's impossible for me."

Then the boy went off one time. While he was out hunting, going all around, he saw two men. Then they found him.

"Ah, Hidden Man! They say he's married now, and we came to see our daughter-in-law. Now that's what we came for. Ah, it's truly good. Now we'll watch over her while you go around."

Then one said, "Now, we want some roasted corn to eat, and some squash, so that, ah, we might eat well; and something to smoke."

Well, then the boy said, "Well, can you possibly come tomorrow?"

Then one said, "Ah, it will be that way. We'll go. Now, Hidden Man, when it gets to be evening, when the sun goes down, you'll tie up the dogs. Oh, this one, my brother, and I are afraid of dogs. We're afraid of dogs, but we'll go there. <Also you must bank the fire in the fireplace so that it burns low—just enough to see one's silhouette, that someone is sitting there. And spread sage where we

are going to sit.> When we eat, we want to see our daughter-in-law, the poor thing. Now, we'll come in the evening."

They departed. Then the boy went. Then he arrived. Then he told the young woman his wife, "My fathers are going to come. There are two. They want to eat something and to smoke, to eat corn—roasted corn—and squash, and to smoke something. You must tell your father about them." That is what he told the young woman.

"Yes, it will be that way."

[To her father,] "His fathers are going to come. They're coming to see us. They want to smoke."

"Ah, it will be that way. I'll get things ready."

Then this man, the poor thing, began mixing tobacco. He was not able to get around, but only sit on his bed.

Now they tied the dogs up. Then they spread sage out on the floor. "This is where they'll sit." <And then they fixed the fire so it would burn low.>

Then the boy went outside. It was getting dark now.

Then the two men saw the boy. They were coming. They were talking.

Then one said, "Hey, we have arrived. Why, surely it's a good thing. We're going to eat something from our daughter-in-law."

"Now come!" Then he led them inside the lodge. Then they sat down where the sage had been spread. Then they sat down.

Then the women dished out roasted corn and squash for them. They placed the food before them. But first the man filled the pipe. Then after they smoked, they began to eat, eating roasted corn and squash. Oh, they were thankful. They consumed everything.

Then one said, "Now, daughter-in-law, we are full. We've eaten your meal after we smoked your father's tobacco. Now it's good. Now let's go! We're going back over there."

Then they went outside.

Well, after so many days then he saw them again.

"Ah, here we come again, Hidden Man, so that we might eat. Ah, it's certainly good that our daughter-in-law can cook for us. Now we'll come again. But we want to know why your father-in-law doesn't get up."

Then the boy said, "Why, his legs are paralyzed. His legs don't move well. It's too difficult for him."

"Well now, we'll doctor him when we come. He'll get well. He'll start getting around again. It's nothing. We scrutinized him. It was good to smoke his tobacco. We just felt good." This is what they were saying. "Now we're going to come again. You must have things ready and our daughter-in-law will have a meal cooked."

And then the boy came back and told his wife, "My fathers are going to come. They're going to doctor your father to make him well."

Then the young woman was thankful. Then she was glad.

She told her father and mother, "This boy's fathers are going to come again. They're going to doctor you to make you well, so that you'll be able to get all around at last. They're thankful for having smoked your tobacco."

Then this man said, "Ah, hand that to me! I should get ready!"

He began mixing the tobacco. He got everything ready.

Then the boy went outside there. When it was sundown he tied the dogs up as they had done before. Then he went to where they were. They were talking as they came, talking. "Now here we have come. Our daughter-in-law must have everything ready for us to eat roasted corn. And now it's ready. Let's go!"

They went to the lodge. They entered. Now they sat down where the sage was spread out, as they had done before.

Food was set before them. Then they began eating well. They consumed everything. This man then fixed the tobacco for them. Then they also smoked.

Then one told Hidden Man, "Tell your wife, 'You must lay your father here where we're sitting.' We'll doctor him. He'll get well."

Then this boy told the young woman his wife and her mother. They made a bed for him. They laid him down.

Then one said, "Alright, I'm going to be the first one to doctor you."

Then he got up and rubbed his hands in a circular manner <with sage between them>.[1] He took hold of one leg, then the other leg on the right, too. Then he pulled out a snake, a bull snake.

1. An act of purification.

Now this man: "This is the one that crippled you." Then he laid it down. Then he sat down. "Now it's your turn, my brother."

"Ha, now I myself will do it." Then he did just what his brother had done. Then he took out a bull snake, too. Now this one was the female kind.

"These are the cause of your not being able to walk around. And, Hidden Man, you'll wrap the two snakes up and throw them away. Now we're going. Well, sometime later we'll find each other again."

And when it was morning the man who had had the crippled legs walked around inside. Then he was tremendously thankful, being thankful that he was able to walk all around again after they had made him well—after they had taken away his crippledness. "Why, I'm thankful that I'm able to walk all around here again!"

Now while this young man was traveling around, the two men found him.

Then one of them said, "Hidden Man, we have come purposefully." Then they gave him two arrows. They gave him two.

Then the man said, "Now when you travel around, if some difficult situation confronts you, this is what you're going to do: you'll nock one of these arrows and you'll shoot it up into the air. Then we'll come. Whatever the problem is, we're going to take care of it for you. Now this black arrow is going to watch over you. Whenever you travel around, have it with you. Don't forget this quiver you have, and keep the arrow in it together with the other ones."

Now as the young man was traveling around, he saw them again. Then the two men saw him.

Then one said, "Say, the village that's traveling on the hunt is turning back. They're coming. They're hungry. Children have died, starving to death. They're traveling this way. They're coming back home.

"Now truly I have come here. Tomorrow I'll take care of things immediately. Your grandmother and your mother-in-law shall make arrows! Oh, you should make many of them! Now we're going to call the buffalo. The buffalo are ranging close by here. They're headed this way toward your village. They're going to come. Now you're going to shoot them. You'll butcher them and take the meat inside all these lodges to be sliced and dried. And you'll place pieces on these scaffolds. There's going to be plenty. Now we'll be shooting them, too. Now, you and the old man your father-in-law, get yourselves ready!"

This boy went home. Then he told his mother-in-law.

"Now, grandma, you'll sharpen the arrowheads."

They did not tell how many days passed [while they prepared]. Now there was a huge number of bundles. There were bundles of arrows all over.

Then they said, "Now tie up the dogs! The buffalo are coming now. There's a multitude of them. They're headed this way toward our village. Now this old man and I are going to shoot them."

When morning came—early in the morning—the ground was rumbling. And here there was a herd of buffalo coming! Oh, there was a multitude of them coming to the edge of the village!

And this man and his son-in-law killed a huge number of them when they were killing them. Then there was a line of carcasses there. And here the other two <star fathers> were shooting the buffalo from out of sight, so that the buffalo did not see them. Then the herd of buffalo passed by. There were carcasses scattered all around here and there.

Then they began butchering them and taking the meat into different lodges, the vacant lodges, and putting the meat on scaffolds. Ah, there was plenty! There was no lack of meat!

And, oh, as the boy was going all around, he saw someone there: there stood a man. He was barely able to walk. He was staggering as he came.

Then this boy Hidden Man went to meet him. Then he said, "Hey, hello!"

Then this man said, "Everyone traveling in our party is *so* pitiful. Children have died, starving to death. And everyone among us is hungry. Now the group is returning. But we came ahead. Everything was ruined for them. They're tired, but they're coming on anyway. Oh my, I'm so tired! I'm so tired, too!"

Then the other one said, "Now be strong for a while! Our village

is close by. You must come there! We're living there with the man
who is now my father-in-law"—whatever his name was. "I'm with
the young woman who is his child." Then he said, "Be strong! You'll
make it."

Then this boy quickly turned back. Then he arrived.

Then he said to his wife, "Tell your mother, 'Boil meat!' Now
they're coming. There are four men. The group that went on the
hunt is returning. They turned back half way out. Children have
died, starving to death. Now there are three others following the
one coming ahead. They're tired and hungry. But this one coming
close by is going to come here. Let him drink only soup first! Then
later you can set meat before him. You'll get everything ready for
him. As soon as he has eaten, then he'll turn around. You'll give
him some dried meat. Then he'll take it to the three who are coming. They'll eat some. Then he'll take meat farther on to the others
who are coming. This is what my fathers told me."

So now that is what she did: then she boiled ribs. Then they
also roasted ribs over the fire.

Then the man who was coming appeared. Oh, he was barely
able to walk, and when he looked, oh my, in this village here there
was meat hanging from the scaffolds! There was a huge quantity of
meat there. Then he hurried along, coming faster.

Then Hidden Man led him to the lodge where his wife was.
Then she dipped up soup for him. He calmed down. Then they
placed meat before him. He ate.

Now the boy said, "Now turn around again! You are strong now.
You are sturdy now. There are two bundles of dried meat here.
You'll give some dried meat to those three men who are coming. But
then you'll take the rest of it to the group that is coming. As soon
as you arrive there with it, you'll tell the people, 'Make a fire, a big
fire!' And then you'll throw the dried meat onto the flames. You'll
become lively after having been sick and hungry. You'll pass the
meat around. You'll place it before them. You'll distribute this dried
meat. One pile will go around evenly! <It will increase and there
will be enough for everyone>."

And then that is what he did, just as I said.

The boy came back. Then he ate. Then this man went and took
the dried meat, as he had told him, just as I said.

Oh, later the group arrived in the village. This Hidden Man had made everyone lively again, and now the women were making dried meat [out of what was in their lodges].

Now that is what he did.

« « «   » » »

Once when he was traveling around, when he was going around hunting, well, wherever he was going, he crossed the water, wherever it was, to the other side when the ice was floating on the river.

Now he sat on a hill. While he was looking all around, he saw a single buffalo. There it came, oh, as it grazed on grass. Oh, as he looked all around he saw that there was one stand of trees nearby and just beyond there was another one. The two stands were facing each other [forming a sort of corridor].

Then this boy thought, "Oh, before that buffalo comes through, I'll go down there. I'll wait over there. And as soon as I eye it between the two stands of trees, I'll shoot it."

Then that is what he did: he waited over there. That buffalo came into the open space between the two stands of trees. As soon as it got there, this boy shot it. The arrow glanced off. As he chased it, shooting at it again and again, he was unable to bring it down and kill it. And here it led him far, far off as he chased it!

Then there was a lodge. That is where the buffalo was going inside. Now the boy caught up with it.

Once it was there inside the lodge, it said, "I have led Hidden Man here. I'm barely alive. He has wounded me all over."

And there inside someone said, "Now sit down! Now that's nothing at all. You'll get well."

A man was inside. He called out, "Come in!"

Then this Hidden Man entered. There sitting against the wall was the one he had chased and had been shooting, <a bull named Big Star>. Also sitting there was something, whatever it was. It had sharp bumps; it also had arms and a mouth. It had long teeth. <There was also a man sitting there, and there was a heart hanging there.>

The man said, "Aaah, Hidden Man, you have come now, but you never think, 'My uncle lives over there.' It's good that you have come. Now sit down over there!"

Then he was seated. Food was placed before him. Then he began to eat.

Then the man said, "Hidden Man, I called you purposefully since we who live here are always hungry. On this earth you are outstanding in the ways of hunting. And I am hungry as I sit here wanting something to eat. You never think, 'My uncle lives over there,' and you never come." That is what this man was saying.

And here the man was evil, doing different kinds of evil things and killing various ones. Whoever had holy power would lose it to him.

"Now you lie right here. This boy, the poor thing, is mine for running around to perform errands."

A little boy went in front of them as he scurried around. He was about so tall.

Then the man said, "Say!"

After they had lain down to sleep, this boy Hidden Man thought, "I wonder why I came. I don't like being around this place."

Now it was morning, and this man—I don't know what his name was, only that they just say "this man"—he said, "Now you're going to hunt for a white bighorn sheep. Ah, it'll be prominent among them. Ah, the horns—I want one of these horns for a horn spoon so I can drink water with it. I want you to bring that."

Meanwhile this young man would go around hunting, killing deer because the man wanted to eat something. "But don't eat any! You'll spoil the taste of mine!" [he admonished Hidden Man].

Then Hidden Man would bring the meat to him. Then he would set it down for him. "Now throw it away! The meat might be spoiled." That is what he was doing.

First the man wanted it; then he did not want it. Now this Hidden Man, the poor thing, was rather hungry. He was left out [when they were eating].

Meanwhile his in-laws were looking for him while they were waiting. "He must have been killed by the enemy." His two star fathers also looked for him, but they did not see him anywhere.

« »

"Now, you are going to bring this white bighorn sheep to me. Oh, it's difficult to find one, but I believe they say that nothing is difficult for you when you hunt things. That's the reason I want you to kill that white bighorn sheep for me."

Well, this one, the poor thing, set out to go off. But he was *so* weak when he went, since he was so hungry!

As he was going along he found one. Why, he barely killed it and then he slit its legs behind the knees. He wanted to carry it on his back.

Then it became too difficult for him. He was *so* weak! It was too difficult for him to get up.

Then he heard something there, up above where he was going. "Heeey, heeey, Hidden Man, where are you?"

Then he thought, "Why, here they're looking for me!"

Then he arose. Then he barely took out the black arrow, and then shot it up into the air. There was a thud on the ground. There stood his fathers.

"Ah, you have erred. We have searched everywhere on this earth looking for you. And here this is where you have come! This is where you must like living "

He said, "Why, this is how it is. This is what happened."

Then they said, "Yes, well, we know that man."

Now one of them made a fire. He took a rib. Then he placed it over the fire.

He made Hidden Man vomit after they gave him medicine to drink [as they doctored him]. Then they made him strong again.

"Now eat!"

Then the boy began eating. They made him strong again.

"Now leave this sheep here! I'll kill a different one" [one of the men said].

Then they went on. Then they killed a different bighorn sheep. The other one put it on his back and then they went on.

"This is the place. That's the lodge."

"Now take the meat inside!"

Hidden Man said, "As soon as I go inside, he'll say right away, 'Bring me some water!' That's what he's going to say."

Then he entered, but the two men stayed outside.

There inside the lodge the man said, "Hey, Hidden Man, whatever were you doing! I'm starving to death, and I'm dying of thirst. Whatever were you doing!"

Then the boy Hidden Man said, "Why, it's certainly difficult to find a sheep of this kind. One can't just bump into one easily. I had to look for it. That's the reason it took a long time."

"Ah, now bring me some water! I'm dying of thirst."

Now that he had been made a slave, this Hidden Man picked up a pail, an empty pail. He went out. After he had gone outside there where the two men were, one of them snatched the pail [and got the water for Hidden Man].

Then he said, "This time when he does it—after he drinks a little water and says, 'Throw it away!'—you throw the water in his face! [Say,] 'This is what you have been doing, tiring me out.' You aren't going to do it anymore."

He took the water inside. The man drank a little.

"Now throw the water away!"

Hidden Man said, "Hey, this is what you always do." Then he threw the water on him.

Then his two fathers who were standing outside came running inside. When this man saw them, he was afraid of them.

"Now this is how Hidden Man treats me," he whined.

Where he sat on top, there the heart was hanging. <One of the men threw it onto the fire. After it burned the man died. He was killed.>

And that thing in the corner—one of the fathers kicked it. It slid across the lodge. It was the one that had long teeth. Then they pierced it with its teeth. Then they killed it. They threw it into the fire.

Then this buffalo Big Star said, "Oh, I want to live! Poor things, this is how it was when we lived here as slaves."

"Now you go on quickly! We heeded you when you called us to come help you, when the human beings were starving. We heeded you when we came, when the humans who had been traveling around looking for buffalo were coming back to their village.[2] Now go on quickly! Don't turn around at all! We might kill you, too."

Then this buffalo bull went out. Then he went off.

Then one of the star fathers said, "Now go on quickly! Don't ever turn around!"

Then this bull said, "There may be a day when I [a buffalo] may be among you people, and I'll kill someone."

"Oh, go on quickly!" They scolded the bull.

Meanwhile there were carcasses lying around. The men destroyed the holy things that this evil man had there.

"Now let's go on quickly!"

Then they flew off to the village. "Your in-laws are weary, and your wife has a child for you. She's weary from having waited for you."

Then Hidden Man went to his home.

Then they cried when they saw him. His grandmother was living yet.

Ah, his little boy was growing up; the little boy, the one he had of his own, was growing up.

Now this man was named Hidden Man. The meaning of it is 'not to be going around plainly.' It signifies that he is around, but he is not obviously there. But he is around, but people do not know his ways, the good ideas that he has. What he does is good, always doing good deeds for others. Now this is the meaning of the name Hidden Man. He is around, but he cannot be prominent.

Now this is what I used to hear when my grandmother told the story—when they talked about Hidden Man.

2. One of the star fathers reminds Big Star, the buffalo bull, that they had come to his aid when he had wanted to help the starving people by bringing the buffalo herd to the village, where Hidden Man and his father-in-law could slaughter them. Subsequently, after the evil man had enslaved Big Star, the bull helped the man enslave Hidden Man, the star fathers' adopted son.

16

Baby Chief and the Two Holy Men

This is another story, similar to the preceding one, of a poor boy pitied by two holy men who are said to be stars. These men are apparently identical to those in the previous narrative, for although their association with buffalo is not as fully developed, they bring the buffalo herd to be slaughtered and they themselves eat no meat, only vegetables, just as the characters did in the narrative of Hidden Man. Beginning with a protagonist who leaves the party as it goes off on a winter communal hunt, the plot develops in like manner. Again the villagers fail to find buffalo on their hunt and return starving, only to find that Baby Chief, the poor boy, has obtained plenty of meat. The theme of the story is thus buffalo calling, in which Baby Chief's spiritual fathers aid him in time of tribal need. Moreover, because he saves the village, the poor boy is raised to the status of chief.

Now I will tell another story. It is an old story from long, long ago when our people were coming upriver. However, where it happened I certainly don't know.

There lived a poor boy in a village where our villages used to be dispersed, a poor boy who was pitiful and had no relatives, the poor thing, who wandered around the village and went into different lodges where they would feed him. Whenever he went into a lodge to spend the night, they fed him. And then he went someplace else. <Oh, he was a handy boy. He hauled water and wood for people and he watered their horses.> This is what he was doing. Why, he was pitiful, the poor thing.

And the chief—the one who was chief, the man who was the leader—had a young daughter. Oh, she was beautiful, a beautiful young woman. And there were many young men who courted her, each one wishing that he might marry the daughter. But her father did not want her to marry them. "Oh, I don't want you to marry and be with any of them. I myself have selected a man for you to marry."

Then this young woman said, "Now quickly tell me who he is!"

Then he said, "The poor thing, this boy who wanders around—the poor one . . . the pitiful one—that's the one I want to be my son-in-law, the one I want to call my son-in-law. He has no relatives. Ah, I just feel sorry for him, the poor thing, when I see him."

Then this young woman said, "Yes. Now I'll do that. We will marry."

Then they called this boy. Then he entered the lodge. Then they fed him.

This young woman then sat down by him. Then she said, "We purposefully called you to come here. My mother and my father want you and me to marry—for you to be my husband and for all of us to be together. Since you have no relatives and wander alone around the village, my mother and father want us to be together."

The young man sat there pondering. "Yes. Poor thing, I am indeed poor."

Then this young woman said, "Now that doesn't matter. We'll be together."

And then that is what she did. Then this favored child—the young woman who was the chief's child—and this poor boy married. Now they were together.

Then the crier called out to the village. "Our chief—our leader—now has a son-in-law. He now has a son-in-law. The poor thing who wanders around the village—the poor boy—that's the one she's with. They got married. Now the poor boy is married."

Oh, the entire village was happy. But there were many young men who had had their eye on the young woman [and were jealous]. Then they said, "I wonder why she wants to marry him when he is poor?" That is what all of them were saying.

Then they erected a tipi for the couple. They put up wood and dried meat for them. The lodge of the chief's son-in-law stood out in front of this village.

[Then it was time for the village to move.] "Now we're going to go over that way. We'll move on. We're going to move out."

Well, then they took away from the newly married couple the things that they had given them. Then the camp moved out, leaving the couple behind. The poor boy and his wife walked alone in the rear as the village traveled on. They had no horse.

Then the couple reached the new camp. There they again had a lodge in the new village. "Now here is your lodge. We've got everything ready for you two."

Then the couple went inside, and then this young woman began cooking for themselves.

That is what was happening day after day.

Well, then one night this boy said, "Now I think I'll go up a hill. I'll go up that hill in the distance and look all around."

Then the young woman said, "Alright."

Then the boy ran over there. He went up the hill.

Then two men came. "Yes, it is us, Baby Chief. You who have the village now—you who are the son-in-law of the chief—you are the leader now. You have the village. We're the cause of it. We felt sorry for you when you were wandering around the village pitifully. Now we're the cause of your getting married the way you are.

"Now tonight after everyone is asleep, oh, you should bring all your things here—all the things the people have given you: dried meat, guns, all the different things that they gave you. You should bring the lodge, too. Now we're going to put up the lodge for you. Now when everyone in the village gets up in the morning, there won't be a tipi. They aren't going to find the tipi.

"Now do that! As soon as it gets dark and everyone is sleeping, you two hurry! Now meanwhile we're going to help you."

Then the boy went back to his lodge there in the village. Then he entered where the young woman who was his wife was. Then he told her what they had been instructed to do.

Then he said, "Say, that's what we're going to do. After everyone is asleep tonight, we'll take all our belongings away. There will be a lodge over there. We'll go. That's where we're going to go. And when everyone in the village starts out on the move, we'll stay here. We won't go anywhere."

Then the young woman said, "Now I'm satisfied with that. It'll be that way. We'll do it."

Then everyone went to sleep. After they were all sleeping, the couple got up. They gathered their belongings together. Oh, they began carrying their belongings off. Then they came to a valley. It was a deep valley. There was a stand of trees in it, and there they put their belongings down.

And there was a lodge there, the lodge that had been theirs back in the village. There the tipi was, at the base of the valley wall. Then the couple went down to it.

Then these two men said, "Don't make a fire until after the village has moved out and traveled on. Then you can make a fire at night. But don't make a fire now! Don't do it!"

Then the couple went to bed.

Oh, it was a long time before the people in the village discovered that the couple was gone. Then the sound of the people's voices was audible while they were looking for the couple. But it was to no avail: they could not find the couple. Then the sounds died out as the people were moving off, as they went, as they were moving off wherever they were going.

Then this young man said, "I'll just take a look."

He went up the hill there to look all around. Oh, there was the former camp site. There was no one at all around. Then he went down the hill.

Then the young man said, "Now let's make a fire!" He made a fire. He began roasting dried meat. Now it got dark. Then this boy went after wood.

Then the two men came again. One said, "Now, Baby Chief, we're going to tell you. Oh, we want your wife to boil fresh corn, roasted sweet corn. And squash. Those are what we want to eat. And also ground beans. Cook a meal!

"You have a dog. Tie it up. Don't turn it loose!"

Well, then this boy brought a stake [with which to tie the dog]. Then he told his wife, "When it gets dark again, I want you to boil roasted sweet corn and squash and ground beans—all these things. But leave out meat or dried meat! Leave them out for now! My two fathers are going to come to eat. They want to eat corn—sweet corn—and squash. And chokecherry pudding. Now that's what they want to eat."

Then the young woman said, "I surely have everything. It will be that way."

Now it got dark again, and then this young woman boiled roasted sweet corn, squash, and ground beans. Oh, it got dark. The young man went outside. He looked, and there they came at a distance.

"Hey, Baby Chief!"

Then Baby Chief said, "You two will eat."

"That is certainly good. You have plenty of food. Don't go anywhere! You two stay here! You won't be hungry. They won't find you. No one will find you. They aren't going to find you."

Ah, the two men had arrived. Then they were fed, and the two men began eating, oh, eating the squash that each one wanted.

"Hey, this meal we have eaten here is sure good. Now let's go! It isn't enemy territory. There's no one wandering around. Anyway he and I live here, too." That is what the two men were saying as they were making this young woman forget things so that she would not know.

"Now, daughter-in-law, we're full. Now we'll go!" Then they went out.

Now winter passed, when it always gets cold and when the village traveled around with his father-in-law the chief and his mother-in-law among the group. And then when spring arrived the two men returned.

One said, "Say, the band that went out west is returning. They're coming back. <They're starving. Their supplies and food are all gone. The snow has been deep. They're having a hard time.> They're talking about making camp again here where the village was previously.

"Now tomorrow you'll cut a chokecherry bush and you'll begin making arrows. This young woman knows how. Make lots of them! Now we're going to shoot buffalo, and you'll butcher them. But we'll help you two. After two days you'll be finished doing it."

This young man then began cutting sticks from a chokecherry bush. Then he began making arrows of them. Oh, there was a large number of them!

And one of the men said, "Now there sure are plenty of them for when the buffalo come here. The people who are returning are hungry. They didn't find anything on their trip.

"Now don't make a fire in the morning. You're going to see the buffalo when they come down this coulee. We're going to shoot them. Don't make a fire in the morning."

Oh, the next morning there was a multitude of buffalo coming down the coulee. This young man began to shoot them. He felled them one after another. Now, oh, the carcasses of the ones they had shot were strewn around there.

Then one of the men said, "Now the herd has gone up the hill. The carcasses are lying over there."

Now this is what the couple did: this young man and young woman, helped by the men, began butchering the carcasses. But these two men—I don't know what their names were—said, "Now this matter of meat is finished." They finished their butchering.

Now these two men left for wherever it was that they lived. "Now we're going. Now, Baby Chief, you have plenty. The camp is coming. The camp is returning to this spot.

"One man is coming ahead. He's alone. He'll come here. You must wait for him. There also are others coming. There are three coming here. The one is coming ahead of them. Wait for him as he comes! He'll come here."

Then this young man did that, waiting and watching for however many nights it was. Then he saw a man. Over there came a man in the distance. He was barely able to walk. The young man waited for the man who was coming.

He said to the one coming, "Hey, here you are!" when they encountered each other, each happy to see the other. "My wife and I live over there."

"Hey, our camp is coming. We're all starving. And they're discussing whether we should camp here where we camped before. Hey, we thought that the enemy must have killed you two! It's sure good to see you now."

"Now come quickly! Eat a meal!"

Well, then they went to where the tipi was. Why, meat was piled up all over inside! Oh, there was a lot of meat! The man who came was amazed at the sight of it.

Then the young woman boiled meat for him. Then he ate.

"Now take this dried meat! Let those men who are coming behind you eat it. When you go back and reach the camp that is returning, you should do this: have them make a big fire and have them put a small piece of dried meat on the fire, and when they smell it they'll become lively.

"Now from this bundle of dried meat that I'm giving you, you'll give each person one piece. After you have cut a piece of the dried meat, it will increase in quantity as soon as you cook it. And that's what is going to happen. That's what you will do."

Then the young man gave him a bundle of dried meat. Then this man turned back. He went on and on, and there came the three men.

Then he said to them, "Hey, hurry! The boy who was poor and his wife—the two who separated from us—are living over there. Oh, they're living in plenty! There's a huge quantity of dried meat and meat piled up there. There really is plenty. You three cook this! Now in the meantime I'm taking this dried meat back to the camp that's coming. This is what he said to do."

And then these men who were coming boiled the meat, and it satisfied their hunger.

And this man took the bundle of dried meat to the camp that was returning, where everyone was starving. Then he arrived with it.

"Now this is the story of the poor boy. Oh, there's plenty where he and his wife live. There's a huge quantity of dried meat and meat—there's a lot of it. He had this bundle. Now this is what he said: 'You people make a big fire! You'll cut this piece of dried meat, and then you'll put it on the fire. And the smell of it will make whoever is sick and whoever is starving feel well again.' That's what the main one [Baby Chief] said when he told me."

And so that is what they did: then they made a fire, oh, a big fire. Then they threw a piece of dried meat on the blaze. Oh my, when the odor arose, the ones who were starving and were sick, the poor things, then became lively again.

Now the one man began passing around the dried meat, giving each person a piece to boil. Then after they did this, they all got full. "Now, you who are in a hurry, go quickly!" So that is what he did when he gave them the dried meat, distributing it to everyone.

When they boiled it, oh, the meat increased in quantity, and they got full. And then they came on, traveling back.

They arrived there near where the couple was living and made their village. Then people began coming to the couple's lodge to take the dried meat from the poor boy and pass the meat around. And then everyone got full again. Then things became good.

Then the couple took their possessions up the hill and lived again among the people in the village.

<And the chief said, "Well, my son-in-law is going to take my place. He's going to be chief of you people. Now he's going to be leader. If it hadn't been for him, a lot of people would be dead now—they would have starved to death.">

Now this boy was named Baby Chief. Now this is the end of the story of him.

These two men then did various good deeds as they traveled around. And the people told about them—that the two men were among them, and what they did when they saved the people. There are good stories about what these two men did.

17

The Young Man Pitied by the Spotted Buffalos

The plot of this myth is the familiar vanquishment of an evil father-in-law, here a man who uses his daughter to lure young men to his winter encampment, where he sets them impossible tasks, then kills them when they fail. After one young man, the protagonist of the story, determines to learn why previous youths who followed the girl have never returned, he is aided first by five animals that impart their powers to him, enabling him to overcome the hurdles put up

by the evil father-in-law. Then the story continues a theme
from previous narratives of associating buffalos on earth
with stars. When the son-in-law is given impossible tasks,
the young man is aided first by a buffalo cow in human
form and then by seven spotted buffalos who are in fact stars
that have come down to earth in animal form. It was these
buffalo stars that had endowed the father-in-law with his
power, represented by a black rock, and now they are the
ones who must overcome him for his abuse of it. The story
was told to the narrator by his grandfather Short Bear.

It was a long, long time ago when our people lived there <in the
southeast> where we migrated from, long, long ago. And they told
this story when they were coming up the river. They told the story.

Now our grandfather used to tell stories. He had stories. My
grandmother was that way, too.

Now there once was a village, a big village, in which Arikaras
lived. And there was a man—it was a man—who lived alone in the
badlands, who lived alone with his wife and daughter. The young
woman, his daughter, was pretty.

He lived there in the badlands during the winter. He had lodges
there: he had two big earth lodges, and one of them was small. The
large one was their dwelling.

And when summer came the family would return to our villages along the Missouri to live among the people, and the man's
daughter would be courted by various young men.

And when it began to get cold in late fall, he would go back to
where "I always go for the winter. I have a nice place where I live.
I'm not in want of things like wood and water, and there's plenty of
game so that I eat well." And then the family moved back there.

Then a young man who liked the daughter and who had been
courting her would follow the family. The family would return to
where they lived in the badlands with this boy following the young
woman he was courting.

But then the young man would be given difficult tasks by this
man. And finally he would be killed. The man would kill him.

This man must have been doing that many times. He would

come to the village in the summertime, and then he and his family would return to the badlands as they always did.

And then one time a certain young man said, "Now I must find out. I wonder why none of the boys who follows her ever returns here. Anyone who has courted this young woman has not returned. And when his parents look for him, he's dead."

And this man [who was the father of the young woman] would say, "Ah, the enemy must have found him. They must have killed him. We looked for him, but he didn't come back." And this is what he always said when he was explaining things.

It began to get wintry now, just about wintertime. "Now we're going where we always go for the winter." Then he went off. Then the family moved back there.

And then this young man followed them. The family must have left two days earlier; then the young man went afterward.

As he was running along he went up a hill. When he looked out over the land there, he saw the trail where they had gone. Then this young man went on.

As he was going along, there they sat over yonder. There sat over yonder a bear, a mountain lion, an eagle, a rabbit, and an ant. There was a dead buffalo lying there [in front of them]. Oh, the buffalo was big!

Then the young man passed by them. Then he turned around. "Say, what's going on?"

As he went to where they were, this bear got up. Then it said, "Yes. Now it's good that you have come. We want someone to butcher the buffalo we have here and to distribute the meat evenly to us. That's what we're sitting here waiting for."

Then this young man said, "I'll do it for you. It isn't difficult for me to butcher it."

Then the young man began butchering the buffalo. He finished doing it. "Well, now, what's going to happen?"

Then the bear said, "You'll give me one hind leg and a foreleg. And you can also do the same for this other one, the mountain lion. Give him a hind leg and a foreleg. But now I don't know what these others are going to say."

Then the eagle said, "Now you can give me the back, and I'll eat it. I'll peck on it."

And the rabbit: "Now you can give me the ribs. I'll eat them. I'll nibble on the ribs. They're what I always eat."

Now the ant said, "Now this head is what you'll give me. It'll be my home. That's where I myself will live inside."

Then the young man divided things evenly as he laid them down.

Then the bear said, "We're indeed thankful for what you have done for us here. Now we'll bless you. We know why you've come here. The man who has the young daughter has already gone by. We blessed him previously, but now he's gone too far. His actions are bad. <He doesn't want anyone to marry his daughter.> He's killed all the young men who have followed him. Each one has died after the man has had him killed.

"But now we're going to bless you. Whatever you desire is going to happen. What you have done for us is good."

Now this mountain lion: "And from me here you'll have the gift of bravery over the enemy as you travel about. The ways of the warpath are not going to be difficult for you."

And now the eagle said, "Now I'm giving you the power of hunting. I'm going to watch over you. I'm going to be hunting for things for myself, too. I'm thankful for what you've done for me."

Then the rabbit said, "I feel the same way, too. I'm thankful for what you did. Now you'll be fast. No one will be able to overtake you when you run. Now whatever you chase will not be hard for you to catch. And you'll be able to do whatever you want."

Then the ant said, "Now I, too, am thankful for what you have done. Now no matter what it is that has been hidden, it won't be difficult for you to find, just as I find it as I travel about. That is my power. Even though something is well hidden, I arrive there and find it. I'm the one to get there first. And I'm giving you that power. I'm going to watch over you. I'm going to make the trails for you that you and I are going to travel. Now make haste! Quickly!"

Then the bear said, "Now when you go on and reach the man's lodge, when you arrive there, this is what he's going to do. Oh, there are two big white wolves sitting outside. They're tied up. They'll start to attack you when you arrive, but he's going to come out. He'll stop them. The wolves are the ones eating up each of the boys. Whenever he gives a task to a boy and the boy doesn't accomplish it, then he tells the wolves. Then they kill him. And then this man butchers him, and [whenever anyone comes to the lodge] he feeds the person human flesh. [He says to the visitor,] 'Now this will be the food that will be cooked first. And you and I will eat it. We'll eat it up.'

"Now whatever task he gives you that he wants done, tell me, and I'll take up the task myself."

And now this mountain lion said, "Now whatever task he gives you, you must go to do it, and it won't take me long to go wherever one must go to accomplish it."

Now this ant: "Now you and I are going to marry the daughter of this man who is preventing her marriage. Now we're going to marry her. It won't be hard to accomplish. Now go quickly!"

Then this young man went off.

And he arrived there. There were earth lodges. There were three lodges. They lived in the large one.

Then the young man went to the door. The big white wolves were sitting outside by the doorway. Then they started growling when they saw him.

Then the man came charging out of the lodge. "Why, it's my son-in-law! The wolves are barking." [To the wolves:] "Sit down! Be calm!

"Now, son-in-law, come inside!"

Then he took the young man inside. "Now sit down!"

Then the young man sat down.

Then the man brought out a pot, a black pot. Then it began dancing. It was dancing around. Then his wife came and she picked it up. Then she took it outside and after making a fire out there she began to boil meat in it. Here it was human flesh! Then she brought the pot of meat inside.

Then the ant told the young man, "Holler! Those two [your animal guardians] will then eat up the flesh."

Oh, this bear and the mountain lion [who were now invisible spirits,] ate up everything. They drank up all the soup.

Now that holy man watched the young man. [But he could not see the bear or the mountain lion.]

The young man said, "Now I have eaten."

After a little while the daughter brought dried meat and corn balls inside for the young man. Then this young man ate well.

Then the father-in-law told him, "Now you can sleep right here."

Something was sitting there in the corner [where he was to sleep]. It was blue. It had warts. It resembled a toad. Then it began to get angry.

The young woman slept on a bed high off the ground on the other side of the lodge, while her father and mother slept on a lower level. So it was impossible to reach her bed.

Then the ant told him, "Sleep awhile! It isn't difficult. We'll get there where she sleeps."

Then the thing sitting in the corner began to move around. Then it began to croak. It sat there with its mouth wide open as it croaked.

Then the bear said, "Now wait! Bring that! Give me the stick that's lying there!"

Then the young man gave it the stick, whatever kind it was.

Now when the creature sitting in the corner opened its mouth, the bear thrust the stick into its mouth. Then it was impossible for the thing in the corner—the one making the croaking sounds—to close its mouth.

Then the man got up from bed [because the creature was making so much noise] and made a fire. "What did you do to it?"

He said, "I didn't do anything. I don't know what that thing is, the one making the noise, with the stick in its mouth."

The man took the stick out. "Why don't you behave, you who are moving around angrily!"

And then the young man said, "If it starts to get mad again, I'll cut its throat."

Then this man became frightened. He was becoming fearful of his son-in-law.

After everyone was asleep, the ant said to the young man, "Now you and I are going to go over to where the young woman is sleeping."

Then the two of them went to her bed. Then the young man got into bed with this young woman, the one whose parents opposed her getting married and who made it difficult for suitors. <But before daylight the young man got down from her bed and went back to his own.>

Now sometime later this man said to the young man, "Now, my son-in-law, I want to eat elk. I want the hide of a white one. My old woman will tan it and I'll wear it when it gets cold."

This young man said, "I've never seen a white elk, but I'll look for one. As long as I've been hunting, I've never seen a white elk going around."

Then the young man went out. Then he went up onto a hill. And then the eagle flew up into the air above him and looked all around. Then a white elk was found. The young man killed it. He brought the meat, and these two who were always together—the bear and the mountain lion—helped him carry the meat back. They were getting near the man's lodge as the two animals packed the meat on their backs. The young man took it on inside the lodge by himself.

"Now here's what you wanted."

Then the man stared at it. Oh, he stared at it! The elk was white. "Now here it is. And it's big! This fur and the hide are what I wanted." Then the man began to butcher it.

It was sometime later, and then the man gave the young man another task. It was wintry now, in the dead of winter. Then this man said to him, "Now, son-in-law, I want to eat some plums. Go after some for me! Let me have some plums to eat!"

Then the young man said, "There aren't any plums growing on bushes in the winter. When it's in the middle of winter—I've never seen any plums on bushes in the middle of winter."

"You talk too much! Go on quickly!" Then the young man was given a sack.

Then he went off. There was snow on the ground as he traveled along the coulees which had wooded slopes.

Then he cried as he fasted. There was a clump of plum bushes there. It was a big stand of bushes.

Then a boy came out of the bushes. He said, "My mother is calling you. Follow me!"

Then he followed the boy. The two of them went into the brush. There there was an earth lodge in the brush. It was a big lodge. The two went into it. There sat a woman. She was cooking a meal. She was boiling dried meat.

"Sonny, you who are traveling around, now sit down! Why, you must eat something!"

Then this young man sat down. Food was set down for him and the boy, and they ate.

"Ah, now what's the matter?"

Then he said, "The man who is my father-in-law wants plums. Now where indeed are plums growing during the winter!"

And then the woman said, "Why, he's gone too far this time. He's going beyond his limit with the things he's requesting. We're the ones who blessed him. [We gave him power.] He was pitiful when he stood alone on top of different hills crying. Now he's going too far. What he's doing isn't good.

"Now I'll do something for you. Spread out the robe you're wearing! And then go outside and bring back a plum bush. Take it up there where the smokehole is [and hold it over the opening]. As soon as I begin singing, you'll shake the bush."

Then that is what this young man did. Then he took the bush up onto the roof of the lodge, and then this woman began to sing. He shook the bush over the smokehole.

Oh, there were thuds as the plums fell down through the smokehole.

And then the woman said, "Now surely there are plenty of them. Now put the bush back into the hole where you dug it up and set it upright!"

And then that is what this young man did.

Then he went back into the lodge and gathered the plums lying there on the robe.

"Now go quickly! He might discover what you're doing. I don't want him to know about it. Now go! You shouldn't say anything. Say only, 'They were there on a bush. They must not have frozen.'"

This young man was very swift indeed. He arrived back at his father-in-law's lodge. Then it was not long before he entered it. The wolves meanwhile were calm as they sat there. He took the plums inside. Then he laid them down.

Then he said, "Here are the plums. They must not have frozen. They were on a bush. I picked them hurriedly. There aren't any plums on bushes in the winter!"

"Yes, yes," the man was saying. Then he began to eat.

Then the young man said, "Eat them up! Don't leave any!"

Oh, this man gorged himself. Now he was barely able to eat up the plums.

Now it was not long before the father-in-law said again, "Hey, I wish I might eat some Juneberries. Say, son-in-law, go find some!"

Then this young man said, "There aren't any Juneberries growing on bushes in the winter! Why, you're just making it difficult!"

"You talk too much, son-in-law! You must go look around for them. You won't lose anything by it."

And so this young man went off. He went to where his mother lived [she who had helped him previously], and then he put the matter before her. "This is what he wants now."

And then she told him they would do as they had done before.

After he brought a Juneberry bush to the smokehole on top of the lodge, he shook it. And hanging there on the bush were Juneberries! Then he began to pick them off the bush [and dropped them down through the smokehole onto the robe below].

"Now take them quickly! Don't divulge anything!"

Then he went off. Then he arrived [at his father-in-law's lodge].

"Now here they are. You must eat them all up! Don't leave any!"

Now this man was becoming rather fearful of his son-in-law. He was barely able to consume all the Juneberries when he ate them.

And then sometime later the father-in-law said, "Say, it's getting warm now. The time is approaching for us to return to our village. Now look for a spotted buffalo for me! And when you bring the hide back, this old woman will tan it. Then we'll go back to our village, and I'll wear the spotted buffalo robe when I go around."

And then the young man said, "Why, there aren't any spotted buffalos among the ones I've ever seen! The only kind I've ever seen among buffalo is a white one, but I've never seen a spotted one. But I'll look around anyway."

Then the young man went back to where his mother lived. Then he told her, "Now this task is too difficult for me."

"But it isn't difficult," she said. "Go over there to the east! They'll be there in a valley. There are seven of them. They are spotted buffalos. If they start to run off, you should yell out, 'My mother Red Bear Woman sent me and this is what she said: "You will comply."'"

Then this young man went off. While he was running along, he climbed up a hill. There they were in the valley below: they were all nice looking; they were spotted. Then they began to run off. "A human being is coming!"

Then the young man called out, "I didn't come of my own accord. My mother Red Bear Woman sent me. This is what she told me to say when I came."

"Yes. Alright." Then they stopped. Then they came back to him and sat down.

And then one of them asked, "Now what has happened?"

Then he said, "My father-in-law made this request. [He wants a spotted buffalo like you.]"

"Hah, he is surely going too far now. That man is the one we blessed. He was pitiful when he was crying throughout the night until the morning came. But now his actions are wrong. This is the end of the blessings that we have given him.

"Now this is a difficult matter, but we'll do whatever we are capable of doing. <We're not from this earth. We really live in the sky. But we knew what you were doing and so we came down here to help you. Every so often we come down to this earth as we have done now. Your situation is a difficult one, but we'll try to get rid of this man.>

"Now go <over there into the hills and> bring back a black rock. If we succeed in splitting the rock, we are going to be able to kill him."

Then this young man went up a hill. Then he found the rock and brought it back.

Then he said, "Now here it is."

Then one of the spotted buffalos said, "Now we're going to hit it. If we split it we're going to be able to kill the man. But if we fail we'll all be dead. <He has power just like this rock.>"

Now these seven buffalos began butting it with their heads to see which one would hurt its neck [attempting to split it].

Then the oldest one—he was an old buffalo bull—said, "I thought that one of you young ones would be the one to split it. Now I don't know what my strength is, but I'm not really strong like I used to be. Now I don't know what I'm going to be able to do. Maybe I'll strike it. Maybe I'll do the job right."

And then he did that: hurting his neck, he split the black rock.

Then he said, "Now there's no obstacle. Now we have overcome him. Now we have got ahead of him."

[To the young man:] "Now you should take one of these other buffalos with you. The eldest one [is strong, but he] is not really fast. But the next oldest one is the fast one. He runs swiftly. Now you two will be the ones to go.

"Now when the two of you arrive close by the man's lodge, you'll twist the arrows that you have and stick them into the buffalo's fur where it is thick. This buffalo will tell you then what he's going to do."

Then this spotted buffalo [turned into a man, and he] and the young man came running. When they got close to the lodge, the one turned back into a buffalo—oh, one that was spotted! Then it said to the young man, "Stick the arrows that you have into my fur where it's heavy. I'll hemorrhage from my mouth. And you go up to the lodge and holler. Say, 'I've driven the buffalo here that you wanted. I found it. And now I don't have any arrows. Perhaps you can help somehow. Maybe you can do something.' As soon as he comes hurrying out and gets close, I'm going to hook him with my horns."

So that is what this young man did. Then the two of them came on. Ah, then this buffalo was staggering around as they went up to the lodge! Then the young man began calling out, "Hey, what are you doing? You must hurry out to help me! Here's what you wanted! I have no more arrows!"

Then this man rushed out of the lodge. Then he was laughing when he looked at the spotted buffalo. [He went back inside and] then brought his arrows out. Then he went close to the buffalo, which knelt on its forelegs. It appeared to be dying.

When that man came up close to it, the buffalo jumped up and knocked him down. Then it began goring him. Then it hooked him in the stomach. It yanked his arms off and then his legs. It tore out all his intestines.

<Then the young woman and her mother came outside. They began helping the young man.>

Then the buffalo said, "Now quickly burn him! Now let those two wolves go quickly! Let them run off!"

Then the wolves went off running. They had been captives.

"And now I'll go on since I have a long distance to travel. Now burn the ground where his blood is! If you don't burn all his blood, he'll come back to life. He won't be good then. He won't be afraid of us. Now do everything I have told you!"

Then this buffalo departed quickly. Then it ran off.

Then these people burned the man's body, oh, after the young woman his wife and the old woman his mother-in-law piled up wood. Oh, they burned him! They burned everything up where he lay after he had been gored to death—they burned his intestines and everything.

"Now let things here be as they are!"

Then the young woman and her mother took the various robes and things they wore, and then they all returned to where our villages were.

Then the people said, "They've come!"

Then the young man said, "We've done away with that man. Here this is what he was doing! He did away with the young men, killing them. He was the one mistreating them."

This woman [who had been his wife] said, "Oh, poor me, I was a slave. He kept us as slaves. He said, 'If you don't do as I tell you, these two wolves will eat you up.' Now that's the reason we were living there doing what he told us to do."

18

Red Dog and the Four Stars

This myth is a combination of two motifs: an explan-
ation for the configuration of four stars set close together in
the southern sky and a recounting of the feat of Red Dog,
a man who had power to call the buffalo. Together they
maintain a persistent mythical association of buffalo and
stars. The plot is tied together by a young woman who first
marries the leader of four star men who bring prosperity to
her family and her village, and then allows herself to be
seduced by the dauntless young man, Red Dog. After her
seduction, the star men foresake the village. The young
woman entreats her husband to return by placing a pipe in
front of him four times, but each time he steps around it,
alternately from each side, creating a winding path. This
pattern is replicated when the stars return to the heavens. A
famine occurs after the star men leave, and the remainder of
the story is an account of how Red Dog succeeds in summon-
ing a herd of buffalo to alleviate it. Hidatsas tell a similar
story of a man named Yellow Dog, but their version lacks the
star association as well as any reference to a constellation.

When we used to live in villages there to the east, it was not
really far from Fort Clark. It was where our villages were clustered
farther downriver. The people there were Arikaras. These I am
telling about were Arikaras, not Hidatsas or Mandans.

There once was a young woman <an only child> whose parents
loved her, and different men admired her, wanting to marry her.
But she refused. She did not want to get married.

And one day some men arrived. There were four of them. Then
they came to the door of her lodge. They were carrying meat, either
deer or some other kind. They entered. Then they put the meat
down at the holy area on the west side of the lodge. Then three of
them went back out, but the other one, the leader, remained there.
And here this one became the husband of that young woman.

Now this man was doing the same thing repeatedly, bringing the family meat and different things.

When summer came things were good when the people planted their gardens—when they used to plant gardens of corn, squash, and beans. There were no potatoes then; but corn, squash, and beans—these were the things they planted. It was good then.

Now, as is usually the case, there was a dauntless young man who began pestering this woman. After courting her, he finally slept with her.

Now one night afterward the four men who were always coming to the family's lodge came again. They arrived. They came inside. Then they put the meat down. Now the one who was the leader continued walking. Then he went outside. Then they all went outside. Then they went off again toward the east.

This young woman went after them and caught up with the man she was married to. But they just continued going on, not stopping <or even answering her when she spoke to her husband>.

And so the young woman went to the leading doctor. "Fill my pipe for me!" Then he filled it with tobacco.

Then this young woman went off again. She overtook the four men way off there. She laid the pipe down in front of them, wanting her husband to turn back. Then he went around it. Now he continued on; he just went on again.

Now she did that four times [setting the pipe down in front of them, but each time they went around it and continued going]. Then the young woman gave up. Then she came back; she arrived back at the village. She felt downhearted, too.

Then there was a famine. Ah, the people could not find any buffalo when they went out onto the prairie to hunt. They were starving now.

And this young woman became angry. "You're the cause," she said of the young man named Red Dog, the dauntless young man who had seduced her and secretly slept with her. Then this young woman became angry. Then she stormed out to look for him.

Meanwhile that Red Dog became sickly and, ah, would just sit around. Now he was sick.

Then this young woman went to him angrily. Then she said, "Now you yourself are the cause of your being the way you are. And you're the cause of our people's hunger because of what you did to me when you deceived me [by sleeping with me when I already had a husband]. Now you're the one who is the cause. Now what are you yourself doing to save the people?"

Now this Red Dog got up. "Yes. Now that's what I did."

Well, then he stood up and shook himself. Then he changed himself [to a big man]. Then he told his father, "Now announce to the people, 'All of you in the village, search through your things, where you used to put your dried meat and store it! Ah, give me a piece of fat, even if it's small!'"

And so the people did that: then they searched through their things looking for a piece of fat.

Now there was a little girl who was walking around there. She wore a necklace with a turtle on it. It was a small turtle that she wore around her neck. Then they took it away from her. There inside it was a piece of fat. It was a small piece inside the turtle. When the turtle had been blessed by rubbing fat over it, the one who did it must have put some fat inside it.

"Here it is."

Then they took it to Red Dog. "Now we've found it, and this girl has saved us."

"Now make a fire!"

Then they made a fire, oh, a big fire!

Then he prayed to the powers. Then he threw it into the fire. Oh, it looked as if there were meat boiling. Then everyone in the village who had been starving became energetic.

Then Red Dog said, "Now after four days someone should go off to the top of the hills. There he'll look to see what's happening. Maybe good fortune will come our way."

Oh, while they waited, four days passed. Then two men went off. They ran there.

And then there was a multitude of buffalo that had come in a herd.

Then one man reported, "Now there is a big herd there. The buffalo are coming close. Well, what are we going to do?"

Then the men went out from the village. Then they slaughtered the buffalo. Then the people became reinvigorated after they ate their fill.

But this Red Dog then married that young woman he had seduced. <She became his wife. And her first husband went off.>

Now sometime later the village moved.

Now there was a trail there. There used to be a trail. They called it Winding Trail. It was there [where the young woman laid the pipe down four times and the men walked around it from behind each time. The pattern of their path was the winding trail.]

But these men—why, here these men were stars! There were four of these stars. They stand over there in the southern heavens. Now they are the ones. The woman was the one seduced by them.

Now the tribe moved, but this Red Dog was holy. He was holy, too, the one who had been blessed by a dog and had been dauntless.

Now this is the extent of what I know. Short Bear used to tell the story. But there are others who tell it. They know it a little differently. I hesitated to tell it since someone else will perhaps have it a different way when he tells it. But the way I have told it is just the way my grandfather Short Bear used to tell it.

19

The Young Man Who Became a Snake and Carries The Antelope

This narrative is a conjoining of two stories now common to the Arikaras, Hidatsas, and Mandans as well as many other Plains tribes. In the first story a young man breaks a cultural taboo against eating snake flesh and subsequently becomes a snake himself. A companion puts him in the Missouri River, where he stretches from Eagle

Nose Butte to the Killdeer Mountains. Herein is the explanation for why hunting parties made offerings to this snake in order to cross the Missouri safely. This story has a ritual significance for Hidatsas not found among Arikaras (Bowers 1965:359–60).

The second story is an account of supernatural powers bestowed on Carries The Antelope, a young man so named in recognition of his hunting prowess and habit of carrying antelopes into the village on his back. After thunderbirds take him up onto one of the Thunder Buttes, he saves their children by killing a gigantic two-headed snake in the water below. In gratitude the thunderbirds give him their powers and he becomes a bird himself. But the snake in the Missouri River from the previous story takes from him all his bird ways except the powers to flash lightning from his eyes and to control rainfall. Reputedly of Hidatsa origin, this myth exemplifies the widespread motif of cosmic conflict between thunderbirds and underwater beings. For Hidatsas it explains certain rituals as well as the origin of their Low Cap clan (Bowers 1965:360–62). It has no ritual significance for Arikaras.

Now I am going to relate an old story that they used to tell— what I used to hear about things that happened when we were migrating upriver. I do not know where the village was when this story occurred. I do not know where it was.

Two young men went out hunting and were going all over hunting for game. They say that after they had hunted, they started for home. They had not found anything. Now they were hungry as they were coming back.

Then they came to a certain place where there had been a prairie fire. The land was burned off. And there lay a snake. It stretched a long way. Its body was high.

"Now, say, let's go around it over there where its head is."

But they could not reach the end of it.

Now they went along the side of it. Then they walked the other way toward the end of its tail. <They were going and going. But

there was no end to it.>

Then one said, "I'm tired. Also I'm hungry. Let's stay here overnight! And in the morning we'll go looking for our people."

And then the other boy said, "Say, surely I'm starving to death. It sure smells good. I'm hungry. This one is a fish. It smells like a fish does when it's cooked. Why, I'll eat it."

Then he cut it. Then he sliced the meat. Then he began to eat the snake meat.

But his friend said, "We certainly don't eat snake. Why, even if we're hungry, what you have done is not good."

"Hey, I'm truly starving," he said as he ate.

Now they lay down to sleep. One lay on one side of the fire and the other lay on the other side of it.

Now when it was morning the young man got up. His feet were spotted all over, and his hands were also spotted all over.

Then the other young man said, "Now, look! After I told you not to do it, after I didn't want you to eat the snake, this is what has happened to you."

"Hey, it's certainly nice. When we reach our village and I roll my leggings up, my legs will be spotted when I go around the village. The young women will admire me when they see my spotted hands."

Then as they were coming along, the young man said, "Say, I'm tired." He felt heavy as he came.

Then he said, "Let's stay overnight here!"

Then they lay down to sleep again. The one could not do anything when he was becoming spotted. The other one was the one who was now making their fires.

"Surely I told you not to do it—that you should not eat the snake. You didn't listen to me. Now look! What has happened to you is not good."

Then they came on again. Then the young man became worse. His entire body was spotted that way. Now his legs were barely able to step forward. Then they stayed overnight again. Wherever they had gone, it must have been far off.

《   》

Now in the morning the young man said, "Now, brother, I can't get up. I am whole: I don't have any legs; I also don't have any arms. Only my head remains separate. But I want to tell you, don't be afraid of me. You must drag me close to the edge of the Missouri River. Lay my head facing there to the east. And the end of my tail will be there by the Killdeer Mountains, and my head will be there at Eagle Nose Butte.[1]

"Now you people will be coming across the river to this side. Whenever you come to cross the river, you must give me a corn ball. And then I'll surface and make a bridge for you, and then you'll cross on top of me. But you must give me a corn ball; and then all of you will cross. Also when you come from the other way, you should do the same thing.

"Now I am half Mandan and half Hidatsa. Now I want you to do this for me. Whatever you ask of me will come to pass."

Now this young man cried as he mourned for his friend while dragging him. He dragged him to the edge of the water. "Now this is what you said, brother." Then he rolled him into the water. The young snake man went into the water.

Then the young man came up the bank and returned home.

Then he told the people about it: "This is what happened. My brother became a snake, a water monster. He ate snake flesh. I warned him against it. He didn't listen. This is the way it was. Now he has disappeared. He is no more.

"But this is what he said. 'When you people cross the river, give me corn balls, and I'll take you across. Corn balls are what I liked the taste of when I was living among you.'"

《 《 《   》 》 》

Now here is where the story of Carries The Antelope commences. This young man must have been one who had good fortune

1. This hill is located on the west side of the Missouri River, south of the present city of Mandan, North Dakota (see map 1).

Plate 5. Thunder Buttes, McKenzie County, North Dakota. Photograph from the early twentieth century, courtesy State Historical Society of North Dakota.

whenever he went hunting, whenever he hunted for various things.

And one time he was led farther west, over there to the area around what we now call Mandaree.[2] That is the place there. A tall hill was there—the hill that was there.[3] That is where Carries The Antelope stopped to camp overnight. Then Carries The Antelope made a fire. "I'll stay overnight here, and then I'll begin to hunt." He spent the night there.

Then it became daylight, and when he awoke he was in a different place. When he sat upright here he discovered that he had been carried up to the top of a butte by thunderbirds!

There they were, two of them. Here they were young ones! When they looked around, lightning flashed. And when they flapped their wings, sparks flew out from under the wings while he watched them.

"Ah, I wonder what happened for me to be lying here on top of this butte."

And then one young thunderbird said, "Now!" Then the rain came. Then drops of rain fell while it thundered.

Then one—here it was a young male—said, "My father has given me permission to tell you that you won't die. You'll go back to your village.

"But this is the reason you were brought here where we are living. My father here has been saying, 'We're depending on you. Nothing is going to be difficult for you as you go around, as you kill different things when you're hunting. Now we're depending on you. That's the reason we brought you here where you are now.'

"Now that's my sister there. She's a young female and I'm a young male. Now my mother and my father and my uncle are all coming. They're coming here to see you where we are now.

"Now whenever it's time for us to leave the nest and begin flying, our downy feathers drop on the water of the lake down below to the west. There's a snake in the water. It has two heads. One comes up over there in the west, and the other comes up over there

---

2. A community established in 1955 in the Western Segment of the Fort Berthold Reservation after construction of the Garrison Dam. Many residents of Elbowoods, which was flooded by the dam, settled here.

3. It is generally identified as one of the Thunder Buttes west of the Missouri River southwest of Senish, North Dakota (see map 4).

in the east. There are two of them. Then the one here eats us up
<just when we are big enough to provide good meat>. I don't know
how many times this has happened.

"Now this is the reason that you have come here—that our
parents brought you here. Now you are going to kill this snake.
Now if it does happen that you do this, you're going to have done a
thankful thing. The powers will look favorably upon you.

"Now this is what is going to happen. We'll prepare you. Our
parents will give you two arrows which you're going to use."

Then it got dark again while he waited. Then it was morning
and it rained again as it thundered.

Then the thunderbird boy talked; he said, "Come closer! Now
I'm going to tell you."

Then this man sat down by him.

"Here are the two arrows that you're going to use." Oh, they
were sharp arrows! "These are the ones you're going to use. Now
everything is ready. Early in the morning, when it begins to dawn,
it's usually foggy. My father says, 'The air is not clear.' But now
you're going to watch over there in the east: that is the place. There
is where the first one comes up. When the head comes up, it's a
really large one. Right underneath its jaw, below the base of the
throat, there is a black spot. That is where you are to shoot it.

"And when the other head comes up, you should do the same
thing.

"Meanwhile we are going to help you. The other thunderbirds
up above will weaken the snake by shooting bolts of lightning. And
then you'll shoot the arrow accurately."

And then this young man got ready. Then he strung the bow.
Now he sat beside a stone by the ledge, on the side where it usually
came up.

Then the <big yellow> head appeared where the thunderbird
boy had said. Now it opened its mouth as it went angrily at the two
young thunderbirds. The young man shot it where he had been told.
The arrow went straight to that spot. The arrow disappeared.

Then the head fell back. Then it made thumping sounds as it
rolled down the side of the cliff.

Then the young man went over there to the west side. Now the

head came up there. He did the same thing again: he felled this
head, too, while the thunderbirds above were also hurling lightning
bolts at it.

Then, after it rained, the sky became clear. Then the sun came
out. There it lay on the prairie in the distance: there was a long
body; there were two heads.

Now the thunderbird boy said, "My sister and I are going to
take you. You'll hang onto us and we'll take you to the base of the
hill. Now you are to butcher the thing lying there, cut it up, and
spread its flesh around. Now birds from all over this earth are going
to come and eat it. They're going to eat a meal.

"Now my father, my mother, my uncle, my grandmother, and
my grandfather are going to talk to you. Now grab onto us. Our
wings are close together."

Then they brought him to the base of the hill. They set his feet
on the ground. Meanwhile the relatives of the thunderbird boy and
girl flew down. They swooped low. After he was set down by them,
this young man Carries The Antelope butchered the snake. Oh, he
cut up chunks of meat and then laid them on the prairie. Then, oh,
all different kinds of birds flew down here and there. Then they ate.

It clouded up again. Then he saw them. There lay what they
call flat wood, paddles to whip things as when lightning strikes.
One strikes [an enemy, for example] with it, and then one has done
something. Then one has performed a great deed. These were the
ones.[4]

Then the thunderbird boy said, "Now there are seven of them.
Now all of them are new except the last one, which is old. You'll
take that one. You'll use that one! This one is really the strongest
one. It's already old. It's been there a long time. They've had it a
long time. These others are all new. They aren't really strong. They
aren't as swift."

Well, then he asked, "Do you want to return to your village or
would you rather be among us here? We want you to come be

---

4. "Flat wood" designates a paddle-shaped coup stick, approximately two
and a half feet long. Such sticks were attached to the outer part of village
sacred bundles.

among us for a while. Now there remains one more thing that we want you to kill for us. It's there in the water. Its tail is here close by, but its head is far off down the river. Now you should attack it at its head! Kill it for us, too! Oh, we'll be thankful if you do that for us. Then you can go to your village. We'll take you.

"Now things won't be difficult for you whenever you want to go against the enemy. You'll have the powers to get everything you want, no matter what the powers may be."

Now when the rain came the young man and the thunderbirds flew over the valley yonder as they were looking for the water monster lying in the river—the one who had been put into the river after he ate the snake meat that I told about previously.[5]

But the one lying there in the river knew what was happening when it was being spied upon by Carries The Antelope. It knew it. Then the one there in the river surfaced. It thought, "Approach close to me! Then I'll grab you." Then that is what it did when the water always rose—when the water rose and got deep. That is how it was when the water rose.

And then Carries The Antelope, as he was flying overhead and looking all around watching for it, saw it. There its head was, close to the river bank. Then he landed. Meantime the thunderbirds were flying around in circles, watching Carries The Antelope. He landed and lurked about, wanting to trick it.

But the one in the river was watching Carries The Antelope. When Carries The Antelope went toward it, it smacked him with its tail. It snagged him in the mouth. It took him underwater. Ah, the ones up above were shooting lightning bolts at it as he was taken underwater.

Now the snake there under the water was the young man who had previously eaten the snake meat. And then he said, "Now, brother, you have done wrong to lurk about, looking for me. I know what you have done. You are holy, and I am that way, too: I am holy. Now I have overcome you by catching you. Now I beseech you:

5. Carries The Antelope has now been transformed into a thunderbird, one of the powers conferred on him.

let things be as they are! Don't do this again! Now I'm going to take
your powers away from you."

Then the two of them went into a sweat lodge. Then the snake
man began making this Carries The Antelope vomit things up—
whatever his powers were, whatever the powers were that he
possessed. Then he changed him.

Then the snake man said, "Now you are going to go to our
village. Now don't do it again! I'll know. Things won't be difficult for
you. But now I have deprived you. But there remains one thing
that is too difficult for me to do: you still have the power to shoot
lightning bolts with your vision, of having lightning in your eyes
when you look around. But I'll give you the power of shed buffalo
hair. You'll tie it over your forehead, and it won't lightning when
you look around.

"Now go back to our village!"

Then he brought him to the surface and doctored him. And
then Carries The Antelope went. He returned home to his village,
wherever the Hidatsa, Mandan, and our own Arikara villages were.

Now that is what that man used to be able to do. Whenever he
looked around, his eyes flashed lightning. And that shed buffalo
hair is what he had tied on his forehead. Now people feared him.
Whatever he said would happen always happened. And when there
was no rain, the people filled a pipe when they wanted rain to
moisten the gardens. Then he would do it: he called the rain, and
then it rained.

Now the people took good care of him. He was accorded high
social status. Things were not difficult for him: he had the power
for success in stealing horses and hunting for the enemy. It was
natural for him to be a leader, to be a chief. Now Carries The
Antelope was the one, the one I have told you about.

When they used to tell this story, they would not tell it in the
summer when the thunder was coming.

It is not known where this man went after he died. He said,
"Now I'm dying. But I'm going to be coming back to do what I'm
supposed to do. Remember to give me the pipe sometimes. Oh, I'll
be thankful <and give you rain>. Offer me the pipe <when you want
it to rain>!" Now that is what the old people used to do when there

were spirits around.

Now today we do not have those powers. We are negligent. I know a little of what they used to tell me. I usually do what I should and He[6] always grants me what I beseech of Him, what I want.

20

Mice Mouth, the Boy Blessed by the Mice

The Arikaras, like surrounding tribes, saw the mouse as a potential source of power, particularly the ability to slip furtively and quickly into and out of difficult situations. A historical observer of this attitude toward mice was the fur trader Henry A. Boller, who recounted that in 1858 Sioux visitors at Fort Berthold were so troubled by the many mice running over them at night "they got up, lit their pipes, and declared they could not sleep because the mice were Great Spirits" (1959:171–72). The following story tells of a young man rewarded with their power after he saves a mouse couple's children. Like many such tales, this one is also a narrative about the abuse of power; the recipient uses it for evil and the people are ultimately driven to put him to death.

They used to call this river the Heart River. That is where the villages once were when our people were migrating this way from down below in the south, they used to say. Now it is not known how long they lived there after coming to its banks, but they stayed a long time.

---

6. The Chief Above *(neešaánu' tⁱnačitákUx).*

≪   »

Then there were no deer in the vicinity of the villages, after they became scarce because of so many boys going around hunting.

Well, then the chiefs, the ones who made the rules, said, "Surely it's difficult here. Let's move farther on to where there is game! Let's go there!"

It was some time in the spring, when the weather usually gets warm. Then the people moved off. When they were migrating closer up this way, they came up onto the top of a ridge.

Now one young man had remained behind in the village, where he was going around among the lodges. "Later I'll go where the people have gone."

While he was going around he heard a woman crying inside an earth lodge. A woman was crying. This young man went there. Then he entered the lodge and there sat a woman crying.

And then the young man said, "Ah, what's the matter? Did they leave you behind? What happened that they left you?"

Then this woman said, "No. They didn't leave me. But they took my children, who are with the group that has gone. They took mine. They are the ones I'm crying for. Now is it possible for you to bring my children back?"

Then this one said, "I'll go. I'll do it. If it isn't too difficult, I'll do it."

Then the woman said, "Fine. The men who are in the lead have a white buffalo robe and in it are my children. Now is it possible for you to bring my children back?"

Then this one said, "I'll go. It's difficult, but I'll do it if they're willing to unfold the white buffalo robe." Inside it is where the medicines were kept. That must have been how they kept their medicine long, long ago. "I'll return if it isn't too difficult for me."

And then this young man came after them. He came up onto the hills there. Then the people were on top of one in the distance. Then he arrived where they were. They had turned the horses loose to graze. "It's far where we're going." <And the horses needed food and rest.>

Now this young man arrived there. Then he said, "You chiefs who are sitting here, I want you to unfold that robe. I want to see it. I want to pray to the medicines in it."

"Yes. Now do that!"

Then that is what he did. Then he untied it, and there were four mice. There were four mice lying there in it. Then he furtively took them up and put them under the robe he wore. Now he retied the medicine robe. Then he quickly left the group and went back to where he had been. He vanished all at once.

Before long he came quickly into the deserted village. And then he went to the lodge where the woman had been inside. Then he entered and there she sat. Also there sat a man. There were now two inside the lodge.

"Now here they are. Are they the ones?"

Then she said, "Yes. They're the ones. Oh, now we're so thankful to you. This is the one who is my husband. These are our children."

Now these two talked to the young man. "Now the ways of the warpath are not going to be difficult for you, nor will whatever you may want, no matter what it may be. You aren't going to have it difficult."

Now the other one, the man, jumped up. He just flew against the young man on one side. On the young man's cheek there was now the image of a mouse. The other one, the woman, did the same thing on his other cheek.

"Now we're thankful to you. You aren't going to have it difficult. Whatever you want you'll find it. And you'll take it and you'll have it. <And when somebody talks about you, you're going to hear it. You'll know.>"

Well, then the young man came after them. Then he caught up with the people as they were moving on. And, wherever it was, they camped there. And the ways of the warpath—horse stealing and striking the enemy—were not hard for him. <His relatives were proud of him.> Perhaps he married. They never mentioned that matter.

Well, then he began to do bad things. He was a bad person when he was stealing the wives of other men. After some man would marry a woman, here he would steal her. Then he would elope with her. Then as he was doing these things, people began to dislike him.

And whenever a baby would cry, its mother would say, "Stop crying! Mice Mouth will come." When Mice Mouth discovered it, he snatched the baby and bashed its head on the ground. He killed it, just as he was killing many of them. His actions were evil.

Now there was one man who was violent. He was strong. He was confident of his strength. Then one day he said, "I've just been hoping that Mice Mouth and I might encounter one another and that I could work him over." That is what the man was saying.

That man went off somewhere one time. Then he began trapping. Now they used to dig a pit. It would be a deep pit in a trail habitually traveled by deer. <The pit was covered so that the trap could not be seen.> And then when a deer passed over it, it would fall into the pit, and then it would die after it was trapped inside. Now sometimes, too, a coyote or some other animal would fall into it and be killed.

That is what this man was doing: then he began digging a pit. While he was busy doing it, he looked up and there standing above was the man called Mice Mouth. He had an antelope skin cap over his head.

Then the man in the pit said, "Ah, you're the one I have been looking for. It's certainly good that you've found me here." Then the man got out. "Your actions—the things you're doing—are bad. You've hurt the feelings of many people in this village of our tribe. Now we're going to fight."

Then Mice Mouth said, "If it has to be that way, let it be. If you want it that way, we'll fight."

And then this man put his bow and arrows down. The other one put his bow and arrows down, too.

Now they fought there, each struggling with the other. Now when this man who had been trapping was pushed backward, he kicked Mice Mouth's bow and arrows away so that he could not snatch them up. And it was the same way with the other one: when Mice Mouth was pushed back, he did the same thing, kicking the man's bow and arrows away.

But after they had been struggling with one another for a while, they calmed down. Now neither one of them was beaten.

This man, after Mice Mouth caused his eyes to swell, was barely able to see. Then he went off. Then he went back toward the village. As he was going along he called out for someone to help him.

People came for him. "What's the matter?"

Then he said, "Mice Mouth and I found each other. He must be as strong as I am."

Then they took him into the village.

Now this Mice Mouth was tough. No one was able to do anything with him. Whenever they talked about him, here he would hear it! "Now we'll spy on him. We'll kill him." Here he would know it!

Now a group prepared to go on the warpath. "Let's go on the warpath!" Then they set out. There were many of them.

Now they always had corn balls made of ground corn flour. Oh, that is what the man Mice Mouth liked, ground corn flour. They had it.

As they were going along, they saw Mice Mouth. He was running by in the distance. Then he went into the water. There he crossed to the other side. It was a lake.

"There goes Mice Mouth."

Then they began to call him. He came running.

"Hey, it's certainly good to see you. You must just be wandering around."

Then he said, "Yes. Why, I usually just wander around. I don't live in your village anymore. You people don't like me." That is what he was saying.

"Now we've brought this for you. It's what you like to eat."

He was overjoyed when he ate it. Then he gulped a mouthful.

"Now!" Then they grabbed him and tickled him. Then he choked. He fell over unconscious. Then they killed him.

Then they went on, and after they had traveled around they started back for home. "Now let's go to where we killed Mice Mouth. Let's see if he's there yet."

Then they arrived there at the lake that he had gone into. But he was not lying there. The mice must have come. They must have picked him up. They must have hidden him.

Then the party came back home. After they returned, they said,

"We killed Mice Mouth, who has been bothering us. We left his body. He was lying there. He was dead. But when we came back, we said, 'Let's go see him!' And then he wasn't lying there! We don't know what happened. We don't know where he went."

He had died. They had killed Mice Mouth. His actions—the things that he did—were not good. Then the people hated him.

21

The Young Woman Who Married an Elk

This story exemplifies the power of elk to charm women and to lure them from their husbands. At the same time it is a story of power bestowed on a man who makes himself pitiful—here the aggrieved husband mourning the loss of his wife—and who is given war and hunting powers that enable him to achieve chiefly status through successful exploits.

Now it is not known exactly where this story occurred, but it was when the people were migrating this way from the east. I do not know whether these people coming from the east were Hidatsas, Arikaras, or Mandans, but I do know the story of what happened.

Now after a young man married and he and his wife were living together, the young man's father told him, "It certainly would be good if you were to go out hunting, if you were to go on a hunt." That is what they used to say.

Then this couple—the young man and young woman who had recently married—got ready to go. Now they must not have had horses. But they had eight dogs.[1] Then they packed their gear on

---

1. In another version of this story, told in English, the narrator says that the couple had seven dogs.

what they used to call a travois, which the dogs pulled. They had
various things, all of them light in weight.

Then they set out toward the west. "Over the hill" is where they
used to say it was—that is where they used to live.[2] Then they
went west, over there where the land was wooded and where buffalo, elk, and antelope roamed, not where people lived.[3] Game must
have liked the wooded country there.

Now this couple made camp where water was close by. Then
they built what they used to call a hunting lodge[4] and picketed
their dogs. And in the morning the young man would go out hunting, wandering off somewhere, and bring back a deer or antelope
after he had killed one. When he would come back to the camp, the
dogs would get up, happy to know that he was returning.

Shortly after he returned with meat, the young man and his
wife would eat some of it after it was cooked. Then the young
woman would begin drying the rest of the meat, and the young man
would go off again.

The dogs watched. They watched over this couple. At night they
were untied so that they could bark at coyotes coming up close to
the camp.

Now finally the couple had a large supply of dried meat. Then
the young woman told her husband, "I feel like going home now. We
have been here a long time, and now there is plenty of dried meat."

Then the young man replied, "I think I'll get just a little more!
Make some more dried meat, and then we'll go." Then the young
man went off hunting. He wouldn't come back all day since he went
far off searching for game.

2. The expression 'over the hill' is a reference to the Arikara village at
Fort Clark, occupied by the tribe between 1838 and 1861. It is also used
sometimes to refer to the former villages along the Missouri River south of
Fort Clark, when the tribe lived farther downstream (see p. 84).

3. Here and in other Arikara stories the expression designating 'wooded
country out west' refers to the badlands country of western North Dakota.

4. This lodge, termed *akanaanuútu'*, was a conical shelter built on a
foundation of four forked poles covered first with branches, then with a
layer of grass, and finally with earth. The semipermanent earth-covered
lodge was built by a hunting party when it planned to be camped in one
place for an extended period. (See Wilson 1934:411–15.)

So the young woman took one hide and staked it out. Now she was scraping it to take the hair off. They did not tell whether it was a deer or buffalo hide. Then the wind came up and brought a nice odor. Then the young woman began to look around.

There in the distance stood a young man. She looked at him, but did not know him. Oh, there was a nice odor brought by the wind.

Then the young woman picked up her things and went into the lodge. After a while she came out. He was not there. He must have gone.

Now the dogs began to growl when they saw the strange young man. Now the young man kept doing this, coming to the spot for however many times it was.

That night the young woman told her husband, "I want us to go home. I don't like it: I've been seeing a strange person. He might be an enemy. Maybe he'll kill me or make me a slave."

Then the young man replied, "There certainly is no one around here. I certainly know the country here, and no one is going around. But now we'll go home. I think I'll just go out once more! Let me go hunting once more and then tomorrow we'll go back home." It was the next day that they planned to return home, and when the young man left to go hunting again for the last time, he said, "Now we'll truly go home."

Later the strange young man whom the young woman had been seeing came to the door of the lodge. Then he said, "I've come after you. Hurry! Let's go!"

Then the young woman jumped up. He must have mesmerized her [with medicine]. Then she began to follow him. The dogs meanwhile were growling. Then he took her off, eloping with her. Then the two went off, with her following him.

Later the husband of the young woman returned to their camp, and when he looked for his wife, she was not there. There lay the things that she had been sewing, or whatever she had been doing. The dogs were whining.

Then the young man said, "You dogs are holy. Now tell me where she went!"

Then he untied them. Then the dogs jumped up and followed

the trail of the young woman and the strange young man.

The husband went up onto a high hill, and there in the distance went the two, the strange young man and the young woman who was his wife.

Then he told the dogs, "Now go home from here! I don't know what I'm going to do, but I might bring her back."

Then the dogs stopped, but the young man went on in pursuit. He caught up with the couple. Then he got ahead of them. And here to his surprise it was an elk!

Then he thought, "I'll shoot it." But when he shot at it, the arrow glanced off. It did not penetrate the hide. It would not pierce it.

He followed and followed the couple, shooting at the elk until he used up all his arrows. Then the couple went up a hill. There was a valley below, and in it was a lake. That was where they were headed.

Now no matter what the young man did, when he approached his wife she paid no attention to him. She followed the one ahead of her, and here it was an elk!

Then the elk went into the water. Then the young woman went into the water, too. They both went underwater.

Then the young man [who was her husband] cried and cried while he was at the edge of the water. Oh, then it became dark.

Just before morning the young woman came to the surface. Then she said, "You must go home now. We can't be together again. It's difficult where I live now. And now you must go! When I was anxious for us to go home, you didn't heed me. Now what I didn't want to happen has happened. And you yourself are the cause. Now go!

"But if there is anything that you want—good fortune on the warpath or in hunting—you should come right here. You should tell us what you want.

"Now after winter has passed and the weather begins to get warm, bring me a dress, a belt, and a pair of moccasins. You'll lay them here. Bring them for me!

"Now you are going to marry another young woman. She will look just like I do. It isn't going to be a long time off.

"Now go! Make haste! Go!"

Then the young man hastened to go back to gather his things. Then he returned to their camp. He arrived back at their camp. He gathered everything up. The dogs were there, and then he loaded the gear onto them and led them back.

He arrived there, wherever our village was, wherever it was. Then he arrived at night. He entered the lodge. Then he lay down to sleep. Everyone was already sleeping. No one knew when he returned.

In the morning when his father, mother, and sisters arose, there the young man lay.

"All of you get up quickly! Look! Here's a pile of dried meat. He must have brought it. Our daughter-in-law must have gone somewhere else. She must have gone to her mother's lodge." That is what they were each saying.

Then the young man arose. Then he said, "The daughter-in-law you're looking for is not here. This is what happened. She and another eloped. An elk is the cause, when he took my woman. And then this is what she said to me: 'You yourself are the cause.' She had wanted us to hurry back home, but I didn't do it. My hunting delayed me. I was having no difficulty in killing all kinds of game. I liked that. I was enjoying it.

"Now that's what happened. She lives there now. She lives in the water there where the hills are clustered." He told them the place. "That's where she is living.

"And this is what she said: 'Bring me a dress, a pair of moccasins, and a belt. After the weather usually gets warm, when it usually gets hot, that will be the time.

"'But now you will marry another woman. She will look just like I do. It isn't going to be a long time off.'"

Now it happened that way: then he and a young woman began living together. She looked like his former wife.

Now after the weather usually gets warm, after the earth usually gets warm and the green grass comes up, when it was hot, the young man led a party on the warpath, and he took a dress, a pair of moccasins, and a belt, just as his former wife had said. They went on, and then they arrived right there near the lake.

Then the young man left the party. "And now I'll go off for a while. I'll look all around." Then he went over to where the lake was.

Then he said, "Here are the things you asked for."

Then she surfaced. Then she said, "You have pleased me. And now, what you have wished for will happen. Nothing is going to be difficult for you. Whatever you seek you will find."

Well, then this young woman went underwater, and the young man went back to where his companions were.

Now he subsequently did as she had said, counting many coups on the enemy. Then he became a chief. After he had everything—after he and his father had many horses—he began to own the village.[5]

Now this is where it was. This is what happened. I do not know whether the story belongs to the Arikaras, or Hidatsas, or Mandans. I never found out.

22

The Young Man Who Was Given Elk Power

Several themes are combined in this story. Two of the most common are the abduction of a young woman by an animal and the ability of animals and humans to transform themselves into one another. Here a bear assumes human form and mesmerizes a young woman whom he takes away. While mourning the loss, her husband is pitied by the spirit of a dead elk, which endows him with the power to trans-

---

5. The expression 'to own the village' means to be its chief and have social and political control of it.

form himself into that animal, known for its strength and
virility. It also instructs him how to charm women with a
whistle that imitates the call of an elk, illustrating once
again the elk's sexual power over women. The drama cul-
minates in a test of strength among the three most ferocious
animals: the bear pitted against the young elk man and his
brother, who has the power to transform himself into a
young buffalo bull.

Now I am going to tell a story. This one that I will tell is a true
story.

Now a young man got married to a young woman after they had
been going together.
"Now let's go on a hunting trip out west!"
I don't know where the village was.
Now they gathered their gear together. They had dogs to carry
their belongings. And then they went off.
Oh, then they camped somewhere in wooded country. They had
a lodge, either a wall tent or a tipi, whichever kind of lodge it was.
And then the young man would go out hunting and bring back
deer, buffalo, or antelope, and the young woman would make dried
meat and also tan the hides, while they were preparing for winter.
That is what they used to say one did in the fall.

Now one day while the young woman was in their lodge, a man
just came up to it. Then he said, "Now come! I've come after you."
This young woman just sat there. Whatever it was that he did,
the man made her forget everything. Then she followed him. They
went off, wherever it was that they went.
There were three dogs there. They were growling angrily. They
were tied up.
And then the young man came back to the camp late in the
afternoon. He brought back meat, but his wife was not there.
"I wonder where she is? Maybe she went after wood." As he was
looking all around, he thought, "Maybe she went after water." She
was nowhere around.
Then he untied the dogs. "What is it? Where did the one who

looks after us go?"

Now these dogs were whining. They headed over there toward the west. When they got to the edge of the woods, they stopped.

Then this young man said, "Now I know. Now here's the way she went!"

Then the young man took the dogs back and tied them up, and then he went all around, crying as he looked in vain for his wife.

While he was searching around, there lay something on the ground! It was the remains of an elk that had apparently been there a long time. Its bones were there. Its bones were there. The skull was there with the horns still on it.

Then he thought, "They always say, 'Elk, you are holy.' Perhaps you might pity me."

Then he began crying out there where the elk's bones lay, going around them and crying.

Oh, finally he was satisfied. Then he lay down and slept.

A man touched him. "Now, I've come to tell you. I know what you are seeking. You're seeking your wife. Your wife is not lost. This is what he's been doing. Why, now he's overstepped his limits. A black bear is the one. He took your woman. But he hasn't laid a hand on her yet. He's the one responsible for taking her away. He lives over there. His den is far away. This is what he's been doing. He has a large number of women whom he has taken.

"Now tomorrow gather up some provisions! But make your pack light for yourself! In the meantime, go! Go home! When you get there, you should ask your father to make you an elk whistle, one that imitates the sound of an elk. Your father knows how. It'll take two days.

"After four days have passed, you'll come with your brother. Your brother is exceedingly powerful. You'll come with him.

"Oh, the one who has your woman is extremely holy. But we are going to help you, too.

"Now do these things quickly! Hurry!"

Then this young man started out. Then he went back to his lodge. Then he untied the dogs. He packed some moccasins. Then he came on. Then he arrived at the village after dark.

Then he lay down to sleep. While he lay there, it became day-light.

When his father arose he said to his mother, "Get up now! Our son has come back. Our daughter-in-law isn't with him."

And then this woman, his mother, got up. She began cooking.

The young man was awakened by them.

"Why, hello! What's the matter?"

He replied, "Well, this is what happened. A bear stole my woman. This is what happened.

"Now, father, hurry! Make me an elk whistle! They call it a double whistle, don't they?"

This one, the father, began making it.

Later he said, "My son, I have finished. Here it is. Oh, it sure has a good sound."

"Now my brother and I are going to go."

Then his brother said, "Yes, we'll go. My brother and I will go. We'll go looking for her, wherever she is."

And then they went off; these two brothers, who were still young men, went off.

Then they arrived where the camp was. Everything was the same as it had been. Then they began cooking dried meat over the fire.

Then this young man started to leave. He said, "Brother, let me go for a while to the elk there in the woods!"

Then he went. Then he arrived there and cried all night. When dawn came, there sat the elk spirit in the form of a man.

Then he said, "What you have done is certainly good. There's nothing preventing us now. It's good that your brother has come, and that you are together. Now, it isn't going to be difficult.

"You and your brother are going to go. You'll go to the west this way! There will be a creek on level ground, where the land is nice. You'll tell your brother to wait for you there in a coulee. Then you'll go on, into the middle of that country, and then you'll blow your whistle. It's a wooded area there. You'll blow the whistle. You'll do it again. Blow it three times Then after the last time, the fourth one, you'll go to the edge of a creek where she is, where the den is in the woods.

"Now the young women will come out. Your wife will be in the lead when they come. Then you and she will come here. But you'll tell the others to go to their villages.

"Meanwhile that bear is going to come. He's going to chase after you. Oh, your wife is the one he's after! That one is his favorite.

"Now you two come! Hurry to where your brother is, where he's waiting for you! Both of you are going to fight the black bear."

Then the young man went back to his camp. Then he told his brother, "Now come! We're going to look for my wife now."

And so they went there, wherever it was, wherever the creek went through the level land.

Then the young man said, "Now, brother, you stay here for a while! Let me look!"

Then he went on. And now he had the elk whistle, just like the elk had said. He blew on it. Oh, he did it again. Then he moved closer. He did that once again. As he moved closer, he blew on it a fourth time.

Within a short time the women and young women came running out of the woods. His wife was the one in the lead.

"Oh, I lost heart waiting for you. But you have finally come! Now back there in camp, my mind went blank. When I came to my senses, here I was, here!"

"Now quickly, let's go!"

Then he and his wife came back, running as they came. The young man looked back. There in the distance came the big black bear.

Meanwhile, the other young women had scattered, each one going in a different direction to her village.

But the black bear chased only this one, chasing after the couple.

Then the young man said, "Now go on ahead! Go on!"

While the young man and his wife were coming, the bear caught up with them. Oh, the bear was huge! He gained on them by jumping through the air.

Then they arrived where the young man's brother was.

Then he said to his wife, "Now quickly, go down the bank! Go down the bank! Now the bear and I are going to do it."

Then the young man swung around. They used to say that 'one
flung himself down onto the ground.' Now when he flung himself
down, he transformed himself. There stood an elk, after he had
transformed himself. Oh, the elk was huge! The bear was that way,
too: he was a gigantic bear.

[Then he and the bear went at each other.] When this elk
lowered his horns, he pierced the bear's neck. Then he stuck his
horns into the ground and went round and round, trying to extract
them, while the bear was digging his claws into him. When he was
scratching him, the bear tore some of his hide off as they fought and
fought.

Then this elk jumped up. And then he threw the bear down onto
the ground.

Now he was tiring. This elk who was a young man said, "Now
brother, I'm tired." Then he went charging at the bear. Again he
stuck his horns into the ground when he pierced the bear in his
neck and pinned him down.

Then his brother said, "Now that's what I wanted you to say,
what you just said." And then the other one flung himself onto the
ground. Then he became a buffalo, what they call a calf. This one
was a four-winter-old buffalo.

He ran into the bear. He gored his stomach. He continued going
on, and there in the distance swung around. Then he came charging
back. Then he began hooking him.

Then the bear said, "You two have at last beat me. Why, you're
both exceedingly strong! I thought I would overcome you, but you've
beat me. Well, now you've beat me. Take the woman! Ah, I prized
this woman. But you've beat me. And you've killed me. It won't be
long before I am dead. Now, all of you, go on!"

Then the young men brought the young woman back to the
camp. They gathered things up and then returned home. They
arrived there at the village.

Then they told about it: "This is what happened. A bear eloped
with this woman. But these young men brought her back."

Now this is how the story goes. It is one my grandmother used
to tell me. The story, as I told it, was told to me three times.

23

The Young Man with the Feathered Staff

*Common in Arikara tradition is the theme of the young
dandy who has never ventured away from home but finally
goes on the warpath without weapons and performs hero-
ically. In this story the boy's success is attributed to supernatural power, represented by a staff of bird feathers that he
always carries and whose origin is unexplained. Sometime
after telling this story, the narrator remarked that the
episode in which the young man enters the underwater lodge
and encounters four bears of symbolic colors was formerly an
account of the acquisition of bear medicine. In this rendition,
however, such an interpretation is obscure since the young
man rejects the bears' overtures.*

Long, long ago when they were migrating this way, the Arikaras
were a numerous people.

Now, there was a village, and the young men in it were always
traveling around, hunting and going on war parties, always going
in groups, however many there were when they went out. But there
was one young man who was about sixteen winters old. He stayed
in the village whenever he went around. He just never went off
anywhere—he just never went out hunting. He did nothing but
just stand around here and there on top of his earth lodge acting
proudly. He just never looked for things, never even going on the
warpath.

But he carried a staff wherever he went. All kinds of feathers
hung from it. They were placed randomly on it, all kinds of feathers—from the magpie, crow, meadowlark, and other kinds of
birds—that hung from the top when he carried it around. The
staff appeared to be spotted when he held it upright as he walked
around.[1]

---

1. Among Arikaras and their kindred Pawnees, a spotted animal, and by
extension many other spotted objects, was mysterious and holy. Thus the

At night he leaned the staff against his bed. It leaned there against it, and as soon as he arose in the morning he would go out to stand there on the top of the lodge, just as the young men used to do when they acted proudly. He stood there on top and he held that staff.

The young man also had a friend. But his friend was active, going all around, going around hunting and going off on war parties. But this other one was just passive, as they used to say, never going on a war party and never looking for things for his mother and father—just walking around in the village where people made fun of him.

Then one day the young man said to his friend, "Let's go on the warpath!"

The boy's friend said, "Alright, we'll go. But you certainly must have a bow and some arrows, and a quiver. Now in the morning we'll go."

Early in the morning, when it was daybreak, the other young man came hurriedly into the lodge of the young man with the feathered staff. "Now is he up?"

Then the parents said, "He's still in bed. He's still sleeping."

"Now get up! We're going on the warpath."

"Okay, that's the way it will be. But surely there's no hurry. We'll eat first and then we'll go." Then he arose.

The two of them began to eat after his mother cooked for them.

"Now we'll go on the warpath," the young man said.

Then his father said, "Ah, it's difficult to travel around on the warpath. You have no bow and arrows! You have no arrows! What are you going to do when you go on the warpath?"

"Ah, but we're going anyway."

Now the two of them ate everything.

Well, then his father said, "Here are my bow and arrows. Here are arrows. Here's a knife, too."

"Ah, I don't want them. They're too heavy to carry around. They'll tire me out. Anyway we're going now."

reference here to the spotted appearance of the staff implies that it is holy and has power for its owner.

Then he and his friend set out on the warpath.

Somewhere along the way while they were traveling, the young man said, "Say, it sure is hot! Let's swim awhile there in that lake!"

Oh, they arrived there. Then the one young man got into the water and swam; but when the one who had the feathered staff got into the water, he sat on top of it. He looked like a duck sitting on the water. He sat there on top. He did not sink down into the water at all.

His friend said, "Surely you said: 'We should swim!'"

"Yes, and surely I *am* swimming!" But he was just floating on the water.

"Now, let me wash myself and then we'll go on!" Then he went underwater.

Oh, he did not surface. Then there he stood in the water over on the other side of the lake. "Now let's go!" Then his friend ran around the lake to him, and then they went on.

While they were going, the one with the feathered staff said, "I wonder how it would be if the enemy were just to come charging over the hill to attack us?"

His friend then replied, "Don't say that! Something might just happen. You don't have any arrows to fight back with, and they would kill us. Don't say anything like that again!"

"But that's certainly why we came on the warpath. Now that frightens you."

While they were going along, they came to a cliff. There was a lake below it and the water was splashing against its side. Then they sat down on the bank.

"Surely we should hide."

"Hey, why should we be hiding here and there? That's why we came on the warpath. Why should we be hiding?"

Then he continued, "Say, I just want to fast here. It seems that there is some plan to this thing: the water splashes against the cliff here, and I want to know what is behind there. Now, how many days does it usually take when one fasts?"

Then his friend said, "It usually takes four days to fast."

"Yes. Now, that's what I'll do."

Then he walked backwards over there. Then he cried as he came back. Then he came to the edge of the bank. Then he said, "Now, my friend, my brother, I've spent one day."

Then he went backwards again. He stopped over there in the distance. Then he cried again, crying as he came back. He came to the edge of the bank. "Now, my friend, I've spent two days."

Then he did it again: then he cried as he came from over there. He came along the edge of the cliff. Then he said, "Three days have passed."

Again he walked backwards. Then he stopped there in the distance. Then he cried, crying as he came. He came to the edge of the bank. Now he said, "Well, the fourth day has passed. Now I want to know why the water splashes against the cliff here."

Then he jumped over the cliff. He disappeared into the water below. Then the water became smooth while his friend, the poor thing, cried. "My, now he's done away with himself. I wonder why that is?"

<Soon, just about the time the sun was setting,> the young man was coming along the edge of the bank over there in the distance. He was singing as he came.

"Hello," he said.

"Why, say!"

"There's nothing down there. There's nothing in that water. When I went underwater there was a lodge there. I went inside it. There was a man sitting there. He was sitting where the door is. He filled his pipe and brought it to me to smoke. I said, 'I don't smoke.'

"Then I went farther on. There was a man sitting over there, too. He said, 'Hey, my son, <I'm glad that you've come>.' He was a bear, <a black bear>.

"'"My son." You certainly can't say that. I'm not your son.'

"Then I went on farther. There was another one who said the same thing. He was white. He said, 'My son, sit down right here!'

"I said, 'You can't be the one whose son I am.'

"There also sat another one. He was also a bear; that one was red. He also said, 'My son, my son.'

"'I certainly am not your son. My father is still living.'

<"Then there sat another one, a yellow bear, who also called to me, 'My son, my son.'>

"Then I came out. I came up the hill when I arrived here. Well, now let's go!"

After they had gone on and on, the young man said, "Say, my friend, I wonder how it would be, eh, if the enemy were to harass us—if they were to come up all over the rise and attack us?"

He had no more than said that when, oh my, there was a thundering sound on the earth as the enemy did come up into sight. Then the two young men ran. The one who had the bow and arrows ran far ahead, but the one who had the feathered staff pretended that he was not fast.

Oh, the enemy gained on him as they were shooting at him, but the arrows could not strike the young man. The enemy were unable to do anything to him.

Then the young man pretended to drop the feathered staff that he had. One Sioux man quickly snatched it up. Then the young man swung around and chased the one who had taken the staff. While he pursued this Sioux among the others, they were shooting at him, but they were unable to hit him at all. Then the Sioux were yelling, and now the one who had the staff with all kinds of holy feathers hanging from it was running away from the young man chasing him. But the enemy were not able to hit the young man when they were shooting at him. He was too quick as he darted all around.

Then the Sioux began to yell, "Give the staff to him! We can't do anything to him. Why, he's holy!" That is what they were saying.

Then this man stopped. The young man was given back the staff [by the Sioux man,] and then he went off. And there his friend stood on a hill in the distance. He went to where his friend was.

Then these enemies, the Sioux, withdrew. Then they went off. They watched the young man.

Oh, the young man reached his friend. He said, "Say, it was fun when they were shooting at me. I don't know where the arrows went when they shot at me, but they couldn't do anything to me. And then the one fellow took my holy object. Now, let's go home!"

Then they were coming back. As they came, the young man said, "There's a village close by here. Oh, it's a big village, too! Now I'm tired." He was pretending to be tired.

said, "There's a village close by here. Oh, it's a big village, too! Now I'm tired." He was pretending to be tired.

He said, "Now when it gets dark tonight, you must go into the village. There's a bunch of horses there. They're off by themselves. After it gets dark, you can go there. Head them off! They're yours. When you run them off, I'll lead the enemy the other way. Don't wait for me! As soon as you take them, depart while it is night. Drive them on while it's dark. Don't wait for me! But drive them on.

"Now, I think I'll sleep awhile! And when I wake up, [I'll attract the enemy, and] then I'll go on [and catch up with you]."

Oh, as they approached the village a dog was barking in it there in the distance.

"Peek over the hill! There's a huge village."

When the one who had the arrows looked where the village was, oh, he saw a large Sioux village with horses standing all around in it!

Then the young man with the feathered staff said, "Now, there on the other side of the village is where the horses are. They're apart from the others. That's the bunch I mean. Head them off! Run them off from there. Whip them and drive them off quickly. Don't wait for me! I'll sleep awhile, and then I'll wake up, [acting as a decoy,] and then go on."

Well, it was late into the night, when everything was quiet, after the singing in the village had ceased and everyone was sleeping.

"Well, now go quickly!"

Then the young man with the arrows jumped up and went where his friend had told him to go. There the horses were. There were eight of them. Then he mounted one and whipped the others. Then they went off.

Then he guided the horses in a bunch. Then he drove them on as he had been told to do. While he was driving them as he came back, it began to get daylight, just as the young man had said: "This is what you'll do."

About this time the young man with the feathered staff awoke when the Sioux came over the hill in pursuit, yelling, "The horses have been stolen." Then he went over yonder on the prairie.

"Hey, there he goes," the Sioux called out. Then they chased him as he went out of sight over a hill.

When the Sioux ran up the hill, the young man had already run down it and then up another one. There he stood on the other hill in the distance.

Well, then they raced their horses. After they ran up the hill after him, he had already run down it, and there in the distance the young man went up yet another hill. In this way he led the Sioux in a different direction from his friend, who now got far away.

Now the young man drew close to the Sioux, but then took them in a different direction while they chased him. Then he quickly disappeared from sight down another hill.

And then finally the Sioux horses tired. There the young man stood on a distant hill. He was motioning for them to come to him.

Then the Sioux said, "Why, surely this young man is holy." They turned back. Then they returned to their village.

Then the young man went on. Then he reached his village [at night]. Then he entered his lodge, where his father and mother were. Then he lay down to sleep.

In the morning his father [who had previously gone outside,] came back inside. There it was, against the wall: there against the wall was the staff with the hanging feathers that his son owned. Then the father said, "Now, old woman, get up! Our boy must have returned. There is the feathered staff that he always carries in his hand. He must have returned."

There the young man lay sleeping on his bed. "Hey, wake up now," said his father.

Then the son said, "Alright, I'll get up." He got up. He washed his face all over. He ate.

"Now what happened while you two were out there?"

And then the young man answered, "We reached the different places in the country where I wanted to go. And now my friend is coming, driving the horses that we stole. He has two of them for you, father. He's coming with them. He'll arrive tonight. But I came ahead."

Now when it was dark his friend entered the lodge. He looked at him. "Hey, I left you sleeping!"

"Yes, but I passed you. Then I came on and arrived first."

"Now here are the horses."

Then he said "Give two of them to my father. And you keep the others."

Now that is what this young man did. Now he was holy as he grew up. Oh, he was exceedingly holy! He never used to go around on the warpath, but no matter what he did was good whenever he did something. <When someone was ill—hemorrhaging, for example—they would go after the young man. He then took his feathered staff with him, and the feathers blessed the sick person and he got well.>

Now, this young man was named Having Feathers On The Staff—He Has Feathers On The Staff. Oh, he had all kinds of feathers on his staff, ones from all the kinds of birds that blessed him—the eagle, hawk, all the ones that fly around. They were what was holy for him while he lived.

24

The Man and His Bear Child

A common Plains motif is the mating of a human with an animal, resulting in a human offspring. In this Arikara version of a northern Plains story, a young man who has intercourse with a she-bear and the child who results from the union are both given power by the bear after they treat her with respect.

I am now going to tell a story about one of the things that happened long, long ago when our people were migrating upriver. Now it is not known which tribe of people it was that I am telling about, but I heard the story from the one who was Bear Goes Out.

He was named Bear Goes Out. Ray Gough.[1] Now I am going to repeat his words.

Now when the people used to move around, when they were moving upriver, they would build a village somewhere and live there a long time. When the supply of game was depleted from hunting and when there wasn't any wood after they had used it all up, they said, "Well, let's move somewhere farther upriver again!" And then that is what they did. That is what they used to do.

Once there where the village was, two young men went hunting. While they were out hunting, they came to a valley. Deer used to come out of the brush there in that kind of valley. While the two men were sitting on top of a hill overlooking it, evening was coming on.

Then one said, "Say, look! I see something. Let's go!"

Then they went down the hillside. In the trees in the valley, there in the valley, there was a spring. And there lay a bear, oh, lying there on its back. It was just sleeping soundly, snoring while it slept. While they were looking at it with its vulva exposed, one man got an erection.

"Say, I'll have intercourse with her!"

Then the other one said, "Don't do it! The one lying there is holy. Something might happen to you."

"Hey! I'm truly a man!"

Then he mounted the bear and did it to her. This bear must have liked it, since her legs were opening wider. Then he finished doing it.

Then he said, "Say, I feel good now."

The other one said, "Let's run off! When she wakes up, she'll kill us both."

Then they went on.

Now some years later—perhaps it was four winters, perhaps five—the people set up a village. Then these two men went hunting again. The village was in the same place.

"Let's take a look at that place where you had intercourse with

---

1. His nickname was *kaáxIt* 'Blackbird.'

the bear."

Then the two young men went. Oh, they went onto the hill where they had been previously. There in the distance was a little boy going around, running about here and there. There in the distance by the edge of the woods sat a bear.

Then one said, "Look! There the two are."

And then the other said, "That little boy going around—I just think he's my son. Let's go over there!"

Then they went. As they were going, as they were going closer, this boy came running up.

"Oh, father, here you are! You've finally come. I've been waiting for you. My mother said, 'Your father will take you to your village. It's been a long time that I've cared for you—since I've been rearing you. Now you go with your father! Let him keep you!'"

Then he said, "Well, that's the way it will be. You and I will go."

Then he ran again to where his mother was. Then this bear got up. Then she went down the hill. She went into the brush. Then the boy ran to where his father was.

"Now let's go over there to our village!"

Then the two young men brought him. Then they brought back the boy, however many winters old he was. When he spoke, the boy was sensible and knowledgeable.

Well, then the father said to his parents, "This boy is my son. This is what I did previously."

Then they said, "Now, it's alright. We'll rear him. He's our child."

Now they took good care of the boy.

Now sometime later, however many winters it was that the couple had kept him, the boy said, "Father, my mother is saying, 'I'm coming [to visit]. I want to eat something. I want to eat some squash and corn. I want to come. I'm going to come early in the morning.'"

Then the young man told his friend, "His mother, the one whom I took sexually, his mother, is going to come. She wants to eat some squash and corn—fresh corn."

Now she <one of the sisters of the young man> boiled squash and corn.

Then someone yelled. "Hey, a bear is charging! It's coming this way!"

While she was coming at a run, she did not act as if she were angry. When she came at a run, she came into the village. There she went, straight to the lodge where they were keeping her son. She went to the door. She entered. She sat down.

They treated her respectfully. The sisters of this young man began to paint the bear. Then the young man's father arose and placed a feather on her. Now she was clothed [with symbols of honor].

Then they gave her a bowl of squash—what she wanted to eat. Oh, then she began eating fresh corn. She ate up everything.

Then this boy said, "My mother says, 'They're taking good care of my son here. I'm going now. I've eaten and I'm thankful for what my in-laws have done for me. And now you shall find some power for something good. I myself am giving it to you.'"

Now she went to leave. Then the bear went out. Now they cried, crying for the bear.

Now, as this boy and his father went around, the boy grew older. When he was becoming a young man, he said, "Father, I want us to sit on that distant hill. I want to say something."

They went up the hill there.

Then he said, "Father, my mother is dead. My mother no longer exists. But she did say this: 'You're a man now. You're becoming a young man. Your father, the one you are with, is taking good care of you. But toward the end nothing is going to be difficult for either of you when you and your father are going to go all around. But now I'll die.' This is what she said."

Now they cried as they sat there. They stopped crying. They came home.

Then his father said to his parents, "Your daughter-in-law, this one's mother, has died."

Now the young man's grandmother and grandfather mourned for him.

Now the young man got older and then he married. Now meanwhile this man [his father] married someone else.

Now for a long time as the tribe traveled around, things were not difficult for him: the ways of the warpath and horse stealing, the various deeds they valued most during those times. Now, however long a period of time it lasted, the one who told me this story did not say.

Now this is the end of his words.

25

The Young Men and the Snapping Turtle

Another story widely distributed on the Plains tells of a party of young men who climb onto the back of a gigantic snapping turtle and, unable to get off, are taken underwater. This Arikara version illustrates the fate of skeptics who do not respect, and so do not fear, the mysterious or holy. After the young men are taken underwater, where they are henceforth destined to live, the lake becomes a holy site and thus a source of potential power and good fortune for anyone who prays and makes offerings there, just as it is for the boy in the original party who out of respect refuses to join his companions and later mourns them on its bank.

This story that I am telling, which occurred long, long ago, is what I heard from someone—one of the stories they used to tell. He told about a snapping turtle that was really big; it's not known how big around it was.

When a party was out going around on the warpath, however many there were in the party, they just did not find anything. Then they started back home. "Let's go home! We haven't found anything."

As they were returning, they came up a hill. The land was nice. There sat something. It resembled a rock; it was big and grayish white.

The party went up close to look at it; among them was a young man, as there always is someone in a group, who was a nonbeliever, one who does not believe in things.

And here this object was a gigantic snapping turtle! Then it moved around, and then it started off after it put out its arms. Here it had arms and legs. Then it went off.

Then the young men, however many there were, followed it. Then one [climbed onto it and] stood on top of it.

Then he said, "It's sure nice here. Come up on top!"

Then the others climbed on it, too, except for one who became frightened by it. He said, "Certainly this turtle is holy. You're going to do something to yourselves."

"Oh, what does he know! You should stand here on top. Anyway it's nice. It's carrying us."

It was moving while they stood on top. And here this thing was a turtle.

Meanwhile the young man went alongside it as it went on.

Now the turtle went a long distance after they got on top of it. Over there on the flat prairie was a lake there in the distance. It was a big lake. That is where the turtle was headed.

Now the lake got to be closer.

Then the young man going alongside the turtle said, "Now see what I was saying! It's headed toward the water!"

Then one young man started to get down, but then his foot was stuck. No matter what he did, when he tried to move his foot, his foot was stuck. Then it became impossible for the others, too, when they wanted to get off. Then it became impossible for them. The turtle had a hold on them.

Then this turtle went to the bank of the lake, and then it began to go into the water while the young men on it tried to jump off. They were not able to do it, however, and then it took them underwater while the other young man who had not got on top of it went along the bank there crying and crying into the night.

When morning came, one of the young men came to the surface.

Then he said, "Brother, go home now! We're unable to do anything to come up out of the water. It's holding us, and it's difficult where we are now. It's impossible to turn back again. It has taken us. But it's good for you: whenever you go on the warpath, come to this spot where we are in the water, and tell us whatever you want. Now we'll watch over you as you go around. Now do this! Go home! We can't turn back. And tell them in our village what has happened and that we ourselves are the cause of it. It's no one else's fault."

Well, then this young man who was talking—the one they had had as their leader—went underwater.

Then this young man came home. Then he returned to wherever our villages were.

Then he told about it: "This is what happened. Their feet got stuck to it when they stood on top of its back there. And when they tried to get off it, their feet were stuck to it. Now they live in the water. There's a lake there. It's a big lake there where I was together with my brothers [i.e., companions].

"Now this is what they told me: 'Whatever you desire, come here and tell us. Now it's difficult; we can't turn back.' Now this is what they said. And here I have come back alone."

"Now the lake where I used to go was holy."[1] And if one had anything to offer, he set it down as he prayed to them where they were in the water. And what happened afterward was good; they were granted whatever they desired.

Then our people migrated this way, closer toward this country here. Then they began to stop going there. Then this was the end of this tradition, [of going to the place where] the young men, however many there were, had stood on top of the turtle.

---

1. Here the narrator is repeating the words of the person who told him this story.

26

The Young Woman Who Married a Horse

*A form of doctoring power prevalent on the Plains was
horse medicine. The narrator's grandparents possessed it,
and this story, told by his grandmother Squash Blossom,
accounts for the origin of hers. Of uncertain provenience,
either Arikara or Cheyenne, the legend became part of the
Arikara tradition. The narrative follows a familiar pattern. A young married woman is abducted by a horse that
assumes various forms, and after she subsequently takes on
the traits of her new animal husband she cannot return to
her people. The horse husband, pitying the woman's former
husband, gives him the power of horse medicine—the herbs
and songs necessary for curing sick or injured horses—as
well as the sanction to kill and eat wild horses in times of
famine.*

Now I am going to relate a story that my grandmother used to
tell. Maybe she is listening now, the poor thing, to what she used
to tell when she and I were living alone when my grandfather had
gone somewhere, and she told the stories she had learned. My
grandmother had medicines. My grandfather had horse medicine.
This story I am going to tell is what she used to tell me.

This is an Arikara story I am going to tell about what happened long, long ago when a band of people—perhaps Cheyenne or
perhaps Arikara—was roaming around. When they were moving for
the winter, they went toward a river. They were seeking an area
where wood was plentiful and there was water. Those were the
things that were valuable then: water and wood. Wood was important above all else—and an area where there was game for the
young men to hunt.

Now there was a young woman, a very young woman, who was
beautiful and lovable and who was purchased for a certain man.
Now she was married <and they set up their own lodge>.

Once when the band had moved to a new location, after the

people had set up camp and this young women needed to bring water for whatever she was doing—probably boiling meat—she ran down to the creek.

She was having difficulty finding a place where she could dip water from the creek. Then there was a white object there. Then she thought, "It must be a stone." It was a nice-looking one. Then she put her foot on it. She dipped water. She returned to camp. She began to cook a meal.

Now sometime later a group of young women in the village went down into the valley to collect wood. Then this young woman went down with them. They hurried as they went around looking for it.

When the women went back up to the village, this young woman remained down there. She wanted to lay back over her load of wood in order to strap on the bundle.

Then a young man came up beside her. He was a handsome person.

Then he said, "I have come here to fetch you. I'm the one who is watching over you. I have come because I want us to be together."

Then the young woman said, "Truly I don't know you, whoever you are."

Then he said, "Certainly you know me. You wanted to dip water. It was difficult for you, and I put myself there so that you could step on me to dip it. I'm the one, that stone."

Now this young woman stood there thinking.

Then the young man said, "Now go on!"

Then the two of them went to the territory of the wild horses. And here this man who had taken her there was himself a horse!

Now back in the village the husband of the young woman arrived at his lodge [after he had been out hunting]. "Where is my wife?"

"The young women went after wood, and she went with them. She hasn't returned yet."

Then his family asked the ones who had been her companions. The young women said, "We came back up. At that time she was picking up her wood. We thought she must have returned already."

Then they ran down into the bottomlands, and there lay the

wood she had intended to pick up.

"Oh, the enemy must have made a captive of her. She's beautiful—a nice-looking woman. [They wouldn't kill her.]"

After they had looked for her, they forgot about the matter. Her husband became accustomed to her absence.

Sometime later, perhaps four winters afterward, when it was about the time that spring usually arrives, the people were roving around, and then the young men said, "Ah, there are wild horses—ponies—roaming around here. Oh, there are many of them! And there's one among them that is different. When they run, it leads. And that leader is human. It's different in form from the others, and oh, it's fast! Now it's something extraordinary."

Then they got ready. And they mounted their fastest horses. Then they went off. "Let's go see the ponies!"

There they roamed in the distance. Oh, the herd was spread out.

"Now go over that way; you men go in a group to the other side! When you get there, these others will be over here. We'll encircle the ponies. We'll rush up the hill. Let's catch the one in the lead to see who she is, to see if she's from an enemy village! We'll corner this young woman."

When they had done this, one man threw a rope over her head. They brought her down; then they tied her up. Oh, she was wild! She was strong.

Then all the wild horses ran off, except for a black horse that was turning around and around, whinnying. There were four colts there, too. Two of them were big, and two were small. They were palominos. Oh, they were beautiful!

While this stallion was running back and forth whinnying, the young woman said to her captors, "Now, there's nothing I can do. I know why you've caught me. Now, my husband, come forward!" Then she called him.

Then her husband came up. She told him, "This is what my mate the black horse said: 'Henceforth things will not be difficult for you as you go around. You will have nice horses.'

"Now, here are medicines for you to use when you doctor a horse that has been hurt. Here are the ones you will use when your horse tires. And here are the ones for when horses are swinneyed and when they break a leg. Now he has given you these songs, the Horse Medicine songs.

"Now I can't do anything. My mate has given you these powers. The colts you see there are my children. They're all calling to me, 'Tell him! Tell him!' That's what each one is saying.

"Now I'm beseeching you. I am no longer good [i.e., human]. It won't be good if I try to mingle among people again, since I'm the way I am now, having hair all over myself. Now do this: turn me loose!

"Now no matter what you may think of those wild horses, you can kill some when there is a scarcity of buffalo." There must have been many wild horses that used to roam there in the country to the west.

Now the father of this young woman cried; her father cried, and her mother and her brothers cried.

"Now there's nothing that I can do about my condition. But I'll see all of you. That's what my mate told me to tell you."

Now they turned her loose. Over there in the distance the horses ran over the hill, and then the party of men returned to their village.

Then the former husband of the woman married another young woman. This one resembled his wife who had eloped with the horse. And then he began to have his own children. He was no longer poor. He now had all sorts of things. He always got the things he sought for himself. Whatever used to be difficult for him was no longer that way.

Now this is what I used to hear from my grandmother when she told the story.

27

The Boy Given Power
by the Bighorn Sheep

Among the Pawnees a common source of supernatural
power was the animal lodge, an underwater or underground
earth lodge in which animals of various species met and
performed their rituals just as the Pawnee doctors did in
their Medicine Lodge. This Arikara story is about a similar
underworld lodge, one at the bottom of a deep blowhole
inhabited by bighorn sheep. The scenario is familiar: in this
account a man is pitied by the sheep but abuses his power
and loses it to his would-be victim, here his stepson. The
latter is saved by the sheep, who in turn pity him and direct
him to kill his evil stepfather. The story closes with two
vignettes about a horse that contributes to the young man's
power.

Now I am going to tell a story that the old-timers who lived
long, long ago told me. One that they told me occurred there in the
country to the south, where the Santees lived. Now I certainly don't
know exactly where it was. They told about a blowhole there. It was
located on nice, flat land. Animals did not know it was there; and
then all of a sudden one would fall into it. Then it would be flung
back up and land on the flat ground over in the distance. The
animals that roam around—rabbits, coyotes—accidently had this
happen to them. One would drop into the hole and then be hurled
back up. It would be thrown over in the distance somewhere.

People did not know about it, but once someone found out about
it. Men used to go by there when they went out on the hunt, when
they were traveling around in a party. Then one time a young man
who was a skeptic went there. Sometimes a rabbit would be found
lying there after that had happened to it—after it had been flung
out by the wind. Then it was killed. Or a coyote would be killed. An
antelope might fall into it, and then it would be thrown onto its
back over in the distance.

Now this young man folded up his robe. Then he threw it down into the hole. After he had stood there awhile, the robe he had thrown down into it quickly appeared. It landed on the level ground over in the distance.

Then this man enjoyed that. He did it over and over.

Then he began telling people about it. The village must have been somewhere close by. That is how they found out about it when they were going by it.

Now one man went there. Then he began fasting there by the hole as he walked around. The others were afraid of it. But this man went there and fasted.

Well, I don't know what happened there—whether or not he was given a blessing—but something must have happened to this man who had bad ways and was always hateful.

Well, there was a young woman whose husband had died. She had a boy who was ten winters old. And then this man who had fasted there at the blowhole married this young woman.

The situation was not good, though, for the man began to dislike her son. He looked for a way for there to be an accident in order to kill him.

Now one time when they were going along, going together in a large party to hunt, this hole was nearby.

Then this man said, "I killed a deer over there. The meat is there. This boy and I will go, and he can carry the meat back. He can come back. Then I'll go on hunting for awhile again." This is what he said when he told his wife.

Now this woman, not knowing that this man disliked her son—that he disliked the boy—consented.

Then early in the morning the two of them went. They took a dog along. It pulled a travois. The man went there where the meat was. He loaded the basket.

Then he said to the boy, "Let's go over there for a while! There's something mysterious over there."

Then he let the dog go. Then it took the meat back to the camp.

But this man led the boy there.

"Look! This is where it happens."

Then he folded up his robe. Then he threw it down into the hole. After a while the robe was thrown up over there in the distance.

"Look! Look at it! Go over to the edge!"

When the boy went up to the edge of it, this man shoved him. He threw him down into the hole. Then he picked up his robe and went on hunting.

Meanwhile this boy flew down into the hole. Well, here there were trees growing [on the sides of the hole] down below there; and as it was planned, as he went down, there was a certain tree. Then the boy landed on it, there on a branch. That is where he got caught when he landed astride a limb, and now he seated himself comfortably as he cried.

Now it was difficult for him to see. Up there where the mouth of the hole was, it looked like a star standing there. Down below it was dark.

And while this boy, the poor thing, was crying, the wind was just whistling.

Then some things just flew to where he was sitting on the limb. They were two bighorn sheep.

Then one said, "Lie down on my back, here where we are!"

Then, the poor thing, this boy lay on its back. Then the two sheep flew down the steep bank.

Oh, I don't know how far they took him, but then everything was different. It was a different country.

As they sped with him, there was a lodge there. Oh, it was a large lodge, in which there were different kinds of bighorn sheep: a white one, a yellow one, a red one, and a black one.

Then a man came up to them. He said, "Why, grandson, you who have come from a distant country, now I know what happened. Here is where we blessed the man who did this deed, here where you dropped in. Oh, it's difficult. What he did is not good. And it's difficult to get out.

"Now we're going to give you power to do to him what he did to you, for you yourself to do away with him. You'll kill him. The way your father has treated you is not good. And they are the powers we gave him, the holy powers that he has. Now we'll take those powers

back. You'll do away with him. And we'll give to you the power we
gave to him.

"Now these rams are going to take you back to your country.
Now when you go, you'll arrive there where your mother, the poor
thing, is crying. She's looking for you. When her husband returned,
he said, 'The boy came back a long time ago. He was led by the
dogs. Meanwhile I went hunting again. Anyway he has no sense. He
must have gone in another direction. Perhaps he's been made a
slave.'" That is what the man had said, when in fact he had thrown
the boy down into the hole.

"Now you're going to go. This is what you're going to do. When
you arrive there where your mother lives and you go inside, you'll
say, 'Mother, I have returned. Make a fire! He'll be ashamed when
he sees me.'

"Meanwhile this man is going to go around spying on you. But
he isn't going to be able to do anything to you.

"Well, when you are going around, look for a dark bay horse for
yourself, one with yellow stockings; and the belly will be yellow, and
its eyes will be red. That kind of horse is like this bighorn sheep.
It's swift. It won't slacken its speed wherever it goes. Now that will
be the kind you'll seek for yourself. You're going to go all over.
When you find it, that one will be your riding horse. That one is
going to be the one to help you. When you want to do something, it
will be your companion when you two do it.

"What we've planned for you is true. Now these sheep are going
to take you back."

There they stood: there were four bighorn sheep. One was red.
One was black. A black one, a red one, a yellow one, and a white
one.

"Now these are the swiftest ones. They're going to take you back
to where you came from. It's far away."

Then one of the sheep said, "Now you're going to grasp our
horns. We're going to run furiously. The black bighorn sheep is the
one you're going to ride on first, during the night. <He stands in the
east>. This one, the yellow one, will carry you on his back the next
morning. <He stands in the south.> And then the red one <who
stands in the west> will carry you on his back. And when you ride
the fourth one, the white one <who stands in the north>, you'll

arrive there where your country is.

"Now get your strength, all the strength you have!"

After the boy mounted the black bighorn sheep, well, then they ran off. This one was in the lead as they ran around and around up the sides of the hole.

Now one night passed. Now he rode this other one, the yellow one.

Now night passed, another night, and then it was the red one's turn.

Now three nights passed, and as he rode the white one, they flew up the side of the mouth of the hole. Oh, they collapsed, each one just puffing. Here it was such a long way that they had come!

Well, then they said, "Now this is the place where your mother lives. Well, we're turning back here. There's nothing for you to worry about as you go. We're watching over you. Well, now go!"

And so this boy went where they told him to go. Then he went.

As he went that way, there was the village there, where he arrived and went along the trail between the lodges. This is what they had said.

Then he entered the lodge. There they were in bed, the man and his mother. He sat down at the west end of the lodge.

Then he said, "Mother, get up! Make a fire! I have returned."

Then this woman replied, "No, whoever you are, you must be making fun of me! My boy has died."

She arose and then made a fire. There sat her son, whom she was glad to see.

Then that other man felt ashamed. He thought, "You must be exceedingly holy! But I don't care where you are going to go, I'll kill you." This is what this man was pondering. He was angry after he saw the boy again.

Now when this boy was becoming a young man, when he was going around on the warpath, he then found the kind of horse he was looking for, a dark bay. It had a yellow belly. Oh, its eyes looked like the eyes of a bighorn sheep. It was truly sturdy! This one was now his riding horse. It was his favorite horse to ride. This was the one he now used whenever he went on the warpath or when they chased buffalo. Oh, it was a fast horse!

Well, during this period when the young man was going around on the warpath and counting coups on the enemy, he was already married. He was taking care of his own children. Now his mother was already an old woman.

Then one day they began to play the hoop and pole game. They began to play the hoop and pole game. Then that is what he and the man who was his father—the one he had as a stepfather—did. Now they were throwing the pole as they shot at the hoop.

Well, this young man was now the one whose pole landed closest to the hoop.

"Oh, I had got rid of you and now you have come back!" <This man was angry, and> while he was thinking about how he might kill him, this young man swung around just as they had told him, "This is what you're going to do when you kill him." He hit the man on the temple.

The man fell to the ground. <The other men left the field.> Then the young man dragged the man out of sight. Then he cut up the man's body. He cut up the flesh.

Then he said, "You beings of the earth, all you birds flying in the air, here's a meal for you, something for you to taste."

Then the birds came flying to the place. Oh, now the spot where the man lay was black with them. Then the birds ate up that man.

And the people did not get angry. They had not liked what the man had been doing. They had not liked his behavior. Well, now this young man had done away with him.

Now as time passed, when this young man became older, he had a song that he sang when he rode that riding horse. When he would sing his war song while riding, oh, the horse became lively as he sang the song, whatever it was! And there was the village he would circle around.

But now this horse was an old one, and now he was an old man, too.

Well, that man died, the one who had gone around as a young man. The horse, the poor thing, was old now. Its hooves were crippled.

Now among the young women living there, there was one who said, "Oh, I know the song that the man who used to ride this horse used to sing when he sang—when he sang his war song while riding. I know the song. [I'm going to ride that horse.]"

One of her companions said, "Don't do it! [That man was powerful. He was holy.]"

Then this young woman mounted it. Then she began to sing the song which that young man used to sing when he sang his war song.

Then this horse became lively. Now it raised its head. Then it moved its ears around. Then it began prancing as it became sprightly, acting lively as it used to do when the young man rode it, turning around and around when they were running, like it used to do when they were running away from the enemy.

Then the young woman, the poor thing, was thrown off by it. It threw her off at a distance over yonder, knocking out the young woman who had ridden it.

"Oh, what's the matter?"

Then her friend said, "She was singing the song which that young man used to sing when he rode that horse. I told her not to do it, but she didn't listen to me. Then it threw her off."

And whenever the village would travel as a group, the old horse would follow. Even when they left it behind, it would just come to where the children of that young man lived and linger around their lodge.

Well, then the village moved somewhere, wherever it was. And two young men had been out hunting, roaming all around, [and now returned].

"Here's where they must have gone. Here are the tracks."

There they sat. "Let's smoke awhile and then we'll go where they went. Here's the trail, and we'll follow it."

Now while they were sitting there, it just got dark. Then they heard singing.

"Hey, there's someone going around. Let's find out who it is. We'll get together, and then we'll all go to wherever the village is."

Then he came. As they sat there, then he came toward them. He was singing. When he came near by, he passed close by the spot here where the two young men were sitting. No one was riding it. This horse itself was singing. It was singing as it went.

Then they said, "Say, that's the horse the young man used to ride."

And then these two young men learned the song. Then they followed the horse. Then it took them to where the village was. Then it went there. This horse knew where the young man's children and wife lived. Then, while it lingered around their lodge grazing, these two came there.

Then they said, "Say, the old horse led us here. We were sitting there when it was late in the evening, when it was getting dark. Someone was singing. The sound could be heard plainly as it came toward us. 'Why, if it's someone wandering around, we'll all get together.' Now here it was this horse, the old horse! We followed behind this one that was singing and arrived here where your horse's village is."

Now that is what this horse used to do: the fast horse used to do many good deeds.

28

Young Hawk and the Power He Lost

The theme of this story is how power, once given, can be withdrawn if the recipient does not use it. The protagonist is once again an indolent young man, upon whom a hawk mysteriously bestows the power of fleetness. On his first and only war party, the young man appears to be foolishly slow, then miraculously fast, vanishing only to appear suddenly elsewhere, thereby securing the party's success. Once back home, however, he reverts to his indolent habits and subsequently the hawk takes his power away because he is content to be lazy.

Now I will tell a story that I heard—what I used to hear when they told stories. Maybe others heard it from the old men I used to listen to when they told stories. There were many stories that have been lost.

Now the story I am going to tell is about a boy who was four-teen or fifteen winters old when this occurred. He was not inter-ested in anything: in going along with a war party or even going hunting—not even in going hunting. He was not interested in manly things. When the young men went around, he was just silent when he was told, "This is what one does. This is the way we men do things. You are becoming a man and you yourself should get some power while you're growing up." But this boy didn't pay any attention.

Now one time something happened, whatever it was, and the boy said, "I'll go on the warpath."
A party had already gone off.
"I'll follow behind."
His father said, "Now that is really good. Don't let them get the best of you. Whatever they do, you do it, too."
<Then his father gave him a bow and arrows and a knife. But the boy refused them. "Oh, I don't need them. They'll be in the way too much if I have to carry them around.">
Then the war party left the village. After they had gone off, this boy went off following them.
And as was his custom, he just wouldn't do anything. Whenever the party stopped, he would eat. He would sit there way off some-where on the prairie. He would walk around on the prairie at a distance, looking all around. That is what he would do.

But, oh, this boy was fleet!
Then scouts were picked out. When the scouts went out early in the morning and were scouting around in advance, they saw some-thing. Then it came toward them. When it came closer to them, they saw it was the boy. Then the scouts said, "Surely we left him behind

in camp. He was still lying there in bed, a left-behind, when we came scouting."

This is also what he did again when they went out. The boy was sleeping when the scouts went out, when the four young men went out to go scouting and to look all around. And then someone was coming, coming toward them. And there it was he, that boy. They were bewildered when they saw him.

Now he said, "It is located close by. There's a big village here. Oh, it's a big village!"

Now that was what he told them, but these scouts did not see the village.

Then they came back to the camp.

One of them told the leader, "There's a big village here."

Now they did not know it for a fact. It is what this boy had told them.

Then this boy said, "There's a big village here. Oh, it's a big village! But these scouts didn't see it. They were lying when I heard them saying it here just now.'

Then this boy said, "When you stop to camp, hurry if you wish to steal horses. Now, hurry!"

Then this boy suddenly vanished. They no longer saw him.

Then the party went on. They got up and went.

The village was close by.

Then the boy said, "There's the village there. Oh, it's a big village!"

Now they selected the horse stealers who were held in highest esteem. "He will be the one to pick out some horses."

Now they selected them. Now they were ready.

"Drive them here!" [they told the horse stealers.] "Then we'll help."

Then that boy said, "Now everything is ready. When you go [you don't have to go into the village]; there are horses close by over there [just outside the village]. Drive those horses here! Then we'll drive them off. When you two groups get together here, then we'll go on."

When the group drove the horses off, oh, there were many of them! They herded them together to where the rest of the party waited for them and then each caught a nice-looking horse to ride.

Then one of the men asked the boy, "Aren't you going to ride one yourself?"

Then the boy said, "No. <I'll go on foot. I don't know how to ride.> You all go on quickly! Go over there to the west! Don't go north! Go over there to the west! They're going to chase us. There will be a lot of them when they come."

The party ran the horses off.

As the party was coming along, it began to get light.

Then this boy said, "There's a lake over there. It's a big lake. Scatter the horses in among the bulrushes! The bulrushes are tall. The horses will be hidden in among them. The enemy will come, but I'll lead them in another direction."

Now they stared at him.

Now there was the lake. Oh, it was a big lake! That is where they drove the horses. They drove the horses down into the bulrushes along the shore. The men sat down in different places there among the plants.

Then, on the ground there was the sound of the enemy coming. Oh, when they were going around on the land above the lake, they did not see anything. But these men were there among the bulrushes.

Then there were two riders coming toward a rock, and by it is where this boy sat. Then the two Sioux came up to this rock while they were talking and making signs. Meanwhile the boy sat behind the rock and watched their faces. They did not see him.

They moved off. The two of them went over there in another direction. The boy waited. As soon as it became dark [he jumped up and called to the party], "Now drive the horses off quickly! They are still chasing us. They'll catch up with us."

The men came out. They drove the horses out as they came.

Before long it was getting light, and the enemy was overtaking them.

Then the boy said, "Hurry! Whip the horses!"

Then that boy was coming in the rear. His horse was trotting along.

Then those Sioux who were coming up hollered, "Hey, we're going to kill this one. He must not know how to ride." That is what they were saying.

Meanwhile the party whipped those horses as they were running.

And then the boy rode over there in another direction on the prairie. He was looking back repeatedly.

Then the enemy was chasing after him and shooting at him. They could not wound him as they pursued him.

Then he rode down the hill while those riders pursuing him were on top. There in the distance on the other side of the creek valley, there he went up the hillside.

Once again they ran after him. Now when they were about to overtake him, he rode down the hill and disappeared.

"He must surely be around here. When he goes up the hill there, we'll run him down."

There, on the hill on the other side of the coulee, there in the distance, he went up and over it again.

Finally the horses the Sioux rode became tired. "Ah, something is strange. He certainly must be extraordinarily fast!" Then they turned around.

Meanwhile the party with the horses ran on with them.

Then the Sioux gave up. Then they turned back.

As the party with the horses came, there was a tree line. They drove the horses into the woods.

And then they said, "Ah, they must have killed the boy, the poor thing. He shouldn't have gone that other way. He went over there, poor thing, and they must have run him down. They must have killed him."

Then suddenly the boy came out of the brush.

"They were running me down, but they tired their horses out." Then they fed him.

Then he said, "While I'm eating, you fellows will go on. You'll go on quickly. You'll run at the same speed when you're going in the morning. But I'll go on later, as soon as I've eaten."

Well, then the party mounted their horses. Then they whipped them.

But this boy was still eating. He ate everything. Then he came
on. He arrived back at the village first. But the ones who were
driving the horses were still coming.

The boy entered his lodge. He lay down on his bed.

Then his mother said, "Hey, old man, someone has entered. He's
entered. He's gone over there to the boy's bed. Make a fire to see
who it is!"

"Ha, poor thing, he must be tired. They don't know how to go
out on the warpath. Maybe our boy is tired."

Then the old man made a fire.

Ah, there lay the boy, lying on his bed.

"Hey! Here you've come back! Now what happened?"

Then the boy said, "The party is bringing some horses, but I
came on ahead. They'll arrive here. They're bringing horses."

"Don't you have any?"

"Surely they'll give you some."

Morning came. It was just at daybreak. The party drove the
horses—a large herd of horses—into the village. They were singing
a praising song. They were telling of the boy Young Hawk: "Now
this is what he did. This is what he did for us," as they were singing
the praising song for him and the deeds he had performed while he
was with them.

And the old man, the poor thing, was happy about it. "And here
our boy was valorous! And here the party is calling out his deeds,
praising him in song for what he did!"

Then they said, "Now call his father! Let him choose some
horses! That one is the cause of what the boy did."

Meanwhile the boy lay there on his bed in the lodge.

They told his father, "Choose some of these horses! This is what
your son did," they were telling him.

Now he selected some horses from however many there were.

Then the boy got up.

His father said, "Now there they are. They've given those horses
to me."

"Now what did they say?"

He said, "Now this is what they said."

"Yes."

Now the boy never did go on the warpath again. That was the last time.

Then the boy lived among his people and he became a man.

And one time when the women were picking corn and squash— when they harvested their crops in the fall—he was inside his lodge.

Then he picked up a robe. Then he went outside into plain sight and looked all around.

Oh, then a bird whistled from up above as dust rose. And there stood a man. Young Hawk did not know him.

Then this man said to him, "You certainly are stubborn. I thought I would make a man of you. But you're not interested in manly ways. You never just venture off. And I'm the one who's the cause of the things you did when you were successful on the horse-stealing expedition.

"Now you must want to be poor. Now you'll at last be poor."

Then a hawk whistled as it flew around after the man disappeared.

Then this man [Young Hawk] cried as he mourned. "Now surely I didn't know; and here you were the cause of those things I did— you were the cause of my having been a warrior!"

Well, later Young Hawk said, "Now this is what happened to me. That's what happened to me. I myself am the cause." That is what he used to tell.

This is a Pawnee story. It is not one of our Arikara stories.

Now this boy never did have good fortune again. He never married; and then many years later he died of old age.

29

The Origin of the Arikara
Crazy Dog Society

A popular organization among young Arikara and Hidatsa men was the Crazy Dog Society, notable during the past century of reservation life for its Doorway songs. Groups of young men would go from door to door in the village or camp serenading young women with these songs, whose lyrics told of love. The origin of the Arikara society is recounted here. Its source was an animal lodge of dogs said to be located at Dog Den Butte in McLean County, North Dakota. The society derived from a dog chief's son who married a human being.

Now I am going to tell another story that I used to hear. It occurred when our villages were there in the country to the east. It occurred in the winter, in the winter when it is very cold, in midwinter.

There was a village and in it was a family that had a young daughter. They loved her. She never went anywhere, but just remained at home, where she was always sewing.

At night when the family was ready to go to bed, when they said, "Let's all go to bed," after they had piled up the wood they would burn during the night, a dog would come into the lodge. Oh, it had the mange. The dog was ugly. And it sat on top of the young woman's bed. In the morning they opened the door, and then they whipped it as they drove it out. It was doing that for some time, however long it was.

Then the young woman became pregnant. Then she was going to have the baby. It was getting to be the time to have it.

Then her family asked her, "Oh, were you talking with anyone?"[1]

---

1. An idiom for having sexual intercourse.

Then she said, "No. I don't know why I'm this way, pregnant as I am." She was telling about herself, "I know that I didn't talk to anyone."

And when summer usually begins, when the ground gets warm, the young woman began to have pains, and then she bore puppies. There were four of them. Oh, they were cute, and they were spotted.

Now her mother said to her brother who was ten winters old, a boy of ten winters, "Ah, throw these dogs away! Let them freeze over there! Why do they ridicule her?" That is what the mother of the young woman was asking over and over.

Then the boy picked the dogs up; then he took them out. When he was taking them, he took a liking to two of them. Oh, they were spotted. He wanted to keep them.

Then he fixed a place and put the two puppies inside it. And the ugly dog—the one that was their father—would be inside keeping them warm.

In the morning the boy would gather together scraps of food and leftover soup from the family's meals. Then he sneaked them outside. And here he was going there to feed the puppies.

Then, after winter, it became summer—when it becomes summer, when the green grass comes up. This young woman thought, "I wonder what my brother is doing when he takes the meat and other leftovers outside? Where is he taking them?"

Then she followed him. There the little puppies were. Oh, they were cute! They were spotted. There, too, was the mangy dog they had been throwing outside. Then he put the food down for them, and then he came back.

And then the young woman saw him. Then she said, "Why, here my brother is feeding the dogs that I bore! He's keeping them over there. But he must have thrown two of them away."

Now one day, early in the morning, she heard someone singing at the end of the village, where he was singing. Then the young woman went outside. Then she went there, and there they stood: a young man and two boys beside him.[2]

---

2. The dog father and the two puppies in human form.

Then the young woman came back. Then she picked up a shawl, and her bag, whatever it was. Then she went over there. And there they were going in the distance. Then she followed them, walking behind them as they traveled <to the northeast>.

Sometime during the evening the two boys ran back toward her. Then one of them said, "Mother, you should turn back. My father says, 'Let her turn back! She certainly didn't treat you well, the way she treated you.'"

Then the young woman said, "Now it was that way, it is true. But I certainly didn't know that you were the ones. If I had known it, it wouldn't have been that way."

Well, then the two swung around. Then they became dogs when they ran behind their father as he went on.

Then the two came back after two days. One then said, "Mother, are you hungry?"

She said, "Yes, I'm hungry."

Then he said, "Now, my father has killed a deer over there. You can take whatever parts of it you want—whatever you will eat. My father has made a fire. When you get over there, you'll feed yourself. We'll all be going slowly. We won't leave you."

Then the young woman went, and there lay the deer. It was just as he had said: there was a fire there, too. Then the young woman began to roast the meat. Oh, she got full, and then she took meat for herself. Then she went on again.

While she was going, following them at night, the two little boys came running up to her. One said, "Tomorrow we'll arrive where our mothers and fathers, our grandfathers and grandmothers, and our uncles live. We're getting near there." It was now close by.

Then this one went there. Both the dogs ran there where they lived.

Morning came. Then the two came back. Then one of them said, "Now, mother, when we go up this rise, you'll see a hill, a hill way over there standing alone on the prairie. That's where we're going. That's where the village is. That's where my grandmothers, grandfathers, and uncles live. That's where we're going."

Then they all kept going. Then the two ran off to it again. The young woman went up a rise. There in the distance was a hill.

Then they all kept going.

Now when they were close to the hill, the boys came up. Then one said, "Mother, we are arriving there. Now, mother, be ready! When we go inside, when we and you enter, you sit over there on the left side. You must sit by the doorway. <That's where my grandmothers, grandfathers, mothers, and uncles sit.> Don't sit there on the other side, on the right! You must sit on the left side!

"Now they are going to talk first. We'll tell you whatever they're going to have planned."

Then they arrived where they lived in the hill. There was a doorway, and then they went inside. Then she sat down where they had told her.

Well, then they began their meeting when they saw the young man, who walked ahead of the two boys. Now he reached the west side of the interior. Then he was handed a pipe, which he smoked and smoked.

Then one said, "Now you are going to explain why this young woman has followed you here."

He said, "Yes. I chose to marry this young woman. Now here is what happened. Now her brother—the brother of this young woman—saved these two boys of mine. Now you are going to decide what is to happen to her."

Then the ones on the right side said, "Surely the young woman should be dead—she should be killed. What she did to the two offspring that she bore for this chief's child sitting here with the two boys was wrong."

The other ones sitting on the left said, "That surely cannot be. She certainly did not know what happened. This one himself erred. This young man erred when he did not present himself clearly as the dog he is, just as this young woman is clearly a human.

"Now she shouldn't be killed. It won't happen. We will side with the young woman so that she won't die, but so that she may turn around and go back to her village.

"But now we are going to bless the boy who is her brother. We are going to bless her brother."

Then they called the young woman. Then she sat down by her two sons.

And then one said, "Now it happened that way: he himself

erred."

The young man said to the young woman, "It is my own fault that I didn't tell you what I had done. I myself erred. I myself am the cause. But now you are going to turn back and return to your village.

"Now we are going to bless your brother. We are going to give him powers so that he won't be poor, so that your brother won't be poor. Whatever your brother wants will come to pass. Whatever he undertakes is not going to be difficult for him. We'll go with him. We'll watch over him. When he sets out on the warpath, he'll have no difficulty achieving what he desires. It will come to pass.

"Now your brother will take these powers from us. He is going to learn these songs. These songs will come to him mysteriously."

Well, then that is what he did.

He said, "They are going to take you back home. These four will return you there. And this is what you'll tell your brother."

Then all day, from morning until into the night, they were bringing the young woman back, and then all night until just before morning. It did not take long.

There the chiefs were meeting inside.

Then her mother said, "Old man, our daughter has returned."

It was morning now. Now she said, "Now this is what happened. We erred; and the one who chose to be my husband himself erred. He himself erred. For whatever reason, he didn't make his identity clear when he came, and consequently we lost two children.

"Now they're going to bless only my brother here. Now things won't be difficult for him. Now he's going to have these songs, which are to be sung at night so that the enemy won't come close—to be sung at night so that the enemy won't attack us. Now he'll keep these songs."

Now the boy achieved these things after he became older. He had all sorts of valuable things since he was a brave for whom nothing was difficult. When he went on the warpath, too, horse stealing was not difficult for him after he had been blessed by the dogs.

Plate 6. Dog Den Butte, McLean County, North Dakota. Photograph by Raymond T. Haas, 1990.

«   »

Now this occurred there near Devils Lake. The hill stands there prominently. The hill stands on the prairie when we arrive there [Dog Den Butte]. That is where the dogs were meeting and where they lived.

Those sitting on the right side were coyotes with strings plaited in their braids. Those sitting on the right were the ones who had strings of otter skin plaited in their braids. Now they were the ones who were mean—the ones who had otter skin strings plaited in their braids.

And those over on the other side of the coyotes were kit foxes, the ones who had defended the young woman and had led her back home.

Now the songs they used to sing were the foremost ones. And we called the songs Whipping the Door. They used to call the members of the society Crazy Dogs.[3]

The Hidatsas had a Hidatsa Crazy Dog Society, too. That is what I used to hear. The Hidatsas still sing the songs.

And I know the Doorway songs—the Crazy Dog songs—because my grandfather, old man Short Bear, used to sing them. He gave me the right to know the songs.

30

The Origin Of The Hidatsa Crazy Dog Society

This version of the origin of the Hidatsa Crazy Dog Society, told to the narrator by his Hidatsa father-in-law John Hunts Along, differs from other published accounts,

---

3. In published sources this name has also been translated as Crazy Horse (Lowie 1915:670) and Foolish Dog (Curtis 1907–30, 5:150).

*which more closely parallel the preceding Arikara story.
Here Coyote is said to have been banished from the animal
lodge at Dog Den Butte because he had aided the Hidatsa
people when the animals attacked their village. Subsequently
Coyote went to live with the Hidatsas and introduced the
Doorway songs.*

The Hidatsas own this story. I used to hear the story that I am
going to tell from my wife's father.[1] This is what he told me—what
the Hidatsas were like when they were camping in different places
in the area around Washburn.[2] That is the area where the Hidatsa
villages were, wherever they were.

There was a young man whose family esteemed him. He had
four sisters and his mother and father. He had many relatives. They
thought highly of this young man, and he was handsome when he
wore the leggings with beaded sides and the shirt fringed with scalp
hair that his sisters made for him. Things were nice for him as he
went around.

He always used to go up a hill in the distance. It was a hill
where he would sit on top and look all around. His sisters would
cook a meal. Then they would call him. He would eat. They would
comb his hair. Then again he would go up the hill to sit on top, to
sit there [in his special place] and look all around. At sunset he
would come down. This is what he was doing.

Now one day when he sat on top of the hill, a meadow lark
came flying to him. Then it landed in front of the boy [and turned
into a human] as he looked at it.

Then this bird said, "They sent me to tell you: from all over this
wide earth the animals that are mean—the deer, antelope, elk, and
different kinds that you people kill—are going to come here to fight.
They're the ones that don't like it. Now they're going to come to

1. A Hidatsa named John Hunts Along.
2. The historic Hidatsa villages were clustered on both sides of the Knife
River, extending west from its confluence with the Missouri River, as well
as the area bounded approximately by the contemporary towns of
Washburn and Stanton, North Dakota.

attack you. The bears, the elk, the different kinds of animals that bite—the ones that are fierce—are going to kill you people. They're going to come to your village here.

"Now be ready! That's what the birds flying up above told me when I came from up there in the sky. That's what they told me to tell you so that you will know. Now get your tribe living here ready! Build a palisade! Put up four rows. Make arrows! It won't be long until they come to attack."

Then it flew up. Then the young man arose. Then he went down the hill. He ate a meal. Then he forgot what he had been told.

And the next morning he sat down on top of the hill again. Then it came there to him again. It was the same bird.

Then it said, "You did not tell what I said. Now hurry! Now hurry and tell the people what I told you! If I come again and you haven't done what I have told you, all of you will die."

Then this young man went down the hill. Now, as he had done before, he forgot after he ate his meal.

Now again morning came and he went up the hill to where he had been sitting and sat there on top. Then it came flying to him. It was the same bird.

Then it said, "You have failed. Now this is the last time that I will come here. Now I'm not going to come again to remind you. Now quickly do what I have told you!"

Then this young man picked up a piece of sage. Then he put it into his braids. He went down the hill. He ate.

Then his sister said, "Brother, why did you put sage into your braids?"

Now he said, "Yes, you've reminded me. I've failed twice. Now this is the last chance. The sage I have in my braids is to remind me. Now you've reminded me of it.

"A bird told me. A meadow lark said, 'You Hidatsa tribe living here, get ready! You're going to die if you don't do what they told me to tell you to do. Now hurry! Quickly put up a palisade! Let there be four rows. Now make arrows! From all over this entire earth the fiercest animals living here are going to come to fight. They're headed for your village here. You're all going to be killed.

Now for that reason, I have come here to tell you.'

"The bird is the reason that we ourselves are living here."

Then his father began announcing it. And then that is what they did: then they put up a palisade. Then it went around the village. There were four rows of posts. Well, then they began to make arrows.

Now the village was ready. Everything was ready where each man sat, where he sat against the palisade.

Now, meanwhile over there at that lodge named Dog Den, there is a butte there where the animals all gathered together.

Then Coyote Chief said, "Now, I won't go with you to attack that village, where you're going to fight that village of human beings. I have among them one I have blessed. He is my child. When you see someone painted white all over, he's the one. He's my child.

"Now be prepared! He'll kill you. He'll shoot you. The young man is my son. That's the reason I don't want to be among you."

"Ah, but you're afraid." They ridiculed him.

The bears and buffalo, the different kinds that were fierce, started out. They came to fight where the Hidatsa villages were clustered. Then it became foggy [from their breathing].

Meanwhile that Coyote Chief scurried off. Then he quickly circled around. He arrived where the Hidatsa villages were clustered.

Then he said, "I have come to do something for you people. Now they're coming to attack your village here. They'll count coups on you. Well, but now I have come here to help you in some way. Now bring me sage!"

Then they made a fire. "Oh, keep building up the fire!"

When they brought the sage, they passed it over the blaze of the fire there. And there the sage branches turned into arrows. Now these were the holiest ones. When one would shoot someone with one of them, that person would fall over dead. He would bloat up.

Then the bears and the buffalo, the fiercest ones, charged, going up against the palisade. They knocked down the outer row of posts. Now, meanwhile the people were shooting at them. And the man who was painted white all over, after he had gone up onto the top of an earth lodge, knocked an animal over every time he shot at one.

Now only one row of the palisade remained standing. Then one
of the animals, either a bear or an elk, began to call out, "Now so
far they have wounded many of us. The one on top of the earth
lodge is the one who is striking us. Now before things go any
further, let's get away before we do anything! They have killed a lot
of us."

Then the bears, buffalo, and the different kinds of fierce animals
retreated.

But Coyote Chief washed the white paint off himself. [Here he
was the one who was painted white all over!] Then he ran where he
was going.

Meanwhile, when the animals were arriving back at their lodge
at Dog Den and were acting holy as they doctored each other where
they were wounded—where they had been shot and were hurting.
While they were getting well from their medicine, there sat a bear.
It was an old man bear [who had not gone into battle].

And then they said to him, "Now you'll be the one to watch for
him. I think that Coyote Chief who was inside here was the cause
of our being killed. Now it will be unfortunate for him if he comes
back here. Now we're going to kill him. Now be ready! Get ready!
You are holy. If anyone comes and smells like a human, we are
going to kill him."

The bear just sat there watching for him as the coyotes were
coming. Then he said, "No, [this one doesn't smell like a human].
No."

The main one, Coyote Chief, the one who had been fighting,
[knew what was going to happen when he returned and] here he
picked up a mushy squash. It was mixed with corn. "Yes, now, old
man, I've brought this for you to taste." Then he put the squash into
his hand.

Then the bear began to eat the squash, eating it and eating it.
Then Coyote Chief made him forget what they had told him.

"Hey, it sure does taste good, and I feel good after eating it. Oh,
there was no one around [after everyone went to fight]. It's your
own fault that you all went to fight the humans. It wasn't good
what they did to you all."

Here that bear knew Coyote Chief was the one who had been shooting them! Now they got together <since the two of them were good friends>.

"But who might it be? There's no one around. Now I've become good and full. The squash tastes really good!" That is what the bear was saying. Well, now this is what happened.[3]

Now when the animals inside learned of this, they sent this Coyote out. "Go on! You cannot stay here inside this lodge again. Now be among those humans you sided with!"

Then Coyote came.

That is the reason that the Doorway songs are among the people, sung at night when [the young men stay up and] the dogs watch over things.

These songs are the ones of the Fox Society, the Fox Way, sung when the dogs watch over things so that the enemy <and wild animals> do not come close to the villages where they are singing at night. Now this is the reason the Hidatsas are always talking about the Crazy Dog Society.

Now this is the Hidatsa story.

31

The Origin of the Round Dance

This story accounts for the origin of the Round dance, a popular social dance among Plains tribes, said here to have come to the Arikaras from the Crows. Its Arikara name, čiikaáhUx, means 'drinking' and, according to the tradition here, both dance and name derive from the vision of a sickly

---

3. The old bear, who was slightly fearful of Coyote, forgot to smell him when he was eating and then did not want to do it afterward. Although he knew Coyote Chief had been the one shooting the animals, the old bear wished to pretend that he did not know it.

young man who vomited whenever he ate food. One time,
after watching a boar being butchered, he dreams the ani-
mal comes to him in human form and gives him medicine to
drink and a song to which he should dance after eating
meals. Subsequently other songs of this type come to the
young man from the boar. There is seemingly no end to
them, according to the narrator, just as when a boar drinks
water there is seemingly no end to its drinking.

Now I'll tell the reason for the custom of this dance that they
used to dance long ago. I certainly don't know about its origin from
my own experience, but it is one of the stories my grandmother used
to tell me. Sometimes she would just tell me something.

Once I asked her, for whatever reason it was, when I just asked,
"Grandma, what do they mean when they say "drinking"? When
they begin dancing they go in a circle when they sing. Does it mean
that one must be drinking something, eh?"

She said, "You're right about its meaning that. It refers to
drinking. This is how the custom came about."

There once was a young man—whatever his age was my grandmother didn't know, she said—who became sick again and again.
He would eat something, and as soon as he had eaten it, he vomited
it right up. He vomited up what he had eaten. They didn't know
what the reason was—what animal he might have been marked by.

This is what people used to say: that when an animal [had been
seen by a pregnant woman, it] marked the child, and then later in
life some illness befell him. But there used to be medicines that the
doctors possessed, and the doctors would treat a person and he
would get well.

Now this is what befell this young man: he would eat something, and then he began throwing it up. <His family got a doctor
to treat him, but the doctor could not cure him.>

And then one day they killed a boar and butchered it. At the
same time this young man sat there watching them do it, watching
them butcher the boar. There lay the boar's head. The young man
stared at it as he sat there, just staring at the boar's head.

After awhile he thought, "I wish I could eat a piece of the meat—the pork." The pork looked good—it looked tasty. "The meat looks tasty. I wish I could eat a piece. The meat must taste good."

<But he did not dare eat any. He was afraid to eat it after they cooked some of the meat, thinking, "If I do eat, I'll vomit it up.">

Later, after it got dark, everyone went to bed. But the meat lay there. Everyone else had already eaten some of it—his mother, father, grandmother, grandfather, brother, sister, and the man who was there doctoring him—the one treating him.

And while this boy slept, he had a dream. A man came into the lodge. Then the man came up to the boy where he lay on his bed, where he lay there sick.

This man then said to him, "Now I have come. I want you to know. You were staring at me while they butchered me. But now it is my fate that you people must eat me, and you were wishing to eat some meat, but you were afraid to do it. Whenever you eat anything, you just vomit it up. Now I am going to doctor you."

And then this man who had come inside knelt down. Then he brought out a wooden bowl. He put something in it, whatever it was. He set it down. Then he put water in it. Then he stirred it. As he stirred it, it got foamy. It looked like soap suds.

Then he said, "Now, I am going to pity you. Now I want you to drink this. When you drink it, you'll have this song. Then there will be nothing the matter. There'll be nothing wrong. You need not be that way again, no matter what happens to you. When you drink it, you'll begin singing this song. Now then there isn't going to be anything wrong with you—and you'll be well if you aren't afraid to do what I'm telling you to do."

Well then this young man who was sick thought, "It doesn't matter. I barely live from one day to the next. Well, I guess I'll drink it."

And then he began drinking it. Then he did it: oh, then he consumed all the foam.

Then this man there said, "I'm the one you have drunk up here. I'm the one. It is nothing for me to eat anything. I don't know of any time when I ever threw something up. When I eat something, I eat it. Now you are going to be that way."

And then this man continued, "Now this song is the one you're going to sing. When you're about to eat, you'll sing this one in your mind. Then the misfortune will leave you. It won't bother you again."

[After the man taught him the song], well, then this young man did it himself: he sang it. Then he sang this song. The lyrics are, "I'll be the one when you drink; I'm the one, this liquid." That is what it says.

> Now I'll be the one when you drink;
>   When you go around,
>   When you go around.
>   Then you'll drink me.

Now this song that I sang is the one.

Then the sick boy awoke. As he lay there, he said, "Mother, are you awake?"

Then she said, "I'm cooking a meal." It was his mother.

And there sat the man who was doctoring him. He was brewing medicine.

Then this young man said to him, "Wait awhile! My mother is going to prepare a beverage that I'm going to drink." Then he said, "Now, mother, come here for a while!"

Then his mother came.

Then he said, "Put water into a wooden bowl! You'll stir that tongue around in it. You'll proceed to stir it around in it. When it gets foamy, I'll drink it. I'm going to sing a song. A man has blessed me for when we are going to eat. Now this is the end of my sickness. Nothing else will happen to me.

"And this man who has been doctoring me—you must not feel hurt in any way. The man who came to me in my dream helped you when he came into the lodge. Now I'm going to get well."

Then this boy drank it up. While he was singing, the tongue had become foam. Then he drank it up.

Well, then his mother began cooking and dished up food for the boy. He ate.

His family now waited for some time for him to begin vomiting. Then time passed there. He did not vomit.

Once again he ate.

As time went on and he continued to eat all right, the family gave presents to the man who had been doctoring him. Now the man returned home. And then this young man got well. Then he regained his strength after eating. When he ate he never again vomited up things. Then he got over his sickness.

Now this is the source of this song. They call it Drinking, when one dances to the singing. And that is what this young man did: when he was drinking he was dancing while he was seated.

Now this is the reason. Right there is where the custom started. Then they began the Drinking songs.

Now the Crow tribe is the one that brought the dance. This is the reason the Crows know how to sing these songs. Today they call it the Round dance, but actually the name is Drinking. Whatever the foam was that he drank, when that young man was made to drink the foam—that's when it began. When one drinks, then one dances.

Now this is what I used to hear. My grandmother told me the story. A boar was the one that had the power. It said, "I'm greedy. When I eat I don't know when I vomit things up, and I just eat everything."

Now this is the end of the story.

32

The Origin of the Pawnee and Other Grass Dance Songs

In post-reservation Indian communities on the Northern Plains, the Grass dance was an innovation introduced from the south that gained vast popularity, replacing most of the surviving men's societies. Two forms of the Grass dance were introduced among the Arikaras: one came from the Santee

Sioux, the other from the Pawnees, both about the same period, 1870. The following narrative is a composite account of the origin of various groups of Grass dance songs formerly current among the Arikaras and today partially remembered by only a few older individuals.

The Pawnee Grass dance was brought to the Arikara by Pawnee Tom, who helped an influential Arikara named Enemy Heart to inaugurate the dance among his people (Murie 1914:629). The songs introduced by Pawnee Tom and Crazy Horse, another visiting Pawnee, are now known to Arikaras as Pawnee songs. The myth accounting for the origin of the Pawnee Grass dance is told here. Ray Gough, an Arikara, learned the story when he lived among the Pawnees sometime during the early part of this century. It tells of a poor young man who is taken into an animal lodge of birds, where the thunderbirds (eagles) and crows teach him the form of the society and its songs so that he can introduce them to his people.

Two sets of Grass dance songs that originated among the Arikaras themselves at the turn of the century, when there was a brief revival of native traditions, were those of Red Star and Crow Ghost. Their origin is briefly discussed here after the Pawnee myth. Both Red Star and Crow Ghost lived in the Beaver Creek district of the Fort Berthold Reservation and had dreams in which they were given songs. Red Star's came to him from Thunder while he lay fasting on a hillside, and Crow Ghost's songs came to him while fasting at a series of graves after the death of his wife. Although the narrator states here that he never heard the full account of how Crow Ghost received his songs, the translator recounted how they came to him from crows, and in fact all of Crow Ghost's songs tell about that bird.

This narrative concludes with brief, general comments on singing among the Arikaras today and how the narrator came to learn the songs he knows.

Pawnee Songs

Now I am going to tell why these dancing songs, the songs that belonged to the Pawnees long, long ago, are now among us.

Now when the Pawnees lived in villages in the country to the south, there was a boy who was pitiful after his relatives had died, whoever his kin were—his father, mother, sisters, and brothers. He had no one. He was poor and would go around alone, wandering around the village, going into different lodges wherever someone would feed him something [for doing chores for them, like watering their horses or cutting weeds]. He would eat and spend the night while he would just wander around the village, poor thing, after he had been left alone.

Well, one day while he was sitting there, sitting on the roof of an earth lodge, something caused him to make up his mind. "I think I'll go somewhere! I think I'll just die somewhere out on the prairie! Or perhaps the enemy might even kill me."

And then this boy left. No one saw him when he departed from the village, when he just walked off. He didn't know where he was headed. After he went off he wandered all around this country, the poor thing, eating Juneberries, plums, and chokecherries, wherever it was that he went. He didn't care where he went; he just went out on the prairie. He was just wandering around.

Then he went up a hill and sat on top of it. Then he lay down. "I think I'll lie down awhile! And then I'll go off somewhere again." He was looking for some way that he might die.

After he had lain there sleeping, he jumped up. When he awakened, he jumped up. His life was transformed[1] when he awoke and got up. The country was different. He did not know the country, but he went on.

"Ha, this is what I am seeking for myself!" That is what he thought.

While he was going along, he heard something. It was the sound of drumming.

---

1. An expression signifying that he has been pitied by a spirit being and is about to receive power.

"Why, I wonder what it is?" He did not know what caused the drumming sound.

Then this boy went toward the place where he heard the drumming, where he thought it was. Now it was close by.

Then he heard singing. As he went on, the sound became louder.

There was a hill there. And here it was a lodge! And here this hill was a lodge! Over there was where they were singing.

When the boy reached the lodge, a man came out. The man had seen him. Now he began to stare at the boy. Then he turned around. He went back inside the lodge.

This boy stood there. He thought, "Whoever are you? Perhaps you live here. Perhaps you're wandering around just as I am." That is what he was thinking.

And there inside the lodge the man said, "The one we have been waiting for has arrived. Here he is."

Then one of those inside said, "Now bring him inside! Let him come in!"

Then the man came out. He said, "Say, now come inside! Follow behind me!"

Then he and this boy went inside. The boy followed him.

Now when he entered there sat a man on the left by the door. He had a pipe, and men were sitting there in different groups, as they sat around in different groups.

Then the boy followed the man. Then he was given a place. "Be seated here!" There sat a group of men.

Oh, by the last group over there on the left is where the drum was. Here that is where the drum was! A group sat over there. Here they were the ones singing! They were the singers.

He sat down, and then the man said, "Now quickly, let him smoke!"

That man over there by the door filled the pipe. He brought the pipe to him.

Then the boy began smoking as he sat there. He finished smoking.

Then that man brought the boy water. He made him drink.

<Then the man had him take water in his hands and put it on his head, blessing himself with it by stroking movements.>

Then the one who was telling him what to do instructed him. He said, "You are going to eat now. These men have invited you. They have called you." Here this man who was telling him things was the errand man.

Then this man got up. Then he sat down right here where the boy sat.

Then he said, "Now I want you to know this. We called you purposefully when you came here. Over there where you wander around in your country, you are pitiful. There is no one. You have no close relatives. Your father, mother, and other family are all dead. You are left alone. That is why we called you, in order to do something for you." That is what he was saying to him.

"Now you are the one we selected here to carry out certain customs for us. You people don't have this tradition. You don't know it. You are going to take it to them. You'll tell them what we want done. You'll do it for us.

"These whom you see here are the ones. These are the foremost ones, here where the drum is and where these are. They are the thunderbirds whom you hear when the thunder claps and it lightnings. And here they are the ones sitting here! Now they are going to talk to you, too." That is what he said.

Then the man arose. He said, "We want you to know that this is what you are going to do for us."

Then he told the boy. Then he said, "These large birds that fly around have the right to the place here where we stand—the different kinds of hawks and this eagle that you see. The ones sitting there are eagles, and the ones sitting there are the birds with white heads. And that one, the favored child, is my favorite one. That one is mine.

"Now, these seated here, the scouts, these small birds that fly all over this world, are mine. They tell me, 'This is what is. This is what is happening,' when they report different things to me. Now they told me that this boy was certainly pitiful, the poor thing, when he was left alone. He has no relatives. This is the reason we have called you to sit here. This is what we want you to do for us.

<"When somebody has lost a loved one—a mother or father or sister or brother—your society must invite that person, bring him

in and feed him, just as we have done for you. There are four things
to do whenever you talk to someone who has lost a loved one: give
him a pipe to smoke, water to drink, water to bless himself with,
and food to eat. That's the way you treat mourners.[2]

"And these songs that you are about to learn—each one is a
prayer. When you go to war you pray with these songs. Or if you
are going hunting, you pray with them. If you look for something,
you must pray. These are the songs.">

Then he continued, "Now this group is the one that's going to
teach you the songs."

Then he was placed by this group. Then they began to sing.

(Now right here I don't know how many songs there were, even
though I know the songs. But I don't know how many songs there
were. I don't want to tell lies.)

"Now, everything is done. Now you have finished doing it here.
Now there is one more thing." Then they taught him the song to be
sung when someone takes the meat out of the pot—when someone takes it out of the pot in which it is cooking to offer it to the
Heavens. Now, there is only one song; they have only one song
when the offering is made, and that is what he was given. "This is
what you are going to do. This is how it will be done."

Well, then they told him, "Now here is the end. This is the end
of what we have given you. Now we are going to take you home. It
won't be long before you marry a woman. You'll have children. Also
you won't be poor any longer, the way you were before when you
were going around. It's different now. You are going to have good
fortune when you go around on the warpath and on the hunt.

But it is the way of the eagle to hunt around. Now they are
going to take you. You are going to go back to your country, for you
to be where you rightfully belong."

Then they brought him back. Here it took four nights for them
to bring him! But I don't know how long the time was that he was
there; how many days it was I didn't learn.

2. This ritual, still practiced today on the Fort Berthold Reservation, is
called 'wiping the tears of mourners.'

They brought him back to the village. Then these Pawnees in the village saw him. "The boy who disappeared has come back." They were glad when they saw him.

Then he told them, "This is where I was. This is where I went." Then the men gathered together. Then they took notice of him.

Then he gathered the men together. Then he began telling about what he had been taught. Then he began singing. Oh, these men liked it as they were singing and learning it for themselves. Now they learned the ways that he had.

"Now this is what is going to be." This is what he said. "This is what is going to be," as he taught them step by step.

Then it was settled: "Now this is how it's going to be for us as a group. There will be a dancing society in which you'll wear a porcupine hair roach with the tail of a whitetail deer.[3] You'll wear an eagle feather on your head when you go around on the warpath. Such a person is a favored child.

"Now, this jackrabbit, the fast one; and this coyote, who hurries up things. . . ."—then he told about each one at a time. "Now this foreteller, the magpie, who foretells things after he has looked all around—whenever there is a dead buffalo lying there, then he influences the birds, and so they begin arriving there to eat it."[4]

Now this is what I know. After he returned, this young man found good fortune, and got married and had his own children. He was no longer in need of horses.

Now this is what he said: "This is how it will be."

Now it isn't known how long the young man practiced these customs, carrying them on for the birds. The eagles and thunderbirds were watching over him carefully, so that he continued to find good fortune for these Pawnees.

Now truly our life here on this earth is not permanent, and when one reaches old age, he dies. But now these Pawnees have told each other from one generation to the next.

3. The distinctive headdress of the Grass dance society.
4. In Pawnee tradition magpies are the birds most successful in finding food and are generally associated "with the near presence of the buffalo" (G. A. Dorsey 1904a:337).

« « «   » » »

Well, a man used to come here to Fort Berthold. He was half
Pawnee. He was a mixed blood. Now he was married here. I don't
know what his name was. I never found out what they used to call
him. Before anyone spoke English yet, they said Pawnee Tom.
Pawnee Tom is what he was called. The men who used to be living,
when they referred to him, always said Pawnee Tom. Whatever his
actual name was I don't know. I don't know if anyone who is still
living knows that.

Now this man is the one who used to bring the Pawnee songs
here, the ones in which they pray to the Heavens. Now those are
the holy ones, in which the Pawnee lyrics of these songs tell of their
putting their faith in the Chief Above. There were thirty-eight of
these Pawnee songs that the man called Pawnee Tom brought here.
But Pawnee Tom was the name he went by.

Well, I don't know if any Arikara was also named that.

Also, there was another one, Crazy Horse. It was the same with
him. He used to bring songs here when he came to dance. The
Pawnee lyrics of these songs are about Night, and about the ways
of war and horse stealing.

There must have been many of these songs, but Ray Gough used
to say that the number of these Pawnee songs was thirty-eight.

Red Star's Songs

Now there used to be another man here named Red Star. When
he fasted as he lay out on a hill while it rained all night and all day
he received power, whatever that power was, to call the rain and to
tell it to go in another direction. That is what he was able to do.

And one time when there used to be dances at Beaver Creek, he
did that as the lightning and thunder came. It was a *very* severe
storm when they were dancing at Beaver Creek. Everyone got
frightened when the rain was coming.

And that man Red Star, the poor thing, went outside. Then he
stood in the west and sang, waving the rain by so that it would go
in another direction. Now that is what it did: then the rain passed

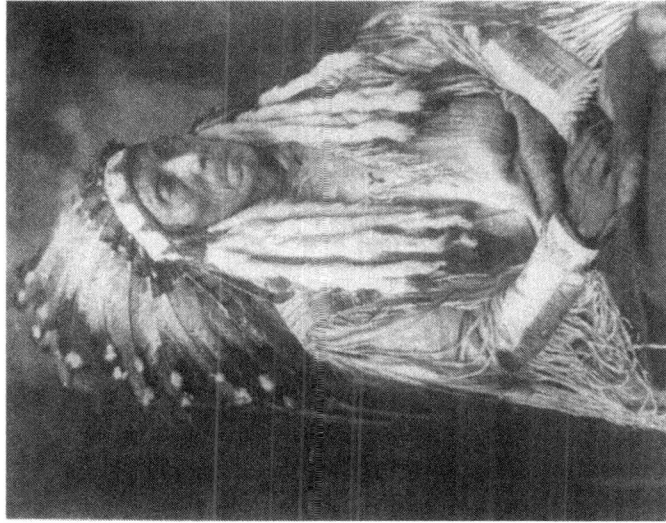

Plate 7. Two early twentieth century Arikara ceremonial leaders. *Left*, Crow Ghost. Photograph ca. 1920, Butler Studio of Bismarck, courtesy State Historical Society of North Dakota. *Right*, Red Star, holding a men's society staff and dance whistle. Photograph ca. 1912, courtesy State Historical Society of North Dakota.

by us. The rain went over there to the north. It only rained a little where they were dancing at Beaver Creek. Now that is what he did there.

There was another time when that happened, too. I don't know if Red Star did it that time; they didn't tell who it was. But that is what Red Star used to do: he would call the rain.

Now my grandmother's brother had that power, too. Looks For The Enemy was his name. He was also called Horse Above. The holy birds—the thunderbirds—also gave him power when the thunder comes.

He used to say, "After I die I'll be the one who comes when my father Rain and my grandfather Thunder come. I'll come among them."

That is what he used to tell my grandmother, the poor thing, the one who raised me.

This Red Star also had the right to ritually smoke the drum. Before they were going to dance, they would smudge it.

This is what they did: they gathered together the members of the dance society. Then he smudged the drum. Then they sang a song. I know the song that Red Star used to sing when he was pleading and praying to Thunder that everything would be well, that nothing bad would occur, that no misfortune would happen, and that no one would get hurt accidentally when things just happen.

Now this is the power that Red Star had.

Crow Ghost's Songs

Now that Crow Ghost had some kind of power, too, whatever the power was.

When the woman who was his wife died, the poor thing, then this Crow Ghost was alone. And so at night he cried at her grave, when he fasted there at night. I don't know how many nights he did that. Then he went to a different cemetery, and there he began fasting again.

Now that is what that man Crow Ghost did. I don't know how many times he did that, but he fasted at no fewer than eight graves.

I saw the house here where he used to live, where he lived alone. He used to live west of where my father, the old man, lived. The house where Crow Ghost lived was close by.

Now the boy who was Crow Ghost's son [Morgan Jones] was our in-law. I don't know the meaning behind his name, Riding, the name which they called him. Riding. It means 'to ride, to ride a horse to go somewhere.'

Anyway, this that I have told about his father fasting is what he told me. He would have told me the entire story, but we were going to Garrison and had a flat tire. <This is what he was telling me as we were driving along. "I'll tell the story as we go.">

When we had the flat, we got out and fixed the tire. Then we drove on. Now we were hungry and so we forgot the story. We arrived in Garrison. We ate and then I bought some things. <Afterward we began singing and forgot the story.>

Comments

Now the number of Red Star's songs is fifteen, and the number of Crow Ghost's is twenty-two. There must have been many more songs. Today we usually sing a few of them, but we forget the words of the songs. They don't sing the words properly, the words in the songs that give them their meaning and tell the reason the song was made. It is the same way with the Pawnee songs: when the Pawnees used to go around and pray, each of these Pawnee songs was a prayer. They used to sing these songs sometimes. Ah, it's a long time since they used to sing them.

Well, I lived where my house used to be when the old ones were living, close by the other side of the Missouri River. I lived over there on the south side, in Beaver Creek. That is where our settlement was, there on the other side of the river.

Now one man, Ray Gough, used to come there. He was named Bear Goes Out. That is what his Arikara name was. But they also called him Blackbird [his nickname], whatever they meant by that bird name when they called him Blackbird. He is the one who used to tell me things.

And then there was Crow Arrow Feather, who was named Ed Lockwood. We used to sing at his house. And Many Crows [Peter Sherwood] is one who used to teach me songs and sing these songs. And our deceased uncle Red Trees [Stephen Wash] used to sing these songs at dances. Harry Gillette, or White Shield, taught me a few songs, too.

I usually sing. The younger fellows don't want me and those my age to sing the old songs. They want us to sing only new songs. But I don't do that. I don't usually sing them—but only the ones I know, the Pawnee songs that came in a dream.

Now when the old generation went off to boarding school, when they were there at Carlisle Indian School, they would not come home for a long period of time, until they finished and graduated with a diploma. Then one could come home. Now that is what some of our people did. All of them who went there are dead now. They were the ones who brought back some of the songs we have among us that came from different tribes at Carlisle and other places and are their songs.

But here where we live there are Crazy Dog and Taroxpa songs, and Fox Society songs. That is all.

33

The Pawnee Woman and the Scalped Man

This is one of many stories about scalped men, individuals who had fallen in warfare but later revived, only to find themselves permanently scarred and destined to live thereafter in isolation in the opaque world of spirits because the scar represented their transformation into spirit beings called tshunúxu'. One folkloric portrayal of the scalped man is a character who is a potential source of miraculous power.

*This role is illustrated here, where a scalped man discovers
a young woman who has fled her village during an enemy
attack. He marries her and subsequently endows her brother
with power for success in war and hunting.*

Now I am going to tell a Pawnee story that is also an Arikara
story. We understand Pawnee when we are talking. When the
Pawnees say something, we understand it. And it is the same way
for them, too: when we say something they understand it.

It happened somewhere, I do not know where, long, long ago.
There was a Pawnee village, and the enemy came to fight. During
the battle the attackers made it rugged for them.

Then one young woman ran off. Then she ran off from the group
when the enemy was counting coups on them and killing them, and
half the people in the village ran off in all directions. This young
woman carried a small boy on her back. Then she ran into a ravine.

While she was hiding in different places, it became night. As
she went on, there was a cut bank over there. Then she went into
a recess in it. Then she sat down after she was in it.

Where the village was the enemy had scattered out and were
around fires that they had made here and there as they remained
overnight. There were fires here and there when the young woman
looked.

Then she thought, "I'll stay inside here for a while. Then when
the enemy goes off, I'll get out. I don't know where I'm going to go."
That is what the young woman thought over and over.

Now there was a sound on the ground that came her way. Oh,
it passed by. Then it came back. Once again it passed. Then it
stopped right here over where she was in the recess.

Then someone sat down. Then his legs hung down; his feet hung
down. Now she saw his feet from where she was there inside.

And then the one who sat on the edge of the bank said, "Now I
am the one they call Sees Him Everywhere.[1] I'm the one named

---

1. The narrator translated this name as Looking At Himself, but the
translator felt that Sees Him Everywhere was a better translation. The
latter is the one used here.

Sees Him Everywhere. Whoever you are who is inside here, get
out." That is what he was saying over and over.

Then he got up, and then he quickly disappeared.

It was not long before he quickly came back. He came back
again. Then he sat down where he had been sitting just as he had
done when his feet were hanging down. "Now here I am. I'm the one
Sees Him Everywhere." That is what he was saying.

Then this young woman thought, "Now surely I wonder who you
might be, you who are coming here. I am hungry."

Then the boy cried. The little boy, however old he was, cried
since he was hungry.

Then this young woman said, "Now whoever you are, Sees Him
Everywhere, my son and I are hungry."

Then the one sitting on the edge of the cut bank, Sees Him
Everywhere, jumped up. There was the sound of footsteps as he
went off. The young woman who was in the recess heard him.

After a while there was the sound on the ground of him coming
again. He sat down. Then he said, "Now here I am. I'm the one Sees
Him Everywhere. Now come! Here's some food for you to eat."

The young woman was afraid of him. "Now it doesn't make any
difference if we starve to death. He might pity me," she thought.
Then she came out.

There sat a man. He was a very young man. Oh, this young
man sitting here was dressed nicely! Then he said, "Now eat!"

Then the baby boy and she began to eat since he was hungry.
Oh, they ate the roasted ribs and dried meat that he brought for
them, eating everything!

Then he said, "Now follow me! It isn't far to where I live."

Then that is what the young woman did: then she followed him.
Oh, this scalped man led her to where his dwelling was. <There was
a disguised door on the hillside that opened into his lodge.>

He said, "This is where I live."

Then they went inside. Oh, it was *very* nice indeed there with
a fire! It was warm.

"Now sit down right there! Now none of your people are close
by. The people of your tribe have gone far off. They have gone *far*
off indeed, after what happened when many of them were killed.

<"Now you must know me."

"Yes, I knew you when you were still young. You were a little boy yet," she said.

"Yes, it happened the same way to me. I was captured, and then I ran away. They captured me, and I got away, and then they killed me. They didn't notice, but I wasn't really killed. I didn't die. Someone came and picked me up—revived me.

"But now I'm not supposed to be among people, not able to go back to our people. I'm different. I have a different way of life.[2]>

"Now if you want, I'll take you. We'll go. Your father, mother, and family are still alive. They are looking for you."

Then the young woman remained there overnight after she and the boy had eaten well. Now the young man must have been good.

Then he said, "You and I will go. We'll all three go. But I want to be together with you, to marry you. And whenever you want something, you must go off—you must leave the village and we'll meet and go off. And you'll tell me whatever it is that you want, whatever you desire."

Now he must have married her. Then he must have taken her back to wherever her band of Pawnees had made their new village. Then the young woman went there to rejoin her people.

Then the scalped man said, "Now this is your home here. Here is where your father and mother live. They survived. They were not struck. The ones who were battling were the ones who were killed, but these living here now are the ones who separated and fled."

And this woman arrived at the lodge of her family. "Why, mother, father, I have come!"

But the scalped man had warned her in the meantime, "Don't tell on me. Don't say, 'Sees Him Everywhere and I are together.'"

Oh, her father and mother were glad. They were all thankful and happy when they saw her.

Then she said, "I went off there and I hid. I was inside a recess in a cut bank. We were hungry and so we got out and came on. We ate Juneberries and chokecherries. Those are what we ate. We were just starving to death."

2. For a discussion of the scalped man in Pawnee and Arikara folklore, see p. 51 herein and Parks 1981:47–58.

Then her family cooked for her and the boy, oh, who now ate!

Now for a long time this young woman would do this: when the men went out on war parties and her brother went off with them—whenever he would do that and go off—then this young woman went far off from the village. She and her husband met.

"Now my brother is going on a war party. You must watch over his movements. Let him find something for himself."

And then she came back, while her brother was going on the warpath.

Ah, no matter what he did, nothing was difficult for her brother. Then he had a great reputation after people talked about his deeds and his being a brave warrior.

Now, it is not known how long this young woman and the scalped man named Sees Him Everywhere were married.

Now what I have told here is a Pawnee story. My grandmother used to tell the story when she reared me.

34

The Young Man with the Broken Leg and the Scalped Man

This story illustrates once again the scalped man as a potential source of power that can be conferred on someone who is pitiful. What is unusual here, however, is the teasing, jocular manner characterizing the scalped man's exercise of his power. His humor is manifested through irony and suggestive illusion, both of which are subtly depicted in the narrative. In a nearly identical Pawnee story the scalped man has the power of ventriloquism, which he uses to create the scenes that are here achieved by suggestive illusion.

Now I am going to tell a story. It is a true story that occurred when our people were migrating upriver. I don't know exactly where it occurred—whether it was here on this river [the Missouri] or whether it was on another river in the country to the north, where they used to go on the warpath.

One time a group of young men, however many there were, went out, going on a war party. And here another war party had gone in the same direction earlier. Now I don't know how many days they had been out going around, but then they reached a certain spot. There was a river valley there. It was nice land with trees all over. The land was rolling.

"Now let's camp here for a while! And then we'll go on. Let's go look around for something that we can eat!"

Then that is what they did: then they made a hunting lodge of willow saplings and got their camp ready. Then they completed the lodge. It was a big one since there were many young men. After they had gathered wood, they built a fire. Oh, after it was dark they remained awake telling stories. There was a fine rain outside. It was raining.

Then the leader said, "Isn't there any water?"

Then the errand boy said, "Say, there isn't any water. It's all gone. Let me go! I might be able to go to the bank of the river in this valley."

And then the errand boy went down to the bank. Then on his way he picked up stones. Then he was throwing them ahead of himself since it was dark. He did not know where the water was. Then there was a splash as a stone struck the water. That is where he went. There the river was flowing.

This boy was about to dip water over there at the edge of the bank when someone said, "Don't dip water there! Go a ways over there to the west! There the water is better. There is blood in the water there where you're standing. They killed us here. Dead bodies are lying all around where they killed many of us."

Now this boy who had gone after water just stood there. Then he went toward the one who had spoken.

Then the voice said, "Why, say, we came here on the warpath long ago. While we were going home they found us and then we had a battle. But I broke my leg. They didn't scalp me. I broke my leg. That's the reason I'm sitting here in the water. I hid here where I'm sitting."

"Ah, now I'll lift you onto my back. I'll take you to where our party is."

"I knew when you all came. You began talking. Then I knew when you came here for water. I thought that if you were to go there to dip water, I'd call to you to go to another spot. I can hear you men when you're talking."

Then the errand boy said, "Now let's go!"

Then he put the wounded man on his back. He lifted him onto his back. Then they went to the lodge where the men were inside.

The errand boy said, "You sit here awhile! Let me go inside and tell them! They might shoot us thinking that you must be some enemy. Let me tell those inside!"

Then he took the water inside. Each of the men drank. They were roasting ribs over the fire.

Then this errand boy said, "I want to ask something of you men here. I just want to find out something. Now tell me, are you brave men?"

"Yes. We wouldn't be going around here if we weren't brave. That's the reason we're traveling here, because we're brave. Why do you ask?"

"Alright, that's what I wanted to know."

Then he hurried outside again. Then he came back inside carrying on his back the man with the broken leg.

"Now this one is one of our people."

Then they tied the man's leg to a wooden splint while the leader of the party doctored him by applying medicine to his leg.

Well, now he roasted a rib for them to eat. Now they began eating. Then this man with the broken leg began to tell the story. "We were returning to our village when we encountered Sioux. We battled. Then there were dead bodies lying all around in this valley where we battled. My leg was broken, and then I ran into the water. I hid there. There are three men there in the water—three, I think. When one jumped into the water, they killed him. Now those are the ones whose blood is mixed in with the water in the river."

« »

Now it was morning. Then the leader—the one who was the main leader—said, "They'll leave wood for you. There is plenty of dried meat. And fresh meat. They'll leave water for you. Now we are going on, and when we arrive back at our village we'll tell your relatives—your mother and father. Then they'll come after you."

Well, then those were the things they put down for him: wood, water, meat, and dried meat. "Well, we are going now." Then they started out. They went off.

Then a long time passed and no one came there. One morning when he awoke, his supply of wood had mysteriously diminished; so also had the water and the dried meat hanging there. All his supplies were nearly exhausted.

Oh, there now was only one piece of dried meat left. Then he took it down. Then he began to roast it. His supply of wood was also nearly gone.

After eating at the dried meat, he left a piece of it. "Now in the morning I'll eat it." Then he put this piece of dried meat under his pillow.

"Now in the morning I'll eat it. But if no one arrives before long, I'm going to starve," he said as he sat there in the evening. Now it was getting dark. He sat inside his lodge. He cried.

While he was crying for himself, a person just came inside. "Hey, why are you crying? What's wrong?"

"Oh, I'm crying for myself since I'm not able to do anything. My leg is broken. A party left things for me, and now all the things are gone, wherever they went. My stack of wood is gone. The water is gone. And the meat—the dried meat—now it's gone."

Today was the day to eat the dried meat that he had saved under his pillow, but when he got up there was no dried meat there. Now this was the day when he cried for himself. This was also the day when the scalped man came in, wondering, "What's wrong?"

"Hey, now go fetch water!"

Then the young man said, "I don't have any water. My leg is broken. I can't go."

"Let me see where your leg is broken!"

Then he felt the leg all over. "It certainly isn't broken anywhere. Go bring some water!"

Then this man with the broken leg got up. Then he went and, oh, he picked up a pail. He went down the hill over there in the distance. He dipped water. Then he came back.

Now as he was about to return, his leg broke again. He fell over, spilling the water.

Then the scalped man began to laugh. Then he said, "Hey, get up quickly! I'm dying of thirst."

"No. My leg broke."

Then the scalped man came down. "Let me see your leg." Then he turned the leg in the other direction from which it was broken. Then he was laughing again, too.

"Go on now!" He had healed him.

Then they went on. Then they entered the lodge.

Then this scalped man said, "Say, at least make a fire!"

Then that one with the broken leg said, "Why, I don't have any wood."

"Well, let's go to my lodge for a while! You know where my lodge is."

"I don't know, and here you have your lodge close by!"

"You were certainly in there," he hollered.

Then they went there. They arrived at the scalped man's lodge. There was a fire there. Oh, there also was a rib cooking over the fire.

The scalped man said, "You must stay! Let's tell stories!" That is what the scalped man was saying.

Then this man with the broken leg was looking all around.

The scalped man said, "You said, 'I'll bring you some wood at last.' There it is."

There it lay against the wall in the scalped man's dwelling, and there on a line hung dried meat. Here he had been the one stealing the things!

The scalped man said, "Bring it for me at last! But I brought it." He was teasing the man as they sat there and he doctored the one with the broken leg.

Well, then this scalped man said, "I think I'll go to our village for a while. And don't go outside! Don't walk around outside! But stay inside. There is a hole to look through, to peep out. Now, I think I'll go to our village for a while. I'll tell them, 'He must be well.'"

Then the scalped man vanished.

Oh, after awhile he returned. Then he came inside his dwelling. He had corn and moccasins.

"Your father gave these to you. He said, 'Take them! And he'll put the moccasins on.' And your mother had this corn. Then she said, 'He'll get well where you live when he eats some fresh corn with you.'" This is the way the scalped man told it to the young man sitting there with the broken leg.

The scalped man began to roast the corn, and they ate.

Then the scalped man said, "I think I'll go to our village for a while! Do you want anything? What shall I tell your father?" He was saying these things to him.

Then this young man with the broken leg said, "Surely they haven't said anything."

"You have certainly been away a long time. They must have thought that you were dead. Truly I told them that we are living together. They know that we're living together." The scalped man was telling him these things.

Then he vanished.

Then in the morning he entered the dwelling. "Now, hello. We had a meeting. And then I arose. I said—I think that a village is coming here to where we are. They will camp here where you and I are in this valley. I told them, 'It is alright—that it would be good if you people were to do that, to camp here. There is water.' I told them, 'My brother and I live there.'" This is what he was saying as he was fibbing.

The boy with the broken leg said, "Hey, it will certainly be good if the village comes here and we see my father and mother."

"I have certainly told them that you're living here. They know." This is what the scalped man was saying.

Oh, sometime later, after however many days it was, the scalped man said, "Why, say, look! There's the camp. They must have arrived. Surely they said, 'We'll go there.'"

Then this young man with the broken leg arose. When he looked out, there was a village there, with men watering horses and standing around fires here and there. The scalped man and the young man with the broken leg surveyed the scene.

Then the scalped man said, "Let's go!" Then the two of them went there.

There was a man crying there. He was crying. Then the scalped man said, "The one crying is your father. He's your father. Your mother comes once in awhile."

The village was sleeping. Then his mother came into sight, and they were all glad to see one another.

Then his father said, "Are you returning?"

Then the one with the broken leg said, "I'm going to go back over there for a while, and when I'm ready to return, I'll tell both of you."

Well, then his parents were thankful to see their son.

Then he vanished. He was now like the scalped man. Then he arrived back at the scalped man's dwelling.

Then the scalped man said, "Did you go to where your father was crying?"

The one with the broken leg said, "Why, I did go, and there was no one there."

Oh, the scalped man began laughing. "Yes, that is what always happens," he was saying over and over. He knew how to say things.

After so many days the scalped man got ready to take the young man home.

Then the scalped man said, "Now you are going to go. Now you'll get ready to go home. Now it's good. Let the village come back awhile! When they camp there, you'll go there."

Now the one with the broken leg was waiting.

Then the scalped man said, "Now it's true this time. It isn't the way it was before. The village is the way you used to see it. It wasn't true before. Now this time it is true that the village is coming here. They're going to camp here where we are. Don't do anything! Don't talk about me when we go to your father and mother's lodge.

"But now you have already seen them. You dreamed an image of them. Now this time their coming here as a group is real. The way you saw things before [in your dream] is the way they're going to be when you see them now."

Then they both went. There was his father crying.

The scalped man said, "Now speak to your father!"

Then the young man went, and there was his father. His father was happy to see him. "Now let's go over there! See your mother!"

Then the two of them went to the lodge. All of them were glad to see the young man. His sisters were happy when they saw him.

Then he said, "I'm not going to come home for a while. Later on I'll come back. Now, I want to go back for a while to the dwelling of the one who pitied me."

Then his father said, "Now surely that is a good thing. Do that!"

Then he said, "My friend wants a knife and a black rope"— whatever a black rope is.[1]

Then they gave him the rope, and the knife and tobacco.

Then the young man went off. Then the one who had had the broken leg vanished. Then he entered the dwelling of the scalped man.

Then the scalped man said, "Ah, I was watching over you. What you were doing was good. You have brought me some kinnikinnick to smoke. Now I have what I have wanted. I have the rope for horse stealing. Well, in the morning you're going to go home.

"But now I'm going to impart something to you. The way I have treated you is the way of my medicine. It is my power to do things in a joking way. But now take care of yourself! Live well! Don't do the things I've been telling you and showing you! Don't do them! You'll take care of yourself."

And then this is what he did: when it got dark again, the two of them came there. Then they arrived at the lodge of the parents of the young man with the broken leg.

Then the scalped man said, "But whenever you go on the war-path, you must come to where I live. It won't be long now before

1. Pawnees, and presumably Arikaras as well, braided black ropes from buffalo hair. Among their many uses, men wore them tied around the waist over a buffalo robe (G. A. Dorsey 1904a:352; Weltfish 1965:362–66).

your village is moving."

And then that is what they did: after a certain period—it was
not very long—after time passed, then they went on. The group
proceeded to move.

Then this young man who had had the broken leg married.

Meanwhile he had the power to doctor people. When someone
broke an arm, then he doctored him. Then the person got well after
having gotten hurt. He had good medicines. So people depended on
him.

The scalped man said, "Don't talk about it! Don't say anything
like, 'He lives here.' Meanwhile I have blessed you, after Night gave
me the power.[2] And now you're going to live well. You have grown
up. Now you'll rear your own children."

And that is what he did.

Now whenever it was, he died, the poor thing. When this one
who had the broken leg was dying, he said, "Now a scalped man
was the one who blessed me. He blessed me. And he said, 'When
you die, we'll die together.' Now it must be that way. Now he must
have died, too."

Now this is how the story goes.

35

The Seven Scalped Men and the Hunter

*To become a scalped man, a person need not have lost
his scalp. When falling unconscious in battle, the loss of*

---

2. Night is a spirit of the northeast direction in Arikara religious
symbolism. This spirit brings rest, and restores and refreshes all things
(Gilmore 1929:95–120).

*any body part, as this story illustrates, was sufficient to
transform the victim into a spirit being, should he revive.
Any disfigurement received in war rendered him "no good"
and thus unfit for human association. Also demonstrated
here is an important characteristic of the spirit world: the
lack of tobacco there and the spirits' desire for it to smoke.
Spirits frequently beseeched a pitiful young man for tobacco
and in return conferred power on him. This theme recurs
throughout Arikara traditions and in part explains why the
smoke offering was integral to all ritual activity in which
spirits were invoked.*

Long, long ago when our villages were there in the south, a
group of young men was out hunting. They were going through
rolling country. It was wooded land. They had each killed a deer,
and this one young man who was with them drifted off from the
others when he killed a buck, and then he butchered it. Afterward
when he looked around he discovered that here the others in the
party had left long ago! Now they had left him.

Then this young man packed the meat on his back. As he was
going along he lost track of wherever it was that the party had
gone. He then forgot where the village was. This must have been
the first time he had gone out hunting. He did not know the lay of
the land yet as he went out hunting for the first time.

As he was going along late in the evening it became dark. As he
went along he thought, "There's no point to going on any farther. I
might wander off to some distant place. I might as well spend the
night right here, and then in the morning I'll start looking for the
village, wherever it is."

And so that is what he did.

Then as he proceeded he began imagining things. "Surely
someone is talking." Then he stopped. Then he lay the meat down
on the ground.

Then a man came running up beside him. Now the man stared
at him. Then he went around and around the young man, looking
at different parts of his body. When he was going around him, he
said, "Ah, surely I'm just imagining that this one is a human."

Then he hollered, "Hey, One Leg, where are you?"

Then another one came, too. Then there were two of them.

After he stood there awhile, then he hollered, "Hey, No Hand, you must be coming. Look, this one is something else!"[1]

Then another one came. Then there were three of them.

Now again: "Hey, No Ear, where are you?"

Then he came. Then there were four of them.

And then he hollered, "Hey, No Nose, where are you?"

Now they numbered five.

Once again he hollered, "Where are you, No Leg?"

Then he came running up beside him. There he had one leg! He was hopping all around.

Now he called out again, "Where are you, No Fingers?"

Then he came running up to him. Now there were seven of them standing there.

As this man gazed at them, he hollered, "Hey, all of you going around, why is it that you aren't going back to our village?"

Now the ones who were standing there ran off. They vanished. Oh, then they went off. And here one of the men took the meat.

And when the young man wanted to pick up his meat, it was not there. "Now, you who were here, you took my meat. Something is wrong!"

One had no ear. Two of them had a leg cut off. One had an arm cut off. Another did not have a foot. Another had no fingers. Another had a nose cut off. Each one was disfigured.

<"I'll follow them to see where they have gone. I'll find them."> Then he went where they had gone.

After he had gone a ways there was a river there. As he went on, as he got close to it, there was a cut bank there. Then there was singing, the sound of it coming from the edge of the water.

This young man stopped, and then he went down the bank. As he was looking all around, there was something protruding. A root was sticking out. Then he pulled it. Then a door opened, and there they were singing.

He gazed at them as they sat there singing.

And then one said, "This song will be yours, No Leg."

Now the one with one leg jumped up and began hopping around.

---

1. That is, "this one is a strange being who is not one of us."

"Now this song will be yours, No Hand."

Then they sang again. Then they were dancing.

Meanwhile the one sitting there singing—the one with no nose—was the one singing. When they looked up and saw the young man, they said, "Hey, he's come inside again." They all piled up on the one who was singing.

Then this young man went inside. Then he sat down by the fire. There was a fire in the middle of the room. There lay the meat he had had. A rib was roasting over the fire.

Then one of them got up and sat down again. And also another one. And then they all got up and sat around. Then the one who had been singing, the one with no nose, sat upright. <"You boys, don't do that! You almost killed me again.">

Then No Nose said, "Now you have found us. It was planned that we should find you. We're the ones. You lost your way after your companions went off. Your village is close by. But we're the ones who have called you. We've arranged it.

"And here you are a warrior! And here you are brave! You're not afraid of us. And yet we're all deformed, we who are sitting here. We were going around on the warpath, and we were killed. And then Night pitied us who were living. Now here is where we're living.

"And now that we've called you here, this is what you're going to do for us. Why, we want to smoke tobacco. It's hard to obtain.

"Other things aren't difficult. Now these are the powers we'll give you. Now you're going to doctor anyone who aches. This medicine is the one you're going to use. <If someone breaks a leg, you'll use this medicine. If someone can't stop bleeding, you'll be able to stop it. If he has a fever or freezes his hands, you'll be able to cure it.>

"And the ways of warfare aren't going to be difficult for you. You'll have those powers on the warpath and over the enemy; you're going to know how to do everything. And we'll be around. We'll be watching over you. Wherever you go we'll be around and we'll be seeing you.

"Now this is what I want you to do for us: we want to smoke some tobacco. It's pitiful for us here. Things are indeed difficult for us.

"We brought this meat for you. Here it is. Now you're going to eat."

And so that is what happened. <The one who had no ear was the cook and the one who cut the meat up.> Then they set food in front of the young man. Then they dipped water for him.

"Why, you would have smoked our tobacco. But it's impossible; we don't have tobacco. And that's the reason we brought you here, for you to do something for us so that we might smoke. Now they're going to take you to your village."

Then the young man ate.

Then they began to sing the song of each one of the men. <When they sang the song of No Ear, he got up and danced around. Then they sang One Leg's song and he got up and danced. And No Feet. Each had his song and his medicine. No Hand had lost his hand when it froze, and now he had a song and medicine for that.>

"Now you know these doctoring songs. Now things aren't going to be difficult for you. Whatever you want you'll be able to do. It won't be hard.

"Now after you have eaten, these two young men will take you to where you came from, to where your village is. Now you must not divulge anything after you arrive back at our village. Don't say, 'I saw them.' We surely are not good now. We are disfigured.

"But Night must have thought that we should live awhile yet. This is his plan, what we have done for you. But you must not mention it to anyone. These young men will hear you if you start to say anything. Then if you do it, that will be all: you'll lose the powers we have given you. And it can't be repeated.

"Now do what we beseech of you—tobacco! After they have taken you home and you have arrived there, and when you are ready to return after four days have passed, you'll bring it and you'll come alone. Don't come with anyone else. This is what you'll bring. Bring the tobacco here. Now whatever remains to be learned of the power we have, we'll give it to you."

Then the two took this young man outside. It was not long before they had taken him to the village. They carried the meat for him.

Meanwhile his companions were fearful that the enemy had

found him and killed him. "Perhaps he's lying dead somewhere. He must be dead. They must have killed him."

Then he just walked into the earth lodge. "Say, I lost my way after you left me. Now I have finally come back. I've finally found you."

Now sometime later he said, "Father, I want tobacco."

Well, then his father mixed it for him, whatever kind of tobacco we used to have among us. Today we have this kinnikinnick, but I do not know what kinds they used to mix together when they mixed kinnikinnick then.

Then this young man took it. <Then he met No Hand and No Fingers, who took him back.> Then he went to where his adopted fathers, the ones who had blessed him, were. He arrived crying. Then they embraced him.

"Now come in!"

They took him inside.

"Now here is the tobacco you said you wanted."

Oh, they were glad! Then they began to sing and dance out of thankfulness after they smoked. <They offered the pipe to the east, to the south, to the west, to the north, to the earth, and up above. "Now we have tobacco for our ceremonies. We have ceremonies in the spring in order to have rain and good weather during the summer.">

Now they continued to give him powers. "This is what you'll do. This is what you're going to do when you're doctoring. This is what you'll have to say."

Now the blessing they gave him was a great thing. And this is the end of the story, of what they used to tell me.

And then they took the young man back. He arrived back at his village. And then this young man became a great warrior who performed many deeds and who married. Now things were not difficult for him: stealing horses, counting coups on the enemy when on the warpath, and doctoring. When someone was ill, he was called and then it was not long before the person got well. When someone broke a leg, it was not long before he got well.

Now that young man lived among us and traveled all around for a long time, and then he reached old age.

Now this is where the story as I used to hear it ends. Some say the Pawnees tell the same story.[2]

36

Wakes Up The Hills and
Red Shield, the Scalped Man

Another role in which the scalped man character appears is that of the provider—not the bestower of power, but the supplier of culturally valuable items (horses, scalps, and eagle feathers) that increased the social standing of the beneficiary. In this story a scalped man named Red Shield from time to time furnishes a young man named Wakes Up The Hills with these articles, which the latter portrays to people in his village as booty that he himself has captured on the warpath. In this way he rises to the status of chief.

I'm going to tell a story that occurred when we used to travel around long ago, when the Arikaras used to travel around on the hunt over the open plains where buffalo, deer, and antelope roamed, where different kinds of wildlife were plentiful.

One time after banding together, a group of young men went off. Then they went far off. Then they stopped to camp. Then they built a lodge and prepared things by going out hunting and bringing back game. They knew how to make dried meat while they were camped.

After they had rested, the young men went on. I don't know where they were going. Wherever it was they were traveling, as they were coming along, one young man separated from the party

2. A Pawnee version of this story is recorded in Weltfish (1937:238–40).

while they were hunting early in the morning. There weren't any deer roaming around. And so he went over there to a hill, a big hill. It was a high hill.

Then the young man went up the hill. While he lay on top looking all around at the wooded hillsides, he saw a clearing. There were trees here and there in it, but otherwise it was clear land. Standing off there in the distance were three deer grazing. Then he looked the situation over. "I'll go around this way. If I get up close, I might kill one."

While he was watching them they became frightened. One fell over. It fell down. Before long a person appeared. Then that person went over to where the deer lay. Then he stopped to look. He looked over this way where the young man was lying on top of the hill.

The one I am talking about—the one I am telling about lying on the hill watching this person—was named Wakes Up The Hills.

The person was rapidly turning this way and that. He had something on his head. Then he was looking at this young man: it was as though he knew where he was lying. He watched the young man. Then he picked the deer up quickly. Then he ran off after packing it on his back.

Meanwhile the young man lying on the hill was watching him. The person appeared here and there among the trees on the hillsides. In the distance was a hill with a cut bank, and then he went up it carrying the deer. Then he disappeared.

Then this young man who was lying on the hill ran down. Then he went to where the man he had watched—the scalped man—had gone up the hillside.

Then he got there. There were stones lying around, the stones he had stepped on, one above the other, so that no one would know where he went. And there was a tree root sticking out of the side of the hill. Then he did it: then he pulled it, and a door opened.

Then he went inside. There was an entryway, and then this young man went inside. I don't know whether he alerted him, but then he went on, going down an incline. Then there was the smell of smoke. When he got to the end, there was a fire there. And there sat the man butchering the deer he had killed.

Then the young man said, "Now I have come. Are you one of our tribe?"

The man sitting there did not say anything. He was startled while he was butchering.

Then the young man said, "Now I have come here. Are you one of us? I'll shoot you if you don't answer me."

The man who sat there said, "Yes, I am one of our tribe. Now I sort of had a premonition that you were coming. And yet I doubted it. And now you have arrived, and it is good. It's good that you're not with someone. Now sit down! We will eat together."

Then they began to butcher together. Then they piled the meat around. Then he said, "Here is this pile for you."

There was a rib over the fire. Now Wakes Up The Hills was hungry.

And then he said, "Now I recognize you when I see you."

He said, "Now that must be it. I am named Red Shield. I died long ago. I was killed. But Night had compassion on me so that I could go around here. I know that you and your party are staying nearby. I know it. And I always go to our village, to go around to see you all. But you don't ever see me because I come as a spirit. And now you have found me, and I am thankful. Now stay!

"After it gets dark, we'll go to the valley. Now your party must hurry. You all must go! The enemy has arrived. They're coming this way. Oh, I want to tell you so that you'll know that there are many of the enemy! They're coming this way, here where you're staying. And the enemy camps are following behind the warriors. Now you and your party must leave quickly! Otherwise they'll find you and count coups on you."

Well, then they ate, and he was happy.

"Now let's go to where your party is camped! When you arrive there, you must say, 'They're chasing me. Quickly, let's run away! They might find us. The enemy is coming near.'"

And then they ran toward the camp.

Then they arrived there. Then Wakes Up The Hills said, "Now quickly, let's run away! Hurry! The enemy is chasing me. They saw me. Let's go quickly!"

Then the others who were camped there got up and left their things behind, whatever they had, such as dried meat. Then they ran off, and no one remained. Then the scalped man was alone now that he had fooled them, thinking "They mustn't find me."

Then the party ran back to where our villages were and told about it. "This is what happened."

Now sometime later the young man Wakes Up The Hills said, "Now I think I'll go! I think I'll go on the warpath alone!"

Then he did that: then he went out alone when he went on the warpath. He headed toward where Red Shield, the one he had befriended, lived. Then he arrived there.

Now Red Shield said, "I knew that you were coming. Now that's good. Now sit down! Now tonight I'll go out by myself. The enemy camps are close by."

Then Wakes Up The Hills said, "Yes, I want a horse—perhaps even four."

"Now I'll do for you what you want. In the meantime don't go out! Don't go outside! You must stay inside here!"

Then they ate a meal. They ate.

This young man Wakes Up The Hills asked, "Will it be tomorrow night when we go—when we go home?"

Then this Red Shield said, "It'll surely take two days at least; two days, and then you can go. But now you're here, and you want me to return right away. If I did, the people in the village might find out that you were really only close by. You haven't been gone from the village long enough on the warpath. But you'll stay two days and then you can finally go back. In the meantime I'll get things ready."

Then this scalped man Red Shield went out.

Then just before morning he entered. He made a fire and then he said, "Now get up! There are horses for you over there. The ones you wanted are standing over there in the brush. I have put the four horses there for you.

"But I want you to take the black pinto to my son and my wife so that it can perform deeds for them.[1] This black pinto is nice looking. Now this is what I want you to do for me."

Then this Wakes Up The Hills said, "Now truly it will be that way. I'll do it."

---

1. In former times, spotted or pinto horses were rare and consequently highly valued. They were thought to have unusual or mysterious power.

And two days later Red Shield said, "Now go!"

Then the two of them returned together. They led the horses back to wherever the village was. When they arrived there, Red Shield, the scalped man, turned back and Wakes Up The Hills took the horses into the village.

Now he told of his own bravery. "This is what I did. The Sioux must have gone on a hunt. They were camped there. This is what I did: I ran off with the horses."

And while he was telling about it he said, "But this boy is pitiful. He no longer has a father. He and his mother can only look at the horses belonging to you people. Now I am going to pity them by giving them this black pinto to work for them."

Shortly afterward he did it: then he gave the horse to them.

Meanwhile the other one, Red Shield, was making plans.

And subsequently there were many occasions when Wakes Up The Hills gained good fortune by visiting Red Shield's dwelling.

Then Wakes Up The Hills became ill.

Now, years later, after Wakes Up The Hills had become a man, after he had become an old man, he said, "Now I'm telling it to you, my relatives, and you tribesmen here. You all know it: I have found all kinds of nice things. Nothing was difficult for me. Now I'll tell you. It was not on my account. It was not my own doing. You all know that Red Shield died. It was long ago. Now I found him. I found him. That is where I used to go whenever I went away, when I went out to look for things. He was the one who found the things for me. Now the black pinto that I gave this woman had belonged to this boy's father. He gave the boy the horse, but I pretended to be the one giving it to him because his father had told me to do it; he told me not to betray him.

"But he must now be an old man like I am. Now you all know it: Red Shield is the one who did those things, the things that I did when I became a chief among you. Now I'm leaving you. But this is where he lives; this is where I found Red Shield."

And now the woman who had been his wife said, "Let us go to see Red Shield."

Then they went there after Wakes Up The Hills told where he

lived. Then they arrived there. The door was wide open. He must have gone somewhere else long ago. He had left. He had built another dwelling. And then he had left everything just as Wakes Up The Hills had said: "This is how it is. This is how the land lies. This is how the door is situated."

Now that is what happened: they did not find him. After they mourned they came back home.

Meanwhile this man Wakes Up The Hills died. He died. But the scalped man lived. He was holy, and things were not difficult for him.

Now this is the end of the story.

Narratives of the Past

Of Historical Events

37

The Separation of the Hidatsas
and Crows

Centuries ago the Hidatsas and Crows were a single people living in what is now central North Dakota. The most common tradition accounting for their separation and the subsequent migration of the Crows to their present home in Montana stems from a dispute among a group of hunters over the apportioning of a buffalo paunch. The incident, according to the narrator, reputedly occurred near the present town of Stanton.

A historically accurate English translation of the Arikara name for the Crow tribe, tUhkaáka' (literally 'crow village'), is moot today since contemporary Arikaras differ in their identification of the words for crow and raven. Mr. Morsette insisted that kaáka', the bird associated with the Crow people, is the raven, while čiripístš is the actual term for the crow, even though many contemporary speakers reverse the identifications. Based on historical evidence, however, Mr. Morsette is probably correct.

Now I am going to tell a story that the Hidatsas and Crows tell about.

Long, long ago there must have been many Hidatsas in that country north of the Missouri River. That is where the Hidatsas must have actually roamed around. That must have been the land they favored.

Now, on the other side of the river, deer and antelope must have been plentiful. But in that land to the north there must not have been so many buffalo. The buffalo must not have roamed around

361

there.[1]

One time when the young men gathered together, they said, "Let's go across the river to that land over there. It seems that there might be some deer or buffalo there."

Then they crossed over the water to that land in the south. While they were going they saw a buffalo. "Now look! Just as I said, there are buffalo ranging close by." Then these Hidatsas killed the buffalo. Then they butchered it. Then each one was given meat.

"Now divide this paunch up! Now do that! Divide it! Cut this paunch thus!"

Then this one young man jumped up. Now where it was thinnest is where he sliced it. Then he saved the thick part, which was nice, which tasted really good. Then he sliced it where it was thinnest. To one group of those sitting there, "Now here it is for you. Divide it among yourselves. Cut it up! But this piece we'll keep for ourselves. We'll divide it among ourselves."

Then one of them said, "Surely you gave us the piece that is not good. It's thin. It isn't thick. It doesn't taste good. The piece you took is the best one. Now you certainly are stingy.

"Now you can stay here, and you can eat that paunch alone. But now we here are going to go west, where the buffalo range."

And so that is where the Hidatsas split up.

One of the ones who went off said, "I am just like the crow, wandering around that land over there just as the crow flies around looking for food for itself. Now I'm like that crow when we are going." Now this is the reason that they are called Crow Village, these Crows in this land now called Montana.

But then the Hidatsas did not go. They are the same ones who live here [on the Fort Berthold Reservation today]. It is because of their being stingy with the thickest part of the tripe.

Those Crows who live over there were truthful when they went west, for they do sound like the crow.

---

1. On several occasions the narrator remarked that Arikaras did not consider the country north of the Missouri River to be good hunting territory. It was a region where wolves were said to be numerous.

‹   »

Now this is what I always used to hear when they talked about it. But perhaps there is someone else living who knows the story and tells it differently from the way I tell it.

38

The Arikara Separation from the Pawnees

On at least two occasions during the late eighteenth and early nineteenth centuries, large groups of Arikaras migrated south to live near the Pawnees. Their last documented residence there was with the Skiris between 1833 and 1835. This tradition undoubtedly derives from one of those periods of residence together.

I am going to tell about when we Arikaras lived in that country there in the south. We lived together with the Pawnees. The Pawnees must have still been a large group of people then, and it must have been the same with the Arikaras.

Now we all must have lived in a combined village. The Pawnees who lived there must have secretly hated the Arikaras. It must not have been a good situation.

Anyway, whenever a young Arikara man courted a Pawnee girl, the Pawnees would catch him. Then they would whip him. They would knock him unconscious After they had beat him up, he would return to the Arikara camp.

But when a Pawnee would come to where the Arikaras were living—where their young women were—he would be treated well when he went among them. The Arikaras did not harm him.

When the enemy came and attacked the Arikara village, the Pawnees never came to help during the battle. But it was different

whenever it was the Pawnee village spread out on the south: when
the Sioux came to attack it, the Arikaras sided with the Pawnees
during the battle.

And when the buffalo would approach close to the Arikara side,
the Pawnees would come and join them whenever they slaughtered
the buffalo. But when it was otherwise with the Pawnees, the
situation was not good. The Arikaras would not get any help. When
the buffalo approached close by the Pawnee village, the Arikaras
never received word; no one ever told them, "The buffalo are approaching close by." The Pawnees did not treat them well.

So, after a long time, the leading chiefs said, "What the Pawnees are doing—the way they are treating us—certainly isn't good.
Now let's separate from them! Let's go to some other territory so
that we may live better! Let the Pawnees live here! They aren't
getting better. They aren't good to us."

Well, then the Arikara chiefs met in council. Then they planned
it. Then they called the Pawnees. They said, "We are separating
from you. You haven't acted nicely. You haven't treated us well. We
always take your part, and we always share with you. Whenever
buffalo approach close by, you don't do the same. Now you'll be
living here alone. And now we are going. We'll be living better there
where the prairie stretches on, where the buffalo roam."

And there the Pawnees thought, "Surely don't do it! Let's continue living here!"

But the Arikaras did not consent.

Then they brought their wives. The tribe came there to Fort
Pierre, where there were the four Medicine Lodges. That is where
the village was. They lived there a long time.[1]

Then they came this way again. Then they lived in another
location for so many years again.

Now again they came on, coming up this way to here where we
now live. Now they refer to that place as "there over the hill" [Fort

1. According to Arikara tradition, when the tribe lived along the Missouri
River in the area of what is today Fort Pierre, South Dakota, there were
four tribal Medicine Lodges. Actually, Arikara occupation of this area
preceded the historical visit to the Pawnees described in this narrative.

Clark]. Now that is where we Arikaras also lived.[2]

Then again they came to a location close to where our village was.[3] Then they camped there for what must have been four winters.

Then they joined the Hidatsas after the Hidatsas called for all of us to get together so that we might defend each other. The Mandans were the first ones to get together with the Hidatsas. And that is when we Arikaras crossed the Missouri River. My grandmother was fourteen winters old. At that time my grandmother was just a girl when they crossed the river and the soldiers were garrisoned by our village.[4]

Now today we are living here where the white man has taken us. We are living scattered out on our allotments here on the north side of the river.[5]

39

Hidatsa and Arikara Relations

For more than a century Arikaras, Hidatsas, and Mandans have shared a common reservation, but individual

2. The Arikara occupation at Fort Clark extended from 1837 to 1861.

3. Fishhook Village, called in English Like-A-Fishhook. After leaving Fort Clark, the Arikaras spent the winter of 1861–62 above Like-A-Fishhook Village. The next spring they began building two villages across the Missouri River, directly opposite Fort Berthold. After a Sioux attack in the summer (1862), the tribe abandoned those villages and moved into Like-A-Fishhook Village to live there with the Hidatsas and the Mandans. The Arikaras built their lodges on the north side of the village.

4. Fort Berthold.

5. The narrator is referring to the allotment of lands and settlement of Arikara families on separate tracts that occurred between 1884 and 1886. Most of the Arikara allotments were on the north side of the Missouri River, but there were some on the south side in the area of the former Beaver Creek district.

tribal identity has remained strong. Throughout the entire
period each group has maintained its own discrete com-
munity. Before allotment, when they all lived together in
Like-A-Fishhook Village, each tribe had its own section,
and subsequently each has had its own area and distinct
communities on the reservation. In spite of more than a
century of progressively increasing intermarriage and mutu-
al participation in reservation government and social and
economic activities, relations between Arikaras and Hidatsas
continue to be marked by rigidity and occasionally by barely
concealed hostility. In the late 1970s this tension was openly
manifested in public remarks by the tribal chairman, a
Hidatsa, who charged that the Arikaras did not belong on
the Fort Berthold Reservation but rather should be living
in Oklahoma with their Pawnee relatives. Those charges
prompted the narrator to record the following narrative to
set the record straight, reminding Hidatsas that Arikaras
had once saved them from an enemy attack and that over the
course of reservation life Hidatsa behavior toward Arikaras
has never been above reproach.

Now I am going to tell a story. I am going to tell about the
Hidatsas, who for whatever reason are always saying things about
the Arikaras.

I am half Arikara and half Hidatsa. I grew up mingling with
the Hidatsas but I lived among the Arikaras. I know how to speak
Arikara. My grandmother and my grandfather Short Bear were the
ones who reared me.

Now when these Hidatsas moved toward us after they appeared
there at Devils Lake,[1] they must have just come to the river there
at Washburn. The village was on a bluff on the east side. It is a
high bluff bordering on the Missouri River. There was a high bank
on the other side of the river where the sun would strike it. Now
the village was on the bluff.

---

1. Hidatsa traditions ascribe their origin to Devils Lake, where the tribe
emerged from an underground world.

Meanwhile the Arikara village was close by, on the bank on the other side of the river. The Arikara village was over there by Fort Clark, the one they always tell about.

Then one time the Assiniboines came to fight and attacked the Hidatsas in their village. Then they caused the Hidatsas to panic. Then they were chased off the bluff. Old men and old women just threw themselves over the high bank, getting hurt everywhere.

Well, then one young man went into the water. The water must have been deep. It must have been sometime in midsummer. Then he rode into the water, going to where the Arikaras lived.

Then he arrived at the earth lodge in which the sacred bundles were kept [the Medicine Lodge]. After he went inside, he reverently moved his hands over a sacred bundle, saying, "Yes, holy, holy." That is what he was saying.

Then the Arikaras inside said, "I wonder what he means—what he is saying?"

One young man must have spoken Hidatsa. "Ask him. What does he mean?"

Then this young man who spoke Hidatsa went up to him. "What are you saying? They want to know."

"Ah, I have come. I want you to help us. The enemy has attacked us Hidatsas in the village where we live. They have made our people panic. All the old women and old men are hurt. They don't care about themselves and just throw themselves over the cliff. The Hidatsas have been panicked by the Assiniboines."

Now these Arikaras said, "Hey, we should help them. We're mingling together now." Long ago we must have begun splitting into different groups and some of the young women began to intermarry with the Hidatsas. That must have been the way it was long ago.

Then the young Arikara men, the ones who were dauntless, charged into the water. They arrived armed where the fighting was. Over there from the rear they chased the Assiniboines down the bank. After they got to the base, the Assiniboines ran away. The Arikaras were killing them as they drove them off, and when two Assiniboines stopped, they were killed. Also another one stopped when his horse tired; they also killed him. They ran full force.

Now one Arikara was named Fears The Fire. He was an older man. He always used to ride a black horse with a white belly. The black horse had a white spot on its belly. And here it was among them! When some Assiniboine was killed, then Fears The Fire would go over there and scalp him. That is what he was doing, scalping one dead Assiniboine after another.

Now the Arikaras pursued them so far on foot, going about as far as the present village of White Shield. Then one man said, "Let's let them go! We've certainly killed many of them."

It was now late in the afternoon. Then they came back home. After they returned, the Hidatsas began summoning them. And here the Hidatsas had boiled meat! Then they invited the Arikaras. That young man who spoke Hidatsa told everything that the Hidatsas said.

Then, when a man was coming along, one man asked, "What does that one have? Is it meat?"

Then they asked him, "What are those things you're bringing?"

Then he said, "They're scalps. Right after you fellows killed someone, I scalped him."

Then he asked, "How many are there?"

Then he said, "Say, I don't know."

Then they began to count. The scalps that were piled there numbered thirty-one. "Now we saved half of them for the Hidatsas, and we'll take half." Now that is what happened.

When they ate they consumed all the food. Well, then the Hidatasas gave the Arikaras things. "You have saved us, doing what you did for us when you took our part. Now here is a horse. You'll lead it away." Well, then that is what they did.

Then the Arikaras got into the water. Then they crossed the river to where they lived in the area of Fort Clark, this location that they always tell about. That is where the Arikara village was.

And today when the Hidatsas get inflated ideas about themselves, the Arikaras really talk about them.

And then they began to call that man, the one who ran over to the Arikaras, *Waaxubaa*. Its meaning is 'medicine' or 'holy way' in Hidatsa. Now that is what they told me.

Now right there at the old village [Like-A-Fishhook], at the time after the three tribes—Hidatsas, Mandans, and Arikaras—joined together, this is what they used to do. When the Sioux came to attack on the other side of the village, where the Arikara section was, the Hidatsas would not stay with the Arikaras to defend the village. The Mandans were the only ones who stayed with them. Then the Hidatsas would run into the water. Then they crossed over to the other side of the river. Only after the fighting was over did they begin to come back up the bank to the village. That is what they used to tell.

When the Arikaras used to dance—when they were dancing Touch The Foot[2]—the behavior of the Hidatsas was bad. They came to the smokehole on top of the dance lodge, where they could look down at the dancing and see the Arikaras, and then they threw the bullboat down through it.[3] Then it fell on the fire in the fireplace. Then they began to throw feces down, too. Then they scattered everyone. That is the way the Hidatsas behaved.

Today when they want to be the best dancers and the best singers, they forget that the Arikaras were the ones who protected them.

Now after there became peace, after the Custer battle and after warfare ended, the government soldiers came. Then they said to us, "You were really truthful when you said that you wanted to work together with the government and that we would 'put our heads together.' But these Hidatsas did not help us at all. They did not enlist with the soldiers. Nor did the Mandans.

"Now I want them [the Hidatsas] to move over there to the east. They can live somewhere there in that land by the ocean. They refused the president, and he was begging them to give him boys to be enlisted with the soldiers. And the Mandans, too."

And then Son Of Star said, "This is what I'm asking of you: I don't want it to be this way. Young women—Hidatsa women are intermarried with our young men, and Arikara women are married to Hidatsa men. And it's the same way with the Mandans, too. And now we're intermixed. I don't want you to do that."

Now three times the representative of the president came,

2. A social dance popular among Arikaras at the turn of the century.

3. Bullboats—tublike boats made from buffalo hides—were stored on top of earth lodges, and during inclement weather the bullboat was placed over the smokehole to keep rain out of the lodge.

wanting the Hidatsas to be turned over to him. Now Son Of Star, who was called Standing Star, did not consent to it.[4] Now it was three times that he came here.

Then the representative said, "Now the president is going to keep the chiefs. Whatever you want, your chief will tell me. And then your chief—the one you have as your leader—and I will plan that.

"Now there will be a school here. The children will go to school at Fort Stevenson."[5] Stone Hill is what they used to call it. That is where the soldiers were garrisoned, and when they left that is where the children began going to school.

That is where my own father went to school when he was growing up and becoming a young man. And when they used to talk about Good Voice [Reverend Charles Hall, the Congregational missionary]. He did not have any other name. Good Voice was the only thing they called him. In Sioux the name means 'good voice.' 'Good voice' is what it means. He was able to speak Hidatsa. He also spoke Arikara.

I never talked to that man when he went around, but I used to see Good Voice there in Elbowoods. They called the community Among The Hidatsas because the Hidatsas had their houses together at the agency, where legal matters were handled—where land matters and different kinds of issues were taken into the agency, and they were worked on for a person, and they were done for him.

I went around that town. I used to go there to Elbowoods. They also called it At The Bend. At The Bend is what they also used to call it. Now there is where I learned things when I went around as a boy while I was growing up.

4. The name of Son Of Star, the leading Arikara chief at the time, was *sákaa'A naaríčI* 'Standing Star,' but among Arikaras he was generally referred to as *kawikaá'* 'Comes Last.' The narrator used the latter name where Son Of Star, his usual English name, appears in the translation here.

5. Fort Stevenson was a military post established in 1867 on the southeastern edge of the Fort Berthold Reservation near the Missouri River. In 1883 it was abandoned and immediately became an industrial arts school serving children on the reservation. It was closed in 1894, when the main part of the plant burned down.

Now at that time the president said, "This is the way things are going to be. They are going to give you rations as long as you live, as long as you are getting food. And you'll be given whatever you want. Now they are going to give you a team of horses to drive your buggy. And if you should want oxen, they'll drive them to your homestead to till the ground where you plant your squash and corn."

And sometimes a person planted oats. He planted them so that the horses could eat them during the winter.

Now there were many people who were given horses. The government also gave them a mower that was to be used by more than one family, to be shared. First one family would use it, and then another had its turn. It was the same with a rake and a plow. At first the people did not know how to use these tools when they were given to them. Then the government farmer began to teach them. They used to call him 'the hurrier' because of one white man. He rode around on horseback telling the Arikaras things: to work, to plow, and to cut hay. And to rack up the hay so that one would have a stack of hay for the horses to eat during the winter. Now this is how it was.

Now at Elbowoods the president said, "Chiefs, what is it going to be? Do you want to live here or do you want to go off to the west?"

Then the Arikaras said, "We'll remain here. These Hidatsas can go west somewhere."

And then the Mandans said, "Our favorite land is there on the other [south] side of the river. That is where we'll live, there on the other side."

Then this is what they did: then they then began to build houses. The Hidatsas moved close to Elbowoods and lived there. When they used to tease the Arikaras, they longed to steal their songs at the dances in the old village [Like-A-Fishhook]. That is what they used to say.

At the combined village the Hidatsa children learned to dance. But then the older ones took up the way and they began to dance, too.[6] Then the Hidatsas built a lodge. It was a large Hidatsa earth

6. A reference to the Grass dance, which about 1870 the Santee Sioux

lodge. The Hidatsas and Mandans used to dance there, and the Arikaras and Pawnees used to dance in another lodge. They used to say that.

Then the man Buffalo Bull's Paunch—he was the Hidatsa chief—said to his people, "Now surely let it be! What you are doing is not good. You used to tease the Arikaras, making fun of them when they were dancing. Now that's what *you* want to do. Let it be!"

But they did not listen to him. They were determined to continue their dancing.

And then the chief of the Hidatsas died. Then Buffalo Bull's Paunch, who had been chief together with another one, died.

Now this Crow Flies High wanted to be chief of the Hidatsas. They did not favor Crow Flies High. So they said, "There will be three candidates. And the one who comes out on top of the other two will become chief. And that one will be in the lead."

Then they said, "All of you who favor Crow Flies High to be chief, go over there! And those of you favoring Lean Wolf, stand over here!"

Now the ones who favored Crow Flies High were in a bunch over there, and Lean Wolf's supporters also stood to one side there. Then they counted. Now Lean Wolf had a larger number of people who favored him, who wanted him to be chief.

Then Crow Flies High lost. Then it became difficult for him and he became angry. "Now I'll go somewhere else. I'm not going to remain here among you." Then he separated from the Hidatsas. There at Fort Buford, on the other [north] side of the river that they call the 'yellow bank' [the Yellowstone River], is where the Hidatsa village was. They lived there a long time. Crow Flies High was their chief.

And then a sickness came. Then different ones died. There also were not many antelope or deer roaming around. Then life became hard. The ones who had Crow Flies High as their leader were now hungry.

from the Devils Lake Reservation introduced to the Hidatsas and Mandans as well as Arikaras (Bowers 1965:91–92; see also p. 323 herein).

They used to call these people *Xoška*. They talked about *Xoška*. Now today no one knows what the meaning of that name is. But they used to say its meaning is 'just going off, with no one stopping him'; 'he just goes off.' He just gets up and goes where he is going. That is what they used to say, whatever its actual meaning in Hidatsa is. It is a difficult word. The younger ones who are living today do not know its meaning; but that is what the old ones—the elderly ones—must have used to say: "The *Xoška*, long ago, just went off where he was going, and he went." That is also its meaning.

Then the president also said, "Surely those others [the *Xoška*] should come back. This is what is planned: all of you are to live together [here on the Fort Berthold Reservation]."

Then word was sent that the *Xoška* should come back. They did not want to, and the agent we had here telegraphed the soldiers there in Bismarck [i.e., Fort Abraham Lincoln]. Then the soldiers went up there and herded the *Xoška* back. The children rode in hayracks and wagons, but the older ones followed on foot for however many days it took them to come there to the village of Elbowoods, where the agency was.

And then that is where they arrived. And that is where the ones who were *Xoška* made their village.

And the one who was my mother-in-law was a baby then. She was born in 1894.

Now this is what I used to hear.

The other people did not like it when they were called *Xoška*. Today they like the word, but formerly they used to get angry. Now this is what I used to hear.

Now the Arikaras never made war on the U.S. government when other tribes were making war on it. Some say that this statement is not true—that we are surely just lying and that we did make war—when they tell stories [i.e., write books]. The Sioux—they were the ones who killed white men there at Fort Rice when they razed the fort. The Arikaras never did anything of that sort. In books, however, it is written that the Arikaras were not good.[7]

Now this is the extent of this story.

40

The Killing of White Horse's Son

*During the first quarter of the nineteenth century,
Arikara contact with white men was primarily limited to fur
traders, who exchanged European goods for peltries trapped
by Indians. Relations between the white traders and Arikaras at this time were often tense and sometimes resulted
in open hostilities. The most sensational incident occurred
during the second expedition of William Ashley up the
Missouri River in 1823, when Arikaras attacked the party.
After the fight, Colonel Henry Leavenworth led a combined
force of soldiers and Sioux against the Arikara villages,
which were shelled by Leavenworth's artillery. Accounts of
the conflict from fur traders and soldiers are part of the
historical record, but nowhere in the record is there an
explanation from Arikaras. The following narrative, one of
many versions still current a century and a half later, offers
a traditional Arikara perspective on this historical event, but
is apparently a conflation of separate episodes occurring
nearly a decade apart. The shelling of the Arikara village
described here can only be a reference to the Leavenworth
assault in 1823, whereas the murder and cremation of the*

7. Here the narrator is referring to the negative portrayal of Arikaras in
the published writings of early-nineteenth-century traders such as Pierre-
Antoine Tabeau (Abel 1939) and Edwin Denig (1961).

chief's son (see also story 106) would seem to be an incident
reported in 1833 by Catlin.[1]

Now I think I'll tell a story for a while. It is a short story that
they used to tell and that I heard.

Long ago when the Arikaras were moving upriver—I am telling
an Arikara story—they would build a village somewhere and live
there for a length of time. After so many years they moved this way
[upriver to a new location].

Now there once was a man who was chief of them. He was
named White Horse. White Horse is what he was named. White
Horse.[2] Now he owned a store. He must have been married to a
white woman. She must have been his wife. They traded for ammu-
nition and food with the whites who brought freight up the river on
the steamboats, buying supplies to trade with the Indians who
brought in the hides of buffalo, deer, coyote, and beaver.

Now one time there was a group of young men, very young men,
who must have gone out hunting. They were coming along, wherever it was, and there was a log cabin [along the river]. And here
there were white men living there, however many of them there
were.

[The party stopped and] then one of them said, "We don't have
any tobacco and our village is still far away. Now the white men
know your father. Go over there! You also speak a little English
since your mother is a white woman. Now go on! Beg for some
tobacco!"

So two of them went, the son of White Horse and another young
man. Then they went. There went the two of them.

They were going and when they arrived at the cabin a white
man came out angrily. He had a gun. "Don't come nearer! Stay
there where you are!"

1. Catlin (1848, 2:182) wrote: "But a few weeks before I left the mouth of
Yellow Stone, the news arrived at that place, that a party of trappers and
traders had burnt two Riccarees to death, on the prairies. . . ."

2. Here the narrator gives a different, interchangeable form of the name
xaačiišawatá. Elsewhere the form is *xaataaká*. Both forms have the same
meaning.

This young man called out, "I came for some tobacco, if you have any for us. Here are [beaver] hides."

The white man paid no heed to his words. Then he shot the young man and killed him.

Then the other young man ran away. Then he arrived running where his companions were.

He said, "They have killed him. They have shot White Horse's son."

Then these men, however many there were, became angry. "Now let us all die, too! Let him not die alone!"

They went for them. Then the white men were killed, but one of them must have hidden somewhere. He is the one who must have taken word, wherever he took it, to the soldiers, wherever they were garrisoned. Then he told about the incident: "The Indians killed all of us. I survived to come here."

Then the soldiers came on the steamboat to fight, bringing cannon with them. They arrived. Then they began shelling the Arikaras. Then they leveled the village, killing and wounding many people. And then there was a battle, but the Indians did not want them to kill us.

Now a young woman was running away [from the fighting]. Then something landed where she was headed as she ran. It was not large. It was a ball. A string stuck out of it. The string was burning. Then this young woman took it off [the ball]. Then she removed the string. Then the flame went out.

Then she told the young men who were in the battle. Then, when one of the large balls landed by them, they snatched it up. Then they threw it at the boat of the white men on the water. Then the boat moved on, and then it went over there on the other side of the river. That is where it landed on the water while they were shooting at it.

Then it got dark. Then the white men ran away. But these Indians buried on scaffolds the ones who had been killed after being shot. Then they began to rebuild the village.

Sometime later the ones [who had been in the hunting party] told the head chief of the Arikaras, "This is what they did to us.

They killed one of us."

Now when White Horse told the government representative of the president [what had really happened], then he became angry. Then he reprimanded the soldiers for what they had done.

Then the white traders said, "Surely they killed the white men in the cabin."

Then the Arikaras said, "It's not true. You yourselves were the ones. That boy came after tobacco, and then they shot him. Then they killed him. That is the reason we avenged ourselves. We were feeling hurt on account of what you did to the one who has our village, the one who is our chief."

41

The Fort Laramie Treaty of 1851

In 1851 the U.S. government brought together represen-
tatives of many northern Plains tribes for a treaty council at
Horse Creek, near Fort Laramie, Wyoming. The purpose
of the council was to establish peace between tribes and
between tribes and the United States, and to establish tribal
territorial boundaries. Although never formally ratified by
the Senate, the document signed there came to be known as
the Fort Laramie treaty. This narrative, which is a descrip-
tion of Arikara participation in the proceedings, is in fact a
conflation of events and personages from the 1851 treaty
council and later negotiations with the government in which
Arikaras took part.

Now I am going to tell you about the things that happened when a representative of the president came here where we were living. This time I am telling about the years when we Arikaras, Hidatsas, and Mandans were already living together and when peace treaties were made, when the white man wanted the Indians to put their heads together and cease their warring—their killing one another, their stealing horses from each other, and all those things that happened long ago. Now the white man's president had taken over the governing of the entire country.

Now here at Bismarck where troops were garrisoned[1]—that is where I am talking about—they brought a letter. There were no such things among us as cars or trains in those times. The letter was brought up on the steamboat when it came up the river to this country here. They brought the letter to where we were living, where we were in the village together.

And my grandmother's father was a white man. <He had a trading post there.> He took the letter and he told about it. Then the chiefs summoned another man. They used to call him Stone.[2] He spoke Arikara and English, and he translated what the letter said for the Arikaras. This happened when that white man was living with my great-grandmother Eagle Woman.

Then Stone translated it. He said, "All the different tribes that are living in this country are going to assemble there [at Fort Laramie] on the Platte River. The president wants you three tribes who live here to send delegates there."

Now the one they used to call Son Of Star—his father was named White Shield—said, "Surely that's good. We'll do that. We'll go. Now no one knows the country there where the Platte River is. We've never gone to that place there. That's enemy country."

And the one named Carries Moccasins said, "But I always go there. My sister is married to a Cheyenne. It usually takes eight days to get there. I know the place where all the different enemy tribes are going to gather. Well, I'll tell you how to go there."

Then they called the Hidatsa named Four Bears, the Hidatsa who was half Assiniboine,[3] and the other Four Bears, who was a Mandan.

And the Mandan said, "Surely that's good. I'll be at the side of

1. An anachronism. The military post that became Fort Abraham Lincoln, south of Mandan, North Dakota was not founded until 1871.

2. His English name was Peter Beauchamp, Sr.

3. When Four Bears was a baby his Assiniboine mother died and no one knew who the father was. He was adopted by a Hidatsa couple who had no children. That couple reared him as a Hidatsa.

the Arikara. We'll go."

But the Hidatsa did not want to go. Then he made excuses. He said, "The enemy tribes we aren't friendly with roam around there. And if they should find us, they'll wipe us out. Just let it be, whatever it is that you wanted to do."

Then the one named Son Of Star said, "It doesn't matter. We're now all the same. But we'll go. I'll go."

Then they selected a particular day. Then they traveled by horse, riding horseback.

They always tell that when they reached the confluence of the Heart River and the Missouri, they camped there on the prairie. Then one young man in the party became sick. He was named Young Fox. He and his wife were together.

And then Son Of Star of the Arikaras said, "Both of you turn back! Go home! He might get worse. But we'll go on."

It took the party ten days to get there. And after ten days they arrived there where the camps were clustered on the Platte River.

And that Hidatsa Four Bears was coming along in the rear, not wanting to go and making excuses.

And then they reached the Black Hills. Then the one named Carries Moccasins said, "Now this is where there are enemies, here in this country. If they see us, they'll kill us."

Now they must have told Four Bears, for he then became frightened. Then he traveled in the middle of the party, and when it became dark he went into the middle of them. He had traveled in the rear, the last one, not wanting to go; but after they frightened him he traveled in the middle of the party as it went along. And when the party camped overnight, he slept in the middle of them. He lay in the middle of the party when they slept.

As they were going along that man Carries Moccasins—he must have still been young—said, "When we reach the Blue Hills over yonder, we'll see the village on the Platte River. That must be the post."

It was evening when they reached the top of the Blue Hills. Then the fort was there in the distance. Then Carries Moccasins said, "Now this is the place."

When the party reached the post, soldiers came riding out at a gallop. Then they said, "Be ready! These men who are coming are going to kill us. They are soldiers."

<But Carries Moccasins said, "No. They're coming to meet us, to welcome us.">

When they came to meet us they said, "Here are your tents. This is where you'll stay overnight. We'll take the horses."

The horses must have been tired. There was a corral, and then the soldiers herded them into it.

There were wall tents here in which they were to stay. Then food was brought for them. Oh, there was plenty of food—meat and all the good foods that the soldiers ate!

And while the party was cooking and eating, there was another tribal delegation camped beside them. And here they were Pawnees![4] Then two of them came over.

Then the two Pawnees said, "We are alike. Now tomorrow the representative of the president is going to speak. And we'll be the first ones to respond. We Pawnees here are going to talk to the president's representative first. <I'm going to be the interpreter.>"

The young man who was speaking was named Young Wolf. His father was a Pawnee and his mother was an Arikara. They used to call him Young Wolf.

Now in the morning they were called at eight o'clock. They went. There was a huge crowd of people there. And the Pawnees were the first ones to speak to the government commissioner during the negotiations when they were making the terms of the treaty.

"This is how you'll live. But we are going to take care of you. The government is going to take care of you for as long as you live."

Now today they deceive us, but at that time he spoke well, with good words.

Well, then Young Wolf said, "Now we are finished. Now, you Arikaras, come! Son Of Star, lead the Arikaras! Now it's your turn."

And then that is what Son Of Star did. Then he began speaking when they were negotiating. And the government commissioner

---

4. There were no Pawnee participants in the 1851 treaty council.

said, "But I want us, poor things, to help each other. The president is the one who sent me to call all you Indians together and to provide for your children to learn to speak English like I do, so that we can understand each other. For however long it may be, the president[5] will be giving you rations. Whatever you want, he will give it to you. And he will fence off reservations for you Indians to live within. The country you Indians now live in will be established as the land for your reservations. Each individual will be allotted a piece of land to live on and to build a house on."

Now these were his words: "For as long as you Arikaras live, the president is going to help you. And your children will grow up learning English so that we will understand each other. The way it is now, we can only understand each other through English. Now this is the way it is. The old ways are past.

"Now I want you to give me your young men to be enlisted in the army in case a war arises, and the Indians will be enlisted so that we can help each other."

Now that is the way things went when they met to negotiate the treaty. Then they shook hands.

Then Young Wolf said, "We have done it. It's now the other tribes' turn to negotiate."

Then the Crows went up onto the negotiating platform. They were the first ones.

Then they said, "This young Indian [Young Wolf] who has been speaking and negotiating—we'll follow his road, too. It will be the same way [for us as it was for him]. It isn't going to be any different. We want to live there where we now live. We are used to living where we are, in the land we know."

And the other different tribes felt the same way. "Now it will be just as the Arikaras who came from the north have agreed. Now the terms of the agreement they made with the government are the ones we want, too. Now there won't be any difference."

Now the council ended.

5. The Arikara term *atípa'*, which is used here, means 'president' and by extension 'U.S. Government.' It is derived from the kinship term *atípAt* 'my grandfather.'

«   »

Then all the tribes had a big dance.

Then this one they call Son Of Star—he was also called Comes Last—said to Carries Moccasins, "Now they are glad that you brought me. If I am given something, even if it's a single eagle feather, it will be yours."

And while all the different enemy tribes were dancing and having a good time and feeling thankful, various persons gave their best-looking horses to Son Of Star since they were thankful to him [for what he had done during the treaty negotiations]. When they were giving them to him, this Carries Moccasins thought, "You surely don't have anything, since you promised to give me what you received, just as you said."

Now here is where this Comes Last made a mistake: he did not give anything to him, and Carries Moccasins became angry. Then Carries Moccasins said, "Now you people can go on your own! But I'm going to do this: I'll go to visit my sister, who lives in Cheyenne country."

After Carries Moccasins went off, the return trip was difficult for the party. They became lost as they were going. Then they were just wandering all around on the prairie and they barely made it back here where our village was.

Now after the party had returned things happened the way they had agreed. The young men enlisted with the soldiers as scouts, Bloody Knife being among them when these who were formerly the old scouts were enlisted in the army. This is the reason for those graves.[6]

And when the time came children went to school there at Fort Stevenson, and they also went to the school of Reverend Charles Hall. Then it was our turn to learn English. That is the reason they made a treaty of friendship there on the Platte River in 1851.

6. The Scout Cemetery west of the community of White Shield.

Plate 8. Views of Eagle Nose Butte, Morton County, North Dakota. *Above,*
Aerial view looking southwest. Photograph dated 1966, courtesy State
Historical Society of North Dakota. *Below,* View looking north. Photograph
by Raymond T. Haas, 1990.

42

The Custer Expedition

During the 1860s and 1870s, Arikara men enlisted in the U.S. Army as scouts at military posts established to secure peace on the northern Plains. Their service was felt by the chiefs to be an important demonstration of Arikara loyalty to the U.S. government as well as providing protection for themselves from their enemies, the Sioux. Although Arikara scouts served at different times at Forts Stevenson, Buford, and Abraham Lincoln, their most memorable assignments were with the two expeditions led by Lieutenant Colonel George Armstrong Custer, who was known to the Arikaras as Long Hair. On the first one, the 1874 exploring expedition to the Black Hills, tribal tradition asserts that it was an Arikara who discovered gold in the Black Hills and that Custer promised the tribe a share in the find, the government to act as custodian of the profits accruing from it. The second was the ill-fated 1876 military expedition against the Sioux. In the ensuing battle at the Little Big Horn River, which took the lives of Custer and some 250 of his men, three Arikaras were also among the casualties.

Subsequently, stories about these expeditions have figured prominently in Arikara oral traditions. Nine of the surviving scouts told their versions in 1912 to O. G. Libby, who published them as The Arikara Narrative, *and today older tribal members still recount the events and sing the songs of Long Hair and the three Arikara scouts killed at the Little Big Horn: Bloody Knife, Bear's Trail, and Bobtailed Bull. The following narrative, the most complete rendition currently remembered, is a conflation of events on the two expeditions, treating them as a single campaign.*

I will now talk awhile about the soldiers stationed here at Bismarck. Over there on the other side of the river opposite Bismarck, [southeast of] the town of Mandan, is where the former military post is, where Custer and his troops started out when he led his soldiers. There at Eagle Nose Butte is where the soldiers were stationed.[1] That is where they started out. That is where Custer led them out to war, wanting to pacify the Sioux who were killing white men in the country extending south.

There were Arikara scouts serving with the soldiers. When they went with the troops, there were many of them. There were thirty.

They started out in the country south of Mandan, and after they went up there to the north, then they [moved south and] went into the Black Hills. At the edge of the Black Hills, they said, "This is where the country is rough. Let's go farther away! It's not good here. The land is rugged. We can't cut through. Let's start heading over there to the west!"

And now this is what I used to hear when the Arikara scouts who were with the troops used to tell about it—when they told stories and I was listening.

Then they arrived there in the Black Hills. While the soldiers were camped there, for however long a period it was, there was a young man called Crazy Red Bear with them.[2] He had another name, too, but I do not know it. He was watering his horse early in the morning, Then he saw that the water was shining brightly where it was coming out of the ground. There were objects sparkling where the spring water came out.

Then he began picking them up. They were pretty rocks when he looked at them. Then he put one on his hat, and another one on his bridle. There they shone brightly.

Then he came galloping back, and then he arrived where the soldiers were camped. And then the officers on guard saw him. As he came galloping his saddle and bridle glittered. Also the hat he wore sparkled.

Then a group came up to him. Then they asked, "What are these?"

And the one we are talking about, the one named Bloody Knife, spoke English. He was half Sioux and half Arikara. He was truly a half breed. Then he said, "Where did you find these?"

---

1. A prominent butte along the Missouri River several miles south of Fort Abraham Lincoln (see plate 8). The landmark is identified with the fort by Arikaras.
2. His nickname.

Then Crazy Red Bear said, "There's water over there. It's a spring. There, way up on top of the hill—that's where the water is coming down. They're lying in the water. That's where I picked them up."

Then Bloody Knife said, "These are the valuable metal. This white man [Lt. Col. Custer] wants to see where you picked them up."

And then they went there, however many soldiers there were. Then they arrived at the spring where this young man Crazy Red Bear had watered his horse. And there they lay in the water.

Then they began picking them up. Then they went up onto the top of the hill. That is where the water was coming out of the ground.

Then the white man Custer said, "These are valuable. They are money. Ah, these nuggets you have found are valuable! Now you are the ones who will share in it, you Arikara tribe, and the government will take care of it for you."

Now there was one Indian and one white man. He said to them, "Now you two take these to Bismarck, there where the tall building is,[3] where the commanding officers are." And then he wrote a letter.

And then these two came. The Arikara, who was named Fortunate One, and the other one, a white officer, then brought those valuable metals. Then they brought them to Bismarck.

Now it is not known what happened from there. I don't know.

But now these soldiers went on. But they put up stakes at the site where the metal had been found. Then they went to the Little Big Horn River. Then that is where they went.

Here where they camped the enemy had gathered! Here they had gathered! There were nine tribes where their camps were clustered. It was one big village where the Sioux waited for these soldiers to arrive. The plan was for them to kill all the soldiers. That is what the two main ones, the two leaders called Crazy Horse and Rain In The Face had planned—and Sitting Bull.

3. An anachronism. This is a reference to the current seventeen story state capitol in Bismarck, North Dakota, construction of which began in 1932 after the old capitol burned in 1930.

And when the soldiers went there they had everything—cannon
and good guns—and there were plenty of cartridges. They drove
horses and oxen, but the troops went ahead. There were 125 soldiers
who went ahead—the cavalry that Custer led. That is what they
used to say: they went ahead of those who had the cartridges and
those who had the guns—and those who had the food. Well, then
the soldiers in the lead made camp.

And there was one scout named Red Star. I saw him. He and
another young man were companions. But he had been out hunting
alone.

Then he said to Bloody Knife, "I killed a deer. While I butchered
it, some men passed by. They were four Sioux. They had horses that
were packing meat. They must have killed deer, too. I think they
saw me—that they might have seen me. Then they rode on by. They
went the other way. I don't know where they came from."

After he returned from hunting, Red Star told what had happened. While he was telling about it, Bloody Knife told Custer.

Now they took him to Custer where he told his story again. Red
Star said, "I don't like having to tell the story again—to have to
repeat it. I saw them!"

And then Custer said, "Six of you will go. Red Star, you'll go
with them to see if you are being truthful."

Then that is what they did early in the morning. It was not
yet daylight when this Red Star jumped up out of bed. Then he
mounted and went off. Then he rode up one of the highest hills.
There in the Little Big Horn valley were the camps. It was indeed
a huge village, with the camps extending in a long line. It was
smoky along that valley.

Then he turned back quickly. Now he arrived back at the camp,
and now the six officers went. Bloody Knife was among them.
Then he said, "I truly went where the camps of lots of people are
clustered! I don't know what we're going to do. When they come,
they'll kill all of us."

Then this Custer said, "What is he saying?" [asking Bloody
Knife to translate Red Star's words].

Then Bloody Knife said, "This is what he has said: 'When they
come for us, they'll wipe us out. <There are too many of them—too

Plate 9. Bloody Knife kneeling by the right side of Lt. Col. George Armstrong Custer, with two unidentified Arikara scouts and a soldier, on the 1874 Black Hills Expedition. Photograph by William H. Illingworth, courtesy Custer Battlefield National Monument.

many people.>'"

Then Custer and his men turned around. He said, "We'll certainly go on. We'll battle them. We'll take them captive."

Then Bloody Knife said, "You surely can't do it! There are too many. They'll massacre us. It's a large village, the one he told you about when he saw them."

Then Custer said, "Whatever I say, it will be that way." That is what this Custer said: "Whatever I say, it will occur that way."

Now these 125 men were the ones to strike when Custer wanted to take the Sioux captive.

But here the Sioux over there had already seen them long ago! Here they were ready when the soldiers went up the hill and showed themselves. Then after peeping over the hill they started coming over the top. Some of the soldiers were now lying on the ground, another group behind them was kneeling, and another group behind them was standing. Then Custer said, "Now you're going to shoot them."

Then Bloody Knife said—then he told the Arikaras; he said, "You go down that hill over there! Don't do anything! But I'll stay here. I've been arguing with Custer. I didn't want it to be this way, but he's obstinate. Now we're going to be killed when they come for us. There are too many of them.

"One Sioux there is calling out. He's saying, 'Go to one side, like Sitting Bull said! There are young Indian men among the soldiers. Don't lay a hand on them! Don't kill them! But only those white soldiers.'" That is what he was saying.

It was not long before the Sioux came up the hill for the soldiers. They were not careful where they were shooting at them. They were running over those who were lying and kneeling on the ground. Then they killed them. Now they killed the commander, and half the soldiers ran off. Then they hid. Half were not killed, and half were killed. Now they killed Custer. Then Bloody Knife died. And Bear's Trail—he must have been named Little Soldier then—and that other one, Bobtailed Bull. Right there now, they were the ones who died on the Elk River [the Yellowstone],[4] where

4. The Little Big Horn flows into the Big Horn River, which is a

the battle was. And now it was over.

But afterward the main column arrived—the supply train and the main body of soldiers who followed and had the guns.

Now there is where Custer erred. This was the plan: there were those coming from the south [under Major Marcus A. Reno], and there was also a large troop of soldiers coming from the west [under Captain Frederick W. Benteen]. They were to rendezvous. My grandfather Chippewa Baby [John Morsette] was there among them [General Alfred Terry's column], who came from over there to the north afterward. They arrived after the battle had ended.

They cut down the soldier Custer, the one who was bullheaded. Well, then these Sioux started off. Then they scattered. Then they went back to where they had come from, going in bodies up the hillsides, traveling off with their gear after the battle was over.

Now afterward the scouts who were enlisted arrived back among our people, too. Now one among them was Running Wolf. Boy Chief and Red Bear, Bear's Belly—there were many of them. Now they were the ones who were with the troops there where the battle was. Now half the Arikaras survived to come home. When their commanding officer arrived, he said, "Now you go home! But I'll chase after them [the hostile Sioux], wherever the groups have scattered. I might head them off."

And then they began burying the soldiers who had been killed and had died. Then they began burying them, all of them working.

And then our Arikaras came back home on horseback.

Now Bloody Knife had died. Bear's Trail died. Bobtailed Bull.

Now the pinto horse that Bear's Trail had ridden came back. It came back. Bear's Trail did not return, though. It is not known how many days it took that horse to come here by itself. That is the one they found. They learned that it was the horse that Bear's Trail had ridden.

Now this is what I used to hear when they talked about it. But some person will have a little different story. Now another one will

tributary of the Yellowstone River, the latter called Elk River in Arikara.

have yet a slightly different story. This is the one I used to hear from Nice-Voiced Elk. This is the story that Running Wolf used to tell, too, this one that I have told.

43

The Eagle Trappers

Eagle trapping was an important activity for Arikara men, second only to war as a means of gaining honor. After the Arikaras had moved into Like-A-Fishhook Village, eagle-trapping parties would travel south and west of the Missouri River to favored locations, where members built their individual trapping pits as well as a hunting lodge in which they all slept. The events described in this story occurred sometime after 1863, when the Sioux were still at war with the Arikaras and small parties leaving Like-A-Fishhook Village traveled the prairies at their own peril. Although the narrator heard this story both from his father and from his uncle Snowbird, this telling follows Snowbird's version.

Now I am going to tell a story that occurred when there was still the combined village, when there were many Arikaras, Hidatsas, and Mandans there in the village. It was the combined village there across the Missouri River.[1] It cannot be seen today. Everything is now under water. It is no longer visible the way things were where the lodges were.

1. The reference here is to Like-A-Fishhook village, jointly occupied by the Arikaras with the Mandans and Hidatsas from 1863 to 1886, and today under Lake Sakakawea. There was no single, specific name in Arikara for Like-A-Fishhook village. Instead, Arikaras later referred to it by descriptive verbal forms such as 'where the old village was,' 'where the village on the river bank was,' and 'where the combined village was.' After moving onto allotments, some referred to it as 'in the village.' A translation of its English name (*čišwátU* 'fishhook') is also used.

That was where he lived, there on the other side of the river, "where the old village was." That is what they used to say.

Now a group of young men set out. They went eagle trapping. Then they crossed the river to the other side, to the land on the south side, here where I live.[2] Where they went was far off.

Then they said, "This is the land of good fortune, here where eagles always fly around."[3]

Then they prepared a site. Then they made an eagle-trapping lodge sufficiently big for all of them to be inside.[4] "Here is where we'll camp for a while."

Then they built traps by digging holes in the ground. Then they laid poles on top. And they finished doing it, getting everything ready as they were preparing the traps that each one would be in.

And then one man, the leader—he was named Bear Charges In The Woods, and he was also called Scabby—said, "Now get things ready for us to sit downwind. Get everything ready!"

Well, then they went off. Each one would say, "This must be a good location." Each one went off in a different direction. Then each of them prepared the hole in which he would sit. The traps extended in a line, each one being quite a distance from the others. They could not just be bunched up.

Now each of the young men did it: he stayed in the trap. I don't know how many days passed while they remained there; no one told how many days they stayed there when they were trapping eagles.

« »

2. The narrator lived in what remains of the old Beaver Creek district on the Fort Berthold Reservation. It was on the south side of the Missouri River. Today most of it is under the waters of Lake Sakakawea as a result of the construction of Garrison Dam and the subsequent flooding of the Missouri River valley on the reservation.

3. In the English version of this story the narrator identified this location as south of the present town of Hebron, North Dakota.

4. In the English version of this story the narrator described the hunting or eagle-trapping lodge as a semisubterranean lodge with four walls and a roof, covered by a layer of posts and then pumice rocks. Grass and finally dirt were layered over the posts and rocks. Compare G. Wilson's description of the Hidatsa hunting lodge (1928:134–35).

And there were those in the group who caught perhaps two eagles, and there were some who caught only one. But among them was one young man who was just having a difficult time. None flew to where he was. He had not caught any eagles in his trap.

Then the one who was their leader said, "It's time to go home now. Let's get ready!"

The next morning the one who had not caught any eagles said, "Now I'll remain here a while longer. Perhaps I might catch one. It wouldn't be right for me to go home. I promised my grandfather I would bring an eagle back for him. And now I've had no success. But I'll stay. Go home! Go on! If I don't have any good luck after four days, I'll go back home and arrive there. I'll stay here alone for four nights and days!"

Well, then they left him. Then the others came back home, but this young man did not come with them.

Then he moved from the trap he had been in, making a different one for himself. He finished it. After the young man had been in it for some time, it got dark. He must have got out of it to go back to the trapping lodge.

And here Sioux were waiting for him! They were blocking his path. Then they began to fight him. Then they killed him. The young man was killed.

But the others returned home. They arrived there.

Now the young man's brother was named Only Brave. "Where's my brother?" he asked when he looked for his brother.

"Well, he didn't return. He remained there alone. He said, 'I'll go home after four days.' He didn't catch an eagle. It was difficult for him, and he decided to stay four more days. 'And then I'll go home.'"

But he did not come back later. And now four days had passed.

And then this man said, "It has been a really long time now. Perhaps something is wrong. Let's go."

And then the young men gathered together, however many there were, and then they set out again. Then they arrived there.

And then it was apparent where he had been. But they did not see anyone when they looked for him. They did not find him.

"Now he must have been killed."

And then they came back again. They returned.

"Young Fox must be dead. He must have been killed."

And then his brother said, "Now let's wait! When it becomes summer again, we'll go there. We'll look for him. We'll find out what happened to him."

And after winter passed, it became summer again. It was some-time later. "Let's go! Let's go eagle trapping! Let's look for the boy! Let's see what happened."

And then they went. Again they arrived there where they had camped. They fixed everything up again.

And then his brother Only Brave said, "I'll stay in my brother's trap. I'll sit in it."

After they fixed up the traps in which they had caught eagles before, this boy Only Brave went into his brother's eagle-catching trap. He set the trap.

Now after however many days had passed—after two or three days—when the boy Only Brave was returning to the eagle-trapping lodge, when he was coming along, he saw him. His brother was just walking over there.

As Only Brave watched him, he thought, "You are my brother." Then he went out of sight in a depression.

Then this Only Brave ran. Then he ran onto the knoll. He did not see anything.

There in the distance was a stand of trees. Then he went there. There a skeleton lay in the brush. There his brother lay in the brush. "Now here is where they must have killed you!"

It was rough terrain where the horses had circled round and round. He must have gone into the woods. They must have attacked him in the woods.

Now he picked up his brother's skull. He brought it. Then he said, "Now, my brother, I have found you. And here you are dead."

Then he brought it back. He brought it to the eagle trapping lodge where they were staying. Then he said, "Now I've found my brother. Here he is. They must have killed him. They must have attacked him in the brush."

It was rugged there where they had attacked him in the trees and had gone around in a circle fighting.

Now they offered smoke to the skull. They put food before it to feed his spirit.

Now two days passed. The party caught eagles after this spirit blessed them. Now his brother Only Brave stood there. The one who was their leader was Bear Goes Into The Woods, or Bear Turns Around; and then Bear Goes Into The Woods said, "Say, this morning we won't go anywhere. We'll stay here in the lodge for a while. It's not windy. It's good when it's windy: the eagles fly around when it's windy. But it's not windy now."[5]

And then one young man went up a hill. "I think I'll look around awhile! Perhaps I might kill a deer." Then he went up on foot. They must have been in a valley.

There were trees all around where they had their lodge. The land was rugged.

He stopped on top. Then he ran down the hill. Then he said, "Say, there's something going on. There appears to be a moving column, and the ones in the lead aren't buffalo. These are different. I think they're enemies."

As soon as he had said that, they hollered. The enemy were circling around. Then they began to attack them.

Then one Sioux called out to the ones inside the lodge. He asked, "Who are you? Are you Hidatsas, or might you be Mandans, or might you be Arikaras? We want to know."

And there was one young man among the Arikaras who spoke Sioux. Then he said, "Now we are Arikaras. We are Arikaras who are camping here. We came here to look for a young man. You must have killed him, and now we've found him."

Then the other one, the Sioux, called out, "Are you a Sioux? You're talking Sioux."

Then he said, "No. I'm an Arikara. But my brother-in-law—they called him Lump Face—the man Lump Face was my brother-in-law. He's the reason I speak Sioux. He's the one who taught me to talk in Sioux."

Then the other one, the Sioux who was calling out, said, "Now

---

5. Arikaras trapped eagles only when the west wind was blowing (Curtis 1907–30, 5:88).

come! Join us where we are! Let's kill the ones in there! How many
are there?"

Then he said, "That certainly can't happen! There are fifteen of
us. I won't leave them. These are all my relatives inside here. But
now you must be brave men. Now I want you to do whatever you
are going to do right now! We're not afraid of you."

Then the Sioux who had been calling out said, "Now that's what
I wanted to find out. Today is your last day. You won't see another
day. Now when morning comes again, you'll be dead."

And then the one inside who spoke Sioux said, "Now that's how
it will be. But I'm not going to die alone. But I'll do that, too: you all
will die, too. I'm holding the hands of the young men here. I'll lead
them myself. You aren't the only one who is brave."

Now it was at this time that the Sioux ran around the lodge
where they were inside, shooting at the lodge thinking that they
would knock it down and flush the Arikaras out. But its roof was
sturdily constructed. There were rocks—pumice—on the roof.

Then they decided to burn the lodge down. But the lodge would
not burn.

Meanwhile Bear Charges In The Woods, that young man inside
the lodge, said, "Now each of you fourteen men load a gun for me!
Now from here where I'm sitting I'm going to shoot one gun after
another. I'll kill those who are running around the lodge."

And then that is what the Arikaras did: then they began load-
ing their guns. As soon as an enemy would appear, he picked him
off when he shot at him.

And here came the main body of the group with their camping
gear. Then they formed into a camp circle when they put their
lodges up, while their men attacked the Arikaras inside the lodge
among the trees.

Then one man began to call out. He said, "They have killed a
large number of us. Let's stop awhile and let them stay inside there!
They'll starve. They'll remain in there where they are. Let them
starve to death! When they get hungry, they'll come out." That is
what he was saying.

But the man inside understood. "He is saying, the one who is
talking is saying, 'Let them stay inside there! They'll starve. When

they get hungry, they'll come out and then we'll kill them easily.' That's what the one who was talking said. But it isn't going to be that way!"

Now the enemy camp was set up, and the Arikaras remained inside their lodge dug into the ground. The enemies were walking around watching the lodge they were in.

Then it got dark.

<Now they prayed to that skull. "We need your help. This is what those people did to you: they shot you; they killed you. Now we need your help today. You are holy.">

After it had become night, one young man said, "I looked. Where we get our water there is an open space. It appears there's a crossing over the creek there where one goes down to it. There's brush on the hillside. One can go up the draw through the trees, get on top of the hill, and then sit down to wait. Let's do that! Then we'll get out of this situation."

Then he said, "Now I'll be the one to go in advance! I'll go. I'll go on ahead first. If they see me, they can shoot at me. They can try to kill me. But that isn't going to happen."

Oh, it was really dark, but there were fires all around, where the Sioux had made fires in their camp. <At the same time it was raining lightly, and the rain would put the fires out and get the wood wet.>

Now this young man clearly found his way. <I don't know what his name was.> Then he got out. Then he crawled down the incline. Then he got to the bottom of the coulee there. Then he dipped water. Then he crawled back.

He entered the lodge. "Here is water. The route is a good one. Now that's what we'll do. Now I think I'll go again! Oh, then I'll cross the water. When you reach the edge of the water, go west there along the bank. The water is narrow there <where I have put a stake in the ground>. You'll cross there. Then go up the hill in that draw there where I said there is brush on the hillside over yonder. Get on top of the hill and then sit down. I'll sit there. I'll wait for you. You'll go there one at a time."

Then Only Brave said, "But my brother and I will be last. You all go first! And my brother and I will go afterward."

After they were going and going, after they had gone down the incline, only he remained. Then he said, "Now, brother, now you and I are going to go, too."

Now they had all taken their eagles, after they had tucked them under their arms. All of them had got out. Meanwhile the Sioux were standing by the fires that were all around, watching.

Now the young man Only Brave picked up his brother's skull. Then he said, "Now, my brother, we'll go. When we arrive at our village, we'll put you in a special place. Our mother and father will see you."

Then he himself got out, too. Then he went down the incline. Then the others were on top of the hill waiting for him. Now he got there. "Now, let's flee! Let's go quickly!"

Then they ran off. Then they traveled all night. Now it was getting to be daylight. They came to the bank of the river here where the village was on the bank, where the old village we used to live in was. They crossed the river.

Then Only Brave said, "Now, father and mother, here is my brother. Here he had been killed! I found him. He's the one who is the cause of our coming home. The Sioux began to attack us in the brush again, but it didn't turn out the way they had intended it to."

But now that same morning the Sioux attacked the lodge at the base of the hill. There were no shots coming back from it. Then one man charged into it. Here there was no one inside! The Arikaras had gone out long before!

Then he came out and said, "They must have gone somewhere long ago. There is no one inside."

Then they broke camp. I don't know where they went.

But our men, the Arikaras, came back. They brought back that young man who had been killed after the party had trapped eagles.

44

The Horse Raid with the Bear Hide

In this widely told war story, the success of a young man who was the leader of a horse raiding party is attributed to his ingenuity, not to any power he received during fasting. Because of his skill and experience, he is thereafter a popular leader on war and hunting expeditions.

Long, long ago there where the villages were, a party of young men, however many there were, went out on the warpath. The purpose was to find some horses for themselves. They went out on the warpath, going off on foot.

Then they found a bear—oh, a black bear. Then they killed it. Their supply of food was low; they were nearly out of the things they had brought: dried meat, corn balls, and pemmican.

Then one of them, the main one, the leader who was leading them, said, "Hey, skin the bear and take the hide off carefully!"

Then that is what they did: then they skinned it and carefully took off the hide of that young bear. <And then they cut up the meat, too, to use for food.>

Well, whenever they stopped to camp overnight, this young man, the leader, spread the hide out to dry. "I'll take it home."

Now it was drying. The hide was getting dry.

Then one day one of the scouts said, "Hey, there's an enemy village of Sioux over there. It's a big village. There's a huge number of horses in it. Oh, we have it already planned. It's a big village."

<Then this leader said, "Well, that's what we came for—to get some horses.">

[The scout continued,] "Hey, there's a stallion picketed there in the middle of the village. <It's a big black stallion, picketed there close to the tipi door.>"

The stallion was nice looking. Oh, there were many horses!

Then the leader said, "[Now we are going to lead the stallion out.] Bring it here!"

<Two young men sneaked into the camp.> Then they brought

it back at night. It was already dark.

Oh, the leader said, "Well, I've already made a plan for this big black horse." It was the stallion.

Then he fastened them to the horse's mouth. He tied the mouth closed with rawhide thongs. It could not whinny.

Then he said, "Now get ready! I'm going to turn this horse loose in the village here. Now the horse is going to frighten all the other horses, wherever they are standing all around. Be quick to catch a horse. We're going to run off with the horses."

Then everyone in the village was asleep. Then the leader and another young man led the stallion to the edge of the village. There were horses standing here and there. Oh, there were many! Then this young man tied it to the stallion's tail: then he tied the bear hide that he had to its tail.

"Now turn it loose!"

Then he let it loose in the middle of the village. Now when this horse became frightened it could not whinny, since its lips were tied the way they were. And then this horse frightened the other horses. After the horses that were picketed—the enemies' riding horses— became frightened, after they broke their ropes and broke loose, oh, then there was a loud trampling sound of the horses when the young men ran them off. The horses ran along the edge of the village to an opening, where the young men drove them out.

Now after each of these young men in the party mounted a horse, they ran off with a big bunch of horses.

And then this young man, the leader, caught the stallion again. Then he took the hide off and folded it up. Then he mounted the stallion and came on. Then he came in pursuit of the party.

Oh, in two days, or however many it was, the party arrived back at the villages, wherever our Arikara villages were. This is what they used to tell. Now the party brought back a big bunch of horses.

This young man, the leader, did that many times. He never fasted to be blessed by anything, but he knew how to plan things. Whenever he led a party or did anything, it turned out well and he saved the day.

45

An Assiniboine Raid

*Historically, Assiniboines had an ambivalent relation-
ship with Hidatsas. They frequently visited Hidatsa villages
to barter for garden produce, but at other times they raided
them for horses and scalps. In this story, a large Assiniboine
war party came to Like-A-Fishhook Village to raid Hidatsas
but instead encountered a group of Arikaras, who routed the
party after inflicting heavy losses on it. The success of the
Arikara warriors is attributed to their animal powers,
especially one man's rabbit power. The powers mentioned
here—jackrabbit, bear, shedding buffalo, and buck elk—
reflect the doctors' societies in the Arikara Medicine Lodge.*

*A notable feature of the narrative style used in this story
and appearing here for the first time in this collection, is its
first person perspective. Many years after the Assiniboine
raid had occurred, in the course of intertribal visiting after
warfare among the Plains tribes had ceased, the leader
of the Assiniboine party told his story to Snowbird, who
subsequently repeated the story just as he had heard it from
that Assiniboine, maintaining the latter's perspective, and
Alfred Morsette in turn has repeated it here just as Snowbird told it to him.*

Long, long ago things used to happen when our tribe was
migrating up this way and the village was moving. When they were
traveling, they would build a village where wood was plentiful and
where antelope, deer, and buffalo were numerous and roamed near
by so that they could go out hunting for them.

Now I am going to repeat the words of my uncle Snowbird
again. The story occurred there when our people were living in the
combined village—what they used to call the old village.

Oh, it is not known how long ago it was, but it was probably in
the fall when the hunters used to go out, when they used to go
around hunting in the country that stretches out near where the

town of White Shield is now.

Then they saw them: there were humans coming. It looked like a herd of buffalo coming. And here the ones I am referring to were on foot. They were Assiniboines.

I am repeating the words of Nice-Voiced Elk. Now, in turn I'm repeating the words of the Assiniboine leader—what he told when he told about what happened to himself.

And then this Assiniboine said, "Say, I wasn't afraid of things. When I went out on the warpath, I'd charge across the water; even when the ice was floating, I'd charge into the river whenever I saw anything. I considered myself brave when I used to travel around when I was young." That is what that man said.

He said, "This one time we came here on the warpath. There were many of us. I don't know exactly how many of us there were, perhaps a hundred. There were many of us when we came to fight you people living here where your village (Like-A-Fishhook) was. We arrived ready to fight here where they used to talk about where the Hidatsas lived.

"Now here they saw us! We ran off. There were so many of us that things were not good when we went there. Oh, there was a valley! Oh, it was wide! There also were trees here and there. It was rolling terrain. We ran to the brush, those of us Assiniboines who went in the war party.

"Oh, then there were bunches of us here and there in the brush, and different ones were performing the things they say to become holy [to become filled with whatever animal power they had].

"Meanwhile, after the enemy arrived they were peeping up over the rises. They were the ones; they must have been Arikaras—the ones who have corn.

"One Assiniboine called out. He spoke in Sioux.

"Whoever it was on your side answered, 'What tribe are you?' Here he must have been saying that: 'Are you Blackfeet or Assiniboines? What are you?'

"Then they said, 'We are Assiniboines. We have come on the war-path.'

"Now the one on the other side: 'Now, Assiniboine, know this! Today is your last day. Now I am going to kill you.'

"He answered, 'Now it will be that way. And when I die, I'll hold the hand of some young Arikara man who is good.'"[1] That is what this Assiniboine was saying.

"Then he called back, 'That won't be.'

"Now they knocked off the Assiniboine who was talking. They killed him.

"'Don't any of you say anything!' And here it was quiet.

"And here one Arikara came up over the end of a hill <in the northwest>!" There was a group of young men sitting on the side of it. There was a shot. "He killed one of us. Then they killed two of our party over there. Also one came charging over the hill in another direction and killed another one of us Assiniboines.

"'Now something is happening!' An Arikara came darting over the hill. He was just like a jackrabbit sitting down here and there. He was watching us. Now here where we were sitting on the bank, this jackrabbit was so holy as he sat there. He turned to face the east. Then as he sat there his ears began doing it: he was moving his ears.

"Then he jumped around. He began to face this other way, toward the south. He sat there facing that way. We couldn't do anything to him.

"Then he jumped around and began to face there toward the west.

"Now again he jumped around. He went over the hill. As soon as he went over it, they came up over the hill and scattered us all around. Now in the valley they killed another one of us. They killed one of us. Now those of us who were fast were the ones in the lead as we fled.

"The Arikaras were now singing praising songs as they turned back.

"There were now thirty-one of us who were left, poor things, and there had been a great number of us in the beginning. Poor things, we stood there crying for the bodies of those in our party who were lying there dead.

"'Now we ourselves are to blame. Let's go home!'

"We barely arrived back. Ah, now right there is the place where they nearly killed all of us. They were Arikaras.

"Now the one we saw turn into a jackrabbit was the one who depleted our shells. No matter how different ones were doing it—becoming holy— they used up our shells. Now he must have gone over the hill. Then they came charging up over the hill. It wasn't possible to defend ourselves when we didn't have any shells. Then there was nothing to do but run.

---

1. An idiom meaning "If I am killed I'll take an Arikara with me.'

Then an Arikara would strike one of us on the head with an ax.

"Now this is how they treated us. They were Arikaras. They were not Hidatsas.

"When we returned, the older people said, 'It's your own rotten fault that those young men are lying dead over there! Those Arikaras are holy.' That is what they said when they used to talk about them. 'When you saw him he must have been a jackrabbit when he made you use up all your shells. And they also have a bear. He does the same thing. And they have a buffalo, a shedding bull. That's what he does, too. And also a buck elk—that's what he does, too. When you use up all your shells, then he chases you and kills you. Be careful! Don't go over there.'

"Now we used to be afraid to just come anywhere near this area. But now when we used to go against those tribes like the Crows [and Hidatsas], they were tough. Then they would begin counting coups on us."

46

Two Kettles and the Assiniboine Horse Raiders

This story was told in response to a query whether there was a specific Arikara name for the Assiniboines who live on the western part of the Fort Peck Reservation in Montana. Although some Arikaras know those Assiniboines as watópA, a borrowing of their own band name (Assiniboine watóp'a or watóp'ana), others have known them by the name of the young man whose exploit is recounted here, one that gained him the name Two Kettles. Thus some Arikaras called those Assiniboines Two Kettles or Two Kettles' Village. Naming a band or village after its chief in this manner was a common practice among Plains Indians.

Now I am telling a story that occurred long, long ago when

there was intertribal warfare here where the village was—where there were three villages combined into one for the three tribes they call Arikara, Hidatsa, and Mandan—and where the different enemy tribes used to come on the warpath. And the ones I am telling about now are Assiniboines, who lived in the west.

Now I am repeating the words of my uncle Nice-Voiced Elk. He is the one whose words I am repeating. He used to tell stories at his home. I used to go there when I went around and he told me different stories. Now I am repeating his words.

After these Assiniboines who live there in the west had gone on raids to the villages of the Crows and Blackfeet and wherever else they had gone, <a group of them got together in the chief's tipi and were talking about different things>. Then one of the Assiniboines said, "We never go over there to the villages in the east where the people of those tribes have corn. Let's go there. Let's go to their villages, even if they should kill us. They are valorous men. They are brave. They will kill us if they should find us. But we'll go anyway."

Now there were thirty-two of them. Then the party came during the winter. It must not have been really cold yet. There was a little snow on the ground. It was snowing a little. Then they came. They came near the river bank here where our villages were, where the combined village was on the bank.

Oh, they were on top of a hill, wherever it was, and were looking all around. Then they said, "That must be the village, there where the smoke is in the distance. We've come a long way from where our village is."

There was a thicket of plum bushes there—I used to see them when I traveled around—and then they went into that thicket during the cold. They fixed up a place there. Oh, it was sheltered. It was warm there. Then they made fires [after dark].

Then one of them said, "Now we sure have come a long way. Now maybe we'll take a horse back."

Then they picked out some men they considered able. "You, you'll be the one to find some."

"You are the ones to go into the village over there. The horses are the purpose of our coming here."

Now one boy went with those young men when they went off. I
don't know how many of them there were. Then they got to the
outskirts of the village. Then it was difficult: there were no horses
in sight.

But this Assiniboine whose story I'm telling—the one who told
this story about himself—then he separated from them. Then he
saw a group of people. There was an earth lodge there, and then
people were coming out as different ones came outside [to urinate].
When they were going back inside, he walked in among them. Then
he hid so that they would not see him.

The horses were standing along the wall of the lodge interior.
They were nice looking.

Then the door was secured.

When they lifted it up, they used to prop a log under it. Two
hides were placed on either side of a pole frame. Now this was a
door [which was suspended from a rafter over the inner entrance of
the entry passage]. It was heavy. When people went outside, they
lifted the door up and set a log under it. And later they let it back
down. To lock the door one pole was laid horizontally over two other
poles that protruded on the inside. Now the door was fastened. It
could not be opened.[1]

But now this Assiniboine was sitting inside the lodge where the
horses were standing by the wall. The people were sitting around
the fire eating and talking. Then one at a time they got up and
went to bed. Why, it was not long before they all began snoring!
Meanwhile there were two kettles of food on the fire.

Then from where the horses were—they were nice looking,
however many there were—he went to the door. Then he took off
the cross pole that fastened it. Well, then he lifted the door up, just
as he had seen the people in the lodge do. He lifted the door up.
Then he opened the door. <Then after bracing the door open he
went back to the horses and removed the rail that held them in.>
Then he slapped the horses. They went out. And then he picked up

1. A brief description of the Arikara earth lodge door is given by John
Bradbury (1817:114). Alexander Henry and David Thompson (Henry 1897,
1:339) describe the Mandan door, which resembles that of the Arikaras. For
a detailed account of the Hidatsa door, similar to the one described here,
see G. Wilson (1934:369–72).

the two kettles of food. Then he went. He went out.

Then he shut the door for the people inside. And then he went over to the horses. They were tied together in a line after he tied them. And then he went into the brush, as he went there in the brush.

Then he had the horses tied together. Oh, the black horse that he led [the one at the head of the line] was nice looking!

He arrived back where his party was camped in the brush. "Now here I have two kettles of food, whatever kind it is. I don't know whether it's dried meat or whether it's ribs."

Then the group of men [who had gone to the village earlier] returned. They had not accomplished anything.

"And what did you accomplish?"

"Why, there aren't any horses there! We had things worked out. We searched everywhere in the village. There are no horses around. They must not have horses!"

That boy said, "Now here are the ones that I myself captured. This is what I did: [the people from one lodge] came outside to urinate and when they went back in, I went inside among them. Then I hid. They did not see me. Then they locked me inside. After everyone went to sleep, I opened the door. I slapped the horses with the cleaning rod for my rifle. I then laid it on top of the bed of a man and woman who were sleeping close to the door. I laid the cleaning rod on top. Then I closed the door. After I brought out two kettles of food, I closed the door. Then I tied the horses and came on. Here they are. I don't know how many there are."

Then one Assiniboine said, "Now we are really *far* away from home. Now let's go back quickly! They're going to chase us. They're going to come. You know now that their horses must be inside their lodges. That's why you didn't find any. These are the only ones we're going to get."

Then they each mounted a horse. Then they ran off toward the river. Then after they reached the bottomland. Then they headed west.

Meanwhile the one who had gone into the village—the one I am telling about—said, **"We did it. Just before morning we were hungry. And here the two kettles of food that I had stolen were filled with squash.**

We got into the brush again. [The leader said,] 'Let's rest for a while! We're far off now.'"

Then that is what they did: they let the horses loose to graze, and then they began to eat. Now the members of the party talked about that boy. He was the one who singlehandedly had saved them. That one was a brave person.

Then one of them said [later, when he related the story], **"But we went on. [Our leader said to the boy,] 'When we arrive back at our village, these horses are yours. You stole them. You captured them. But we're riding yours while we're coming back.'**

"Now as we were going back it was morning."

Then the party went on to the Assiniboine village. They arrived there, and then they began calling that young man Two Kettles. That boy had found a name for himself. Now that happened there in the country where the Assiniboines live.

Now after peace was established and intertribal warfare had ended, the Assiniboines came one time to Fort Berthold for a visit— to tell stories of what they had done and to dance—and then they told about this exploit.

And an Assiniboine man told this story. "It happened long ago when I was a very young man. That is when we came. Now my father is the one who used to tell the story of it. This is what my father did here at your village.

"Now I don't know who the people in that lodge were or even which tribe it was when he stole their horses and picked up the two kettles of food, but you must know which tribe it was."

They said, "Now the ones whose kettles you took were Arikaras. Now they were the ones who tracked you. They would have overtaken you when you were in the brush, but it got stormy when you were fleeing, and then they turned back. They didn't run after you. The storm covered your flight. Then they turned back. They were Arikaras, the ones whose lodge you entered by going among them. You wouldn't have survived if they had seen you."

Now this is what they used to say. This is what that Assiniboine man did. This is why they tell about Two Kettles, the Two Kettles of that Assiniboine village. But on the east side of the Fort Peck

Reservation the people are Assiniboine-Sioux. They are half Assiniboine and half Sioux. And the people living farther west are the real Assiniboines—the "chief Assiniboines," as they used to call them.

This is what they used to say. That is what they used to call these people, Two Kettles, Two Kettles' Village, after he accomplished his deed and became chief.

Well, now this is the end of the story that I have told about Two Kettles.

47

A Sioux Attack on
Like-A-Fishhook Village

Until peace was established among the tribes along the middle Missouri River, Sioux war parties from downriver— from Standing Rock, Cheyenne River, and even Rosebud— continually raided Like-A-Fishhook Village. Although all three tribes at Fort Berthold were objects of these attacks, the Arikaras were most often the avowed target. "To go attack the Palani [Arikaras]" became a rallying cry for young Sioux men during the middle of the nineteenth century.

This narrative recounts one of those raids and its aftermath, one that probably occurred between 1866 and 1876. It is a concatenation of three episodes, the first two of which overlap. The story is a composite of versions told to the narrator by Running Wolf, Andrew Little Crow, and Jackrabbit.

The first episode describes how a group of Sioux, acting as decoys, tried to lure the villagers across the river into a trap where they would be overwhelmed, a tactic commonly used by the Sioux. When a group of pursuing Hidatsas recognized the ruse and started to pull back, several daring

Arikaras dashed ahead and charged the enemy. Three were killed: Bear Goes Into The Woods, Little Crow, and Watonasha. The account of their deeds is largely repeated in the words of Bear's Ghost, a young Mandan who was a member of the party that was crossing the river.

In the second episode the courageous behavior of the three Arikaras who were killed is attributed to their association with the Taroxpas, a warrior society whose lance bearer could not retreat from battle. Little Crow was keeper of that staff. The same requirement apparently held as well for Bear Goes Into The Woods and Watonasha, who the day before the raid had obligated themselves to a manly deed by eating food prepared for the Taroxpas, a custom of that society. After being killed, Bear Goes Into The Woods and Little Crow were scalped and their bodies mutilated, but Watonasha's body was never found. He reputedly became a scalped man—a belief not mentioned here.

The final episode recounts an act of Arikara retaliation that occurred late in the nineteenth century, sometime after land allotment at Fort Berthold, when a group of Arikara men attended a dance on the Standing Rock Reservation. There they were provoked by the exhibition of the scalps of Bear Goes Into The Woods and Little Crow and by the taunts of some young Sioux women.

Now I am going to tell a story—one they used to tell me about what happened here where they were living in the combined village. They say "in the village," where the Arikaras, Hidatsas, and Mandans—the three tribes—lived.

Well, I surely don't know what summer it was, but as I am telling it, it was sometime in the summer.[1] It was the season when it is hot.

Those various Sioux villages—the different enemy groups in the

---

1. In a short autobiographical account, Running Wolf said that this attack occurred when he was eighteen years old—i.e., circa 1874, since he was born in 1856. Three hundred Sioux came to fight (Libby 1920: 204–5).

country extending far off there—had banded together. "Now let's go where the three tribes live and attack them! Let's kill all of them! Let's kill them!"

Now this is the story. Then they banded together after the Sioux villages had gathered.

They say that these various groups of Sioux don't talk alike. Those who live in Canada[2] talk a little differently from the ones who live to the south, and these here at Fort Yates, Cannon Ball, and where Little Eagle had his village talk alike,[3] but those who live beyond there talk differently when those Sioux groups name things. There are many Sioux. No matter where it is, there are Sioux there.

Well, then they planned to come here to attack us where our village was—to kill us Hidatsas, Mandans, and Arikaras. "Let's kill all of them!" I don't know what their reason was for wanting to do it. I don't know what their reason was.

Now one day they saw the Sioux coming out of the brush across the river from where people used to get water when the village was high up on the bank on the north side of the Missouri River.

Then after they came up to the edge of the Missouri, they were shooting at the village up above on the opposite bank. Then they went back into the woods.

Now the men who were daring, the ones who had proved themselves brave when they went around, were saying, "Let it be! Let them go around! They will certainly come across the river, and then we'll avenge ourselves. Let them come across themselves! Who knows what their reason is for shooting at our village."

But now there always are some who won't heed what they are told, and some of these young men sneaked into the water at a distance. After they got across the river, they convinced others. Then they, too, swam their horses across. Then they chased after

2. A reference to the Santees and Sissetons who fled from Minnesota to Canada in the 1860s and today live in Manitoba and Saskatchewan.
3. A reference to the Sioux living on the Standing Rock Reservation. Those living at Cannon Ball are Yanktonais, while those at Fort Yates and Little Eagle are Tetons. Little Eagle was a Hunkpapa chief. The community named after him is in Corson County, South Dakota.

the Sioux.

It was level land there along the base of an incline. It extended
west to a point over there along Beaver Creek, where the ones who
told this story used to live. They went down the coulee, along
Beaver Creek. Then they circled around over there.

Now there were eight of those Sioux men who came along the
bank. There were also eight villagers who went across the river
chasing them.

And here the Sioux had set a trap, wanting it to happen this
way! This was the plan: for all the Hidatsas, Mandans, and Arikaras to cross the river—that all of them would go across. Now
when they reached that other coulee over there, the Sioux would
head them off. There in the east is where they were waiting. Then
they would go around. Then they would head them off and kill all
of them. And then the Sioux would cross the river to fight. Well,
then they would kill all the ones who remained in the village,
however many there were. Now that was the plan. That is what the
Sioux had planned.

Well, it did not happen exactly that way. There were only eight
from our village chasing the Sioux, the ones chasing them on
horses. They went down to the river there on the other side where
the Sioux were waiting.

Now those who went were fearless. There must have been some
Hidatsas among them; they must have been there, too. This is what
Bear's Ghost[4] used to tell, too. He said, **"When they turn around to
shoot at us, we'll chase them again."**

Now, Yellow Legs[5] was a brave man. He was fearless.

Bear's Ghost said, **"I was running alongside Yellow Legs when we
were chasing those eight. Also there were eight of us. They got down into
the water where the terrace is above the river. They used to call it Where
The Prairie Dog Village Is.**[6] **Then right there is where the ones waiting for
the enemy came out into sight. And that is where there was a real battle
with these eight. There were not many of them.**

4. A Mandan, the nephew of Yellow Legs.
5. A Mandan whose English name was Wolf Chief. He was married to an
Arikara woman, *swaátu neešaánu'* 'Sioux Woman Chief.'
6. An area near the former town of Expansion, North Dakota.

"They pulled themselves back. They said, 'There is a huge number of Sioux! Let's go up on this hill! The Arikaras must be coming. They must have come from the other side.'"

These eight men, the ones Bear's Ghost was among, were the ones waiting.

Well, then Bear's Ghost said, "There was a young Arikara man they used to call Bear Goes Into the Woods. Oh, the horse he rode was swift! Then he ran it in among the enemy, riding it into the middle of them and shooting at them. And the enemy ran after him, but they were not able to catch him. They were not able to overtake him. The horse he rode was swift. And so that one would taunt the Sioux.

"A little while later another young man arrived there. He was riding a gray horse. He was an Arikara. I'm referring to Little Crow.[7] He was riding a gray horse. Oh, it was the same way with him: his horse was swift. Now the two of them taunted the Sioux.

"Meanwhile, here we were going away for some reason—perhaps we were frightened to death. We turned back, but this man who was riding the gray horse just went right into the middle of the Sioux. And the Sioux wounded his horse. The horse he rode slowed up. It was not running well after it had been wounded. Then the horse was bloody after it had been wounded.

"Now Yellow Legs said, 'Nephew, tell this Arikara that they've wounded his horse. Let him get away! They might kill him.'

"Then I said—I called out to him, 'They've wounded the horse you're riding!'

"He must not have known it. Then he saw it. He rode away from them. Then he rode up the hill. The horse stopped after spilling out blood. This young man jumped off. He ran up the hill. He stood on top. The Sioux surrounded him as they attacked him.

"Now this young man, this Little Crow, was fearless. They all ran away when he shot at them.

"Meanwhile our horses—the ones we rode—were tired. 'Now let's do something for this Arikara, the poor thing!'

"Now the one riding the black horse when he had previously come riding up—then he whipped his horse on the face and went off. Then he stood there [on the hill with Little Crow]. Then the Sioux attacked that

7. His full name was *kaakaatšuneešaánu'* 'Little Crow Chief.'

Arikara, Bear Goes Into the Woods, too.

"Then when another young Arikara man—they called him Good Dish—also came charging up onto the hill, they attacked him. Oh, the Arikaras were fierce!

"Then another young man came charging, too. It was the same with him: he was an Arikara. Watonasha[8] is what they used to call him, a man who shot with his left hand.

"Now there was a huge number of these many Sioux he had wounded. Our horses were tired. 'Let's go carefully! Let's get away!'

"Now there was a huge number of Sioux. Now they must have been coming.

"Here the Arikaras must also have been coming yet. There were only Arikaras and Hidatsas among the eight of us.

"There was a young man named Drum Beater, and another named Black Robe. These two Hidatasas were killed. Now all of the four Arikaras on the hill were dead there.

"In that area where I had gone all around previously, there was a huge number of Sioux. But the Sioux had not been able to do as they had wanted because it was too difficult. After they had arrived there, no matter how brave they might have been, it became too difficult for them. The Sioux withdrew, and there were many of them who had been wounded and killed."

Little Crow was the one who had the society staff.[9] They killed that one, the young man who was named Little Crow. Now he [and Bear Goes Into the Woods] must have been members of the Taroxpa Society. These two I have been talking about were the ones who were killed.

Now the Sioux had crossed the river. Then they pulled back. "Why, they have surely defeated too many of us! And there aren't many of them who have wounded us! The ones who have come out to fight us are few. Why, if there were many of them, they would

8. This name, the origin of which is not generally known today, is a borrowing from Sioux *mat'o naǧi* 'Bear's Ghost.'

9. The staff, the standard of the Taroxpa society, was a lance wrapped with red broadcloth and decorated with swan, owl, and crow feathers. In battle the lance bearer, a society officer, would thrust his standard in the ground and remain by it, unable to retreat until some other warrior removed it (Lowie 1915:665).

have killed all of us if all of them had come. However many there are, they must all be ready for us. If we had gone closer on the river bank, they would certainly have gotten the best of us.

"These Arikaras are holy. If they call the thunder and if they call the rain," they were telling each other, "if they call the rain, they are certainly going to overwhelm us. We will all be dead."

Now I don't know who the Sioux was who had the idea to attack our village or how many bands of these Sioux there were. I don't know who he was who wanted to kill all the Arikaras, Hidatsas, and Mandans. Now I don't know where he went, or what he did, either.

Now the young men were dead. I myself saw the hill on which they were killed, too. It was not long ago that I wandered around there at the place they used to tell about. The hill is still there. The hill is there. It is a large hill. That is where the Sioux dead lay. They lay on top of the hill. One hundred thirty-one—that was the number of bodies lying on top, the ones who had been killed there.

Sometimes when a man was wounded, the Sioux took him back to their village. Their village was there near what is now called Beulah. There in a ravine is where the Sioux village was, where they were camped. That is where the village was when they arrived to fight.

Now it did not happen as they had planned. But some did die. These were the ones: four young Arikara men who died; and two Hidatsas, the one named Black Robe, and Drum Beater.

This Drum Beater was the father of He Flies. Now she [He Flies's daughter], a woman, is the only one who survives. All the other children of He Flies are now dead. This woman is the only one who survives. That one Hidatsa was named Drum Beater.

But this Hidatsa Black Robe must have been married to an Arikara. He was the grandfather of Black Buffalo Woman [Letha Howard] and Spotted Tail [Albert Simpson], who was also named Slow Bear. Now the father of Slow Bear was a Mandan. But he was half Hidatsa and also half Mandan. They used to say that Black Robe was the grandfather of Slow Bear. Now this Black Buffalo

Woman was the brother of Slow Bear. *Saništaaka*[10] was their mother.

Now this is what I used to hear from the two or three men who told this story that I am telling.

« « «   » » »

Now I am going to tell about what this Bear Goes Into The Woods did. Well, the young man who was named Watonasha was a brave warrior. The two young men were companions.

Now when the Taroxpa Society had its dance and when the members were singing, they had different kinds of food there in the lodge where they met—dried meat, dog, sweet corn, and squash— while they were singing Taroxpa songs.

Meanwhile these two young men were going around the village. <They were hungry.> "Hey, let's eat the food of the Taroxpas!"

Then they entered the lodge where the warriors were singing their war songs.[11] They went around the interior of the lodge where the Taroxpa members sat. Then they picked up a pot of food cooking over the fire. Then they took it outside. "Let's eat their food!" Now that is what they did.

Well, that was the custom. If one did that—if one took the Taroxpas' pot of food cooking over the fire—well, one was obligated to perform a manly act for them, to perform some war deed. He has now promised himself. That is what I used to hear. Now that is what these two young men did.

Well, it was the next morning after they had picked up the pot of food and taken it out.

Now the young woman who was the wife of Bear Goes Into The Woods—oh, she was nice looking, a beauty—and her husband had gone after Juneberries and chokecherries close by on a spot east of where the village was, where the combined village was. They were riding in a two-wheeled cart.

---

10. This name is the term for a species of bird whose identity is no longer known.

11. A reference to a song sung prior to a war party going out on a raid or to a battle. The lyric told that the warrior(s) might not return alive. Also called a death song in English.

Oh, there were many Juneberries and chokecherries that they picked.

Why, then this horse of theirs was getting nervous and whinnying again and again. It looked over in the direction from which they had come.

Well, then it was just about that time when the enemy began shooting at the village from the other side of the river after they had come to the river bank.

Then this Bear Goes Into The Woods said, "Now, my wife, I have loved you. But now this is what I did: I ate the Taroxpas' food. They are brave men. Now whatever I do, I can't be afraid. My wife, I have loved you. Now I'm going to leave you."

The horse was restless. Then he unhitched it. Then he took the harness off. Then he said—he told the horse, "Hey, what is it that you're afraid of? You're swift, and you're certainly strong. I'm the one to die. You're beautiful, you swift horse. I'm the one. I'll be the one to die."

Then he mounted the black horse. It was nice looking. He shook the hand of this young woman. Then she cried.

Then the young man made the horse run at full speed as he came. Ah, the horse was swift as he rode into the village. Then he ran down to where they were crossing the river. Then he rode into the water. He crossed the river.

And then he rode up to the line of battle, where the enemy had come over the hill. Then he arrived. Then he jumped off.

It isn't known what became of the horse, but they brought that black horse back for him. But the one who rode it was dead now. They had killed Bear Goes Into The Woods, but he had first done away with many of them after killing and wounding them and after killing various horses of theirs. Now the Sioux became afraid of that one.

Now that other young man—the one they called Good Dish— that one became a bear. Then he scattered the Sioux. Then he transformed himself into a bear. Then he killed Sioux.

Now the Sioux were attacking this Watonasha, too. This one was just as fierce. But he was left-handed. It was difficult for him because the shells jammed in his rifle. It was one of those rifles that they called red arrows, when breechloaders were first introduced here.[12] Then the gun jammed. The shells were not loaded correctly. Then they killed him.

After the fighting had ceased, the relatives went to look for the bodies of those who had been killed and were lying there. <They found Bear Goes Into The Woods and Little Crow, scalped and cut up, but the body of Watonasha was not there. They could not find him. Then they put the bodies of the two young men on the hill there. That is the way.>

Well, this Good Dish must have returned, but the other three were already dead. Bear Goes Into The Woods, Little Crow, and Watonasha—and the other two, the Hidatsa and the Mandan.[13]

« « «   » » »

Well, years later after there was peace everywhere, the Sioux would tell stories when they traveled around in groups. There at Cannon Ball and Fort Yates and there—I forgot the place where they were recounting stories of various incidents. "Now this is what happened."

Well, the Arikaras went on a friendly visit to the village there at Cannon Ball. While they were dancing there, oh, they were having a good time! While they were there, there were *so* many Sioux!

Over there at a distance [on the community dance ground] was an upright stick. A scalp hung from it. There also was another one over there. There were two scalps with the hair of the two who had been killed.

Then the Arikaras recognized them. One of them said, "This is the scalp of Bear Goes Into The Woods, and that one over there in the distance is the one of Little Crow." The young man Little Crow must have had slightly curly hair. The Arikaras recognized the two

12. Identified by the narrator as a .25–20 Winchester rifle. Because this model was not introduced until 1893–95, however, the likely identification is the .44 caliber Winchester Model 1866, common on the Upper Missouri from 1866 to 1880, the period of this narrative. It used copper cartridges that were red in color.

13. A reference to Black Robe and Drum Beater, both of whom were previously identified as Hidatsas.

of them. I am talking about the Arikaras, whose scalps the Sioux were displaying after they had counted coups on us and killed those two.

Then one of the Arikaras who had holy ways filled a pipe. They made a smoke offering:

"And here we sit, members of our tribe.
  Now you two must smoke.
  Now, you other one, Little Crow,
    we have come here where they have you two.
  Now maybe you will somehow avenge yourselves
    that we may be thankful after what they did to you.
But it's good that they have you in a nice place,"

they were saying as they talked to the ones who had lived formerly.

Then the Arikaras had a good time while they were dancing.

Now a young woman was dancing around where they were. She looked like a doll. That is what they used to say about a young woman who was good looking. Then she was dancing in front of the Arikaras where they sat.

Then one of the Arikaras said, "Now just wait! This one is going to be abused."

There was also another one going around. There were four young women who were showing off in front of these Arikaras, mimicking the actions of the Sioux who had counted coups on these two young men who had been killed.

Well, then the dance ended. Then the one they called Iron Crow, and Running Wolf—the two of them ran off with this young woman who was good looking, the one who had a yellow dress. Oh, she was a beautiful young woman about eighteen winters old. She was about that age. And the others ran off with the other young women when the group came home.

And then Running Wolf and Iron Crow brought this young woman back. This young woman thought, "You two must be going to take me back to it," where our village was here.

It must have been sometime after we Arikaras had gathered together to live dispersed on the north side of the Missouri River. It must have been about the time when the people were living dispersed on allotments.[14]

Then this young woman thought, "You two Arikaras must be going to marry me."

And here they had actually brought her so that the men who were living then, however many there were, could take her sexually. Well, and each one of these men had wives. They were not single men.

It happened somewhere north of Cannon Ball. Face Submerged In The Water is the place where they camped. "Now let's eat first and then we'll go on!" Then they camped.

Then that Iron Crow would come over the hill and name different ones. "Come here awhile!" Then the man would go up. And here that is where they had that young woman who had been showing off. Now right there is where they began raping her as each one took his turn. They finished with her and then they let her go.

The other one who had just been showing off, too—they did that to her as well. There were two of them.

Well, and here someone in the party had run off with the wife of a Sioux man named Standing Elk, too, but they must have given her back. Her Sioux husband must have tracked her down. Then Standing Elk must have taken back the woman who was his wife. She had a baby.

Then the Arikara group came on back home.

Now that is what happened there. Then the group came back home. Meanwhile they had been given things when the Sioux donated to them [at the dance].

Now this is what happened. This is what I used to hear from the old timers when they used to tell stories.

14. In 1886 the last Arikaras moved out of Like-A-Fishhook Village to live on their allotments on the north side of the Missouri River.

48

War Story of Wet Moccasin and Old Bull

This war story tells of another Sioux party that came to attack the Arikaras, this time when the latter were in their winter village in the Missouri River bottoms west of Like-A-Fishhook Village. It is foremost a story about ironies, of two incidents incongruous with the goals of warfare. One of the tragic outcomes of the routing of the Sioux raiders is the fate of two young companions, Wet Moccasin and Old Bull, who were among the Arikaras besieging them. Both young men were shot by their fellow tribesmen: one was caught in the crossfire and the other was killed by two Arikaras who mistook him for a Sioux. The second irony is the fate of two more fortunate men, one Arikara and the other Sioux: each was the sole survivor of his war party, the Sioux the survivor of the raid recounted in this story and the Arikara the survivor of a simultaneous raid some Arikaras had made into Sioux country. As they are returning to their respective homes, they encounter one another and share their experiences.

Now I am going to tell a story that I heard from the ones who used to have stories that they told while they were still living. And the one who told me the story I'm telling here was Nice-Voiced Elk, who I have been talking about. He was my uncle. My father and he were cousins. We were relatives.

Now when the village was there—when it was the combined village of the three tribes here—the people used to move into the woods in the bottomlands in the winter, when it began to get cold. They built a village here to the west, where there was plenty of wood in the timber extending westward.

They would live there during the winter, when the land gets cold, when the ice freezes the river over, and when it snows; and on this occasion the snow on the ground had got deeper again.

Well, and there were seven Sioux who came there in a war

party. It isn't known where they came from when they came to the
village, where the old village was. The country is not the same now:
the land is underwater. Their purpose for coming on the warpath
was to steal some horses.

There was no one living there in the village on the edge of the
bank [Like-A-Fishhook Village].

"Ha, I wonder where the people went." That is what one Sioux
was saying. That is what the Sioux later told Nice-Voiced Elk.

Now they went on. Then they found the trail; and, oh, there
there was a wide trail where the village had passed.

Then they said, "Say, they must have camped in the woods
where the trees are thick, now that it's becoming winter. Now let's
go around the other way! Let's come upon their village from the
north! And if they follow our tracks, they'll think, 'You must be
Assiniboines who have come here.' They'll blame them."

Then they went around. Then they came to the village in the
woods, oh, where there was the sound of the drum while they were
singing songs. But then it was difficult for them to get close enough
to the village so that they could go into it to steal some horses.

Then they said, "Say, let's cross over the river! Let's come at the
village from the other side of the river! And then we'll steal horses.
They must certainly be all around there in the brush." That is what
they were saying.

Then they were conjuring images of horses in the brush. They
were also stepping in each other's tracks as they crossed the prairie
[to make it appear as though only one person had been there]. Then
they went into the brush there in the woods. Then they crossed over
the ice at another place to the other side of the river. Then they sat
down in some brush.

"After they go to sleep, then we'll go on."

Now one youth from the village saw the track there.

Well, in the morning when the young men in the village mounted their horses and rode onto the prairie, there was one track. It
came from over there to the north. There was just a single track.
The track had the print of one foot. But on one side of it there were
holes in the snow. They were looking at it. "I wonder why there's
only this one track and on one side of it there are holes in the

snow."

Then they told some older men in the village about it.

Then the older men said, "It sure is puzzling. There must be many of them who came. They must be stepping in each other's tracks. It must be a cane that's making those holes. Now go follow that track! Whoever they are, they must be somewhere in the brush."

Then they followed the track past the village there in the woods. Then it went to the bank of the river; then it went across the ice. That is what the young men were doing, [following the track].

And here in the brush were the Sioux! Then the Sioux emerged from the brush when the young men exclaimed, "We've found them!" Then the young men chased them.

The Sioux went up one of the hills where those twin hills are, off in the distance. One hill stands apart from the other <and is pointed>. That is the one they went up. I saw it. There are rocks scattered all around on top. And there is where they were on top.

Then the young men surrounded it. Now they were attacking them on the hill.

An Assiniboine was killed by the Sioux. There must have been some Assiniboines among the young men from the village. They must have come from over there in the northwest after befriending some Hidatsas. There must have been an Assiniboine among them. The Assiniboine was shot by them. He must have had an inflated notion of himself; he must have sat down somewhere too close to the Sioux on the hill. He was shot.

Well, then the young men said, "They'll come down when they begin to get hungry."

Then they completely surrounded the hill as they watched the Sioux.

Then the young men raised their voices. The Sioux must have come down. They saw one run away from the hill. Then they ran after him. Then they killed him. And there it was one of those who had been on top of the hill!

Now they killed six. They did not know that there were seven of them. Well, they killed all of them, they thought. Then they came back to the village. One was going to go into the woods, and they killed him, too. Now the dead were lying all around.

«   »

Then the young men came home and were telling about what had happened. They said, "There was one who lay at the base of the hill, where they descended to the foot of the hill. That one lying there is the one he and I killed." Two men were telling about how they wounded one man.

It was not a good situation when they had been firing their guns after it got dark. The Arikaras were also killing each other.

Well, there was one of their young men named Old Bull. They had wounded him. He was now lying inside his lodge. Then he said, "I'm waiting for my brother [Wet Moccasin]."

Then they told him, "We're looking for him, but we can't find him. He'll come back when we find him."

Then that young man Old Bull said, "I want to see him. I'm dying."

Then later he said <after drifting back from unconsciousness>, "And here he has gone first. There he stands. He's waiting for me. And now I'll go."

Then that young man Old Bull died. He died.

Then some men said, "Say, the one that these two talked about—the one they killed at the foot of the hill—perhaps you ought to go there. Take a look at the bodies! He may be one."

They ran there. Then they arrived there at the hill. And there was the young man lying there, that Wet Moccasin, the one in the story these two men were telling: "We killed one where they descended, when they came down the hill. The man lying at the foot of the hill is the one we killed."

And here these two were the ones! "And here we killed our own man, too!"

These two who had killed Wet Moccasin barely escaped getting killed themselves. Now they had killed him, too.

Meanwhile one of the Sioux who had been on top of the hill had survived after he came down. He now went off alone. He had nothing. After he had gone for some distance, however far it was, he was hungry and cold, since it was wintry when he was traveling.

Now this sole survivor was cold and had nothing.

Meanwhile a group of Arikaras had themselves gone on the warpath. There was the same number of them who were killed as there had been in the party of Sioux whom we Arikaras had killed. And here one Arikara survived!

Now the same thing happened to the Arikaras, when they were chased as they drove off some horses. But the one of them who was saved was thrown off by a horse, and then he did not get up. And that was the reason he survived. After the Sioux slaughtered the Arikaras who had gone on the warpath, they thought, "We must have killed them all."

Well, then that man who survived came on back alone. He was an Arikara. He must have had some edible things. He must also have had his weapons.

As he was coming along, there came this Sioux who had survived. Then they found each other. They sat down. Then they told about themselves.

Then one asked, "Who are you?"

Then the other one said, "I'm a Sioux."

"But I'm an Arikara myself. We went over there where your village is. They killed us. But a horse threw me off. I didn't get up. I just lay there. And after all of them went off, I got up. Then I came on. They killed all the rest of our party."

Then the other one told a similar story: "They killed us, too. I escaped. This is the reason: after this one fellow rapidly descended first, after he went, I followed down the hill behind him. As soon as my feet touched the ground—I hadn't taken a step yet—now another fellow landed on top of me as he slid down. Before I could even take a step, he landed on top of me. And here they must have seen us. Here they must have been watching down below there.

"Then they began shooting. They killed all the others in our party. Now I myself lay still. As soon as things were quiet, I got away. Then I came on. I'm tired now. I haven't eaten anything. I just don't have anything, not even a gun. I don't have any shells. I don't have a knife."

Well, then that Arikara gave him meat. "Now eat! But I'll go on." Then he gave meat to this Sioux.

Then the young man, this Arikara, came on. Then he arrived back home.

Meanwhile this other one, the Sioux, must have arrived there at his village, too. He must have told what happened.

Now that is how the people found out that the two Arikaras were the ones [who were the cause of Wet Moccasin being killed]. These two who shot him were older men. Now Wet Moccasin and the one who was named Old Bull were always companions. These two were the culprits when they killed him. They didn't know it. They thought, "The one we killed must be an enemy. And here he was one of us!"

Now this is what happened. Now this is what I myself heard.

49

War Story of Big Bear and Lump Face

Big Bear was a noted doctor as well as an experienced war leader among the Arikaras during the period immediately after the tribe moved into Like-A-Fishhook Village. This story, which is a testimonial to his powers, was originally recounted by Lump Face, his nephew, who accompanied Big Bear's war party when he was eighteen or nineteen years old. Much of the narrative is repeated in Lump Face's own words.

Now, I will tell a story that the old ones who used to live told me—what I used to hear from them when they told stories about what happened long ago when the Arikaras were coming upriver.

There used to be a man called Big Bear, a man who had mysterious powers after he had been blessed with holy ways. And there was a young man—the one whose words have been repeated—who was named Lump Face. Old Man Lump Face is what I used to hear him called. But at the time of this story he was a very young man. This Big Bear was his uncle.

This is an Arikara story that I am telling. This Lump Face must have been half Sioux, though, and half Arikara. But the Arikaras, whom he lived among, raised him. He spoke Arikara really well. But his father was Sioux. His father was Sioux and his mother was Arikara.

I will now be repeating the words of this boy called Lump Face.

"I was a very young man. My uncle was Big Bear. We were going on a war party out there in the west, somewhere out there where the land stretches on and on. We were going on a war party. There were fifteen of us. We were on foot; we were not on horses as we traveled around out there in the west.

"Then we camped. This man we had as our leader, Big Bear, said, 'We'll stay overnight here. It's nice here.' There was water nearby, and there was plenty of wood lying around. 'We'll stay overnight here. We're running short of food—of deer meat. Let's go hunt around for some deer to kill! And then we'll go on. It's time now to turn back and return home. Then we'll return home.'" That is what this man said.

Then he said, "Now, you young men, make a sweat lodge for me!"

Then these young men made a sweat lodge. Then some of them went into it, however many there were. When he was inside the sweat lodge, this man began to sing his medicine song as he prayed to the different powers. I don't know what his powers were.

Then he ceased his singing. Then he was crying out his words as he finished his praying.

Then he said, "Now, young man, open the lodge door!"

They opened the door and then filed out.

Then he said, "Now, young men, be ready! In the morning the Sioux are going to shoot at us. They are ranging close by. They have already seen us camped here. We are going to have a fight in the morning. Be ready!

"Now I'll be the only one they are going to wound. I have been praying that no one gets hurt. That is what I have prayed for to my father.[1] That was my prayer when I cried."

And morning came. The light broke over the land. Then they began shooting at them, firing and firing as they shot at the lodge. Then all the young men got out.

Then this Lump Face said, "Now I'm going to protect myself. I'm not afraid after what my uncle said."

Then he said, **"We killed a large number of them, after shooting and killing different Sioux. They retreated. They ran away. Now my uncle was shot by them here in the chest. He was shot. We laid him down.**

"Then he said, 'Now make a fire!' Then they began to prepare medicine, which he drank. But he was groaning. Blood was coming up. He drank the medicine. Then he became quiet.

"He said, 'Alright, we'll go now. Now watch the moon. As soon as it comes up, if there's a line across the middle—if there's a black streak across the middle of it—I am saved. Then I'll go home with you. But if it's not that way, if this red moon has no line across it—if it isn't there—I'm dying. I will die. Then you must place me somewhere here in these hills. Place me somewhere after I die. Then you can go on home.'"

Now this is what this man Big Bear had planned.

While they were waiting for the moon to rise, he was growling like a bear. And then it appeared the way he had said: there was a black streak across it in the middle. Oh, the young men were happy when they saw the moon. "Now, Big Bear, you have saved our lives. It is now the way you said!"

Then he said, "Be ready! Now let's go quickly!"

Then he arose. Then he tied a bear robe around his waist. He wore a bear robe.

Then this young man Lump Face said, "We will travel slowly since my uncle is wounded."

Then Big Bear did it: as soon as he took a step, he truly began to run and went on at a trot. "Don't leave me behind!"

"Then we proceeded to travel back at night, coming on when it was nighttime. He ran and ran. He never slackened his speed. He maintained a steady exertion.

"There was the moon. As soon as it went out of sight, he stopped. 'Now let's stop here! Now, young men, let's eat!'

1. A reference to his spirit benefactor.

"They brewed medicine for him to drink. Then he began to eat. 'Now sleep! But I'll remain awake.'

"Then we all lay down.

"When morning came, we got up. A fire was made, and then we began roasting meat over it, each person having some. We ate.

"Then Big Bear began to drink his medicine. 'Now, young men, sleep awhile! We are going to run again after dark.'

"And after it became dark, as soon as the moon appeared after coming up, Big Bear tied the bear robe around his waist as he had done before. Then it happened quickly: when he started off, he proceeded to run. Then we followed him, running as we came back. He did not slacken his speed.

"Then when the moon went out of sight—just as soon as it went out of sight—he stopped. 'Now you must have some of your own food to eat,' he said.

"Then they brewed medicine for him again. Then he began drinking it. Then he began to eat. He ate. And then he said, 'Now sleep! Tomorrow we'll travel during the day. We're near the end. We'll arrive at our village. There's no trace of the enemy around. We're safe.'

"When morning came, early in the morning, 'Now get yourselves ready quickly!' Then we came on during the day.

"It was evening when we came to the river bank where our village was—where the village was on the high bank. Then a boat was brought across for us and we crossed over to our village, Like-A-Fishhook.

"And then they took Big Bear into the Medicine Lodge. After they doctored him where he was wounded, he got well."

Now after Lump Face became an old man, [he used to say,] "After I became a young man, whenever I was going to go on the warpath, I would go to my uncle first. Then he would tell me things, giving me all kinds of advice. 'This is what you should do. You should do this! This is what is going to happen when you go on the warpath.' Now that's how he instructed me. Those are the things he would tell me when I went around on the warpath.

"Now when my uncle was dying, they [my aunts] gathered him up and then they placed him somewhere in the woods, and he died.

"Now, while I was still a young man—now, after intertribal warfare had ended and we no longer warred—now things were good: we lived

here peacefully and the different tribes who had been enemies would get together socially."

Now this is where the story ends. I was related to Nice-Voiced Elk through my father. He and my father were cousins. He is the one who used to tell me things and tell me different stories. Now this story I have just told is one that I heard from him.

50

War Story of He Stands Sideways

Despite their frequent conflicts, Arikaras and many Sioux bands were often at peace, and intermarriages occurred between members of the two tribes during those tranquil periods when intertribal visits, generally for trading, occurred. The setting for this war story is a Sioux village, probably on the Standing Rock Reservation, into which the sister of an Arikara man named He Stands Sideways had married. For He Stands Sideways, this is a story about proving himself and gaining the respect of his Sioux brothers-in-law during a visit to his sister's household, when a party of Crows stole horses from the Sioux camp.

Now I am going to tell a story. It is one that my uncle Snowbird [Nice-Voiced Elk] used to tell. I am going to repeat his words again, just as Nice-Voice Elk would repeat the words of the Sioux after he had visited among them. Now he told the story of one man they used to call Blind Sioux. He was named Standing Soldier.[1]

« »

1. The man who used to tell this story was named Standing Soldier, who was also called by the nickname Blind Sioux.

Standing Soldier's father was an Arikara, but his mother was a Sioux. Now this man, the father, was named Stands Sideways. His sister, who married a Sioux, had five male in-laws. The young woman, after marrying this Sioux, had four brothers-in-law, who teased the one named Stands Sideways when he came to visit.[2] Why, his male in-laws teased him, saying all kinds of things: "Why don't I go hunting awhile! Why, I think I'll finally bring some meat for this one!" or "He doesn't know how to look for anything," and making different remarks about him. That is what they said when they teased him.

One night someone in the Sioux camp cried out, "The horses must have been stolen! The horses have been run off. It must be Crows. They're headed over there toward the west."

Then they mounted their horses. Then they tracked them.

Now one of the brothers-in-law of Standing Sideways said, "Sister, don't allow it! Don't allow this man to go! Those Arikaras aren't afraid of anything. We don't want him to get hurt or get killed. Anything might happen. Don't permit him to go!"

Now the man who was married to her said, "I have had four brothers but now our in-law He Stands Sideways makes a fifth one."

And, oh, the Sioux were quick to get ready to pursue the Crows. After they had mounted up, oh, there were many Sioux!

Then this He Stands Sideways said, "Now, sister, I want to go where they're pursuing the Crows. I want to see what they're going to do as they pursue them."

Then she said, "Brother, now I don't want you to do it. But now you can go. This horse is mine. My female in-laws gave it to me."

Ah, this black horse was swift, a nice-looking black horse. It had a white spot on its forehead. Oh, it was beautiful! It was swift.

"Now that's the one you'll ride." Then she got it ready for this man [her brother].

He dressed himself for the warpath. Then he mounted the black horse.

---

2. Among both the Arikaras and the Sioux, brothers-in-law had the right to tease one another in a jocular manner.

«   »

It was certainly true that this horse was swift when it ran. Now he was about to catch up with the Crows.

And here they had run up a hill. The terrain was *very* rough where they were. And when they got to the top of the hill there must have been a large rock sticking up there. In the middle of it there was a depression. And here the Crows had gone into it after leaving their horses. There they were. They were climbing over it up there.

Over there in the distance, where the stone stood upright on top of the hill, is where the shooting was. Then the Sioux began going slowly up the hill, crawling up it.

But now when this He Stands Sideways arrived, he jumped off his horse. The Sioux did not recognize him since he had disguised himself by putting on an enemy capote. The gun he had was a breechloader.

When he scrambled up the hill, the Sioux said, "Now he is the one!" as different ones were talking. Then He Stands Sideways quickly went to the top, and there were all the Crows, dead now, their bodies lying there. They had been killed.

But here there was a single one left who was still shooting at them. And here there was this single one! But over there were dead bodies lying around.

Now this Stands Sideways, ready for battle, jumped over the rock where sat the one who was shooting at the Sioux as they came up the hill. Then this He Stands Sideways came at him from behind. Then he grabbed his hair. Then he cut his throat.

Then he emerged ready for battle from behind the rock, oh my, causing the Sioux to retreat in fear. And here it was he, they discovered, after he removed the hood that he wore over his head! And here it was He Stands Sideways!

This one, the man who was his brother-in-law, was named Bear.

When they saw Stands Sideways, they said, "So it is the Arikara!"

His name was Bear; I don't know what the rest of his name was. They said to him, "That's your brother-in-law. Look! Look at him! And here that's your brother-in-law. I wonder what he did."

And now after he had charged into that depression, oh, the party sang praising songs for the ones who had accomplished brave deeds. Then they came back. Then they were riding on recaptured horses after they had counted coups on the Crows. Then they came back to the Sioux village.

Now that Arikara is the one the Sioux talked about—what he did when he charged into the depression where they were afraid to go after some of them were killed. And here it had been a single Crow who had stood them off! He must have known how to shoot well: he didn't miss a shot.

But this Arikara, He Stands Sideways, tricked him when he charged into it. And here there were dead bodies lying there where he charged through. Then he killed the lone Crow when he came at him from behind. He cut his throat.

That is what the Sioux talked about after they came back. After they returned home, the Arikara was the one they talked about.

Then that Bear—whether he was Black Bear or Red Bear, I don't know—then that Sioux said, "Ha, this is what your brother did. When we were fighting the Crows who were on top of that hill and they were shooting at us, one of them never missed a shot. Then he was wounded after being shot by someone. Why, when that person came charging out, we thought, 'You must be the one who did it.' And here it was your brother who was the one who had cut his throat and came charging out on top of that rock. He made us scatter. And here it was your brother who was the one who cut the throat of that Crow and scalped him!"

Now his male in-laws were not about to tease him. Then that man Bear said, "Let that be all of your teasing him! He outdid us."

And the Sioux had not wanted him to go with the party in pursuit. "This is what he did. Now he has shamed us who are here. Don't say things to him again! Now this is what that man did," the one who was named He Stands Sideways.

He was the father of Standing Soldier. Now none of his relatives among the Arikaras who are living today has taken the name of that He Stands Sideways. That was Black Rabbit's grandfather. Francis Young [Black Rabbit] surely does not know it. No one tells him things like that.

Now this is what happened, the war story that my uncle Nice-Voiced Elk used to tell me. Now this is what he told.

51

The White Horse: A Crow War Story

This story, told to the narrator by his Hidatsa father-in-law, is a Crow war story, undoubtedly passed from Crows to Hidatsas in the course of visits between members of the two tribes and finally retold here by an Arikara, who has preserved its provenience. Thus it is an example of how tales have diffused.

Now I am going to tell a story. It is a Crow story that they used to tell when I would to listen to them tell stories.

One time when the Crows used to roam over there in the west, a group of young men was out hunting and they were butchering deer. Then some other men came in sight, and here they were out hunting also. They must have been Sioux. It was the same with them as with the Crows: as they rode, they were leading horses that were carrying meat.

One young man, as he watched them, saw a white horse among the party. It had a load of meat. It was carrying it on its back. Oh, this white horse was nice looking. The young man admired it. "Why don't I catch its rope!" he thought, wanting to steal it surreptitiously. Now it was dark when they went by.

They must have been Sioux. Nevertheless this group of Crows turned around to go home. Meanwhile this young man continued to wish he could steal the white horse, but the Crows did not want him to do it. "Don't do it! They'll chase us if you do that."

This young man did not heed them. Then he proceeded to head the white horse off. It was swift as it ran. He was shooting arrows at the rope that it dragged.

Well, then after he had gone some distance, however far it was, he saw a village. There was a big Sioux village there, and that is where this party that had the meat was headed. Now, oh, here this village was arranged in a circle. It must have been on an island. Then the party went into the village.

While the young man was watching this and thinking he would catch the rope, the white horse ran on and left him behind, just as it had been doing again and again. Then the horse reached it. There was an open space by the village, and the riders drove the horses carrying the meat into it.

At a distance there in the middle of the village was a tipi. Then that is where the man carrying the meat went, and the white horse followed him.

Now the young Crow lay flat on his stomach while he was observing things, while he was looking everything over. "Hey, what can I do to catch that white horse standing there?" he thought as he spied on it. And then the people began to take the meat into the tipi. It was dark now. Then they turned the horses loose to roam around in the middle of the village.

While he was spying on the white horse, the young man went closer, and there it was still dragging the rope. Then he thought, "Why don't I go to sleep for a while! Then I'll catch you." Then the line of fires began to go out as people went to bed. Then everyone was sleeping; everything had quieted down.

Then this young man went to where the white horse stood. Then he caught it. Then he tied a rope to its mouth [to serve as a bridle]. Then he mounted it. With the dogs barking, the young man ran the other horses out into the open space. But then he quickly turned them around. Then he went in a different direction. Now south is the way he wanted to go. And here there was also an open space there.

When the Sioux woke up, they were yelling, wanting to catch their horses, but meanwhile this young man made the white horse he rode run. It ran into the middle of the open space.

Now, after these Sioux caught their horses, they chased the

young man. They saw the white horse he rode and chased him. And
now where he was headed there was a washout. Then they were
catching up with him. After he swung around, the young Crow
whipped the white horse again. Now here the horse jumped over the
washout, and when it landed on the other side of the bank, it fell!
Its hind leg slipped down the edge of the bank. But then it regained
its footing, and the young man continued going on as the Sioux
began shooting at him. But the washout was too difficult for the
Sioux to cross.

Then the young man continued to come on and on until it was
becoming daybreak. There in the distance he saw smoke rising, and
that was where his companions were camped. Then he arrived
where they were.

"Hey, we thought they must have killed you. You certainly
didn't heed us."

"But I liked this white horse. The white horse was the cause.
This is what happened; this is what I did. I took it away. Then they
chased me. And then there was a cutbank. When this horse jumped
over it, I was scared when its foot slipped. It must not have quite
made it, but it reached the bank. It jumped over the bank.

"Now they're coming. Be on the lookout! They're going to chase
us."

Then they hid the white horse. They put a blanket over it so
that the Sioux would not see it.

Now this is what that young Crow did. It is a Crow story that
my father-in-law used to tell.

Narratives of the Past

Of Mysterious Events

Plate 10. Virgin's Breasts Buttes, Morton County, North Dakota. Photograph by Raymond. T. Haas, 1990.

52

The Origin of Virgin's Breasts Buttes

On the level prairie not far west of Glen Ullin, North Dakota, on the south side of U.S. Highway 94 is an isolated pair of prominent, pointed hills known to Arikaras as Young Woman's Breasts Buttes and over the last century to whites as The Twins or Virgin's Breasts Buttes. The latter is their designation today, a more poetic translation of the Arikara name, and no doubt derives from this story, which explains not only these geographical formations but also the reason why hawks make a cry like that of a human baby.

When our people used to travel around while they were moving upriver, they were living somewhere, but I do not know just where it was. But this story here is one they used to tell. It happened there at the place they call Virgin's Breasts Buttes. It tells why they are called Virgin's Breasts Buttes.

It is a nice place there where the camp was located. A coulee goes through, and there are trees here and there. It is nice land. <The people used to go there on hunting trips.>

Well, one time there was a group of young women. There was a village there. Then they went up onto the prairie to go around digging for wild turnips.

And one young woman carried a baby on her back. It was a young baby. The baby was sleeping, and so she laid it down on the ground. Then she fixed up a nice spot where it could lie while she went around digging turnips.

The young woman must have gone quite a distance away. She must have somehow separated from the others. She must have wandered far off.

Finally she said, "Now I'll go back. I certainly have enough turnips now."

Then she went to where her baby lay. And there it was crying far up above! Then she looked, and the baby was not lying there on the ground! But there lay the shawl that had been wrapped around it! There her child was, flying up there with wings!

Then she began to call it. Then she began showing it her breasts. "Come quickly! Maybe you are hungry."

But it went on up there. It began flying higher. Then this young woman, the poor thing, gave up.

Now after that it is not known what happened.

And after the women went back home, the young woman's husband asked, "Where is the baby?"

Then she told her husband, "This is what happened. It flew up into the sky. Now it's flying around. It's become a bird."

Now from here I do not know what happened.

There are two hills sitting prominently there where the highway passes by today. The two hills are there on the prairie. They are pointed hills. That is where they are. That is where they used to say the young woman's baby—I don't know whether it was a little boy or a little girl—flew up and became a hawk.

And sometimes when a hawk calls out, it seems as if it is a baby crying. I myself heard it when I used to herd horses. When they used to brand around here, there were many horses. We were on a hill there once while the horses were grazing. It seemed as if someone were crying. It turned out to be a hawk flying around. It was calling out as it was making its sound. Now it sounded just like a baby. Maybe that incident is the reason why.

Now that is what I heard. And the two hills are prominent between Glen Ullin and Hebron.

53

The Priest Who Turned into Stone

Formerly, when the people of a village were returning
from a communal buffalo hunt, the priests and others who
had remained at home in the earth lodge village came out to
meet the party. The priests carried the village sacred bun-
dles, and people customarily presented offerings of dried
meat to them to offer to the deities in return for blessings.
This story tells of a priest who is ignored by all the members
of a returning party save for the last couple, who are hurry-
ing home suffering from thirst and hastily give him a tongue
rather than dried meat. Deeply offended, the priest pouts
and turns to stone. This story is admonitory in intent,
emphasizing the gravity of taking proper note of a priest in
prescribed contexts. It is also the explanation of a landmark
whose location is no longer remembered.

Now I certainly don't know where it was that this story happened in the country there, when long, long ago our people were in
the south migrating this way toward where we live today, but I
used to hear about it when they told stories where my grandfather
and grandmother lived—when the old-timers were living. Now I
heard it when they told what happened with these sacred bundles
that they had long ago.

Once after the village had gone on a communal buffalo hunt,
after they had traveled far off, the young men returned to the
village ahead of the others. "Now the hunting party is returning.
The hunting party is coming." There were people who had remained
behind in the village,[1] wherever it was that the Arikaras were
living then.

And then the leading priest—one of the old men who possessed

---

1. A reference to the elderly and infirm who were unable to go on the
hunt.

the holy things, the sacred bundles they had at that time—went out to meet the returning people as the priests would do.

Then someone would be sitting there, and he would say to a priest, "Now, open the bundle for me!" That is apparently what they used to say. When someone had given birth to a baby on the hunt, the old men who had the holy ways prayed for it while they incensed it. Also [another person might say,] "Bless my boy. He became sick while we were traveling around out there." That is what the returning people would do, <asking for a blessing or making an offering of thanks to the bundle>.

But no one paid any attention to this one priest as he went by family after family. Then as he went on, the last members of the party were coming along. As one man and woman came, they stopped; and when the priest reached them, the man said to him, "Sit down for a while!" Then the priest sat down.

"Ah, my wife and I are dying of thirst. We don't have any water," said this man. "But here is a cooked tongue." It was a whole buffalo tongue. Then they put it down for him.

Now it is not known what the priest said—they never told it—but then this couple arose to continue on their way home. They were thirsty for water.

Then this priest picked up a stick. Then he stuck it through the tongue. He felt hurt because no one had offered him some dried meat or had paid any attention to him [by asking for a blessing]. Then he went off. Then he climbed up it. A hill was there. Then he sat down on top of it. After he planted the stick with the tongue on it in the ground, he sat down by it. His feelings were hurt.

Then people began to look for him. "Where did he go?"

"He went out there. He went out to meet the returning people."

That is the reason priests used to go out to meet the returning people: that they would be invited somewhere <and that people would ask them for a blessing and present an offering of dried meat to them>.

Then they began looking for that man after he had not been seen around the village for however many days it was. "Surely you two were the last ones to see him," [they said to the couple].

"Eh, he reached us as we were coming. We were dying of thirst and wanted to come back quickly. So we put a cooked tongue down for him. I thought he would follow and we would all get back and then we would cook something nice for him here in the lodge. When we were coming we were in a hurry. And here he did not come with us. Now I don't know where he went."

"Perhaps he was killed." That is what people were saying.

And here he was sitting on top of that hill. Then they went up onto the prairie looking for him after he had not been seen around for however many days it was. Then they found him. There he sat on top of the hill, on a high hill. It was a high hill where he was sitting on top. There was the stick, set upright in the ground. The tongue hung from the end of it. And there he was, a rock! Why, here this man had become stone after pouting because no one had invited him to take some meat or had noticed him! And he had the holy things—he had the sacred bundle.

Now this is what the other priests were saying: "None of you noticed him. You were wrong to do that. <We have been praying for you people to get plenty of meat. You should have taken out some dried meat for him instead of giving him that tongue.> Now it has happened. You have offended the priest."

Then they offered him smoke.

Now, whatever had happened, he was no longer alive. No one knows what happened after that—only that he disappeared.

They used to call the place Where The Tongue Was On The Hill. They also used to say Where The Old Man Sat On The Hill.

This is what I used to hear from the man named Enemy Heart.

54

The Fight between the Bear and the Buffalo Bull

*This short narrative is a vignette of a fortuitous en-
counter between two awesome beings, a bear and a buffalo,
the most powerful of animals. An Arikara hunting party by
chance witnesses their fight to the death, and once both
animals have killed each other the men in the party show
their respect for them by performing three customary acts:
painting the head with vermillion, placing a plume on the
head, and offering smoke. Afterward, the party attributes its
subsequent hunting success to the honor they have shown to
the spirits of the bear and the buffalo bull.*

Now I am going to tell one story I used to hear from the one
who used to be called Pete Beauchamp. His name was Sitting Bull.
He used to tell stories there at the agency, where he used to work
at night. I would just go to where he lived and he would tell me
stories. He told me this story that I am going to relate about the
people who lived formerly—long ago. I surely do not know how long
ago it was.

Now one time when the young men were out hunting in rough
terrain, they saw buffalo. Oh, there were many buffalo in the herd
there. They lay on a hill watching them.

Then one of the young men said, "It's time now for them to come
[to the stream] to drink since it is past noon. They will drink and
then go up onto the prairie to graze. As soon as they reach the
bank, we'll look for a small bull among them. Then we'll eat well."

Now while they were sitting there, a large bear appeared. Oh,
the bear was big as it came along the bank of the stream! Then it
stopped. Now it looked all around. It looked over there where it
saw the buffalo. Then it moved quickly. Then it went up onto the
prairie. Then it sat down in a clump of buckbrush.

Later, while the men waited, all the buffalo arose. Then one of them just came in the lead. Oh, it was a fine-looking bull about four winters old! It was big. It was in the lead as it came, as the herd of buffalo came on. Then it stopped. It seemed to know that the bear was waiting for it. And then it came on again. Now it was coming to the edge of the hill, and then it stood there near it.

Then the bear peeked over the hill. Then the bear jumped up and charged. Now the bull did the same thing, too. Then they fought. Oh, this bull was fierce! The bear was thrown some distance over there by it. But now the bear was itself just as fierce, as they were fighting and injuring each other.

Now they ceased. Then the bull went backward, and then the bear went up the hill. Now it sat down again in the brush where it had sat before. While it sat in the brush, that other one, the bull, sat down, too.

But then this bear began to become holy: then it raised the dust there where it sat in the brush. The dust was blue. Then the bear ceased to growl.

And now this is what the bull did, too, snorting as it was dying. Now it ceased.

Well, then the buffalo ran off; then they scattered out, running.

Now the older men, who were knowledgeable, said to the young men, "What has happened is not good. These two animals injured each other. The bear must have thought it would have something to eat, but then it became too difficult for it."

Well, then they went down the hill. Then they offered smoke to this bear. Then they gave the pipe to it. Then they painted it.

Then they went over the other way, where the bull lay. Then they said, "Now you two have injured each other." Whatever the bull had thought, whatever it had wished for the bear, they put a soft plume on its head. Then they offered it smoke so that it might smoke something.

Then they said, "Now let's go home! We'll find some deer. What these two did to each other—their injuring each other—is a bad omen. Now, let's go home!"

Then they came on home, and while they were coming they each killed a deer when they killed various ones.

Then they related the incident: "This is what happened while we were roaming around in the west. A bear and a buffalo fought. Then they killed each other. Now they are both dead."

The older men then asked, "Did you do anything for them?"

Then they said, "We painted the bear. Looking for a meal for itself became difficult for it. We also did the same thing for this buffalo, the fiercest one. They both smoked, and we put a feather on it[1] after it tried to save itself. Now we were coming home, and it was not at all difficult to kill deer."

"Now that bear was the cause of that: it gave you good fortune, and you must now be thankful."

Now that is what happened.

55

The Elk Doctor Who Called the Elk

A popular narrative form is the anecdote of a successful doctor's performance of his power to accomplish miraculous feats, thereby reinforcing people's faith in his ability to cure. This anecdote tells of one such performance witnessed by Jackrabbit, the narrator's uncle and a noted singer during the early part of this century. When he was still a boy, Jackrabbit and a companion watched the ritual summoning of an elk by a member of the Deer society, one of the eight doctors' societies composing the Medicine Lodge. This incident, related entirely in Jackrabbit's own words, occurred when the Arikaras were still living in Like-A-Fishhook Village.

---

1. In the Arikara text, literally, 'we clothed it,' signifying that they had attired it with a symbol of honor.

Now I am repeating the words of the one called Jackrabbit. My mother—my father's sister—married him after her first husband died. Afterward she and the one who used to be called Jackrabbit married. He had no other name. I knew him by one name only, Jackrabbit. The man had a good voice when he sang songs at the old village. Now he told the story that I am going to tell. I was young yet. I was not going to school yet. I did not speak English. He told what I am going to relate.

"Among those who lived there in the village were medicine men, the different ones who used to perform mysterious feats.

"Now this boy and I were together. He was named Good Crow. Now I was fourteen winters old, but I don't know how old he was when we used to go around together here in the village, when we were in the combined village.

"Now he said that they were going into the Medicine Lodge to perform. My friend and I used to hear it from his father, or his grandfather, or his uncle, whichever one it was. He said, 'The Deer Society,' to which he belonged, 'is going to call an elk when it performs mysterious acts. Now they're going to call an elk. They're seeking to see if it will happen—if an elk is going to believe them and to see if it will come.'

"Oh, it was just really dark. There was a fine rain. We were lying under the bed by the door, which faced east. We were lying there watching things. A man came out. Or, they were singing while the drum was beating. A man came out. He faced the other way, the west. He stood there. He whistled, 'Uuuuuu.' It gradually faded out.

"He went on, going there. He went to the edge of the bluff on the river bank beside the village. We were hiding so that we would not be seen. It was really dark. He stood close by so that we could see him when he was talking. Again he whistled, 'Uuuuuu.' The sound echoed.

"After a while there in the west there was a whistle. We barely heard it when it whistled. He began speaking; he was singing.

"Again it whistled, and the sound echoed along the river. Now it must have been moving closer. Then it whistled close by. Oh, it was loud! There was an echo after it whistled.

"Now it had whistled twice; now once again it whistled after the human whistled, 'Uuuuuu.' It was barely audible at the end. The sound faded out after it whistled. It whistled nearby in the gardens in the brush.

It seemed that we were actually seeing the elk. Oh, we opened our eyes wide so that we might see the elk.

"The other man began talking, talking, talking. He finished. Then he began to sing. Now it was not clear when the elk turned around. There were rustling sounds there in the brush where it went. Then there was a whistle over there in the distance where the end of the line of hills was, where the brush bordered the hills.

"And then this man turned around and entered the Medicine Lodge. We ran to the door. He began to tell about it. The Deer doctors ran around the inside of the lodge, and then they finished their performance. Now, this is what I saw."

This is what that man [Jackrabbit] said. And I myself heard what he told. That is why I know various stories.

56

The Young Man Who Did Not Believe in Ghosts

Fundamental to the Arikara worldview was a belief in an individual's continued existence, after death, as a ghost— an incorporeal spirit that might lurk around the living and influence their lives. This is the story of a skeptic, a young man who does not believe in an afterlife as a ghost. The experience convinces him that spirits do in fact exist and, moreover, are a source of good fortune when propitiated. Such a story functioned to reinforce cultural values and promote social conformity.

There once lived a boy—a young man—who did not believe in anything. No matter what might happen, he did not believe in ghosts. "Oh, you tell lies. There are no ghosts going around. When someone is killed, he is killed. What is he going to do if he becomes a ghost?" This young man just did not believe in them. He was living alone then.

Then one time he said, "I'll go hunting. I might kill a deer or an antelope," these animals being plentiful here in those times. And then this young man went off. He rode one horse and took two pack horses to carry his gear.

Then somewhere out there on the plains, in the west, wherever it was, he found a place to camp. It was a nice spot. "This is where I'll camp!" There was water there, and also woods. Oh, it was a nice, level place at the base of a hill.

Then he put up a lodge, a pointed lodge. They used to call it an enemy lodge, a tipi. Then he put up the lodge. Then he tied his horses up. Then after making a fire, he began to fix a meal for himself, roasting dried meat.

Now it got dark, and as he sat there eating, someone came into the lodge. His shins were skinny. There were joints all over him. He was just bone. And he wore something over himself. Whatever it was, he wore it over himself.

Then the ghost began to make signs. Then this ghost said, telling him by motions, "I want you to give me some of what you're eating so I can eat."

Then this young man who did not believe in things said, "Why are you going around? And why don't you look around for your own food, just as I do. Don't just think that anyone is going to be giving you food! Go on outside!"

Then this ghost moved closer to where the young man was sitting, begging for food.

Then the young man who was a disbeliever said, "I don't like it. Just say, 'Throw me out at last,' and I'll do it." Then he jumped up angrily, and he and the ghost grappled with one another.

Oh, the ghost was strong as they were wrestling. When it became daylight, the young man got on top of the ghost. And as soon as it became dark all over, the ghost got on top of the young man. Then the ghost became strong.

After they had been struggling, the young man with difficulty finally overcame the ghost. Then he grabbed the ghost's leg. Then he dragged him. He dragged him outside. There was a deep depression over there where he was dragging him, and then he threw him into it. "You're just pestering poor me when I am hungry!"

After he returned to his lodge, the young man began to eat. It was morning, and he ate a meal. After finishing, he said, "Why don't I water the horses first, and then I'll go hunting!" Then he proceeded to do that.

When he led the horses to the water where he was taking them to drink, there on the edge of the bank sat the ghost he had wrestled with. Then he charged the ghost. Then he kicked his ribs. "Now you're doing what you always do. I suppose you think you should be given food!"

The ghost, the poor thing, rolled over the bank, and there he went rolling down the bank.

Then the young man went on and watered the horses. Then he went to his lodge. He roped his best horse. Then he mounted his best horse. He went hunting.

When he would shoot at antelopes he could not kill any. Oh, so he came back to his camp. He had not killed anything.

Now it was morning again. When he went out hunting, he still could not kill anything. Even when he hit an animal he did not kill it: the deer or antelope just continued going on its way.

Then this young man felt like crying. He was now in his lodge. "Hey, why is it? Nothing is usually ever difficult for me, when I want to kill deer, antelope, and buffalo. Why is it that I'm not able to kill anything?"

Then a party of young men came along. There were seven of them. Among them were two older men.

"Now, hello! What are you doing?"

He said, "Why, it's difficult for me. Oh, there are lots of antelope, but I can't kill any. Or any deer or buffalo. Oh, they're plentiful. But no matter how I try, I can't kill any.

"But when I first arrived here, this is what happened: a ghost harassed me, begging for food while I ate. We fought, and I threw him down the bank. There's a deep depression there. That's where he's lying."

Then they went over there.

Then one of the two older men said, "Why, here's where you erred! The man lying down there at the bottom was with us when we were once camped here. It was long ago. This one was sick, and he died. We buried him here. And this is where it was, here where you are, when he was begging for some food to eat. The poor thing, he was sick and then died. That must be the reason he was hungry. That's why you didn't kill anything.

"Now, quickly, let's hurry!" Then they got ready. Then they prepared food for the ghost. They set food down for him, and then filled their pipe and offered it to him.

Now it was morning. "Now, hello! What's going to happen now? Let's go to where you were hunting, where you said there are plenty of antelope."

Then they went. There was a huge number of antelope. In no time they were shooting them and killing them. Oh, there was a large quantity of meat after they brought the carcasses back to their camp and made dried meat.

To this young man who had found it difficult to kill any, they said, "Now you'll believe it. You didn't believe in ghosts. Now you know how it is. This ghost, who is holy, was going to starve you to death, just as the situation was when he died."

For this reason, then, the young man said, "Now I believe it. Here it is that way! Here it is true! Ghosts do hear! Now I believe in them. Now from here on when I go around I shall believe everything. I'll be praying to the sacred powers to bless me."

Now that is what this young man did. The spirits blessed him, and after he prayed to them for what he wanted, it happened that way.

Now, this is how the story went.

57

The Dancing Ghost

*This short story continues the theme of the existence of
ghosts and how they are a potential source of good fortune.
In it a party of Hidatsa hunters, having no luck finding
game, camp near a bed of quicksand, where they are visited
in the evening by a strange being. As they leave the next
morning, they find a skeleton by the quicksand and then
realize it had been the visitor, who is the spirit of the man
whose remains are there. After caring for the skull and
offering it smoke, they experience success in hunting and
return home laden with meat.*

I just don't know who I heard this story from that I am going to
tell. It is one that was told when they used to tell stories. There
were many old men who told them. Actually they were not old men;
the men I used to see when they told stories were still young.

Now one time when a group of young men had gone off somewhere, however many there were, going out hunting to look for
various things—now after they had been gone for so many days,
they came to the bottomland of a river valley, wherever it was.
Then they made a bullboat to cross the water. Then they floated
across. Now they floated across. They came to the other bank. It
was early evening now.

Then one of the men said, "Hey, it sure would be good if we
were to stay overnight after we've crossed the river, and in the
morning we can go back to our village."

"Now that's really a good idea. We'll do that," they said as they
were floating across.

Then they went close to the bank. Then the one who sat in the
front jumped onto a sandy spot. When he put his feet down, there
was soft sand. Then his feet began to mire. And then he sang, "Ho,
heya; ho, heya. I might get stuck in the mud." Then he quickly
crossed over it.

Now the same thing happened to each of the others, but all of them came across the sand. Then they left the boat and went up the bank. It was a nice area there.

Then one of the men said, "We'll stay overnight here." Then they readied everything. Then they put up a hunting lodge—what they used to call a hunting lodge, whatever kind of lodge that was. Now they were inside the lodge telling stories while they were making a meal and meat was roasting over the coals.

Now after a while a man just came inside the lodge. Oh, what he was wearing must have been on him for a long time. When the men looked at the way he was dressed, they could see he had worn his clothes for a long time.

Then the stranger said, "Ah, I'll eat some of what you're eating and then I'll dance awhile. Ah, I like the song you were singing."

Then they gave him a piece of meat as he kneeled with one knee on the ground. Oh, they did not know him.

Then he said, "Now sing it! I want to dance awhile and then I'll go."

Then the men were singing different songs.

Then he said, "No. It's a different song. That isn't the song I like."

Now there was one young man, a quiet one, who was sitting over there. Then he said, "Say, maybe he means the song we sang when we climbed up the bank: 'Ho, heya; ho, heya.'"

Then the ghost said, standing there by the fire, "That's the song that I want to dance to. Now sing it!"

While these men were clapping their hands and singing, "Ho, heya; ho, heya; ho, heya," oh my, this ghost was dancing and dancing. He was whooping as they were singing, "Ho, heya; ho, heya; ho, heya."

"Ah, say, now I'm thankful to you. Ah, I just like that song. Now I'll go." He went out.

"Whoever are you, you who are wandering around?" That is what the young men were asking now, wondering who he was.

Then they went to bed.

Then morning came. "Now let's go back to our village!" Then they went down the bank to where the boat was, the bullboat.

When they came to it, there was a pile of bones there. The skull

was lying there, too. The person, whoever he had been, had got
stuck in the mud over there where these young men had got stuck
before.

"Ah, the poor thing, he must have died. He must have starved
to death after he got stuck in the mud, just like what might have
happened to us."

Then they picked up the skull and put it in a nice place. They
offered smoke to it. After they fixed up a place for it, they set the
skull nicely there.

Then they came on. Now nothing was difficult for them, as they
were shooting deer and antelope on their way home. They had
plenty of meat. Ah, then they arrived back at the Hidatsa camp,
wherever it was.

This story I have told is a Hidatsa story. Now that is what
happened when the Hidatsas were singing, "Ho, heya." It means 'to
hurry up when one is getting ready to throw something away, to be
prepared.' That is what they must have meant.

Now, I have told the story of this song "Ho heya" that I have
sung. Now this is what happened.

58

The Mysterious Snake Seen by Short Bear

*For Arikaras, inexplicable phenomena were considered
to be manifestations of the holy. Such a phenomenon, once
observed, became a topic of conversation, frequently retold
with curiosity and awe. The narrator stated that such stories
or anecdotes were common in the past, and he recorded the
following one, told here in his grandfather's words, to exemplify the genre. The incident occurred when Short Bear was
a young man and the Arikaras were still living in Like-A-
Fishhook Village.*

Now I will tell one of the stories my grandfather Short Bear used to relate about the young men when they went around hunting. He and another young man were always together. His friend was named Bear Paw.

One time they went off hunting there on the other side of the river from where the village of the three tribes was, there on the edge of the bank—the one they always talk about. Then they crossed the Missouri River <heading toward the west, to the Beaver Creek area,> when they went deer hunting. Antelope must have been plentiful in the country there around Beaver Creek, too.

They were going around there on the prairie as they came along during the late afternoon. Then one of them said, "Say, let's stay here! Deer usually come out of the woods in that coulee in the evening. Perhaps we might kill one."

Then they sat down there on a rise.

Then a rainstorm came up. Oh, when it rained, it rained hard!

Then my grandfather said "While we were sitting up there, something was on the prairie where our eyes were focused. It was on a flat. With the sun opposite it, it was shining, and when it started to rain we ran down the hill into the coulee, where there were birch trees. We were standing among the trees. Oh, it was a heavy rain with lightning and thunder. The ground was just really shaking. Something must have come close by there.

"Now after the rain had passed over and it had cleared up, I must have looked off. There in the sky on the edge of the storm, where the darkness of the rain was, there was something swinging around. It looked like a string. The string was swinging back and forth. <It kept going higher and higher.> Then it disappeared!

"Now we just stood there. There was nothing there on the prairie. We ran over there, and there there was a hole. We never noticed what it might be. <We were hungry and wanted to get home. So we noticed the place where it had been when it was wet, and then we rode down to the river.> Then we crossed over to the village.

"<After we got back we told people what we had seen.> And different ones said, 'Say, I saw the snake. It used to come out, and it landed over there. Birds flew around, and when a meadowlark flew by, it was not tired.

But then [after the meadowlark landed near that snake] it was difficult for it to fly up into the air, and then it was eaten up. Now it must have been that thing. It must have been snatched up by Thunder.'"

That is what people used to talk about formerly. That ground must have been holy. But now mysterious occurrences like that no longer happen. That is where they really used to occur, there at Beaver Creek where the people used to live scattered out on allotments.

Now this is what my grandfather told me.

59

The Eagle Trappers and the Scalped Man

When parties of men set out to seek their fortune—to raid, hunt, or trap eagles—the leader generally took along religious objects that he used in rituals to insure the success of their undertaking. In this story of an eagle-trapping expedition, a buffalo skull (addressed as Grandfather) and an ear of corn (addressed as Mother) formed an altar in the hunting lodge where the men ate and slept. During the day, while the men were in their traps, a scalped man would slip into the lodge, scatter the furnishings about, and embellish the ritual objects. Here the Scalped Man appears as a comic character—one of the many roles in which he was cast—and both his antics and the men's reactions to them are sources of mirth. The story suggests how the tensions inherent in the seriousness of ritual were occasionally released as humor.

Back when we used to live in villages, a group of young men went off. They went to trap eagles like they used to do formerly when they caught eagles. They were eagle trappers. Now, however many young men there were, they went off to the badlands, where eagles ranged, out there on the prairie in the west.

"Now this is a place where we might find some eagles."

And then they built a lodge. They used to call it a hunting lodge, whatever kind it was, the hunting lodge. Then they fixed everything up. Now they used to pray to various things. There was a buffalo skull there. They had it sitting there. And there standing upright was Mother Corn. [These formed an altar.]

After the young men had fixed everything up in the lodge, getting everything ready, then each one said, "This is where I'll be." "This is where I'll be," [choosing their trap sites].

"Now all of you fix up the places where you'll be!"

[Then each one fixed up the trap he would sit in, where] he could watch things while he was inside, where he could watch all the other men, too, including the one farthest away [in case the enemy might come]. Then at sundown each one got out of his trap. Then they all gathered together. Now they came back to their lodge. That is what they used to do.

After a person had dug a hole and gotten into it, he laid willow sticks on top. There was a hole where the smokehole would be in the center, where the bait would lie—what they used to call bait, a rabbit. Now after skinning a rabbit, they tied it there. It was tied tightly so that an eagle could not snatch the rabbit away. He fixed things up. Now it was tightly secured.

Now when an eagle landed to eat the rabbit, that was the time to catch it by its legs. Well, then he would break its wings. Whatever it was that they used to do I surely do not know, but it is what I used to hear when they told stories.

But on this occasion those young men, after they had gone to their traps, came back to the lodge in the evening. "There aren't any eagles in this country."

Now they came back to their lodge. After each one had gone off to his trap, they returned to their lodge. Then they went inside where they had left ribs roasting over the fire, thinking "We'll be coming back."

Now the ribs were scattered along the far edge of the lodge. Things were in disarray. Wood was lying everywhere, and this buffalo skull was sooty black after someone had smeared it with soot. After he had smeared it, there it was, black! Also on the

Mother Corn he had drawn a woman's face. And whatever else he had done.

Oh, then time went on with this happening repeatedly. Here the one bothering them was a scalped man.

"It's certainly not good; whoever he is, he's making fun of us, the one doing these things, ridiculing our grandfather Buffalo Skull and our Mother Corn. Now let's find out who it is going around making this mischief, scattering our things all around—the things we were roasting, while we thought they would cook nicely." He had thrown the ribs way over there. He had thrown them over there by the entry to the lodge.

"He must be one who really mocks people, whoever he is. Now let's catch him!"

Then they dug holes close by their lodge. Oh, then early in the morning they got into the holes, after they had arranged things in the lodge to look like they should.

Now it was sometime later. There was the sound of footsteps on the ground, coming fast. He arrived at the lodge, and, oh, he looked all around. It seemed as if he knew they were waiting for him. He put his head inside and looked all around. Then he went into the lodge again.

And then these young men got out of the holes. They went to the doorway. He was muttering in Arikara. And he said, "Why, say, I got everything fixed up for you, ah, so that you'd look nice. Ah, Mother, now they've spoiled the things I did. And this Buffalo Skull that I fixed up—they've changed it back. Oh my, it's certainly not good." That is what he was saying over and over.

He was kneeling down in the middle of the lodge. Then one man entered slowly . . . and then another . . . as they all came inside. The scalped man sat there facing the other way in front of the buffalo skull, talking to it and talking to himself. Then the young men stood in the doorway so that he could not run out.

"Hello! Hey, you who wander around far off, why, I wouldn't wander around if I had a village!"

When the scalped man jumped up and saw these young men, he fell over. Then he died of fright.

Then he was shaken by one of the young men. He never moved.

"Let him lie there! Now quickly, let's be on our way!"

Then they picked up their things, the Mother Corn and the buffalo skull, and then they came home.

"What he's been doing to us—his making fun of us—is not good."

Then they remembered that a young man had died there long ago, and here he was living! I don't know what his name was. But they knew him when they saw him.

Ha, then the young men came home. After they returned home, one said, "Say,"—they meant that one—"he was ridiculing us, and here he must have been living there, and now he died of fright. Now this is what he did when we caught him. When we took him by surprise, he died of fright. He's still lying there, a left-behind. Then we came on."

Then the relatives of that young man went so that they could see him. He was not lying there inside the lodge. Here he had apparently jumped up again and gone off somewhere!

Ah, while they cried, saying "Ah, you yourself are the cause!" one of the young men said, "We should have grabbed him. Then we could have brought him back for whatever might have happened."

Tales

Of Coyote

60

Coyote and Lucky Man

Hungry, always seeking gratuitous meals for himself, deceitful, inept—these are the most common traits of the trickster, Coyote—traits well illustrated in this story.

They always tell about Coyote and his pranks when he wandered around looking for meals for himself.

One time when Coyote was running along, he saw smoke rising up. There was a lodge there. When he went up to it, he looked at the lodge.

Ah, the food smelled good to him. It smelled like boiling meat. "Why, oh my!" Coyote said.

Then Coyote went there. Then he went to the entrance of the earth lodge. Then he made a sound in his throat, "Ha, ha, uha!" as he tried to get the attention of whoever was inside. Now he was making this sound over and over.

Then the person inside finally said, "Say, whoever you are going around out there, you should come inside. Come in!"

Then Coyote went inside. "Hey, it certainly is good that I've finally found you, uncle, while I'm traveling around on the warpath. I've just come from the Black Hills. Our war just ended. We were warring with the enemy, and we counted coups on them." That is what Coyote was saying.

And then this man said—this man was named Lucky Man— "Say, sit down now!"

Then Lucky Man took some meat out of the pot. Then he dished some meat out for Coyote.

And here this is just what Coyote wanted: something to eat. Oh, he began eating while he told stories, telling all kinds of fibs.

463

Finally Coyote said, "Now I sure am full. I'll go now."
"Alright."
Then Coyote went out.

After he went outside, he swung around. "Hey! I wish I could
find something good for myself. I wonder what I should do?" That
is what Coyote was thinking over and over.

"I should hurt myself in some way so that Lucky Man will give
me some meat!"

Oh, Lucky Man had lots of dried meat. Coyote just looked at it
there, wanting to steal some dried meat, a tongue, or, oh my, one of
the many other pieces.

Then Coyote said, "Say!" He charged up to the door. Then he
sang a song there. While he was singing, he was jumping and
dancing around, bothering Lucky Man inside and teasing him. He
sang:

> Lucky Man, I am pleading for your food.
>   Fox is dancing well.
>   Fox is dancing well.

Lucky Man came outside. Then he gave Coyote a rib to eat.

But Coyote was determined to continue jumping around while
he was singing. Again Lucky Man gave him something to eat.

Now Coyote continued to sing:

> Lucky Man, I am pleading for your food.
>   Fox is dancing well.
>   Fox is dancing well.

Now Lucky Man was giving Coyote things—giving him dried
meat and different things.

Then Lucky Man said, "Say, you sure are a pest! You must not
be at all thankful for what I've given you. Hey! Now I'm going to
kill you."

Then Lucky Man nocked an arrow. Coyote, the poor thing, fell
to the ground screaming when his leg was shot. Then Lucky Man
went and dragged him inside. He took the arrow out of Coyote's leg.

Coyote said, "Now, uncle, I just want to be around here because you have such good meals."

Then Lucky Man replied, "Yes, that's alright. You can fetch water for me. And if you stay here for a while your leg will get well."

But when Lucky Man went out hunting, Coyote was greedy and got into things to eat. He ate everything up. And here that is what he wanted: to eat all of Lucky Man's food!

That is the way Coyote was, always telling lies when he was looking for food for himself.

61

Coyote and Beaver

This story portrays Coyote as an upstart, an emulator who thinks he can do the wonderful things that he has seen someone else do, even though he lacks the power. The narrator modified this version to conform to contemporary standards in the presentation of children's stories. An uncensored version is given in story 127 (volume 4).

One time when Coyote was wandering around, he was going along the river bank, wishing he might find a deer. While Coyote was running along, he came to a lodge. The lodge was on the bank.

While he was looking at it, someone inside said: "You must come in! Why should you just stand around outside?"

Then that other one, Coyote, said, "Hey! I wonder who you are, you who are calling me. Ah, where's the door?"

Then the one inside said, "Why, the door is there where you're standing!"

So Coyote went down in. There was a hole there. Then he went inside.

There sat a man. He was making arrows. He was cutting and

scraping willow branches, as he was preparing them. Coyote looked at the man sitting there.

"Ah, so right here is where you live!"

"Yes."

Then Coyote was looking all around at things. Oh, there was not a thing for him to eat. Oh, over there in the corner was a pile of bark.

Then that one said, "Yes, I know what you're thinking about. There isn't a thing for us to eat. But you're going to eat."

Then Coyote thought, "I wonder how you've happened to answer my thoughts. Why, you know what I'm thinking!"

And then that man sitting there said, "Yes, I certainly know what you're thinking. And you'll eat. Sit down awhile! Wait!"

Then this man got up. Then he went and made a fire. Then he picked up one piece of bark. He held it over the fire. Then it became dried meat.

While Coyote watched him, it turned into a piece of dried meat, which he roasted. Then he went and lifted up a stone. Then he began pounding it. Then he made it into pemmican.

Then he went and picked something up, whatever it was, a piece of tallow. Then he held it out over the fire and melted it. Then he mixed it up with the pounded dried meat.

Then he said, "Now eat!"

And so this Coyote began eating as he sat there. Then, oh, while he ate, the pemmican began increasing in quantity.

At first Coyote just thought, "Perhaps I'll eat two handfuls and then I'll gobble it all up."

But then the pemmican increased in quantity. He got full.

Then he said, "Now take what's left over! You can take it home, wherever that is, and eat it." That is what the man was saying.

This Coyote said, "Yes. But you must come to where I live, too. We'll tell stories. Now I should hurry home!"

Then he picked up the dried meat. He took it out. Then he went off, eating as he went.

Before he arrived at his home, Coyote had eaten all of it. He went inside.

Then Coyote told his wife, "Now fix up the room! I don't want a thing inside here. You'll sit there. Let the children go off for a while! A man is going to come. He's a nice man. He and I are going to tell stories."

Bark was lying along the wall, just as he had seen it there where the man lived. Now he was doing it: he was imitating that man.

And then that man suddenly arrived.

"Now come in!"

He sat down.

Coyote said, "It doesn't matter what you're thinking. You're going to eat what you're going to eat."

Now the man just sat there, not thinking of a thing.

Then Coyote said, "Why, I know what you're thinking."

But he thought, "In spite of what you're saying, I have nothing on my mind."

"Now you'll eat."

Then Coyote made a fire. Then he began roasting the bark. Then it began to burn on him. It was not becoming dried meat.

Then this one said, "Bring it here!"

Then he blew on it all over.

Then Coyote began roasting it. Then it became dried meat. Coyote was doing the same thing the man had done. But it was difficult for him to make it tasty. The grease—the tallow—became burnt when he did whatever he did to make the tallow. But he mixed it with the pemmican.

Then this beaver man began eating it.

Then Coyote said, "Now take these leftovers! Eat them after you get back home."

Then this man went out

Then his wife asked, "Who is that man?"

Then Coyote said, "He's my uncle. Whenever I go hunting, I just go to his lodge."

Then they all followed him, Coyote and his children.

"Where's he going? I wonder what he's going to do?"

There was no lodge there, the way Coyote had said, "This is how it is."

Then Coyote stood there on the bank. Then Beaver jumped up

into the air and slapped the water with his tail and mouth.

Then he frightened Coyote, who jumped back into the woods over yonder.

This is the reason a coyote is afraid whenever it sees someone, and then it runs off.